CRYING WITH LAUGHTER

This book is dedicated to Jackie
as is the story of my life to come

CRYING WITH LAUGHTER

My Life Story

Bob Monkhouse, O.B.E.

ARROW

This edition published by Arrow Books Limited 1994

3 5 7 9 10 8 6 4

First published in Great Britain in 1993 by Century
Random House UK Ltd, 20 Vauxhall Bridge Road, London SW1V 2SA

Arrow Books Ltd
Random House UK Ltd, 20 Vauxhall Bridge Road, London SW1V 2SA

Random House Australia (Pty) Limited
20 Alfred Street, Milsons Point, Sydney
New South Wales 2061, Australia

Random House New Zealand Limited
18 Poland Road, Glenfield
Auckland 10, New Zealand

Random House South Africa (Pty) Limited
PO Box 337, Bergvlei, South Africa

Random House UK Limited Reg. No. 954009

A CIP catalogue record for this book
is available from the British Library

ISBN 0 09 925581 2

Typeset by SX Composing Ltd, Rayleigh, Essex
Printed and bound in Great Britain by
Cox & Wyman Ltd, Reading, Berks

CONTENTS

Dear Jackie

I can't remember ever having written you a letter before. Have you ever written one to me? Not that I recall. So this is a first. It will come as a bit of a surprise as it's not only my first love letter to you, it's also the first time you'll ever read it, here, printed in this book. While you've read patiently through the rest of what I've written, correcting my faulty memory here and there, making your usual shrewd contributions, I kept this chapter to myself. You see, I knew you'd ask me to leave it out and I didn't want to do that.

Perhaps you have some idea how much you mean to me but I doubt it. You've often worried about how I'd get along without you, but only because I wouldn't know where everything was or how to deal with the bills and the VAT returns, and what to do when the burglar alarm goes off in the night. Apart from my domestic deficiencies, you seem to feel that I'd manage just fine, absorbed in my writing and old movies and gadgets and books. I don't think that about you. I think you'll find life awfully difficult without me, just as vacant and unfocused as my life without you. That's why I wish you'd stop smoking and take up some sort of exercise and make more friends outside show business and have more frequent health checkups. And you wish I'd cut down on my drinking and my weight, work less, go for walks on the beach and relax more. But we don't nag one another about it, do we? Not because we don't care, we do, but because we don't want to spoil the day.

You've never been good at handling criticism anyway. Perhaps because you are a great cherisher, you need to feel secure in the harmony you create, wanting everyone to be as thoughtful and friendly to you as you are to them. Besides, you have so many positive qualities that any criticism of you seems like nit-picking to me. You're a superb hostess, always looking after the needs of others. You remember people's birthdays and buy them gifts and cards to make them feel cared for. Your love of other people's children makes some of our friends wonder why you never had any of your own, but not those who know you really well.

How would I describe you to someone who'd never met you? Beautiful, tall, blonde, cheerful, smart, funny, industrious, thoughtful, with a great sense of humour: yes, all of that. I'd have to admit that you drive better, slower and more carefully, than I do. You're hurt by indifference and you need to be appreciated for the care you give so generously to those you love. One important expression of that care is your cooking. You dismiss it lightly but I know why you put so much thought and time and effort into preparing the food we eat. It's another way of saying 'I love you'. Saying the words out loud instead, that's a little bit embarrassing. You have such an outgoing personality that new acquaintances often assume that you were once a performer, yet you shy away from the spotlight when asked to pose for pictures or speak in public. Then again, do you remember Hong Kong? While I was explaining to our military hosts that there was no way you'd ever say a few words, you'd already jumped up on the stage and grabbed the mike. You got a lot of laughs too. We were so happy there, living on the twenty-fourth floor of the Mandarin, making love a lot, shopping nearly as much, leaning over the balcony and pretending to be in charge of the harbour, organising the taxis and the Star ferry boats far below.

Above all, you're loyal. You're on my side no matter what I do. You even pretend to be interested when I get theoretical or talk about philosophy or film or music. I try to do the same for you when you tell me about the dreams you had last night. Yes, I do, because that's really the only time you can be bothered with something unreal. Otherwise, you've no patience with the fanciful, the impossible or other abstractions. Science fiction doesn't exist for you. Your taste in books is as practical as your taste in all your interests. You like rules, tidiness, getting round the supermarket fast, clever comedy films, planning ahead, reflexology (sometimes), giving dinner parties, clearing your desk, swimming in the Caribbean, dead-heading roses, exploring our home territory in your car, watching people, unusual clothes, remembering your dad, punctuality, going home, New York City, great Chinese food, long phone conversations, dry white wine, getting indignant about people who take liberties, nail polish, tableware, hard mattresses, oh, and cats, cats, cats, cats and more cats. You never met a cat you didn't like. Neither did I, I suppose.

You hate dogs barking, untidiness, your knees, loud music, watching live drama in a crowded theatre, bad manners, whisky, plots with loose ends, chicken, male motorists who cut you up, yourself for smoking, illness in others, most dressing rooms, printed instructions, fast food, missing Wimbledon or Steve Davis on TV, unexpected callers, cruises, horror films, being late, hot curries, running out of bin-bags, magic acts, dust, the last potato crisps in the packet, trains, slow shopping, bingo clubs, most TV commercials, Swaziland, fancy cocktails, radio studios, and me snoring.

There's nothing in the world I'd rather see than your face. I wake up every morning feeling glad and grateful because of you. I'd forgive you for every rotten thing you've ever done but I can't, because you've never done a rotten thing. You're the nicest woman I've ever met, which makes you the nicest person I've ever met, and I'm very proud that you're my best friend. When two people love and need each other as much as we do, there can be no happy ending. But until then, every day I have with you is a present.

I love you, Jac.

Bob

PS I know, I can hear you – 'Scrap the caddie, Clyde.'

THANKS

are due to some folks not acknowledged by name in the text of this book. I'm very grateful to Helene Olley for checking the accuracy of my memory for dates, names and places; to Joan Prichard for her co-representation, and to David Knapman, Hugh Elphick, Denis Ryland and Richard Blake, all four of whom have kept my finances in order despite my prodigality. I'm indebted to so many people who are now beyond reach. Who will accept my thanks on behalf of Bud Flanagan, Chesney Allen, David Nixon, Gracie Fields, Richard Murdoch, Bernie Winters, stage director Joan Davis and TV producer Albert Locke who gave me such sage advice? Thank you to good friends who encouraged and supported me throughout some of these sixty-five years: Michael Bentine, radio producer John Browell, Lord Westbury, the entire Dave Ismay family, Tabatha Richards, Mitch Murray and his glamorous girls, Jimmy Jewel, Jim Bowen, Leslie Crowther, Mike and Lynne Pemberton and their son Michael, and Ivor Spencer, whose Guild of Professional Toast-masters voted me After-dinner Speaker of the Year in 1987 and again in 1992, making me its only two-time recipient. As for my eight years as Vice-Chairman and Chairman of SOS, our celebrity-based organisation helping those with cerebral palsy, they've been made easy by director Carol Myer and her superb staff and all the famous faces smiling around the committee table. Finally, thank you kindly to the members of the press who have helped me by endorsing my flimsy fame, especially the interviewers and feature writers and some of the kinder critics. I remain beholden.

Foreword

WHAT'S IN THIS BOOK
AND WHAT ISN'T

On the morning of 1st June 1993, I stayed in bed until the temperature was sixty-five and rising. Then I was the same.

I didn't spend my sixty-fifth birthday looking back. Writing this book has given me a bellyful of that. What I hoped would be a nostalgic stroll down memory lane has too often turned out to be a miasmic grope through long-closed corridors.

There's a lot in the past that one doesn't recall until one remembers it, if you see what I mean. Summoning up some wistful or self-serving anecdote is easy. Rewriting history to avoid its uglier facts, no problem. No, the hard part is the truth. And on all the relatively important matters in my life, I have elected to be as honest as I know how. That decision has meant doing it the hard way, dredging up some disagreeable sludge from the waters of Lethe and reassessing it in often painful retrospect. Since I have spent my whole life trying to avoid confrontation with the unpleasant, it may seem a bit out of character for me to do it now. Well, Catholics call it confession and psychiatrists call it catharsis. I call it playing fair with the audience. When you buy a ticket to see a performance, the entertainer owes you your money's worth. Same with an autobiography. Well, it is in my book.

That said, my frankness doesn't grant me licence to acknowledge the faults and wrongs of others. So while I promise to tell you the truth about my life and times insofar as I am capable of doing so, I won't tell you the whole truth about everyone. That would involve a few betrayals of faith. Let others tell their secrets elsewhere if they want to, I really can't. And my publisher's lawyers agree with me.

In particular, in the past I've caused my first wife and my children some distress through my rashness with press interviews and, if you will forgive me, I'll set down no more than the plain facts regarding them and otherwise respect their desire for privacy.

This June of '93 has brought me more than a bus pass. Within my first twelve days as a pensioner I've been blessed in triplicate with a return to dramatic acting in a TV film; my second award as After-dinner Speaker of the Year from the Guild of Professional Toastmasters; and, to the joy of my friends and the confusion of my enemies, the Order of the British Empire. Not being able to believe my luck is keeping me a safe distance from complacency.

Writing an autobiography has been likened to marrying a nymphomaniac. Wonderful for the first couple of months; thereafter, exhausting.

I started in July '92, took time off for writing and taping a couple of TV series and an instructional video on public speaking, plus some other professional engagements, returning to my word processsor with varying levels of eagerness. Eagerness to express myself, eagerness to record the facts, eagerness to get a nasty bit over . . . but never an eagerness to edit. If I'd had more time, I'd have written a shorter book.

Some disillusioned writer once said that the relationship of editor to author is that of razor to throat. I've been fortunate here. No more than surplus whisker removal has resulted. In fact, it was my publisher's enthusiasm over the first half of my writing that vivified the second. As a result, the content of the book you hold is everything relevant to my life that I have to say.

Well, I believe it is.

If I think of anything else, I'll be in touch.

1

WHAT IT'S ALL ABOUT

– As a Boy –

Concerning childhood pain, physical and otherwise, devotion to Grandfather Christmas and loss, vocal and otherwise

In the spring of 1992, Channel Four screened a series of old TV shows under the umbrella title of 'TV Heaven'. One was called 'The Bob Monkhouse Show' from 1958. Not unnaturally curious, I watched. At first, I was amused to see myself aged twenty-nine or thirty, spouting an opening monologue I could still just remember. I was even moved to mixed feelings by the raw brashness of my former self, wondering how I'd feel if I could meet him, whether I'd like him or not. Would I tell him what the future had in store, warn or advise him? Switching off the sound, I tried to assemble in my mind just what he was like, this smooth-faced wag clowning his way through absurd routines with such apparent confidence. My conclusion was this: I'd tell him nothing. No words from a ghostly older self on a visit from thirty-five years in the future could have altered the pattern of his thinking.

Hard as I thought, watching the lucky chap frolicking in his black-and-white mock-Hollywood, I could come up with no trenchant advice that might have deflected him from the pitfalls, nothing to improve his selfish behaviour or cure his bad habits or prevent his lapses into careless stupidity.

With this fatalistic lesson in mind, I began to embark upon these memoirs. At first I feared that my memory, although prodigious on subjects that interest me, might be too inadvertently selective as I delved into my own history, so I turned to old scrapbooks

1

and early press cuttings, boxes of stuff untouched for forty years or so. Whose detritus was this? It seemed to be concerned with another person's existence entirely.

Here: a photo of me in suit I hope I never owned, opening a jam factory in a town I've never visited, surrounded by unfamiliar intruders from a parallel universe. There: a press report about my being unable to take part in a Show Biz XI football match due to a fractured ankle. I've never volunteered to play football in my life. I was giving way to fantasies of having a secret twin when it suddenly struck me. A fractured ankle, yes, 1957, filming a sequence for a TV play due to be screened live from Bristol. It was a 1920s comedy thriller, *The Cat and the Canary* – I'd seen Bob Hope in the film of it when I was eleven – and there was this scene we'd shot on Cobham Common. My vintage Studebaker stalled while fording a shallow stream. I was to jump out, swing the starting handle and then register awareness of being watched from the bushes by the pretty heroine, Elvi Hale. But my foot skidded on the wet pebbles, my ankle twisted and snapped and – the story's unimportant so I won't go on, I'm sure you've got the point. Without the press report of a long forgotten lie about a long forgotten match, the memory of that play and a dozen other associated incidents might not have been triggered. I can't tell you how much that cheered me up.

The prospect of writing a book about myself had been depressing me. Now I realised that it could be a voyage of discovery. Well, rediscovery for me, I suppose, and that's how it's been – a knock-on effect, one recollection stimulating another. Take that fractured ankle, for example. That brought to mind another, earlier pair of fractured bones.

For the greater part of my life my emotions have seemed to live a private and separate existence of their own. They affected my behaviour without doing me the courtesy of announcing themselves to the forefront of my mind, operating instead on some secret level and influencing my decisions and actions in a way that was very confusing to me. Since the everyday self who is writing these words still hasn't a clue what subterranean seas may be ebbing and flowing and washing around my id, I can't always be certain of my honesty. Which brings me to the day I broke my leg.

I was nine years old, running around our garden in Beckenham in an August twilight. Little apples littered the lawn and my left foot crushed one, slipping on it and twisting under me as I fell. My left shin bone cracked and the fibula, unable to take the strain, also fractured. The pain was the worst I had experienced until then and I started screaming. My mother came running out of our french windows, angrily hushing me as she came, grabbed my arm and smacked me round the head, telling me, 'Quiet, Robert! What will the neighbours think?'

Why am I still angry with her for that? Her mistake was easy enough to understand and I am sure that she felt contrite when the facts were known. Here was a woman who hated fuss, who required all outward signs of excitement concealed, reacting according to her nature when her small son apparently lost control of himself and started shrieking. Yet my only clear emotional memory of that incident remains ineradicable resentment.

Did my childish indignation enter the fabric of my identity like a fly caught in amber, never to be changed by the tolerance of maturity? Or was this single offence somehow recognised by my prepubescent subconscious as signifying my mother's total attitude towards me? Perhaps it is that, the instinctive and unalterable sense of outrage at a loved one's coldness typified by one small incident. Or maybe I just hold grudges.

At that same age, my favourite person in the whole wide world was my paternal grandfather, Frederick John Monkhouse, co-founder of the family business, Monkhouse and Glasscock Ltd, with factories in Hardwidge Street, Snow's Field, London SE1 and at Devonshire Works, High Street, Birmingham 12, churning out custard powder, jelly crystals, infants' and invalids' foods, cake and bun mixtures, blancmange and golden raising powders, soup preparations and celery salt, all under the banner of 'Monk & Glass – At Last! At Last!'

Grandpa Monkhouse was a Charles Dickens character; white side-whiskered, rosy apple-cheeked, twinkling blue-eyed and hemispherically paunched. If I tell you that his laughter came in gales, that his rich baritone filled his great house like that of a born orator, that his readiness to like everyone he met was only exceeded by his unstinting love of children, then you will surely suppose that, if I am not wilfully exaggerating, my description may be distorted by the golden glow of nostalgia. As a young man I wondered the same thing and so sought out old people who knew and worked with my grandfather. Their depiction of him tallied in every way with my own.

My great-grandfather was a ship-owner in Cumberland and Frederick John was the youngest of his nine children. At the age of twenty-two he came to London to seek his fortune, first joining a firm of tea importers and becoming manager. When his employers rejected his plans to reorganise their sales department by doubling the number of commercial travellers and giving them increasing commissions in reward for greater sales, Grandpa joined a concern of mineral water manufacturers as a traveller, where he befriended S. T. Glasscock and told him his idea.

While visiting a wide range of grocers in the cause of taking orders for mineral water, the two young men also carried out a private investigation for themselves. In friendly conversation with each of the shop proprietors, they encouraged them to complain about inconsistent lines and seemingly attractive goods of unreliable quality. Within a few months they had compiled what they needed – a short list of products least trusted by retailers and their customers but nevertheless saleable.

'Somewhere on this list is our future,' said my grandpa. They crossed out a once-famous glossy toilet paper, a harsh scouring powder and, to grandpa's amusement, the very tea imported by the company that had first employed him. They all represented entrenched competition and offered poor profits. But prominent along disappointing products were two fairly recent labour-savours: egg custard formula and ready flavoured gelatine.

'Cooks and young wives have to spend hours making custard from fresh ingredients,' my grandpa reasoned. 'Same thing with making jellies, boiling up gelatine, fruit juices, sugar and such. A really well-made custard powder that mixes quickly and gives the same pleasing result every time is bound to succeed. Likewise some kind of fruit jelly crystals. Let's make both under the same brand name.'

They established their little factory in a tiny Bermondsey back street with only a handful of employees and invested most of their capital in development, paying high salaries to three talented research chemists. Six months later the partners agreed that they had exactly the right products and they hit the road once more as commercial travellers, this time in business for themselves alone. Within five years their bright yellow label was a familiar sight on the shelves of thousands of groceries all over the world. Monk & Glass was now employing over one hundred and fifty factory workers and thirty travellers, all participating in profits. In the jelly business, my grandpa told me, it's called being set for life.

He married Miss Kate Jarvis of Faversham, destined to become the grand old lady of my distant boyhood. I have a sepia photograph of her, dressed in the manner of Queen Mary and sitting in a small open carriage drawn by two Shetland ponies, ready to tour her gardens in Forest Hill. She turns a cool and innocent gaze to the camera as if jelly crystals wouldn't melt in her mouth.

Christmas at Terrington, my grandpa's big house in Mayow Road, was a lavish, crowded, well-fed riot. He sent chauffeured cars to fetch everyone so that the grown-ups could drink safely, arriving on Christmas Eve in time for hot toddy and oysters, in retrospect the oddest sort of appetiser but unquestioned at the time.

The twenty-foot tree in the hall was wired to the second-floor balcony to support the weighty profusion of its multi-coloured load: stars and fairies and glittering balls of silver and gold, scarlet ribbons winding round pink cupids, crackers, candy canes, masks, ragdoll clowns and pierrots, all ablaze with cheery little lights. Heaped beneath it, solemn with promise, were a hundred mysterious parcels, one to be opened by each of the children whenever Grandpa drew his bos'n's whistle from his waistcoat and blew it, a ceremony that occurred at hourly intervals and which had me and my nine cousins squealing and sprinting and tearing at paper with an energy that made the old chap cry with laughter.

The Christmas Day banquet began at noon when Grandpa beat a three-foot-wide Chinese gong with a croquet mallet. His butler and two maids helped him to share out masses of food to us all: whole hams and turkeys with chestnut stuffing, suckling pigs, black puddings, veal pies, breaded sausages, great tongues with boats of Madeira sauce, and then mince pies and cream, rich dark cake, lemon tarts, brandy snaps, baked apples in cinnamon, rhum babas, treacle pud and, of course, oceans of custard. Wines and spirits circulated freely and, as the staff cleared away, everyone drifted into what Grandpa called 'the convalescent club', a big withdrawing room full of comfy chairs. My Aunt Muriel and Uncle Bert Trouse would join the hired pianist at the Steinway to sing Victorian duets while the staff brought round China tea and liqueurs. Grandpa never served coffee – he said it made people testy. Then the adults chatted and dozed, the maids took the small children up to bed for a nap and we brats were wrapped up warmly and sent into the garden to test the durability of our larger toys. We knew that Boxing Day would mean a mass outing to see a matinée performance of the Lyceum panto and a farewell supper back at the house when Grandpa would do some conjuring tricks and then ask each child to tell a joke for half-a-crown. I enjoyed that bit most of all.

Once again I feel I must reassure you about such idyllic memories. Those of my cousins who are still living have identical recollections of four such Christmases at Terrington. We also agree that none of us ever felt so well loved than when we sat on grandpa's lap and looked into his eyes.

He was an extraordinary man whose philanthropy was a byword, he was active in countless charities, a Pastmaster of the Worshipful Company of Fletchers, a member of both the Livery of the Worshipful Company of Weavers and that of Needle-makers. Masonically he was Past-Officer of the Grand Lodge of England and also of the Grand Chapter of England. For those of his factory workers who needed such things, he bought bicycles, reading glasses and false teeth. When he died in April 1938, aged seventy-six, over two hundred mourners joined the family at the graveside in Norwood and the number of floral tributes was so great that three coaches were needed to convey them.

The effect of his death on me was profound. I lost the ability to speak and remained more or less silent for just over three months. It was possible for me to make a noise with my vocal chords but it was uncontrollable and unintelligible and it frightened me to hear myself. During my tenth birthday party I made a great effort to use my tongue and lips to produce a little speech of thanks but it was as if they were paralysed and I ran upstairs in tears. Schoolwork was difficult and unkind boys made fun of me. When I began to talk again, it was with a stutter that affected all words beginning with vowels. Even today, the same stammer can return if I am severely shocked.

It may be that most of us love because we need to do so, not because we find someone who deserves it. I believe that the devotion I felt for old John Monkhouse was so total and so enriching that, although it was very unlikely that I could ever have found someone else deserving such adoration, I continued to look for such a person, occasionally deluding myself into believing I had found them. So there was, in the first forty years of my life at least, a compulsion to love without reservation. It was a powerful legacy, Grandpa.

2

WHAT IT'S ALL ABOUT

– As a Father –

*Concerning the birth of a remarkable first son, how he
made his own fun and how I made my own defects*

My first son, Gary Alan, was born on 24 November 1951, after
two days and nights of trying to delay his premature birth. The
pregnancy had only just completed its sixth month and his
chances of being undamaged by his birth struggle were slight. He
weighed two pounds at birth, immediately lost a vital ounce, and
had anaemia, septicaemia and jaundice. He lay in an incubator
together with another premature baby, a little girl. The dangers
of oxygen pressure were not so well recognised in those times and
the baby girl lost her sight. That's about the only time Gary was
really lucky.

I could relate almost every detail of the morning he was born
and of the months that followed, months in which we had no idea
that anything was seriously wrong with our son, but I couldn't tell
you what I was feeling. My emotions were keeping their secrets.

Gary's mother was not so repressed. She was as tirelessly
dedicated to him as I was to her. When we realised that Gary was
not progressing normally we sought advice from the then
foremost specialist in disabilities resulting from premature birth,
Dr Irene Collis. That was the first time I ever heard the word
'spastic' used to describe a physical condition. The doctor
explained that cerebral palsy meant that part of Gary's brain was
permanently damaged, mostly the part that operated movement
in his arms and legs, which were receiving scrambled
instructions. She also told us that she believed he would never be
able to speak. She was quite right. It transpired that Gary was
effectively deaf and unable to use his tongue and lips to produce

speech. He could make a noise with his vocal chords but it was uncontrollable and unintelligible. Unlike me though, he couldn't run upstairs in tears.

Gary's life was to be a sustained refusal to give in to his disability. In him one could see the innocence and vulnerability which the rest of us have only briefly and soon lose. As he grew, it was both terrible and wonderful to watch him coming to terms with his condition while simultaneously expressing the unabashed anger and sorrow he felt as he recognised it. Growing with him was his natural determination, a strength of purpose as unselfconscious as everything he ever felt. Trapped in an increasingly unresponsive and disobedient body, he would remain undefeated by it. I saw Gary in despair but I never saw him surrender.

Dealt such a poor hand, Gary held three aces to see him through: he was handsome with a knock-down smile, he knew exactly how he wanted to use each day and each person, and he loved fun. As early as 1958, when he was seven years old and we lived in Golders Green, this love of fun took the form of comic revenge. We had regular visits from a Gas Board man who came to read our meter every quarter. He was painfully jolly and patronised Gary by ruffling his curly hair and shouting in his face.

'Hello, cat got your tongue? You can say my name if you try! Come on, say Ronnie! Ronnie Burnside!'

'Gary can't hear, Mr Burnside.'

'Oh, he can hear me all right, can't you, son?'

'He can't talk either.'

'Listen, I've had kiddies talk to me who haven't spoken for ten years.'

What did they say, we wondered – bugger off?

The man called round one busy December day and, as he repeated this vexing ritual, my wife left for a shopping trip while I retired upstairs to my little office to complete a script for my BBC TV sitcom, 'My Pal Bob'. If Gary needed me, he could press a bell with the big toe of his right foot. Otherwise, he was helpless, depending on a lap-strap to keep him in his small wheelchair with his wrists individually strapped to his belt. But he wanted to spend the day drawing, holding coloured pens between the first two toes of his right foot. Mr Burnside dismissed us with a wave.

'You go off and leave the lad with me, we're good pals, aren't we, son? Let's see, what are you trying to draw? What's that meant to be? Eh? Is it a house? Say house. You can say house, can't you, son? I'll say this for the kiddie, he may be crippled but he knows how to make his own fun!'

I'd been working on the script for longer than I realised when I heard the closing of the front door announce my wife's return. I greeted her in the hall and we both walked through the kitchen-parlour door to see Gary hanging out of his chair, red-eyed with tears, lungs heaving, giving every sign of having had a seizure. Very alarmed, we sat him up. He looked at us and burst out laughing again, hoarsely because he'd been laughing an awful lot for over an hour and a half. There was no sign of Mr Burnside.

The more we acted perplexed and asked him to tell us why he was laughing, the more he laughed. Then he raised his leg and pointed his toe at the cupboard. At that same moment we heard the cupboard door being thumped from inside and a man's rasping voice calling out, 'Is there somebody there at last? Let me out, please let me out!'

We opened the door and Mr Burnside, weary and sweaty, emerged. While Gary continued to chuckle throatily we worked out what had happened. The man had no sooner gone into the cupboard two hours earlier to read the meter than Gary had hurtled his chair across the floor and slammed the door shut with his foot. It was an old and solidly made door with no handle on the inside. Gary must have sat watching it shake with each unheard blow of Mr Burnside's fists, shaking even more with laughter.

'I've been yelling for him to let me out for half the afternoon!'

'We did tell you he couldn't hear,' we reminded him.

I was tempted to add that the Gas Board man had been right about one thing; Gary knew how to make his own fun.

Once the extent of my son's disability had sunk in, my emotional sublife made its presence known by giving me migraine headaches, something I'd never experiencd before. Each attack began with a kaleidoscopic scrambling of my vision for about twenty minutes. Then my sight blurred and clouded over so that I became effectively blind. A short while later the pain in my head began, a grinding sort of ache that lasted an hour or more but was almost welcome because its arrival was accompanied by the return of my sight. I had these migraine attacks about once every eight weeks or so for about twenty years. When Gary became happily settled at a residential centre administered by the Spastics Society in a very beautiful part of Worcestershire, the attacks slowly became shorter and less frequent.

Then in 1990, after moving to Grangewood in Essex, he fell in love with one of the residents, went through a form of marriage with her and entered the most contented phase of his life. My uncontrolled emotional response to my son's physical impediments subsided and the migrainous blindness hasn't returned since then.

So far. I don't want to say more, lest I tempt my unpredictable psyche. Manifesting inner turmoil as outward affliction is easy for me and my subliminal self, you see. We can do it all the time.

When my wife went into Queen Charlotte's Hospital in July 1954 to have our second son earlier than expected, I was quite calm about it. Or I thought I was. Not having eaten anything unusual, I was surprised by an attack of acute indigestion. I began to belch like Krakatoa and continued to do so every few seconds for just over forty-eight hours, making sleep quite impossible. No medication could stay this barrage of burps. Then, just as I despaired of living long enough to see my new baby, the news came that a healthy boy of four pounds four ounces was crying lustily at finding himself evicted from his cosy billet. In sympathy with my wife's triumph, I was delivered of a massive final belch and then fell quiet at last.

You may say hah, big deal, belching for two days and nights, that's just nerves. OK, but nerves are feelings – and how do you feel about haemorrhoids? I was opening in my first big summer show at the Winter Gardens, Blackpool, in 1957. The impresarios, George and Alfred Black, were favourably surprised at how well I had taken the arduous preparations for the six-month run, showing no sign of stress at the prospect of carrying a lavish two-hour revue twice nightly. Cool as an airline bread roll I was. With my wife and sons comfortably established in a big rented house in Lytham – St Anne's, I had finished writing the sketches and crossovers and solo patter spots as we rehearsed, completing one complicated musical routine only two hours before curtain up. The first night was a smash. Two thousand two hundred people cheered so long and loudly that we took an unheard-of seven curtain calls. After congratulations galore and a thanksgiving supper, I went to bed. Next morning I was walking like Groucho. The doctor counted nine piles, each with its own thrombos, requiring surgical removal. If you've ever been unlucky enough to share this affliction, you'll know how much I enjoyed doing the show for the next three weeks or so. To this day, I can't look at a retreating baboon.

3

WHAT IT'S ALL ABOUT

– As a Husband –

*Concerning the healing power of love upon an old
wound and the need of it to accept two very great losses*

It's been said that each of us makes his own weather, determining
the colour of the skies in the emotional universe which he
inhabits. If that's so, my sun shines in perpetually clear blue
heavens. I am constitutionally and fundamentally incapable of
worry. To me, worrying is like trying to grasp a piece of raw liver
in a bath of engine oil. Horrible and almost impossible.

But if that's true, what part of me put the wind in my
constitution and the piles on my fundament? Who's running
things around here, me or some stranger within? My desire to
understand this ambivalence frustrated me for years. I felt so
uncertain about how I was going to react to each important event
in my life, aware of this separation between my normal serene
self, the me I know and trust who's able to address life's setbacks
unruffled, and the frantic freak inside whose only answer to
problems is to rustle up some random affliction. The solution to
the dilemma presented itself so quietly that it went unnoticed for
years.

The process of falling in love with Jackie began shortly after
the collapse of my first marriage. Having known and worked with
her since 1956 when she joined our office as a twenty-year-old
secretary, you may wonder why it took over a decade for my
respect and affection to become love. After all, I'd had love
affairs during this time; and for that matter, so had she. It just
never occurred to either of us to fancy one another. Besides
which, had I made an amorous approach, she'd have turned me
down because I was a married man and the situation in the office
could have become awkward.

13

When we married on 4 October 1973, Jackie was thirty-seven years old and I was forty-five. She had loved me for six years by then and the healing of the schism at my core must have been complete, although I didn't realise it until Sunday, 12 January 1975, during an edition of 'The Golden Shot' with Willie Rushton and Ray Alan as guests.

What I'm about to describe is a piffling incident by any standard. The format of the show required me to invite Willie 'to shoot the crossbow on behalf of someone who deserves a bit of luck'. He spun a wheel of fortune loaded with letters, I took out the one indicated by the arrow and read it out loud. It was a harrowing little note, describing the plight of an elderly widow in Leicester who was blind and needed twenty pounds to replace her beloved radio, stolen by thieves who had knocked her unconscious. Halfway through reading the letter I began to weep. Later in the show, Ray had his dolly Lord Charles say something very funny and I laughed uninhibitedly for half a minute or more, regardless of the audience.

Afterwards, Dickie Leeman, who produced the series that year, commented upon my vulnerable state and surmised that I'd had 'a tumble down the sink' at lunchtime. I never drank before six pm then and very seldom do now. Neither Jackie nor I remarked upon my behaviour as we drove home from Birmingham. Two days later I was down at Thames TV's Teddington studios, taping 'Looks Familiar' with Denis Norden. One of the nostalgic items in the programme moved me to tell a revealing childhood anecdote, one that's repeated elsewhere in these memoirs. Denis was mildly surprised and said later, 'You were very much yourself on the show this afternoon, you weren't performing, it was really very natural.'

On Wednesday I was in cabaret at the Four Seasons Hotel in Lincoln and found myself telling the audience a long, true and funny tale about myself I had never before used in performance. It scored deeper, friendlier laughs than the regular material that had to make way for it.

We drove on to Cleethorpes next day where I was doubling at night spots called the Beachcomber and the Flamingo. In those days Jackie used to sit out front and watch my act about four times a year, offering valuable opinions as I developed new routines and discarded old ones. That night she watched both shows.

On the drive home she broke the silence about midday. She said, 'You were great onstage last night, you were different, you were like you really are.'

I said, 'It's a bit late in the day, I know, but I think I'm turning honest.'

It's ironic that, in an industry where writers and directors but particularly performers search for ways to protect themselves emotionally so as not to be crippled artistically by rejection, I spent so much of my adulthood trying to get in touch with my emotions, to welcome and be led by them. During the previous eight years of my adjustment to the fact of being loved, warts and all, by the most important person in my life, the dichotomy in my nature had been dwindling until at last there was no longer any breach between thought and feeling. Jackie's strong, consistent approval of me had been a therapy. Deep down in the mind, where no logic or reason can penetrate, love is slowly recognised and surrendered to as the supreme emotion.

When we had moved to our present home, the sixteenth-century farmhouse in a Bedfordshire valley just north of the Dunstable Downs, I was very keen for Jackie's mother to give up her flat in the increasingly dangerous London neighbourhood of Shepherd's Bush and live with us. Lily agreed with mixed feelings. She had lived in the flat with her beloved Bill, Jackie's daddy, and it held precious memories for her. Still, on 21 June 1975, the three of us set up residence in our tiny village and Lily busied herself with local voluntary work for the elderly. At first she was as cheery and funny as she'd always been, but after eighteen months or so she began to show signs of irrational anxiety and depression. She'd scold Jackie for no reason, which caused us all distress. We persuaded her to seek medical help for her fits of melancholy and she responded quite well to the treatment for a while. But there was no preventing the inexorable deterioration of her spirit and early one August morning in 1979, determined not to become a burden on us, she slipped out of the house in her night clothes and went up the garden to our swimming pool.

When Jackie found her mummy's bed empty, she woke me in great alarm.

'The pool!' she said instinctively.

15

I ran there in my pyjamas, saw Lily face-down in the water, waded out to her, pulled her on to the steps and tried to give her the kiss of life, but without success. The effect of her mother's death on Jackie was intensified by the change in what had been demanded of her by Lily's illness, combined with the day-to-day need to support me through the previous two-year build-up to my Old Bailey trial, a misery recounted elsewhere. Suddenly the two greatest reasons for maintaining her strength and stability were gone. I was discharged and poor Lily was dead. For the first time in our relationship, Jackie needed as much help as she usually gave. The same doctor who had done his utmost to help Lily now came to our help with a course of medicine that would help Jackie to get through the difficult months that ended the 1970s. Then, just after Christmas, we went to Barbados for a holiday and her prescription ran out. 'That's the end of that,' she said; and it was.

The emotional chain that has guided my narrative so far has led from my boyhood through fatherhood by way of anger, adoration, grief, pain, joy, anxiety, love, despair and the survival of the spirit. I think this is the appropriate point to tell you that, while I was writing these pages, I had a phonecall from my first wife to tell me that Gary had fallen seriously ill. Within an hour, I learned that my oldest child had died. The coroner's report was of natural causes.

His funeral, a quiet one, was on 14 July 1992. Only a few good friends knew of Gary's death and they were scrupulously careful to keep the news of it from the press. At the request of Gary's mother, some words were spoken by an actor friend who had known my son well. In the midst of our deep sorrow, he was able to make us smile by recalling Gary's insuppressible personality. He said, 'When Gary came to call on you, he knew without doubt that he was doing you a favour. He would never leave without letting you know what he was going to eat the next time he'd manage to call round.' It was a small and typical example of that unconquerable and innocent ego that had helped Gary to endure his awful impediments with such positive strength for over forty years.

A pal of Gary's, at one time his key worker at Grangewood, had spent the final weekend with him and the videotape he made of their activities shows my son at his happiest.

16

You'll recall, a few pages ago, I explained that conveying some of my feelings to you isn't easy for me. This is a case in point. I can't express my emotions in words, explain my sense of emptiness at Gary's absence. What is different is this: I know about it and I can accept it and I can deal with it. It's taken me a lifetime to learn to do that.

4

FROM THE TOP

– Fat Boy –

'From the top' being a show business term for 'Let's take this routine from the very beginning'; we do, as an eight pound baby expands to an eleven stone butter ball and comic motivation is considered

Unpunctual from the very start, I vacated my mother a week overdue and at the inconvenient hour of two in the morning. It was 1 June 1928, and unsubtle hints dropped by my aunts Eckie and Ella in later years suggest that I was the result of a rare coupling after my parents returned from a boozy evening with the Worshipful Company of Fletchers. I'll drink to that.

I was christèned Robert Alan Monkhouse at St Margaret's Church, Beckenham, the younger son of Wilfred Adrian Monkhouse, a scholar at Aske's who became a cavalry corporal, fighting the Turks in the 1914–18 war and who came out of the army with one certainty – that horse exhaust is the ill wind that blows nobody any good. He once told me, 'Never, *never*, walk around the rear end of a horse because their timing is perfect.' That's the only piece of advice my father ever gave me and I've always followed it.

My mother's two sisters never wanted her to marry 'Wammy' – they thought him a glum and parsimonious young man. I knew that dad got his nickname from his initials but always wondered why my mother's nickname was Buddy and her younger sister Eckie's was Hammy. My question was brushed aside. When you're nine years old, everything is none of your business. I was thirty-eight when a Bolton widow saw my TV series 'Mad Movies' and wrote to me offering her late husband's collection of short silent 16mm film comedies for sale. Among them I found three one-reel knockabouts from 1915 featuring slapstick comedians called Bud and Ham. I tried to imagine a forgotten summer evening when the laughing girls came out of a long-vanished picture palace and cavorted on the Norwood pavements in imitation of the movie clowns, creating moments of such silly happiness that they were stuck for life with their sobriquets. With lighthearted Eckie, it was easy to picture; with my mother, utterly impossible.

She was born Dorothy Muriel Hansard and had from her childhood a strong-willed and self-controlled nature, not easily pleased. Facially, I resemble her, even to the moles on our chins, although her features were stronger and more severely set. Her hair, naturally dark until her death, was always pulled back from her face and usually arranged in a roll above her forehead in the manner of Joan Crawford, the rest of it kept conveniently short or in the sort of hairnet that used to be called a snood. Unless something amused her or social politeness required a smile, her expression seemed to fall naturally into one of dispassionate reproof. She spoke well but in a clipped fashion, made immediate judgements of people and events (usually unfavourable), and assumed prejudices like other women collect jewellery.

I can only recall a single instance of feeling her embrace, an occasion so astonishing to me as to remain a clear picture in my mind today. It was on a May afternoon in 1944 when north-west Kent and south London were experiencing an unusually heavy fall of doodlebugs, the unmanned Nazi FZG-76s that were launched from France to exhaust their 150 gallons of fuel over England and crash with their explosive warheads onto targets that were mainly civilian. I'd come home from school early after six of these flying bombs hit Dulwich and it was feared that the College might be a target. As I opened the front door of 168 Bromley Road, another one struck a house in nearby Scott's Lane, sending up a huge coughing thump. In the stairwell of our hall my father had erected a Morrison air-raid shelter, a sort of strong metal table. As I closed the door behind me, my mother called to me to join her where she knelt, leaning halfway out of the shelter and beckoning me. I crouched down and slithered inside on the blankets she had laid there. 'They sent us home early, Mum, they don't seem to realise that doodlebugs haven't got a precise guiding mechanism and . . .'

Suddenly my mother made a sobbing sound, grabbed me and hugged me against her. My face was pressed against the soft material of her dress, a cotton frock patterned with little blue and brown flowers, and I felt her shaking with tears as she choked out, 'Grandma! I'm so frightened for Grandma! Are the bombs falling on West Wickham, Robert?'

I lied as I so often did, telling her that they were passing to the west of the area where her parents lived and flying on towards London. I said that only a few were running out of juice too early and those were the ones dropping on Beckenham, Crystal Palace and Dulwich. This placated her and she released me as suddenly as she had seized me. I was sorry she had let go of me, although this unique display of emotion from my mother had embarrassed as well as amazed me. It was never repeated or referred to. She was more than usually snappy with me for a week or two afterwards.

Our house seemed as big to me as your childhood home probably appeared to you. Jackie and I were driving back from a seaside show five years ago and I realised we were passing through Shortlands. 'Over the next hill we'll come to the house where I was born.' Jackie, who'd always supposed that I grew up in the kind of home she associated with well-to-do folk, could hardly believe how small it was. Nor could I. What I remembered as a great gate to swing on now seemed to have the dimensions of a cat-flap, the long steep driveway more like a wheelchair ramp.

If this causes any offence to whoever lives there now, please, dear residents, accept my apology. You are occupying a very des. res., fully det., sep. garage., with fr. and r. gardens, mature fruit trs., hall, 2 recep., 4 bedrms., 227 bus route. It's just that it was a great big world to a little boy. Outside the french windows was the giant rock that hid a million ants, upstairs to the right was the store room with the workbench upon which my father's hand-built crystal set once picked up 2-LO and I signalled my position in the stormy Atlantic to Royal Navy HQ. Here's the window I'd climb through after everyone was asleep to run naked around the garden in the dark of night. There's the newel post that stopped my first attempt to slide down the banisters and also gave me my first experience of scrotal agony. That's the shelf where my Rupert the Bear annuals were replaced by Richmal Crompton's *Just William* books. Look at this gravel-dashed wall by the back door, do you see the empty sockets where the stones are missing? They were embedded in the skull of my little friend Alan Simpson when he ran, tripped and head-butted the house. To you, it's a place to live. To me, it's a museum of memories.

My mother had some slight artistic talent, inherited from her father who taught woodwork at a Norwood school and carved beautifully. In turn, I inherited my mother's modest gift and she taught me how to draw and paint. When I was six I made a picture of a farmyard which became her proudest possession for many years until the day I failed her. That was the day she took my childish painting out of its frame and tore it to pieces. For seventeen years after that she refused to acknowledge my existence and wouldn't have my name mentioned in her house.

From the time of my birth until his death, my father was a prematurely bald chartered accountant for Phoenix Assurance. While awkwardly affectionate with me, he was much more comfortable with my brother, who was five-and-a-half years older. They shared a passion for cricket, rugby and football. I've always loathed cricket, rugby and football. For my principal education I was sent to Dulwich College where the only things they taught with rigorous dedication were cricket, rugby and football. If they caught you painting they sent you for a cold shower. I consider running an unnatural act unless it's away from an enemy or towards a lavatory.

This distaste for physical action has its origins in my pre-pubescent weight. I was a very fat boy. As a Boy Scout my favourite good deed was helping myself across the road. Despite my mother's efforts to reduce my size with diet and exercise – no sugar, and cycling all over Kent and Surrey – I continued to retain flesh. When the local parade celebrating the Coronation of King George V passed our house in 1937, I was swinging on our gate and cheering as I waved my flag and peered into my tuppenny cardboard periscope. A gypsy family in the procession, red-white-and-blue bunting draped all over their caravan, pointed at me as they drove by and the father yelled, 'Fatty Arbuckle!' I had no idea what he meant but I went back inside the house at once and started drawing, my customary way of withdrawing.

Twenty-eight years later I was to research and produce a TV programme celebrating and defending the great silent film comic,

Roscoe 'Fatty' Arbuckle, whose career had been scuppered by false accusasions of rape and manslaughter. It was nominated for an award. That'll teach strangers to shout at me in the street.

Sports Day at St George's, my first prep school, was hell for me. Aged nine and weighing as many stones, my attempt to run the hundred yard race on a hot summer's day ended with my passing out cold in the final stretch. I remained unconscious for nearly half an hour while a doctor was summoned to revive me. My eyes opened in the school changing room as I heard Mr Beater, our aptly named headmaster, saying, 'All that fat and a weak heart – the boy will never live to adolescence.' I was horrified. From all I'd picked up from the older lads, adolescence was going to be the best part of my life. Haunted by this fear, I began to starve myself, pretending to have no appetite for home cooking. I hiked everywhere, supposing it to be less of a strain on my heart than cycling. Still my adiposity went unchecked. Hating my swollen appearance, I stuck my drawings all over the mirror in the bedroom which I shared with my brother. He'd take them down and I'd stick them back. Eventually he'd hit me and I'd run crying to our live-in maid, Edith Ashby, a plain but merry girl not that much older than my brother. She'd come to work for us aged fourteen when I was five and, though she was not expected to express any opinions, she always took my side. After she'd had a timid word with my mother, our bedroom mirror was removed. Four years were to pass before a doctor, treating me for a cut head, diagnosed my problem as a thyroid condition. In a way that would be considered primitive today, I was encouraged to pop thyroid correction tablets into my mouth as if they were Smarties. My excess lard melted away as I entered upon the adolescence I feared I'd never reach.

And that cut on my head which the doctor had to stitch? I told my mother it was caused by a fall off my bike while riding around after dark. It wasn't the truth. It had happened as the result of a blow. Although it's rather late in the day to write to a father who died in 1957, a year younger than I am now, it might help me to get something off my chest.

Dear Dad,
This isn't an easy letter for me to write. I wish we had loved each

other more. I'm not making excuses for myself but it would have been easier for me to care for you if I had believed you cared for me. I don't mean when I was little. I adored you then. You used to hug me in a way that Mum never did. You once sat me on your knee and told me a story about Hop High, the Red Indian boy, and more than once you let me snuggle up to you in bed on a Sunday morning. You rubbed your unshaven jaw on my little chin and told me you were planting whisker seed. At mealtimes you did silly dances with your first two fingers on the dining table to make me laugh. I always ran to you when you came home but I preferred to be close to you at weekends when you wore that rough Harris tweed jacket with its lovely smell of pipe tobacco. I can picture you so clearly, leaning over the coal fire in our dining room, scraping out the charred bowl of one of your two old pipes, blowing out the dottle of poisonous tarry deposit so that it would fly into the glowing coals to shrivel and hiss away to nothing. You used to say, 'Burn, witch, burn!' and roll your eyes and I'd scream and laugh in happy terror. Perhaps it was when I stopped laughing at such simple things that you began to lose interest in me. As I grew, I began to see how otherwise joyless you were. Perhaps the tiny boy I'd been was your last admirer.

The infantile fun we'd shared, was it a sort of respite for you, a break from your habitual dislike of people? I recall you scowling more, your mouth in that sulky grimace, your front teeth slightly protruding, your chin drawn back, and I hear the rise in your bitter criticism of all our relatives and family friends, not a good word for anyone. You didn't gamble at all or drink much – the two bottles in the sideboard, Charrington's Forest Brown Ale and Dubonnet, seemed to survive from Christmas to Christmas – and as for sex, I doubt that you made more than a clumsy pass at another man's wife after a glass or two during Ladies' Night at Gleneagles Rugby Club. As my humour grew more sophisticated, I'd often make Mum smile at jokes you didn't share. It annoyed you.

Because I sensed your growing disinterest, I turned to her for approval. Then you lost the company of my brother, so much closer to you than I, when the war started and he was evacuated with the rest of the college to Tonbridge, then called up and sent to fight in North Africa. Somehow that seemed to make you even *colder to me and your late-night rows with Mum kept me awake in bed, night after night. Young as I was, I knew that that endless war of words had little to do with its prosaic subject matter.*

'Wammy, must you pick at that leather? The settee's peeling badly enough as it is.'

'I was brushing off a loose bit, that's all, my dear. Something that could have been done when the room was cleaned today, I'd have thought. Was it, by the way? Cleaned?'

'How can I invite friends here with this furniture? It's all peeling and cracking. We live like paupers. No hot water after eight o'clock . . .'

'Once the washing-up is done, we don't need hot water and anyway, it's news to me that we've got all these friends you're so keen to invite.'

'We haven't any, thanks to you. Every friendship I manage to strike up, you manage to spoil it, criticising, sneering, look at Marjorie and Harold. And I can't look Mrs Gamon in the eye.'

'Harold Roberts is my bank manager, not some wartime comrade.'

'When did you have a wartime comrade? You never made friends with anyone in the army.'

'What about Arthur?'

'Horrible, common man. You said so yourself.'

'It's you who won't invite people, not me.'

'How can I, with you sitting and picking bits of leather off the settee? And just supposing someone wanted to wash their hands and us with no hot water? And that awful little Jew sitting there making his remarks.'

'Once and for all, Arthur Freeman isn't Jewish. He's a Mason.'

'And there are no Jewish Masons, I suppose.'

'Not in my Lodge. So just who are all these people you're so desperate to invite? And what are they going to do? Play party games?'

'They can help you pick the leather off that settee while you make your sarcastic remarks about their legs.'

'I never made any sarcastic remarks about Sheila Gamon's legs.'

'You asked her if there was something wrong with them. I've never been so embarrassed in all my life. Marjorie Roberts couldn't believe it.'

'I don't care what Marjorie bloody Roberts believes . . .'

'You can keep that sort of language for your Jewish guttersnipe friends like Arthur Freeman.'

'. . . all I said was, all I thought, there might be something wrong with the woman's circulation. She was breathless and they were mottled.'

'Sheila's legs are always mottled. No one's ever mentioned it until you had to blurt it out. Marjorie thought you'd gone mad.'

'All I did, I thought she was ill or something, I asked her if she'd like a glass of water.'

'Cold water.'

'Yes.'

'If it had been after eight o'clock in the evening, you could hardly have offered her hot water. If you call that hot, it's barely lukewarm.'

'As I recall, you've got a perfectly good gas stove and a perfectly good kettle and you're quite capable of boiling water.'

'That gas stove is older than the settee. It's a wonder you're not sitting in the kitchen, picking bits off that. Staring at Sheila's legs, it was quite disgusting. No wonder we have no friends, at least you're right about that.'

'I never said that we had no friends, what I said was . . .'

'That's exactly what you said not two minutes ago.'

'I didn't, all I said was it was news to me . . .'

'No, I'm agreeing with you, Wammy. You said we have no friends, Harold's only your bank manager, isn't that what you said? You swear about his wife, you drive Sheila away by staring at her legs and making horrid remarks, so how could we expect to have any friends?'

'I didn't mean that, you're deliberately twisting my words. Look, if I said that, which I don't remember saying, I'm only too happy for you to have as many friends as you want, for God's sake. Invite the whole neighbourhood round, for all I care. Have a weekend house party!'

'And let them see this furniture? Thank you very much. You'll do the washing-up, will you? At midnight, with cold water? You'd better ask the man who's only your bank manager if you can afford all the luncheon meat. Or perhaps Arthur Freeman can get it for you wholesale.'

'Don't start up again about the luncheon meat. All I said was *that with the price of boiled ham today, if we're going to go on having so many cold meals in this house . . .'*

And so it went on, never penetrating deeper than an endless skirmish with petty armaments, no real issues addressed, no kindness or honesty in the nightly process of using barely polite squabbling to distract your own attention from the real problem of your life together. Upstairs, I often wept, sensing that I overheard only symptoms of that greater, unspoken disaffection. Did old age bring you any harmony, Dad, or didn't you live long enough? After we moved to West Worthing you began to stay all week in London, coming home for weekends. In some ways I took your place, acting as Mum's escort to the cinema, doing all the things around the house that you used to do, like digging the garden and winding the clocks and creosoting the fence.

Do you remember the weekend that Grandma was ill and Mum had to go and look after her? You and I were alone in the house that Sunday evening. The weather was freezing and fuel was scarce. The bathroom was so cold I boiled water for my bath in the kettle and carried it to and fro from the kitchen to a zinc tub in front of the fireplace in our tiny front room. You were sitting silently at the small dining table, working on some figures, as I bathed in the flicker of the wood fire. As I finished washing and stepped out of the bath, I dropped my towel. You looked up and saw me standing there naked and let out such an angry roar, rising and rushing at me, seizing my right arm with your left hand and hitting my head with your open right hand so hard that I was sent flying backwards out of your grasp against the front wall of the room. My head smacked against the bottom of the window frame and the glass cracked. It knocked me out for a moment or two. While I was lying there, you had walked out of the room and when you suddenly strode back in again, coming towards me, I was frightened. I put my hands up to ward off another blow. We both saw that my fingers were covered in blood from where I must have touched the back of my head. You stopped, there was a pause, then you said, 'Clean yourself up,' and left the room again. My head was bleeding freely and I didn't know what to do. I held the towel to the wound and pulled on my pyjama trousers with the other hand. Then I knelt over the zinc tub so that the blood wouldn't drip on the carpet. I could hear you moving about upstairs, then you came down holding a first aid kit. You folded up some gauze, told me to hold it against the split. Then you wound a bandage around my head to hold the gauze pad in place. All this time, neither of us spoke. When you'd tied the bandage, you said, 'Now get dressed.' By the time I'd gone up to my room and put my clothes on, you'd phoned Dr Lewis.

The doctor, who had previously treated me for chicken pox, put the necessary stitches in my head in his backroom clinic, then went to speak to you in his front parlour. I heard you say something like, 'He's been told to be careful on his bike in the blackout,' so I knew the story. I also heard Dr Lewis say he thought my excessive embonpoint might be due to a glandular disorder. We walked back home in silence and I went up to bed without any exchange other than our goodnights. When I woke up I found my left eye and cheek were discoloured from the blow. You went off to catch your trains – West Worthing to Brighton, Brighton to Victoria, Victoria to Cannon Street – and I cycled to school, too queasy to eat breakfast. Mum was back when I'd got home and gave me hell for going out on my bike after dark. You'd phoned her about it, the cracked window too. Apparently I'd done that, playing about with my brother's old football. I thought you could have done better than that, Dad. Me with a football? As for your reasons for bashing me, you never explained them. I can only imagine that they had something to do with inarticulate emotion.

When we moved back to Beckenham, you continued to overlook me until that extraordinary time when you decided we should spend the day together. You astounded me by coming into my bedroom to open the curtains and announce that, now I was almost fifteen, 'It's high time you had your first shandy in a proper pub. And you're coming with me to that big store in Croydon, Kennards. We're going to buy a new radiogram and some up-to-date records. You can choose those, Robert. And after a meal, anything you want, we'll go to the pictures together, just you and me!'

I could tell you every detail of that day. The radiogram was a re-built pre-war utility model made by Murphy, the records we bought were by Joe Daniels and his Hot Shots, Johnny Clae and his Claepigeons, the Andrews Sisters, Mildred Bailey with the Red Norvo Orchestra, and Lennie Hayton's band playing 'It Looks Like Rain in Cherryblossom Lane'. We ate fried brill and chips in the Vogue Café and saw Abbott and Costello in Who Done It? *at the Bromley Odeon. It was after ten o'clock when we got home but we unloaded the car and brought our purchases into the hall. Then I thanked you, said my goodnights and went upstairs to bed. After I'd put the light out, I heard you and Mum arguing as usual. Foolishly, I crept across the landing and crouched by the first bend in the stairs where I could hear your voices most clearly. I heard you say, 'Look, I gave him a day, my dear, just as you asked. I'm not prepared to go further.'*

After that day we never talked much. It must have been a strain on Mum, trying to encourage conversations at the table that would involve us both. I preferred to draw comic strips and type stories in my room with lots of twelve-inch records of classical music spinning at seventy-eight revolutions per minute. Even today, when I play CDs and tapes of those same symphonies and concertos, I tense up at the points in the music where I used to have to stop the turntable and turn over the discs. It meant taking a few steps across the floor and I knew how the creaking of my bedroom floorboards above your head irritated you.

Were you aware that I passed my Higher School Certificate with five honours? You never mentioned it. When I went off to my first job aged seventeen-and-a-half, you never wished me luck. You weren't around when I said my farewell to Mum and home and used my RAF travel warrant to report for basic training at Padgate. During the difficult times with Mum over my engagement, marriage and the birth of my first son, you remained neutral. Our only contact was the gift you made me of a three-piece suite. I have it still, frequently re-covered and re-upholstered, and Jackie understands why we have to keep it.

When Mum cut me out of her life, you seemed to go along with it. Did you ever try to intercede with her on my behalf? And was it you, I swear it was, whom I saw through my dressing-room window, leaving with the crowd after I'd compèred a first-house performance of the Ted Heath Band Show at the Streatham Hill Theatre? Did you make some excuse to Mum and come to watch me that Sunday evening in May 1954? I think you did, I think that that was the very last time we saw one another, separate and at a distance, a bit like we'd always been since I grew out of being amused by desk rulers that turned into magic wands for Guy Fawkes Day and capering fingers on the table and tickling and having a pretend blackbird peck off my nose. I have to close now, Dad, I've got a book to get on with. It wasn't all bad though, was it? We weren't much of a father-and-son team but we weren't enemies either. And this will surprise you – the best time of all for me was the night when you hit me. For a little while, we were co-conspirators, sharing a male secret, allied in a lie that only we knew about.

It wasn't for long but the feeling was great while it lasted.

Goodbye, dad. I wonder what you were really like.

Your loving son,

Robert

Where were we? Well, I was now in puberty, shedding my cloak of fat, growing to my adult height of five foot ten inches and a bit. At last I could smile at girls without my eyes disappearing into folds of pudge. What was more, I didn't *have* to be funny any more.

Many comedians attribute their choice of career to some childhood cause, such as poverty, peer mockery, isolation, ugliness, rejection or loss. Woody Allen thinks that's baloney. He says 'It's just an inborn thing that some have. Like Jerry Lewis. I think he was born funny. Two babies lying side by side: one will not become a comedian no matter what he does. For the other, it's like it was in the genes.'

Some friends whose opinions I respect have suggested to me that I turned to comedy because I was embarrassed by my spherical shape. They believe I must have set out to make my family and boyhood friends laugh *with* me instead of *at* me.

To the extent that I used my natural ability to be amusing to deflect their ridicule in the early years, that's true, but I've always been a pragmatic fellow. The need to keep up this comic self-deprecation simply vanished with the fat – I felt the motivation diminish as I ceased to be remarkable for my rotundity. And as this compulsion to use humour to cope with my unusual appearance faded away, I was left with a new freedom. Now I could choose to be funny or not.

But I don't want us to get bogged down with psychological theory. Half of analysis is anal. I haven't much in common with those who cry, 'Help! I'm being held prisoner by my heredity and environment!' Whether, as Allen believes, it's in the genes, or whether my own love of being funny grew out of the enjoyment I felt when I made people laugh, I really don't know. What I do know is that I never wanted to do anything else more than I wanted to do comedy. From the day that Edith Ashby took me to see George Formby in *Boots! Boots!* at the Splendid Cinema, Sydenham, on Easter Monday 1934, I was hooked in a way that would have taken the Jesuits the first seven years of my life to achieve. If the purpose of life is a life of purpose, mine never lacked it after that day.

Two talents were apparent in me from a very early age – memorising and lying. The moment I heard anything attractive or amusing, it was as if I already knew it. And the moment that I was in trouble or need, I'd lie in an effort to get a good result.

My parents were fascinated by my automatic memorising of songs from wireless programmes and seventy-eight rpm records. I saw that I was interesting them and began showing off. Whenever family and friends came to call, I was ready to perform anything from my fast-growing repertoire, rattling off Stanley Holloway's monologues, from 'Albert and the lion' to 'Sam, Sam, pick up tha' musket', at the drop of a hat. Callers learned to keep a tight grip on their headgear in our house.

This was 1932, when comedy on the air waves was infrequent in Britain. Fortunately for this four-year-old Memory Man, it was abundant on cheap six-inch records from the Woolworths in Beckenham High Street and my parents bought a great many of them, as much to feed my infant appetite as for their own amusement. A single hearing of Sandy Powell's latest adventure 'At the Seaside' would have me repeating it, word for word, mimicking the accents and the pauses, never missing a syllable of many phrases I wasn't old enough to understand. Thirty-five years later Sandy was a guest star on my Saturday evening TV show and I still felt the need to show off. I started reciting his old sketches to him. He became quite alarmed and asked me what I was talking about. The dear old boy couldn't remember a bloody word.

This precocious ability to retain the exact wording of anything that I enjoyed extended to educational talks on the BBC, one of which indirectly blew my eyebrows off.

Like all kids I loved fireworks and longed for each Guy Fawkes Night. After tea, the fall of darkness would be the cue for my father to become the centre of attention for a change. While my mother knitted and shook her head at such foolishness, he would make circles in the air with the ruler from his bureau, a black cylindrical rod with hexagonal ends to prevent it rolling. My older brother was always embarrassed at Dad's occasional stabs at magic and used to sneer loudly.

After hamming it up, Dad would press the wooden ruler to his ear and ask the Ghost of Guy Fawkes, 'Where have you hidden the fireworks this year?' He would then attempt the ventriloquial trick of answering in a high voice without moving his lips, producing a worrying sound as if he were choking.

This inspired my brother to further jeering: 'Oh, now it's Arthur Prince and Jim! Can I have your autograph?' and 'He ought to do this on the wireless, then we wouldn't have to see him.'

'What does Guy Fawkes say, Dada?' I asked every year till I was ten, although by that age I could see that my brother had a point.

'Guy Fawkes says, "Tell Robert I've hidden them on top of the white toy cupboard!"' and off I'd rush to wherever the location of this magical cache of Brock's finest might be.

When my father died in 1957, my mother's younger sister, my aunt Eckie, took me aside at the funeral. 'Your mother wonders if you'd like a memento of your father. She gave him this new wallet for his birthday this year but he was never able to use it. Take it, Robert.' I took it but I told her there was something that meant far more to me.

Three days later, a parcel came in the post, labelled in my mother's handwriting. Inside was Dad's magic wand. I still have it, of course, but it has never talked to me as I once believed it talked to him.

On 6 November 1936, with the glorious smell of the previous night's Gunpowder Plot still lingering in our back garden, burnt-out carcases of what had been glittering cascades and whizzbangs scattered around the plank Dad had erected between two trestles, I heard a BBC talk about how fireworks were made. It went straight into my eight-year-old memory bank.

My mother was pleased if puzzled at my uncharacteristic

eagerness to clear up the garden. Most of the exhausted volcanoes and fountains were too eaten by fire to serve my purpose but those tough little cardboard cases that had survived the heat were surreptitiously stowed in a grocery bag under the coal in the kitchen shed.

That weekend I bicycled through Beckenham to Clock House Station, behind which was a block of flats where my aunt Eckie lived with my cousin David and, occasionally, my roving uncle Jack. Jack was strikingly handsome and had the sexual appetite of a buck rabbit with satyriasis. Cousin David was a year younger than me but a total rogue. If anyone knew how to get the ingredients I'd heard mentioned in the talk on how fireworks were made, I was sure David could. David, basking in my respect for his abilities, took down the list of chemicals as I recalled them. 'Potassium Nitrate, yeh. Potassium – how do you spell Chlorate? C.L.O.R.A.I.T. Sulphur, iron filings . . .' The completed list looked daunting on paper, like the secret formula of a mad professor in a Saturday morning picture serial. 'It's a pipe, buddy,' said David, who picked up his slang from Little Rascals comedies on those same Saturday mornings at the ABC Regal Cinema. 'My friend Rodge's dad keeps a chemist's shop in Penge.'

I handed over all the pocket money I had been saving up to buy Chrismas presents and, sure enough, Rodge came through with samples of more than half of the stuff we needed. The following Sunday David arrived on the 227 bus and sneaked round to the back of our house with a dozen mystery packets.

'What is David doing in the kitchen shed?' asked my sharp-eyed mother, who regarded my cousin as God's punishment upon her sister for marrying such a faithless womaniser as uncle Jack.

'They're teaching chemical compounds at his school and he's ever so behind so I said I'd help him.' She knew I was top of my class in science. 'If you'd rather we did the tests in here . . . ?'

'Oh, no, I'm not having you making your messes in the house. Out you go and change into your old trousers first.'

In the darkness of our little kitchen shed, with two flickering candles on the mangle adding to the drama, a pair of feckless pioneers set up their laboratory. A purloined cat's saucer and a teaspoon served as mortar and pestle. Portions were measured in an eggcup. Various combinations were tried, a pinch of this, a drop of that – each resulting amalgam twisted into a paper pouch and held over the flame with tongs borrowed from our fireplace.

Sometimes there was a disappointing hot blob of melting stench, sometimes a satisfying hiss and pop and sparkling flare of colour. When we'd found a particularly pleasing formula, one that gave us both the longest blindness in its afterglow, we set about cramming the mixture into the old firework casings from under the coal.

'Jam it in tight,' I advised expertly. 'It's the pressure up the tube that makes it shoot higher.'

'That's why boys can piss further than girls,' said David. I had no idea what he meant so I just nodded and packed more powder into another charred container. When all of our experimental recipe had been hammered into place with suitable items from dad's tool-chest, each cylinder sprouting a string fuse that we had soaked in a solution of potassium nitrate and carefully dried, we solemnly shook hands.

'After you, Professor Howard.' I held out the Swan Vestas.

'I think the honour falls to you, Professor Monkhouse.'

After a dramatic pause, I lit the first fuse. The amateur firework was unbalanced and fell against the one beside it, sharing the spark with the other's fuse.

'Separate them quickly,' snapped my cousin. 'In fact, put them both out and we'll start again, only this time I'll handle the matches. But first, I've got to go for a pee, I'm bursting.'

David opened the shed door and went outside and I, like a fool, watched him go. My vision, accustomed to the dark of the shed by candlelight, now took in the full radiance of an unseasonably sunny November afternoon. Then I was back in darkness again, licking my right forefinger and thumb to squeeze the glow out of the two lit fuses. But I couldn't find them. All I could see was the shape of our Cox's orange pippin tree silhouetted by the sun, an image imprinted on my retina in the second it had taken me to look out of the shed door.

Fumbling for the two lit fireworks which were rolling on their sides, I only succeeded in knocking them off the rocky strut of wood where we'd balanced them and into the shallow plant box below where the remaining fireworks waited.

I peered into the wooden crate, stirring the fireworks, straining to see a spark and still seeing only the outline of our apple tree.

I thought looking closer might help.

As I moved to push my head into the box, rising smoke went up my nose and I sneezed.

That simple action jerked my face downwards as the fireworks exploded upwards. You might say that a sneeze saved my eyesight.

The blast hit me just above the eyes and took off my eyebrows and the first two inches of hair past my forehead. I fell back as the rest of the box blew up and the sphere of flame hit the roof of the shed. I was fully conscious and not yet in pain so I was amazed to see the sky where the roof had been. And I remember that I had begun wondering how I could put all the blame on David when the shock hit me and I started yelling.

The next thing I knew my mother was pulling me out of what appeared to be hell. Thick smoke was billowing. My forehead was beginning to hurt. I heard my mother half-choking, half-shouting, 'This is all David's fault!'

'Good,' I thought, 'that's taken care of.'

Then I passed out. When I came round I was having my head bandaged by Dr Pitt-Payne. I was scared of him because of his name, but at least he made house calls.

It only took about three months for the burns to heal and my hair grew back quickly. It took about three years for my mother to drop the subject. A full criminal enquiry had been set up and every detail sifted and viewed with horror. Responsibility, which had seemed so naturally to be David's portion, had now been unfairly shared.

The only benefit I could derive from the whole of 'what happened to the shed', as the incident came to be known, was days off school while I recovered. Then more days off school because I complained of headaches. My forehead was still pink so I tried to get more days off school by claiming that it was a rash.

My mother sent for Dr Pitt-Payne. He didn't even examine me. He just looked at me sceptically and said, 'I see no rash.'

One last try. I said, 'Perhaps the rash is on the *inside* of my skin.' At least I got a laugh.

5

FROM THE TOP, WITH A FORWARD HOP

– Unlucky Boy –

Three childhood duckings inspire a fear of water and another prolix time warp takes us via Barbados to Borehamwood with one hueless integument and three hopeless hooligans

Loneliness is more painful for an actor because he has no one to witness his misery. It's not so hot for fat little boys of six either. With a brother five-and-a-half years my senior, I had no one close to play with. I'd be his unwelcome shadow and follow him round to his friends, the Tunnadine brothers, who were about John's age, eleven or twelve, and too grown up to bother with me. Ignored, I fell into their garden pond and sucked in half of it before being pulled clear. As the Tunnadine brothers had been peeing into it for most of their lives, I swallowed more than my pride.

On a hot July day one month later, Edith took me with her to visit her friends' farm in Oxted. Until her death last Christmas, she still remembered that there were no other children to play with, so I ran wild on my own, hurtling across the long grass of an unused pasture and then, very suddenly, completely disappearing from her view. I had plunged into a deep cesspit, penetrating the thick crust of bugs, submerging myself and repeating my act as a human waste disposal unit. August was hotter yet and we went on a day's outing to Herne Bay. Still unable to swim, I was persuaded against my six-year-old judgement to float in shallow water on top of a kind of inflated air-bed called a LiLo. Fear made me keep my eyes shut and I had no sensation of movement other than the rocking of the waves.

When I risked a peek, I found myself twenty yards from the shore. Being a bright little kid, I screamed, fell off the LiLo and got on with drowning. This time I managed to gulp a few gallons that were less polluted than my previous ingurgitations. After my father had rescued me, he administered first aid to clear my lungs and stomach. Then he administered a whack round the ear because he'd had to come back into the water after he'd just finished drying himself. I cried with self-pity and indignation all the way home.

By now I'd formed what's turned out to be lifelong hydrophobia. Ironically, I'm writing these pages under a sunshade on the outdoor deck of our home in Barbados. We bought the beachfront land a couple of years ago and had a three-and-a-half storey house built on it. Sunshine, sand and sea, it's the stuff that dreams and travel brochures are made of. Every day, Jackie walks across our little garden of rosy bougainvillaea and tall palm trees, crosses twenty feet of coral sand and swims for half-an-hour. I just watch her.

I hate sand, I can't swim and sun-bathing is out because of vitiligo, a skin abnormality in which irregular patches of skin lose their colour and turn white. The only sun block that'll really protect these colourless bits is Snowcem. No one seems to know what causes this loss of pigmentation. On me, it arrived overnight in 1978 while I was taping a twenty-six week series for the CBS Network at Borehamwood Studios, giving me two depressing afflictions to deal with instead of one. The series was called 'Bonkers' and it was supposed to replace ITC's five years of success with 'The Muppet Show'. A trio of American hobbledehoys called the Hudson Brothers co-starred with me and any weekly guest whose agent was sufficiently unwary. These visitors included Joan Rivers, John Ritter, Phyllis Diller, Don Knotts, Rita Moreno, Valerie Harper, and a score more such devil-may-cares, all misguidedly trusting the producer and finding themselves performing material that was immaterial. The resulting shows were screened at prime time across the USA for four weeks before someone woke up to the fact that an atrocity was being inflicted on a population not yet recovered from the agony of Vietnam. The scripts would have struck me as the most apalling part of the venture had the Hudson Brothers – Bill,

Mark and Brett – not seemed even worse. 28-year-old Bill was then married to Goldie Hawn and I soon formed the opinion that, although almost as handsome as he thought he was, he'd been innoculated against talent. Middle brother Mark had the musical ability to produce competent guitar and keyboard rock but otherwise funned around like an amiable Neanderthal. I think he looked upon my British civility as a sign of brain damage. Armed with a short list of farting jokes, Mark made up for their small number by daily repetition, replete with sound effects. Brett, the youngest and funniest of a genially loutish litter, gave me the impression of being so oversexed he couldn't be trusted alone with a pumpkin you were planning to eat. The measure of their couth may be judged from the alleged incident that had them asked to quit their rooms at the Dorchester, Park Lane, and move elsewhere. According to their version of events, they had invaded the lift at the sixth floor, already occupied by an elderly couple. The old lady noticed the aroma of Mark's cologne, always liberally applied. 'You smell nice, young man,' she said kindly. 'What have you got on?'

'I've got a hard on,' answered Mark, 'but I didn't know you could smell it.'

When I first began my six months in bondage to the brothers, they addressed me as Bobby-Bobby or Monkie.

Within a fortnight my nicknames had changed to Penis Breath, Scumsucker or occasionally Onion Ring, 'Our codeword for arsehole.'

As 1 June came around, I tried to keep my fiftieth birthday a secret, but somehow the brothers always got to know everything that could be used as ammunition. That morning I walked into the studio to be greeted gleefully with 'Here comes Wrinkle City!' Now I had to answer to names like Scrotum Face, Walking Dead and Borrowed Time.

I responded in kind with silly names for the brothers – Bill was Spoon Seeker (he was so vain he actually looked at his reflection in cutlery), Mark was Super Drooper (he'd been foolish enough to confess some difficulty in achieving an erection for the fifth bonk in a row of six), and I called Brett 'Brett' because I said he was too dull to inspire a nickname. No, it wasn't the name-calling that got me down; on the contrary, the horseplay lightened the dark mood created by the script. What depressed me were the pies.

However ineptly done, 'Bonkers' was a slapstick show and I've always loved physical comedy. Each script called for me to take a pie in the face, often several. That was fine with me, I'd done my share of knockabout in pantomime and even written weekly sight gags into my 1965-6 series, 'Mad Movies', committing myself to a regular face full of custard pie, expertly flung from behind the camera by the director, Jeff Inman. I'd say a line like, 'That's the end of part one. I'm not sure what I'll do in part two, but something funny is sure to strike me.' Jeff's unerring aim would put the wet pie splat in my fizzog and I'd wipe off a little piece with my finger, sample it and say, 'Certainly *tastes* funny!' and we'd go to commercial. Not brilliant but we did variations on the gag in thirty-nine shows and we only used thirty-nine pies. We did it in one take every time. Not so with the Hudson Brothers and 'Bonkers'.

The scene might go something like this: as the harassed host of the show, I'd search for the truant trio, find them eating pie behind the scenery and shout, 'So! You gluttons are feeding again! Give me that illegal pie at once! Let me have it, I say!' Mark would fling the pie and hit me in the neck, shoulder, left ear, right ear, hair – anywhere but square in the face. Then he'd say, 'Er . . . what's my next line?'

That meant a studio wait while I hurried away to clean off the mess, perhaps change my clothes, wash and dry my hair, have fresh makeup applied, and return for take two. And take three. And take four.

Over the run of twenty-six shows, my friends in the Property Department kept count of the pies they made out of candlewax, milk powder and dye, each one to be flung or slapped into my determined grin. They made four hundred and three. I can still taste every one of them.

If having all that dyed tallow forced up my nose wasn't enough to put me in hospital, a cabin trunk was. The scriptwriters had devised a joke so weird that only the brothers could have liked it. Each week, a scene in our fictitiously shared dressing room would end with the three hooligans yelling, 'We gotta get outa here! The weatherman's forecast a pingpong storm!' As they ran out of the room, I had to stand firm and say, 'A pingpong storm? How utterly insipid! There's no such thing as a pingpong storm!', whereupon a deluge of two thousand pingpong balls would fall on me.

Versions of this dull joke were used week after week. In the name of comedy, I withstood a bedroom slipper storm, an underwear storm, a hat storm, a throw cushion storm, a kindling wood storm, a wet sponge storm, even a wrecking ball storm. Then came the day we taped a luggage storm. Hanging in a net above my head, in among the soft holdalls and empty cardboard attaché cases waiting to drop on my head, lurked a heavy cabin trunk. How it got there we never discovered but I suspect that my immature co-stars had allowed their enthusiasm for a practical joke to override any unfamiliar caution they may have felt. We reached the end of the scene as usual.

'A luggage storm?' I dutifully yelled with scorn, 'How totally vapid! There's no such thing as a luggage storm!'

Two seconds later I was on the studio floor, knocked out cold.

In the hospital I awoke with concussion, mild double vision and a duck's egg bump on my skull.

Back at work two days later, my chief concern was to keep the medical report away from the brothers. It described the damage as slight and temporary and added, 'The dessication of the cervical vertebra (sic) is consistent with the advanced age of the patient.' I could just imagine my next nickname – 'Dessicated Dick'.

Halfway through some sort of rehearsal with Petula Clark, she took my hands and looked at the backs. 'Bob, have you been sunbathing or gardening?'

'Yes, yesterday evening. I was chopping down nettles.'

'Had you spilt perfume on your hands and face?'

Face? I rushed to a wall mirror and there they were on my left cheek and chin, two deathly pale areas, each about two inches long and shaped like New Zealand. A two-inch silhouette of snowy Spitzbergen had appeared midway between my nipples, both my hands were symmetrically mottled in white and as for my genitals, they'd become a symphony of polka dots and moonbeams.

The Hudson Brothers, typically sympathetic, promptly changed my nicknames to Bleach Features, the Semi-Albino, and Patches.

The first dermatologist I visited told me that the condition might come and go at random and he suggested that I rub lemons on the affected areas. For about a year I smelled as fresh as furniture.

The second specialist was a Bovril-coloured Barbadian lady who told me that vitiligo was symptomatic of a breakdown in my immune system and pointed out that I'd really have had something to complain about if I'd been born black. I couldn't argue with that.

Two years later, in New York during the autumn of 1981, I consulted a skin doctor named Dr Marvin Brodie. We'd become friends during our annual holidays at Sandy Lane Hotel on Barbados, and Jackie and I enjoyed his wit.

I told him how I'd been thinking about my vitiligo and, although the dermatologists in London and Bridgetown had pooh-poohed my conclusion, I believed the disorder to have been caused by stress during the making of 'Bonkers'. It followed that, if remission were possible, such a stress-related condition could be reversed and that relaxation, even quiet meditation, might restore the melanin to my hueless parts. Marvin shouted, 'No doubt about it!' He thumped his desk with each word. '*No doubt about it!*'

'You mean I've found the answer?'

'No, *you* haven't found the answer, *I've* found the answer!'

'What answer?'

'The answer to any schmuck who comes up with an idiotic theory that keeps him happy. I just say, "*No doubt about it . . . !*"'

In the meantime, I experimented with camouflage pastes and masking makeup to hide my piebald face and hands from my live audiences and television viewers. Normal flesh colours gave me the smooth pink look of a survivor from a fire. Using darker shades made my face appear unshaven and my hands unwashed.

Then in 1983 I returned to BBC TV to do a series of game shows and talk shows, and there in her makeup department I found a caring lady named Cherry Alston who solved my problem by using a method I've employed ever since – tanning under a sunbed and filling in my untanned splotches with a patented, realistic brown coating, fixed with a spray of flexible lacquer. And that's why I always look as if I've just come back from Barbados, even though I usually have.

Once again a subject – my susceptibility to accidental misfortune

– has tempted me out of the chronology of my years. We left me half-drowned on a beach as the 1930s were drawing to a close. And me only eleven years old with a world war to deal with. Shame on us.

6

FROM THE TOP

'The Day War Broke Out . . .'

To the south coast for a lesson in heroic gestures, innocent serendipity and a disillusioning outcome

Just before the end of August 1939, my father stood up after Sunday lunch in our Beckenham home and announced to my mother, my brother and me that Hitler was sure to launch a massive surprise blitzkrieg upon London and our house would be on the periphery of it. He told us that he had bought a small house in West Worthing and that we were to move down there at once. I drew a picture of Hitler on a large piece of paper, cut it into a disc twelve inches in diameter and fixed it under the wire frame on our dartboard. Me and my cousin David, we gave Adolf some stick that afternoon.

During the phoney war, that strangely peaceful period that followed the Declaration of Hostilities, I wondered if my father had been right to move us to the south coast. His predicted London blitz wasn't happening but every Worthing lamppost displayed placards exhorting residents to 'STAY PUT'. The inference drawn was of invasion and people were beginning to talk of extended holidays in Scotland and Eire.

The summer of 1940 was uncommonly sunny and I spent a lot of time in our tiny garden at 4 Douglas Close. One July Sunday after lunch, the distant pulsing growl of a plane engine made me look up at the sky to see a Dornier-17 bomber flying very low and slowly over the rooftops and heading towards me. The German plane passed directly over my head, leaving a sooty trail. I could see the outline of a pilot's helmet as the aircraft swept away and a few moments later I smelt the oily odour of the smoke. It was as if the plane were lost, seeking some landmark that would give it a reason to choose direction and get away before the RAF came to see what all the noise was about. Even as this thought occurred, two Spitfires came banking down from over the sea, engines grinding out a lighter note than the bomber.

Immediately behind them, higher and in formation, three Me-109s appeared like shepherds searching for their lost sheep. All the planes vanished inland and then, lower than ever and with its right engine flickering with little rosy petals of flame, the Dornier returned, heading for the sea this time. One of the crew of four was pressed against a glass panel in the bulging forward section and I saw something fall as the pencil-shaped body of the fuselage glided away. The RAF and German fighter planes were scribbling angry patterns in the blue high above and the chatter of their guns was surprisingly loud. By this time, I was on my bike, cycling as fast as I could round the little lanes to see if I could find what had fallen from the Luftwaffe bomber. Lots of people were out of their houses, shielding their eyes as they gazed upward. My gaze was downward. I was just twelve and didn't know the impossibly high odds against my finding an unknown object dropped from one hundred and fifty feet on to a built-up area.

When I saw it, lying in the gravel at the edge of a private drive, I recognised it at once. It was a military mess tin, a grey metal box with a lid, intended to carry rations. It was stamped with the outline of a swastika on one side and a spread eagle on the other. Inside it were three photographs, a coloured stone and a letter in German on yellow paper. The photos showed a handsome young man with close-cropped hair and wearing an NCO's jacket, a pretty young woman posing coyly beside a farm pump, and a fat baby on a rug in a bushy garden. I put the contents back in the box, put it into the basket on my handlebars and cycled home.

I heard later that the Dornier had hit the sea and broken up about two miles off shore. There had been no survivors. No one knew I had the box, which I kept wrapped in my winter raincoat at the back of my bedroom cupboard.

Alone in my room at night I pored over the letter, as if sheer concentration would translate its angular German script into a language I could understand. It seemed to be addressed to someone called 'Fremde', which I took to be the name of the girl in the photo. My boyish imagination took wing and I could picture the desperate airman, resigned to a fatal crash, hastily penning this last message of love to his young wife in Germany and then casting it from his dying craft, entrusting his final words of love to fate, hoping against hope that some intelligent and fearless youngster would find it and devise a way to get it back into the grateful, trembling hands of his beloved Fremde.

Only one teacher at Goring Hall School taught German and was thoroughly hated for possessing such unpatriotic knowledge. He was also given to confiscating any articles he thought unsuitable for children so I was reluctant to show him the original letter. Instead I copied it out, a painstaking task lest I change the meaning of a word with a clumsily reproduced character. When I thought my final fair copy was as close as I could get to forgery, I took it to Mr Hatfield and asked him what it said. He looked at it briefly, put it in his pocket and told me he would see me later about it. When I got home after school that afternoon I found him and Mr Green, our Headmaster, in our small front room with my mother, who was pale with anger. She told me to explain exactly how I had come to write these words on school paper. I blurted out the truth and was sent to bed without supper.

It turned out that the letter was a seditious exhortation to hasten the inevitable Nazi victory by doing all the reader could think of to sabotage the British war effort. The three photographs, said the letter, were typical examples of healthy, strong and friendly German people who wanted only an early end to our hopeless resistance. Ways followed in which the enlightened finder of the letter could aid the German plan to free our precious islands from Jewish and aristocratic domination. 'Fremde', I learned, was German for 'stranger'.

The coloured stone, which I had been thinking of swapping for a cap pistol owned by my best friend Doherty, had been enclosed to help finance the subversive deeds, intended to cover the cost of materials needed for train derailment and firesetting near key railway stations. It was a valuable piece of red jasper, dating from Roman times. My father consulted his solicitor and I was given to understand that the gem had been surrendered to the Crown, whatever that meant. I didn't much care. All I knew was I had a month of extra prep, early bedtime and no going to the Worthing Odeon. Bloody Jerries!

For many years I supposed this singular little incident from my boyhood to be unique. Fairly recently however, in dinner conversation with a man whose father had been in British intelligence during World War Two, I learned that hundreds of such random shots in the dark had been attempted by both sides. Apparently the gathering of small valuables from Jewish families had been part of the Abwehr's policy for funding their spies both prior to and during the war. British agents were similarly equipped with coins or gems which could be converted easily into cash. Once war was declared, the surplus of such items, together with other heirlooms from patriotic German families, was considered dispensable in the cause of the chance recruitment of disaffected Britons to the Nazi cause. Some Luftwaffe crews were encouraged to write individual letters based on suggestions from Goebbels' propaganda experts. My mess tin full of incitement to sabotage was a typical result. Against the background of other wild schemes approved by MI5 and MI6 on behalf of an Allied victory – the injection of Hitler's vegetables with female hormones so that his voice would turn soprano and his moustache fall out, for instance – scattering bits of red jasper and picture postcards over Sussex for schoolboys to find seems pretty reasonable.

This odd interlude had been only a minor diversion from my principal interest, that of finding suitably appreciative recipients for my outpouring of cartoons, stories and jokes. My father worked in London all week and my brother had put his career as an accountant on hold and gone to North Africa in khaki, so my mother and I spent a lot of time together. We listened to the wireless in the evenings as German bombers throbbed overhead on the way to lighten their load over London, grateful for the comedy of Tommy Handley, the Western Brothers and Robb Wilton – '*The day war broke out, my missus looked at me and said, "What good are you?"*' – or twice weekly we took a single-decker green bus into the centre of Worthing, waxy headlights hooded for the blackout and shining down at the road ahead through shielded slits. These were trips to the Odeon, Plaza, Rivoli and Dome cinemas, where my lifelong addiction to the movies grew stronger with films I never expected to see again, let alone projected on the screen in my own house. Still, the overriding passion of my life was my own output of invention.

My mother put up with my obesssional industry, even to the point of financing my never-ending requests for drawing and writings materials, but she must have wondered what she'd begot.

7

A VERY PERSISTENT AND IMPUDENT LITTLE FELLOW

– Aged Twelve to Eighteen –

Following the joke trail from childhood precocity, as first attempts fail to please, early influences inspire imitation, a Carroll Levis Discovery is not made, cartoons and books and gags are peddled, Max Miller invests money and wisdom, and Derek Roy gives employment and encouragement

'I persevere, you persist, he keeps on, they won't bloody stop . . .'

Leonard Henry had me down as a very persistent and impudent little fellow. An almost forgotten comedian now, just as I am destined to become, Leonard Henry was the cat's pyjamas in the 1930s, a wireless wag and the very merry-andrew of Durium cardboard recordings; 'Oh, Nicholas, don't be so ridiculous, I don't like it in the daytime!' He seemed to me the *ne plus ultra* for the receipt of my tenderly constructed jokes. I carefully copied out the cream of my first crop in capital letters on my mother's Basildon Bond and sent the two pages of wheezes and a covering letter to Mr Leonard Henry, Famous Comedian, c/o The BBC, Broadcasting House, London W1. I was careful to point out that I thought he would find 'my jokes newer and funnier' than some I had heard him tell.

My newer and funnier jokes included:

My father was ruined by hard drink – he sat on an icicle. Would you like to buy a half-naked duck? It's fifty per cent down!

*Knitting is something women do so they'll have something to
think about while they're talking.*
*My Uncle Angus is so mean he only bought a bike because he
heard it came with a free wheel.*
*Why does a cowboy bother to wear two spurs? After all, folks,
if one side of the horse goes, so will the other.*
*And now to conclude, a little song entitty-titled, 'If Your Phone
Doesn't Ring, Dear, You'll Know it's Me'.*

A duplicated form came in reply. It said only that unsolicited
manuscripts of plays or stories could not be returned to the
sender without a stamped self-addressed envelope or label. I
wrote my jokes out again, adding my latest inspirations on a third
page, stuff like:

Do you know what a zookey is? It's the key to a zoo.
*Most accidents happen in the house or on the roads. So play
safe . . . leave home and sell your car!*
*I offered the barber a piece of my birthday cake – he took 2
inches off the top!*
*I read that prices will soon go up on a big scale. So if you want
to buy a big scale, do it now.*

I wrote my name and address on a gummed label, stuck a penny-
ha'penny stamp on it, and enclosed another letter to Mr Leonard
Henry telling him that I also made up rhyming monologues and
silly songs which I thought might be worth a shilling each, twice
as much as the sixpenny jokes. And were there any particular
subjects he'd like me to write jokes about?

Three weeks later, having heard nothing, I copied out all the
jokes again and, at the suggestion of our English teacher, Miss
DaCosta, whose sister sang in the Luton Girls Choir and so knew
all about show biz, sent them to Mr Henry in care of the Concert
Artistes' Association in London. Altogether, I wrote nine times
to him at both addresses. Then one day I came home from
Goring Hall School and my mother said, 'Robert, you've got a
letter.'

The notepaper was headed with a simple, red, die-stamped *LEONARD HENRY*.

It read,

Young Man,

Please do not send me any more of your nonsense. For a boy of twelve, you are a very persistent and impudent little fellow. I put you upon your honour to show this letter to your parents. To them I say this: if I had been such an arrogant child, my father would have administered corporal punishment. I say no more.

Yours etcetera,   *Leonard Henry*

At the bottom of the page, in the same red, die-stamped lettering as the heading, was the phrase: *'LAUGH WITH LEONARD!'*

My first brush with greatness didn't faze me. I had also been persistent and impudent enough to send examples of my cartoons to *Mickey Mouse Weekly* and, after a dozen tries, they had published my drawing under the puzzle heading 'Guess the town?' It was a picture of a coalsack with 'COAL' written on it, beside a bottle with 'PORT' written on it. It was clear even than that my creative efforts were to be unhindered by subtlety.

From the back page of every children's weekly paper I could buy came my collection of potential customers, the names and addresses of publishers and printers. To each of them went my comic strips and single picture jokes. One firm in Stoke-on-Trent, R. and L. Locker, wanted Christmas card verses and paid me a shilling for each of the four dozen I submitted: 'No holly in my garden bed, No holly do I miss; Just mistletoe above my head, So I can send a kiss!' Easy money. I sat in the tiny garden of our tiny West Worthing home writing Christmassy doggerel in summertime, looking up to the clear blue sky from time to time to watch Spitfires and Hurricanes as they flew to battle with Stumpff's Messerschmitts, spectacular contests which painted wildly swirling vapour trails all over the sky.

The concert party on Worthing Pier had been called 'The Gay Parade' and each holiday in the 1930s had meant a visit or two to watch Fred Gwyn impersonate a slowly wakening frog, the corners of his mouth stretched down, his splayed hands on the lily pad of his thighs; then he would mime a little boy, newly bought eggs in his pockets, his homeward journey interrupted by the excitement of a Punch and Judy Show, laughing and pounding his sides with mirth, only to slowly change his expression to horror and tears as the broken eggs soaked his legs.

Now the parade, no longer gay, had passed by. The theatre on the pier had closed for the duration, changed its mind and reopened in 1941 with a morale-boosting programme of shows, including a Young Talent Contest. I won second prize, telling my best jokes and imitating Fred Gwyn, with the added froggy refinement of catching a fly with my tongue.

A few weeks later I repeated the performance for Uncle Bill Fraser's Saturday Morning Children's Fun Show at the Connaught Theatre. Uncle Bill paid me half-a-crown. Thirteen years later I was to have the BBC pay Uncle Bill thirty pounds to play the Victorian villain to my clumsy hero in my first television series. Bill would go on to achieve national fame on TV as Sergeant Snudge in 'The Army Game' and critical acclaim on the West End stage, but to me he was never greater than when he pressed that coin into my palm, winked and whispered, 'You've got the makings, my lad, you've got the makings.'

In 1942 my parents and I left West Worthing and moved back to the house in Beckenham, from where I was enrolled as a pupil at Dulwich College. The first friend I made there was a boy named Hurst whose father knew David Lowe, the great political cartoonist, and I begged him to show a portfolio of my drawings to the maestro. They were returned to me a few weeks later with a saddening comment scrawled on the last page: '*Sorry, no real promise here. Lowe.*'

I shrugged off the depression this brought and applied for an audition with the eponymous Canadian host of his nationally famous Carroll Levis Discoveries. A Gestetnered letter instructed me to present myself at nine a.m. on the following Friday at Golders Green Hippodrome. That meant playing truant, but I reckoned the opportunity was worth the punishment. The opportunity turned out to be a punishment in itself.

My act had a precocious shape to it by this time. I planned to

enter from the stalls, removing my raincoat and cap, pretending
to be late for the show. My opening jokes arose from my
unpunctuality:

*Sorry I'm late but I got out of a sickbed to come here today – a
sickbed – one of its legs has death watch beetle.
Then I had trouble with my train ticket – the Inspector said I
ought to have bought one.
You see, I come from a poor home, really poor – my mother
takes in gypsies' washing. We can't even afford coal for the fire
– on cold days my father sucks a peppermint and we all sit
round his tongue.*

More of the same followed. Fred Gwyn's stolen pantomimes had
been replaced by something more original; a silent portrayal of a
boy in a pinball arcade, putting imaginary pennies into the game
machines and trying to influence the behaviour of the little silver
balls by twitching slightly, then jerking spasmodically, finally
degenerating into tardive dyskinesia in a frantic effort to win
something. Trying to persuade the mechanical crane to pick up a
watch, he settles for what it finally delivers – a wine gum. Exit
deadpan, chewing, as the pianist winds up the piece.

To finish my seven minutes, I had what I thought was a neat
idea:

*Ladies and gentlemen, nearly all comedians finish with a song
but at least I'm different – I'm going to finish
WITHOUT A SONG!*

This would cue an arpeggio from the pianist and I would sing to
the tune of Vincent Youmans' famous ballad:

*Without a song – this act would never end,
But if I sang – I wouldn't leave a friend.
I can't go wrong – if I just go along,
Without a song!*

A man sat behind a table in the foyer of the Golders Green
Hippodrome and took the invitation forms from the long queue
of hopefuls who all seemed to have been called for nine a.m. like

me. We were each given a number on a yellow card and told to come up on the stage when called. By the time I crept into the stalls, the back rows were full of us: girls clutching music, men with musical instruments, a yokel, a woman holding a topcoat over her spangled ballgown, little children in tap shoes, a red-nosed chap in a stovepipe hat, even another schoolboy like me. I hoped he wasn't funny.

In the middle of the fifth row I could see the silhouette of the mighty Levis, flanked by two assistants, one of whom moved to and fro from his seat to the stage, the other calling out occasional instructions to the amateurs: 'Louder, please!' 'That's enough, thank you! Next!' 'Move further forward, come to the footlights!' Levis didn't speak. Levis seemed to be asleep.

By five minutes to twelve I had watched thirty-four claimants to fame do their best or worst; now I heard, 'Number thirty-five on stage, thirty-six stand by.'

I stood by. A fat brunette sang 'How I love the kisses of Dolores, Aye-aye-aye, Dolores.' Then it was my turn.

I rushed up the steps on to the big stage, pulling off my raincoat and cap.

Sorry I'm late but I got out of a sickbed to come here today . . .

Levis's aide-de-camp interrupted me by shouting, 'We don't want excuses, just get on with it!' I was badly rattled and didn't know what to do. 'Come along, son, get on with it!' I nodded and went into my second joke:

Then I had trouble with my train ticket . . .

'GO HOME!'

'I wasn't sure what I was hearing. I peered uncertainly into the stalls. 'Pardon?' Carroll Levis had awoken. Like Fred Gwyn's frog, he had stirred and opened his uncaring gaze upon me. He called out to me again with the only two words I was ever to hear him speak.

'GO HOME!'

I went home.

My truancy earned me a caning but the pain of it was nothing compared with the mortification of my pride. I locked myself in our bathroom and sat naked in the empty bath, muffling my weeping with a towel so that my mother couldn't hear it. I had forgotten how to be persistent or impudent. Leonard Henry's cure for childish arrogance was finally administered, in fact and in spirit. I'd make no further attempt to perform in front of anyone ever again.

The next week the *Beckenham Journal* announced a talent contest to be held at the Penge Empire. I applied at once. Some cure.

In 1943 I found Martin and Reid Ltd. Or rather, Mo and Isadore, two hustlers who'd procured a stray load of paper, hard to get in wartime, printed five thousand comics and sold them to Woolworths. Their address was on the back.

My cartoon strips and short stories were not as good as those they had used before, but I was cheaper than Jock McCail, who drew for Thompson's famous weeklies, *The Wizard* and *The Dandy*, and who knew his value. Now my output became prodigious, drawn in India ink on Bristol board on top of an inverted butler's tray in my bedroom, and limited only by the quantities of paper that Mo and Isadore could wheedle from hassled suppliers. Sometimes they found a consignment made from re-pulped bus tickets or newsprint, so blackened by printer's ink that my drawings had to be painted in white on a black background so as to be visible to the readers' perusal; children's eyes straining to make out the adventures such as 'Hannibal the Cannibal – This Darky Fellow Makes You Bellow'.

On my sixteenth birthday, Mo phoned our house from his Bishopsgate office in great excitement. 'Books for the troops! As much paper as we need, by order of the War Office! They want thrillers and American private eye stuff, a bit sexy, not too much. How soon can you do us six or seven? Make it a dozen!' A thought struck him. 'You can write books, can't you?'

I bought my first typewriter.

A year and a half later, author of about thirty terrible pulp novels, I had polished my stage patter enough to perform with several youth clubs who put on amateur shows for local charities. Chief among these was Ernie Lower's West Bees Concert Party, in which my schoolfriend Denis Gifford was the principal comedian. In order to join them, I had to play his straightman, the stooge whose attempts to deliver an uplifting monologue were constantly interrupted by the funny partner.

Ladies and gentlemen, a little recitation. 'There's a little old log cabin, out on the Great Divide . . .'

The funny partner runs onstage with a soda syphon and sprays the audience.

How dare you? You can't go around squirting people willy-nilly!

Mock outrage from the funny partner –

I didn't do it with that, I used a syphon!

Very racy stuff in 1945.

My confidence in my own material had grown with the successful sales I had made to professional comedians. Aged fourteen, I had stood in my bicycle clips outside the stage door of the Lewisham Hippodrome, waiting to approach the comedian I had seen in the first house performance, unaware that Frankie Higgins had come off and gone straight to the pub. He returned just in time for his second house appearance and with no minutes to spare with some snotty-nosed kid. I knew that because he said so.

The following evening I waited outside the pub. As Higgins walked up to its door, I stuck a page of jokes in his hand. A few minutes later he came out slowly and wagged the page at me. 'Where'd you get these?'

'I made them up, sir.'

'Swear to God?'

'Yes, sir. Do you want to buy them?'

He looked at the page, then at me, then laughed.

'I never paid for a gag before. Here you are, you cheeky monkey.'

He took a handful of coins out of his pocket, dumped them in my hand and vanished into the Bunch of Grapes. I counted four shillings and tuppence. I spent a shilling of it to watch the second house show but he didn't use any of my lines. Well, I thought, perhaps he's a slow learner.

Flushed with triumph, I attempted to repeat the operation with most of the comedians who had nearby theatres in their touring schedule – the Penge Empire, cine-variety at the Bromley Gaumont, Catford, Camberwell – but it seemed I'd struck uncommonly lucky with Higgins. 'Piss off' was one of the more delicate reactions I provoked. Then a year later I struck gold, Max Miller, the 'pure gold of the music hall'.

It was back at the scene of my only sale so far, the Lewisham Hippodrome. Miller was making one of his rare appearances at what he regarded as a variety theatre in decline. Standards had fallen to a nude revue called 'This Is The Show', its posters printed in blue except for the initial letters of the title which were bright red. From a distance, all that caught the eyes was:

TITS

By this time the stagedoor-keeper knew me and, after warning me off once or twice, relented and allowed me to stand in the shelter of the doorway when it rained. I had learned not to approach the comedians on a Monday when they were arriving for a bandcall, carrying and unpacking bags, setting props or busy arranging digs. So it was Tuesday evening when I watched Max Miller get out of his car and walk towards me. I held out a page of jokes I had written in what I thought was his style. Before I could speak, Miller did.

'Hello, son, give it here.'

His pen was in his hand and in a moment he'd autographed the back of the page and disappeared through the door.

Wednesday evening was wet and I was soaking in the downpour despite the protection of the stagedoor awning. Miller ran past me, his dresser holding an umbrella over his head. It knocked Miller's trilby askew and I saw that he was bald. Cycling home, I made a mental note to take a joke about wigs out of the list:

Haven't I got nice hair, lady? Sid's got nice hair but not as nice as mine.

(Sidney Kaplan was the bandleader in the orchestra pit.)

But it's all his own, Sid's hair, all his own. You made the final payment on it last week, didn't you, Sid?

On Thursday I waylaid Miller's dresser, on his way to the Bunch of Grapes' off-licence counter. 'Excuse me, sir, would you give this to Mr Miller?' He took it without a word. I waited for an hour or so, rehearsing the gags I was submitting in my head. Clothing was rationed and a purchaser had to have not only the price but the clothing coupons too:

There's going to be no more clothing coupons for old maids. No, well, they've got enough in their drawers they haven't used yet.

Mussolini had betrayed the Allies in supporting Hitler:

Ouch! I think I've got Italian lumbago. That's a sudden stab in the back.

Tinned food was rationed by a system called 'points':

Heard the latest? They say brassières are going on points. I thought they always did.

Suddenly, Miller's dresser came out of the stagedoor. Without speaking, he gave me five shillings and went back inside. I sang all the way home.

Max Miller was kind to me six years later when I was the opening comedian in a variety concert staged at the London Coliseum to raise funds for war refugees. He was topping the bill but had arrived early to rest in his dressing room as his health was beginning to fail. With so many performers in the show, dressing rooms had to be shared and there was no privacy for him, and I overheard him telling the show's producer, Michael North, that he'd lock himself in his car outside and have a snooze. Who would wake him in time for his whack? I volunteered and asked, 'Is the number plate still MAX 1?'

North introduced me and I thanked Miller for the five bob he'd paid me. To my surprise, he either remembered the occasion or pretended to and said, 'I used a couple of your trifles, yeah, and I'd have used more if you'd put your name and address on the page.'

'I appreciate good advice.'

'Yeah? Good boy, good boy. What time's he on?'

North said, 'After the opening and the one song from Vincent Tildsley's Mastersingers.'

'Put me in a chair somewhere.'

That's how the greatest front-cloth patter comedian in Europe, needing sleep and feeling unwell, came to see me do my spot to a cold audience that wasn't ready to laugh. After I came off, I was told to take a cup of tea to his car. When I tapped on the car window, he told me to climb in and close the door.

'You drink the tea and I'll drink this.' He sipped from a silver flask. 'Now, let's talk about what you did on that stage.'

On that chilly evening in 1949 I was given a master class in patter comedy by its greatest living exponent.

Some of his advice might appear obvious and simple, but I've seen star performers forget or overlook such basic principles and wonder why their audience drifts away.

'There are rules, my son. You can bend these rules but you must not break them. First, the people won't laugh if they can't understand you, so keep it simple, keep it clear and sharp so that they can hear you in the back row of the gods, don't shout, just speak up. Second, energy, all good comics have energy, even Horace Kenney.' Kenney's act was as a walking disaster, a hopeless hapless jeremiah, but I could see that Miller was right. Despite the man's glum depiction of misery, Kenney's croaking delivery was crisply pitched and animated. OK, I thought, be audible and lively, got that.

'Now I'm not saying you're not already loud and clear and full of beans, you are, I'm just laying out the rules, see? Three, give 'em the chance to laugh. Just now, they weren't easy but you never gave them enough rope. Wait. If the buggers don't laugh, stare 'em out. You're in charge, not them. Make them have it. When you've got a good joke, and you had very pretty stuff tonight, set it up for them. Say "Come 'ere, listen, listen, you won't believe this, come 'ere!" Twinkle, like you're trying not to laugh yourself. That's infectious, you see. Take them into your confidence, my son. Create an atmosphere. Strike an attitude. Be likeable, be the people's mate, and if they don't take to you right away, act happy as if you don't care. Don't tick 'em off, that's rude from a youngster.' Sure enough, I'd followed one joke that misfired by saying, 'Oh, *you* can laugh! You *can* laugh, can't you?' I wouldn't do that again.

'Rule number four, and this is more important than you think, let them see you taking a chance. Do you know what audacity is? Well, young as you are, the mums'll forgive you, the girls'll think "There's a saucy lad" and men like a fella with a bit of spunk. Don't go too far, mind. Make them do the work, make them figure it out. What's that joke you did about the girl's father when you asked for his daughter's hand in marriage?' I repeated the joke.

> Her father said, 'Have you the means to make a woman happy?'
> I said, 'Yes, they always laugh at it.'

'No, it's wrong, coming from a clean-looking lad like you. The word 'it'. Too brutal, no subtlety. You want to hint at what you mean. And 'means', that's the wrong word for the set up. Try it like this:

> Her father looked at me, he said, 'Have you got what it takes to make my daughter happy?' I thought to myself, 'Oh, yes, I've got that all right!'

'Now pause there. Give 'em the eye. Let 'em catch on what you mean.

> I've got what it takes to make her happy all right! Not just happy – the first time, she laughed her head off!

'See? Not perfect, I grant you, not a classic, but funnier if you put it over right.'

There were more rules that night – about avoiding repetition except where it lends build-up and emphasis, about using movement to create a mental picture, about the split-second timing required to drop the final word from a punchline to begin the next sentence, about sincerity and funny accents and the illusion of danger. Of the many things he told me, precious tips that I've used so often and practical secrets that I've passed on with care to those able to use them, one line he said still makes me smile:

> *Comedy is the only job you can do really badly and people won't laugh at you.*

The kindest of all the comedians to whom I sold my gaglines, one-liners as I now learned to call them, was Derek Roy, the Melody Boy. Derek had the uncanny knack of memorising a script with a single reading and never having to carry pages at the microphone. I first wrote to him in 1946, care of the bandleader Geraldo at the BBC as Roy often sang with him, enclosing a five-minute routine that I had improved during repeated performance in charity shows. He replied with a cheque for ten pounds signed P.S. Thomas, his real name, and a flattering note commissioning 'three more routines like this but with some radio sound effects and lines about my ugly girlfriend'. I worked out a contrived bit where he'd tell the audience about his being pursued by a girl so ugly. . . .

> *. . . her face looks as though her hobby is stepping on rakes.*

Derek then demands that the sounds effects man be instructed to provide suitable noises to make an impressive radio production out of the story. But the man in charge of those noises is the previous boyfriend of Derek's would-be lover and he takes his revenge. Every sound effect he produces is wrong, wrong in the funniest possible way. 'Our first tender kiss' has the noise of a gumboot pulling out of sucking mud, 'her eyes fell' gets two loud balls hitting the floor, 'I bent over her with a gentle sigh' cues the explosive donkey fart later made famous on countless editions of 'The Goon Show'. Simple stuff but it was a riot in its day. Derek sent me twenty pounds for it. I was overjoyed. It went down so well, he did it again. And again I received twenty pounds from him. In all, he used the bit four times on radio, then on the London stage, eventually on TV and on radio in South Africa.

He paid me for each and every performance. No other comedian was so grateful and generous in his successful years.

When he learned he had cancer, his immediate reaction was the same as Roy Castle's would be twenty-five years later, to put the bad news to good use. He blamed smoking and became one of the earliest of anti-smoking campaigners. He died after a distressing tour of Paul Ramond's nudie farce *Pajama Tops*, in which Derek had great difficulty in remembering his lines and had to have them written on props positioned around the stage. Courageous and courteous to the very end, Derek Roy set an example for other comedy purveyors to follow.

8

A VERY PERSISTENT AND IMPUDENT LITTLE FELLOW

– Aged eighteen to nineteen –

Into battledress with a TV debut, amateur dramatics, revue with Benny Hill, a forgery forgiven and a radio audition blessed with fool's luck

Called up to do three years of National Service in the RAF in June, 1946, I remained stubbornly persistent and had very little of the impudence knocked out of me. Our drill corporal was a chest-beating brute, tough enough to smoke in bed face down, and he made life a misery for any recruit who seemed at all educated. After a week of his bullying, I managed to duck out of most of the square-bashing of basic training at Padgate by persuading the Station Adjutant to let me paint murals on the walls of the sergeants' mess and the station cinema. The latter got Mickey Mouse and Popeye, the former Betty Grable and Rita Hayworth.

Despite my efforts to make this painting work last as long as possible, I was due to resume training when another lucky break came along. Assigned to distribute Daily Routine Orders before breakfast, I caught the officer temporarily in charge of postings, a flouncing Pilot Officer with improbably red lips, *dextro tempore*. He'd forgotten to lock his door while romping trouserless with our seemingly macho drill corporal. The corporal never picked on me again while the officer gave sympathetic consideration to my request to be trained in shorthand and typing in London. Duly posted to Uxbridge a month later and in training as a secretary, I applied for a further posting to the Central Medical Establishment in Kelvin House, Cleveland Street, W1, rumoured to be a cushy billet. After a complicated bit of chicanery with a

Station Warrant Officer at Records, Gloucester, involving a permanent cash loan from me to a lady of his ulterior acquaintance who was in urgent need of a £200 abortion, I was deftly shunted into CME in 1947, where the leniency of the unit allowed me to live with my parents in Beckenham and commute, excused boots and promoted to corporal. The service expression of the day was 'jammy bastard'.

Passing an audition for television wasn't difficult because no one wanted to do it. Very few people had television receivers in the late 1940s and the small, hazy screens made watching it a misery, like staring at a monochrome stamp in a fog. Professional performers were not eager to accept meagre fees to expose their ideas to theft and their talent to critical disdain. I applied, was called to Alexandra Palace at once and booked for my baptism of cathode rays on a musical show called 'New to You', transmitted at three p.m. on Thursday, 29 January 1948. Backed by Eric Robinson and his orchestra, I was introduced by 'magicomic' Jackson Green, along with Jack Crosbie (comedy cartunes), Sonya Hana and John Gregory (dancing on air), Elizabeth Sidney (silver songstress) and Toderick Hilton (the singing jackeroo). I was nineteen years old, paid two guineas (two pounds and two shillings) by BBC cheque, which I endorsed on the back and gave to our Station WO in exchange for the time off, and I never met anyone who remembered watching the show including the producer who stayed in the bar.

Getting on to the radio was a very different matter. As professional performers were demobbed by the dozen each week, as ENSA wound down and released its entertainers on to the civilian market, as young amateurs who had found their métier performing in camp concerts came looking for work, so did the long line of applicants for radio renown lengthen.

On two late October nights in 1947 I had appeared in the cast of W. Chetham-Strode's three-act murder mystery *The Day Is Gone* at the Daylight Inn, Petts Wood, in aid of the local War Memorial Fund.

'Individual performances were of a high standard,' said the *Kentish Times* of 7 November, 'but perhaps a special word is due for Mr Robert Monkhouse, whose interpretation of an ex-army major was so full of detail work that it provided one of the most convincing performances I have seen by an amateur. Mr

Monkhouse, a new member of the Proscenium Club company, is a welcome addition.' Mr Monkhouse was already a subtraction. The chap who'd played the police inspector was Kenneth Alwyn, about my age and yet to find fame as a master musician. Ken reckoned we were both ready for the big time and he knew of a more exciting outfit called the Cabin Club, which was preparing an intimate revue to showcase new performers, writers and composers – and in the West End too. Well, near the West End anyway. Westbourne Grove, W11, to be exact, but more to the point, they paid your expenses.

On 14 and 15 November an eight-o'clock curtain rose in the 20th Century Theatre, property of the Rudolf Steiner Association Ltd, and *Spotlight* took to the stage. With Kenneth Alwyn and David Caryll at two pianos, we all took turns, twenty-five of us, in sketches, solo acts, point numbers, dance routines, parodies and ballads. One beautiful young man had a voice to match his blond masculinity but the unsuitable name of Neville Williams. After our first dress rehearsal, an agent named Philip Brown had taken him on, renamed him Gary Miller and was to see him through a brilliant but sadly short recording career until his untimely death from a congenital heart condition. The same agent bided his time with the three comedians in the show. He could spot a good singer but only audience laughter could identify a saleable comic for him.

My pal from charity shows was Phil Burn, a marvellous comedy mime, whose rubber-faced mouthings to gramophone records convulsed every sort of crowd. Philip Brown made him an offer as soon as he came offstage but the happy, sweating, tousled lad grinned a 'no-thanks'. He'd be loyal throughout what was to be a consistently successful career in summer shows and cabaret to the Streatham agent who'd first encouraged him, Rex Leslie.

Item number seven on the *Spotlight* programme was listed as:

> *Sensation on Sunday* . . .   . . . *Bennie Hill*

Benny, a slender young man with an experienced manner and a red tie for a double-take ('Oh, it's me tie, for a moment I thought me tongue was 'angin' out!') was a sensation as billed, but to

Philip Brown's disappointment he was already represented by his ex-army officer turned agent, Richard Stone. It seemed I was the only lost lamb on the green. After the second performance, Philip Brown became my tentative shepherd. It turned out that, as an agent, his limitations were boundless. Since he had once been a BBC producer, I thought he'd be able to put me on the air at once by seeking a favour from a previous colleague. But it seemed that the queue for radio auditions was the sole compulsory route to the ears of Britain. The waiting list was dauntingly long and, Brown said, likely to take a year and a half to clear before he could get me a hearing. I had no patience with that.

My immediate boss at the RAF station in Cleveland Street was Group Captain Thompkins, a senior neurologist and psychiatrist, specialising in the assessment of the RAF's liability to personnel suffering from nervous debility or mental illness. He'd see the applicants for disability pensions each morning, dictate his conclusions and recommendations to me in the afternoon and go home. I'd type them up for his signature the next morning and the process would be repeated. I had noticed that, after the first few weeks of finding my work free of error, he had stopped reading the reports. He just signed them. I composed a letter and slipped it in among the other papers for his signature.

For the attention of: *From Grp.Capt. I.W. Thompkins,*
Mr Michael Standing,   *Consultant Psychiatrist,*
Head of Radio Variety,   *RAF Central Medical Establishment,*
BBC, Bond Street, W1   *Cleveland Street, W1*

Dear Sir,

Many of the young men and women of the Royal Air Force who have experienced psychological damage as a result of their duties respond to very individual forms of treatment. In the case of Cpl R. A. Monkhouse, normal therapy cannot proceed along the lines I have prescribed without first disposing of a monomaniacal obsession which is obstructing such progress. The patient is fixated upon the need to submit himself to a professional examination of his ability as a broadcaster. It would be of great assistance to me and to the RAF if you could see your way to accommodate this frustrated fantasy by granting the young man some sort of test or audition. We could then continue his reparative psychotherapy. I need not add that, as with all such cases and their relief, the sooner the better.
12th March, 1948   *Yours very faithfully,*

While the Group Captain signed his papers next morning, I closed my eyes and whistled complicated bits of Vivaldi, not allowing myself to think of anything else. Even though my attempts to whistle classical themes sound to others like an asthma attack, they make sense to me as long as I concentrate very hard. I was halfway through Symphony P 21, 'Al Santo Sepolcro', in the 'black despair' key of B minor, when I heard the door slam. Thompkins had started his first patient assessment of the day in the examination room and the neat pile of documents left on his desk included our letter to the BBC with an unforged signature appended. I switched to whistling Haydn's 'Surprise' in the optimistic key of G major.

For the next few mornings I was in the office very early, making sure that I had time to open and read all the Group Captain's letters before he arrived. The sergeant in the mail room held all other postal deliveries for me so that I could peruse them and intercept the BBC's reply. In short, I had the situation covered. I got back from lunch on the fifth day to find Thompkins standing by the window, reading a newly opened letter.

'Corporal, do you know anything about this? It just came by hand from the BBC.'

By hand? I felt my stomach double up like a fist. Stepping forward enquiringly, I held out my hand, trying to control its slight trembling. 'May I see it, sir?'

But he was studying the letter.

'It's from a Miss Berkeley of something called "Radio Chimes", whatever that may be. Says a Mr Standing has asked her to arrange an urgent audition for my nominee.' He looked at me keenly. 'How did I come to nominate you, pray?'

'I'm sorry, sir, but with me being underage, well, the application form said "If under twenty-one, name of adult sponsor" and, well, sir, I thought you being my immediate superior, sir, it would be OK, I mean, correct . . .'

'Why didn't you give your father's name?'

'He doesn't approve of my ambitions, sir. Neither of my parents approves, sir.'

That much, at least, was true. I had overheard Dad's complaints about my foolishness in pursuing such an uncertain career and my mother's response, that Robert was going through a stage, that to oppose it was to encourage it, and that although I was bound to suffer disappointment, failure was the best way to bring me to my senses.

Thompkins waved the letter. 'So you gave them my name?'

I took a chance. 'I suppose I look on you as a father, sir.'

Thompkins went, 'Hah!' and sat down behind his desk. 'You very nearly went too far with that last remark, Corporal. I may put up with being taken for a sponsor but I won't be taken for a fool.'

'I'm very sorry, sir, I didn't mean to be disrespectful.'

There was a long silence. Then he held out the letter for me to take. Had I misunderstood him?

'Sir? Do you mean it's all right? That I can do the audition?'

'Oh, I'm not going to stand in the way of a budding George Robey or whatever you think you are. Just make sure you get your work done.'

I took the letter and stammered my thanks, but he flapped a hand in dismissal.

I wanted him to say, 'And one day, when you're famous, don't tell this story as if you made a mug out of me, because you haven't fooled me for a moment.' But he didn't, so I settled for what I'd got. And what I'd got was an appointment in Studio 25B, Bond Street, at ten a.m. the following Monday. 'Bring accompanist if required,' said the letter.

If that story of how I got my radio audition seems like further evidence of my persistence and impudence, the circumstances of the audition itself demonstrate my sheer dumb luck. First of all, my accompanist was right there, working in the building as a clerk. Corporal Stan Tracey, his phenomenal career with the Ted Heath Band and his own great combinations and jazz compositions all in the unforeseeable future, was my best mate. I thought, 'I'll ask him to play one of his show pieces and he'll get booked for a radio show too.'

Secondly, I planned to take Neville Williams along with me as well. Given half a chance, he could try out his superb singing voice under his new name. It was all adolescent optimism but I didn't know any better. Had the normal BBC audition system been working, Stan would never have been allowed to solo and Neville would have been given the bum's rush. But the system wasn't working.

On the Friday before the big day, some late winter bug struck down the man who had been in charge of BBC Variety auditions for just over fifteen years. His method was to mark performers by percentage in the most niggardly way, five per cent being a passing mark and twenty per cent the highest accolade he ever awarded anybody. Most applicants scored between zero and four, never to inhabit the ether. I'll never know what mark he would have given me because the Monday of my maiden speech into a radio microphone was also the first day the man hadn't shown up for work.

While we three must-get-theres waited in the brisk March wind outside a locked entrance in the north end of Bond Street, panic gripped the office of Miss Berkeley and her junior, some three hundred yards south of us in the BBC's Aeolian Hall. Here they were, the two of them, solely responsible for assembling the variety programme 'Radio Chimes', a closed-circuit presentation intended only for the ears of BBC producers over the loudspeakers in their offices. The cast of each weekly edition was composed of first-time performers, as selected by the senior administrator in charge of BBC auditions. But he was either late or not coming at all and there was no one of sufficient authority to sit in judgement on the day's intake of newcomers.

Their crisis was beginning to provoke hysteria when Dennis Main Wilson walked through the wrong door and asked, 'Is this where I get my subsistence money?'

Seeing Miss Berkeley and her assistant in such distress brought out the white knight in him. He calmed the girls down and explained that, while he might be only a probationary producer in Variety Department terms, he was in fact a genuine radio executive, a graduate of the pre-war BBC German Service in fact, and a former Head of Light Entertainment for Nordwestdeutscher Rundfunk, newly arrived from Hamburg. Just tell him where to go, he told them, and he would stem the tide of talent *pro tempore*. The girls were hugely grateful and pressed the key of Studio 25B upon him. He departed amid relieved laughter and reassurances.

The girls could not have known that Dennis was, at that brief stage of his life, an overripe candidate for Group Captain Thompkins' psychotherapy. A kind of nervous breakdown had loosened his screws.

That he made a full and rapid recovery from this shatterpated state can be judged from his subsequent output as perhaps the most innovative comedy producer of his day, producing the early Goon shows and 'Hancock's Half-Hour' for radio, while his television work would include 'Till Death Us Do Part', Terry Scott's best solo starring series, 'Scott on . . .', and 'Citizen Smith'. He would audition literally thousands of future applicants, discover and encourage John Bird, Eleanor Bron, John Fortune, Griff Rhys Jones, Emma Thompson, Stephen Fry and Hugh Laurie, while promoting the best of Britain's comedy writers including the work of a BBC scene-shifter named John Sullivan. But as we stood and watched him in the street, wrestling with the lock and then muttering to himself as he ushered us into a dark studio and vanished upstairs, we got a definite whiff of March Hare. We shrugged at each other, and while Stan began noodling on the Steinway, Neville and I read the notice on the wall.

NOTICE TO AUDITIONEES
STAND ON THE ORANGE MAT AND FACE THE
MICROPHONE. WHEN THE RED LIGHT GOES ON,
STATE YOUR NAME CLEARLY, THEN WAIT. BEGIN
YOUR PERFORMANCE WHEN THE GREEN LIGHT
GOES ON. WHEN THE GREEN LIGHT GOES OUT,
STOP PERFORMING AS SOON AS IT SEEMS
JUDICIOUS FOR YOU TO DO SO. IF YOU HAVE
STOPPED PERFORMING BEFORE THE GREEN LIGHT
GOES OUT, GO TO THE DOOR AND PRESS THE
BLACK BUTTON UNDERNEATH THE LIGHT SWITCH.
DO NOT WHISTLE UNLESS YOUR PERFORMANCE
REQUIRES IT.

We had agreed that Neville should perform first in case the three of us were dismissed as soon as my effort was over. The red light came on and he stepped up to the triangle of scuffed orange canvas stitched into the worn haircord carpet. The microphone was as big as a breadbox.

'Gary Miller,' he said, grinning at me.

A speaker buzzed loudly, went silent, buzzed again, coughed, then a distorted voice said, 'I haven't got you down. How do you spell it?' Gary spelt it.

'Just a minute, I've got to start this list again. Damn! Bloody pen. Sorry. Hold on a minute.' The speaker hummed and died. Minutes passed.

A yellow light came on over the door. We looked at the notice again but it didn't mention any yellow light so we just waited. It went out again.

Suddenly the speaker sputtered and we heard Dennis again, much louder this time.

'Right, not to worry. Press on regardless. G.A.R.Y. M.I.L.L.E.R., eh? No details, you see. OK, OK, space provided, ink flowing. State name of sponsor.'

'Er – Philip Brown Agency, 17 Wigmore Street, W1. Telephone, Langham 4258.'

'Got that, good. Now, switch on green light. Where the hell is – oh, I've got it, I've got it. It's going on . . . *now!* There! Is it on?'

Gary – he was Gary now – nodded to Stan, who led him into a marvellous rendition of 'There Goes That Song Again', a number that was to take Gary back into the British charts for the sixth time in 1961. He finished the song and stepped back from the mike but the green light stayed on. I went to the door and pressed the black button underneath the light switch.

The speaker crackled. 'Jeepers Creepers! What the hell was that? Oh, I see, "Audition over", I see. Well, too bad, bloody super voice. Now what's next? "Percentage", just a second, I've got to fill this in.'

There was another long wait while the yellow light above the door went on and off twice. It occurred to me that this might indicate somebody's arrival outside. We had a similar light in Thompkins' examination room instead of an intrusive bell. Perhaps the queue for auditions was forming in Bond Street. But the tinny speaker clicked into life again.

'OK, all shipshape. You can go, Gary. Next!'

I stood on the mat and faced the mike, script in hand.

'Well, go on then. Who's next? What are you waiting for?'

'The red light,' I said.

'Bugger! I'll get the hang of this before I die. There!'

The red light went on.

'Bob Monkhouse, same agent as Gary.'

'Phil Brown chappie? Langham four two whatever?'

'That's right.'

'Give us a tick.'

I gave him a tick.

'OK, off you go. Oh, sod it, green light switch, sorry.'

The green light went on and so did I.

It was my very best material, tightly routined so as to give me the chance to do lots of accents and funny voices. Other gags were performance bits, requiring self-interruption and fine timing to make them work. Some of my lines still get used by comedians today:

> I said, 'Professor, what's your latest invention?'
> 'I'm wearing it, Monkhouse my boy – a hearing aid, no bigger
> than a farthing and almost invisible!'
> 'How much will it cost?'
> 'Half past five.'

The patter covered my childhood, my failures with girls, troubles in the RAF, clashes with the sergeant, my crazy relatives and so on. I had discovered something elemental about writing comedy for oneself to perform. It presents a double dilemma: how much of your act should be an act? And how much is your life itself an act? To put it another way, how much of what you believe is yourself should you reveal in your jokes? Just enough honesty to make them seem truer and therefore funnier perhaps.

I finished my seven minutes with a comic parody of the Rodgers and Hart song 'There's a Small Hotel', making lyrical alterations which the publishers would never have allowed on the air, although I didn't know that at the time and I don't believe the man upstairs did either.

The last note faded away but the green light didn't. Should I stop performing? Was it judicious to do so? I caught Gary's eye and jerked my head toward the black button that seemed to announce the end of the audition to our unseen listener. Gary pushed it but nothing changed. Stan pointed at himself and mouthed. 'Me?' I shrugged, no longer sure I even knew what judicious meant. Then I turned back to the microphone.

'And now, Stan Tracey will play for you. Same agent.'

Stan did his Gershwin medley.

Nothing. Just the steady gleam of green and a speaker that didn't speak. Stan got up from his piano stool and crossed to the mike.

'Goodnight, everybody, goodnight,' he said with a monocle in his throat, and we slipped out of the studio. Waiting on the pavement were seven or eight people, some with music, one old chap holding a washboard.

'Are we right for the auditions?' he asked.

'Go on inside,' said Gary. 'But they took our washboard off us.'

Nothing happened for a week. Then the phone in Philip Brown's office started ringing and wouldn't stop. It seemed as if every variety producer in the Corporation wanted to book me and Gary for their shows. Philip couldn't take it in.

'But this is the fifth engagement I've been offered this morning, Miss Boxall. And neither of these artistes has passed his audition yet.'

The Bookings Manager had to explain it to him twice.

What had happened seemed extraordinary at the time and like

a bad sitcom idea today. Dennis Main Wilson had given Gary one hundred per cent. He'd then listened to me and awarded me one hundred and one per cent, adding the opinion 'WOW!' Having done that, he'd collapsed in his chair and passed out cold. Stan's Gershwin selection had fallen upon unconscious ears. Someone had found Dennis after a while, the St John's Ambulance men on their usual voluntary duty at Aeolian Hall had been sent for, and Dennis had been helped back to his home and bed.

Meanwhile the wheels of bureaucracy worked on inexorably. Some clerk had collected the audition report, short though it was, and put it into normal channels from which it emerged a week later on two dozen or so desks throughout the BBC Variety Department.

Producers, accustomed to the parsimony of the usual auditioner's marks out of one hundred, now saw what appeared to be the emergence of the two greatest talents of the century. Not waiting for such flabbergasting prodigies to debut in the regular way on the internal 'Radio Chimes', they immediately instructed the Booking Managers, Miss Boxall and Miss Lipscomb, to acquire our services for their shows.

Within the next few days Philip took bookings for me to compère 'Works Wonders' from Leicester, do the top spot on a discovery show called 'Beginners, Please', fill the opening comedy slot on the venerable Saturday night favourite 'Music Hall', be the New Voice of the Week on Sunday night's popular 'Variety Bandbox', become the 'resident comedian' on Thursday evenings in 'Show Time' from the People's Palace, Mile End Road, commencing that 27 May, and join the Ralph Reader team for a new series called 'It's Fine To Be Young' to run from 6 July every Tuesday until 21 September 1948.

I was still nineteen years old and greener than algae. No experience, no wardrobe, not enough material to fill half these engagements, no hope of sustaining the illusion that I was truly a one-hundred-per-cent wow. All I could think of was that letter from Leonard Henry. He was right. I had only got this far because I was a very persistent and impudent little fellow. How much further could persistence and impudence carry me? I should just have to wait and see.

9

RADIO FUN

– Act One –

Commencing two partnerships, touching upon fraternal love and maternal opposition; getting the early bird, getting some dress sense and the luck of getting six million listeners to hear something to my advantage

Within the space of only a few weeks I encountered two of the four people who most affected the rest of my life: my first wife and Denis Goodwin.

Both came to the Central Medical Establishment, the former because the RAF posted her there to work and the latter in search of me. Denis had known of me at Dulwich but never approached me there, being a year younger and in awe of older scholars. Flat feet had kept him from being conscripted and his love of radio had drawn him to the job of selling wireless sets in a London department store called Gamage's. On one such set he heard me rattling off the sort of brisk one-liners that he was trying to write for himself. With a tenacity I was to learn to respect, he spent three weeks tracing me and then simply presented himself to the RAF guard at our entrance and asked to see me. We lunched at some greasy spoon beside Goodge Street underground station while he explained his ambitions and I half-listened, wrestling with corned beef fritters and fascinated by what I took to be an ochre birthmark running from the left corner of Denis's mouth down to his collar. It wasn't a birthmark. It was the stain left by regurgitated iodine. He had found the bottle in his mother's medicine cabinet, its label bearing the skull-and-crossbones symbol and the warning: 'Poison – Not To Be Taken Internally.' He had tried to drink it but choked it up.

'Do you often try to poison yourself?' I asked.

'My father was killed by a doodlebug when I was fourteen. My mother's remarried and I hate him. I get depressed. I want to be a great comedian like Danny Kaye and I don't care how hard I have to work but, I don't know, sometimes it all seems so impossible that I want to kill myself.'

'Killing yourself is not the solution.'

'No, I'd probably live to regret it,' he said and laughed nervously.

After that – and for the next fifteen years of our partnership – I kept a close watch on Denis's moods. He paid for the ecstasy of his frequent bouts of happiness, a delirious state of giggling bliss that had to be seen to be believed, with troughs of the blackest gloom, self-loathing and despair. He was self-centred, generous, both arrogant and self-effacing, clumsy, envious, unpretentious and very confused. On his father's death, his mother, Mrs Evelyn Goodwin, had turned away from Judaism to Christian Science, which didn't help her son with his adolescent sense of identity. Teaming up with me may have saved him from any immediate further attempts to top himself but, in the long run and for his sake, I wish he had found a partner with a steadier and less challenging nature than mine.

Throughout our long collaboration, he was never unaware that his natural reserve and physical awkwardness contrasted with the drive and self-assurance so easily adopted by me. The thousand and one instances of this did not add to his general self-esteem, although they sometimes stimulated in him a compensatory and exaggerated *amour propre* which drove him to some vain and valiant performances on TV and stage.

I came to love him as a brother, far more than I loved my natural brother, whose small regard for me had not increased during his years serving overseas in the Queen's Bays. John was now articled to a firm of chartered accountants and laying the foundations for his future and prosperous career. He would soon woo and marry a lovely wife, raise two fine children and eventually retire to well-earned comfort, where he lives today in Sussex. Since the times I am writing about to the present day I shouldn't think we've spoken to each other more than a dozen times, with total silence reigning from 1957, when he came out of my father's bedroom to make a curt announcement of Dad's death, until 1977 when he and his wife brought their youngsters to see a taping of 'Celebrity Squares'. My friends find this estrangement very sad and Jackie, with her strong tradition of family loyalty, can't understand it at all. Ready for my amateur psychology? I believe that the five-and-a-half-year-old John never accepted my birth and grew up resenting the affection that my greater amiability attracted from our mother. In my turn, longing for my older brother's approval and not getting it, I gave up trying but later embraced this new friendship with Denis Goodwin, hugely fulfilled by the love I was able to feel for him. I instinctively took on the job of being *his* big brother, role-playing what I had missed in my youth. Maybe you think that's a load of codswallop but, hey, this is my book and you're stuck with my opinions.

(On June 15, 1993 I was moved to tears by a letter from John. It said simply, 'Dear Bob, Sincere congratulations on your O.B.E., without doubt the first of its kind for our family. Best wishes, John.' I wrote to him in thanks and we have restored brotherly contact of a kind after so many years.)

Sorry. Back to the plot. While Denis and I met regularly to discuss comedy and compare ideas, I fell in love with an enchanting Ulster girl, a WAAF who'd been allocated to my department. I took her home, where my mother was hospitable but cool and later indicated disapproval. Rallying to the defence of my sweetheart I only provoked a furious row which ended with my mother vowing 'not to let that girl set foot in this house again'. I didn't go home for a few nights, sleeping on a camp bed in the RAF Orderly Room. My mother then modified her hostility and I was allowed to bring my girlfriend to my parents' house again, but I found myself caught in the middle of the domestic equivalent of a Mexican stand-off.

While my mum and my future ex-wife assumed battle positions, I was having a whale of a time, encouraged by my RAF colleagues who indulgently took on my duties so that I could skip around southern England learning my comedy trade. Benny Hill had tipped me off about some of the friendlier venues that would tolerate relatively unskilled performers. Even so I was getting my full share of rejection. The audience at the Ridgeway Working Men's Club, Hammersmith, saw a young man take the stage wearing a drape-shape American suit, hand-painted kipper tie and a white trilby with the brim turned up at the front and they took instant umbrage. I opened with what I hoped was a funny parody of 'The Alphabet Song', a new hit record by Perry Como and the Fontane Sisters:

> *'A' – I'm adorable,*
> *'B' – I'm so beautiful . . .*

A man shouted, 'C – you're a cunt!' and that was the end of my act. At another club in Catford I began another parody of the Bing Crosby song, 'Pennies from Heaven':

> *Every time it rains, it rains . . .*

Two pints of beer shot out of two mugs from two men with but a single thought. They hit me simultaneously in the face and the chest. I stood there dripping. I held out my right hand palm upwards, looked up and tried a singing *ad lib* from the Jolson song, 'April Showers':

> *It isn't raining rain, you know,*
> *It's raining Younger's ale . . .*

That was interpreted as begging for it. Beer was cheap in those days and the local lads enjoyed a target. The contents of every glass and mug in the joint were tossed at me. For a long time afterwards, whenever I wore that Cecil Gee suit for any length of time, the smell of best bitter increased in ratio to my body warmth. And I had yet to learn about clothes, that in those post-war days of austerity, it just wasn't smart to look smart. It was the BBC's most popular ventriloquist who taught me that.

One autumn Sunday night in 1948, Peter Brough and his dummy Archie Andrews shared the number two dressing room for a live broadcast of 'Variety Bandbox', radio's top variety show (Albert Modley was in number one). Peter was standing nearby when the stagedoor keeper told me that the dressing room originally intended for my use was now needed for the extra musicians augmenting an act called Troise and his Mandoliers.

'Look here, son, you can bunk in with me and Archie if you like.'

I was changing my clothes and repeating my thanks when Brough said, 'No, stop that, don't do that.'

'Sorry, was I overdoing the gratitude?'

'Never mind about that, it's the suit, you don't want to wear that. It'll make you look like a smart-alecky spiv. You're doing comedy, aren't you? Well, put your RAF uniform back on, my lad, they can't be unkind to one of our boys in blue.'

I believe that the enormous goodwill felt by the British public towards the armed services doubled my laughs that evening. From then on I wore the uniform for every broadcast and charity concert, even discovering that if I temporarily picked off the corporal's stripes and returned to being an ordinary AC2 (Aircraftsman 2nd class), the crowd's sympathy increased. By the time I was demobbed in 1949, I was almost on the verge of having myself extensively bandaged and carried onstage by stretcher with a nurse displaying my medals on a tray.

Luck seemed to be against me on my return to 'Show Time' in the top spot as its regular closing comedian. I had to follow two other comedians, an ailing veteran whose act fell flat and a young Max Bygraves who physically did the same. Puzzling his listeners but convulsing everyone in the People's Palace, Max strolled up to the mike, took one look at the audience, said 'Oh, my Gawd!' and fell flat on his back as if in a dead faint. He rose to his feet and continued to score with strong material and easygoing authority. I knew I couldn't follow him and I certainly didn't. When my turn came I'd lost confidence in my comparatively thin patter. Boy in blue or not, the people couldn't summon up much more than mercy laughter for me. I came off to a round of apathy, soaked in flop sweat and fighting back tears of humiliation. Roy Speer was the producer, a kind man, and he greeted me in the wings with real sympathy.

'Tough luck, young Bob. Obviously you know.'

'Well, yes, how could I not know? There was nothing I could do to save it.'

He looked at me curiously. 'Save it? Well, you can save it till next week and do it again, can't you?'

'Do it again?'

'No need to waste a good script, is there? Did it go down well? I couldn't listen to you, I was on the wire to BH, of course, just in case they came back to us before the end.'

Since it was plain that we were talking at cross purposes, I shut up and listened. It seemed that my lousy (and, at such a stage in my new career, potentially very damaging) performance would remain a secret between me and the two hundred people in the hall. Broadcasting House had pre-empted the last eight minutes of our show to take a Test Match announcement from Australia. At the exact moment that I had been announced, our listening millions had been switched away from Bob Monkhouse about to score a duck to Sir Don Bradman scoring a century.

My tears of self-pity turned to those of sheer relief. I was awake all that night, planning my script for the following Thursday. Morning brought phonecalls from the press, wanting the story of the rising star who'd been bowled out by the world's greatest cricketer. The fluke publicity was a gift and a perfect set-up for what I planned to do.

Speer went out before our next broadcast to warm up the theatre audience and, at my request, reminded them of how his young comedy discovery had been faded off the air the previous week. Most of them seemed to know. As a result, I came out to very friendly applause and moved to the central microphone:

Thank you, ladies and gentlemen, yes, here I am, back with the act they tried to put a gag on – and heaven knows, it could do with one.
Now as I was saying last week when I was so rudely interrupted . . .

I then moved swiftly to a second mike, speaking like a BBC announcer:

We interrupt this broadcast for an urgent gale warning.
Get out of the flat, Gail, my wife's coming back a week early.

In this fashion, I turned myself into an ill-fated comedian whose best gags were cut by police messages, fat-stock prices, crossed telephone lines and news flashes. The crowd loved every change of accent and running gag and, remembering how effective Bygraves had been with added slapstick, I added to the mock confusion by dropping pages of my script between the two mikes and apparently mixing them up. It won big laughs and fine press reaction. For my big finish I had myself interrupted by the unmistakeable growling tones of Winston Churchill, speaking from Blenheim. Since I couldn't do a good Churchill impression, I paid half of my fee of eight guineas to a young Welsh actor, new to London and whom Speer assured me could handle the comedy well. He only had four lines to do for his four pounds, four shillings, but he was worth every penny. His name was Richard Burton.

As the end of my RAF service drew near, my love for my Irish girlfriend and my desire to become independent of my mother increased. I wanted to propose marriage but I didn't dare. My spate of radio bookings could easily have dried up and I needed a regular income. Goodwin and I still hadn't hit our stride with our writing so I tried teaming with a Beckenham neighbour named Laurie Wyman to script a BBC series for Michael Howard, a bespectacled raconteur of Wyman's acquaintance. Wyman had just been ejected from the army after serving three months behind bars for desertion and Howard had a suspended sentence for embezzlement, so I wasn't impressing my parents with the company I was keeping. Nevertheless, the success of 'Here's Howard' and of my weekly appearances on a BBC Midlands concert party called 'Radio Ruffles' led to an appointment with the Head of Radio Variety.

'Nice work, young man, making a name for yourself very fast. Trouble is, we no sooner make new artistes popular on the air than they desert us to go tootling round the variety circuit, cashing in on their new-found fame. So here's what I propose. You sign a two-year contract to be one of the BBC's two new resident comedians. We pay you five hundred pounds a year plus your individual performance and writing fees and in return you agree to stay put, available to us whenever we want you. Yes or no?'

I said yes to his proposal and my new fiancée said yes to mine. Shedding my RAF uniform at last, my first civilian job was to co-star in an experimental programme called 'It's in the Bag' with the BBC's only other contract comedian, a slender Terry Scott. The show was meant to be funny but the studio audience sat there quieter than a mouse peeing on a blotter.

I was too preoccupied with my private life to worry about it.

My mother had taken the news of my intended marriage very badly. Her behaviour became erratic, veering from icy rage to a sudden, unexpected warmth, as when she invited my fiancée to our house and put an amazing suggestion to her.

'You want a home in England and a husband who can provide for you, I quite understand that,' she said. 'If Robert marries you, we will cut him off without a penny. So why don't you turn your attention toward his older brother? John has a secure future in accountancy and neither Wilfred nor I will stand in the way of such a courtship. Once you've thought it over, I'm sure you'll agree.'

After travelling to Belfast to present myself to members of her family, my bride and I were married at Caxton Hall, Westminster, on November the 5th, 1949, just the day for the fireworks that were to follow before the marriage ended. After weeks of refusing to acknowledge the approaching occasion, my mother was persuaded to attend at the very last minute if only for the sake of appearances. Wedding photographs show her tight-lipped and pale, dressed entirely in black. I must have been as sensitive as a doorknocker. All I cared about was what I wanted, my mother's pain overlooked. As usual in my life, what I can't tolerate, I switch off. Either it becomes invisible or I do.

1950 beckoned with wonderful opportunities. The West End impresario Cecil Landau cast me in his lavish revue *Sauce Piquante* at the Cambridge Theatre, where I shared a dressing room with Norman Wisdom and Tommy Cooper. Cooper's towering figure dwarfed us both. He once took his shirt off, handed me a dark stick of Leichner's makeup, turned away from me and said over his shoulder, 'Do me a favour, write B.A.C.K. on me.' Obediently I wrote the letters across his back. 'There,' he sighed, putting his shirt back on, 'that should end the confusion.'

The show folded after six weeks and I wasn't sorry. By that time, I wanted to kill Norman Wisdom. On the opening night the show had overrun by over an hour and his multiple appearances throughout had been drastically cut to three or four. His outrage was so intense that it still shines from his eyes today when he speaks about it. Working with him became a nightmare. Apart from my work in the show as compère and in sketches with Douglas Byng and Moira Lister, I had to feed Norman in a scene that required him to kick me on the shin several times. Landau had overspent massively and so refused to pay for more than one shin pad. As Norman came onstage each evening, his eyes would glance at my legs and spot the padded leg. He vented his frustration on the other one. I tried switching the pad from shin to shin but Norman's foot always cracked me on the unguarded limb till both my legs were black and blue from knee to ankle. Today he says he can't remember doing this to me but I certainly do. I didn't forgive him for a very long time but, as I'll relate, an unrecorded performance on a Sunday in Birmingham nearly twenty years later would dissolve my resentment in admiring wonder.

The sweetest and loveliest member of our cast also caused some grief. Out of the twenty-four girls in our chorus line, twenty-three could dance quite wonderfully well. Only one danced with an enthusiasm unfettered by ability. The infant Bambi on ice handled its legs better. She was also a walking X-ray, a strand of spaghetti with shoes. The other girls wept and fumed, not because she couldn't dance nor because they disliked her.

'We might as well not be on the stage at all,' sobbed Diana Monk. 'The entire audience ignores all of us and just stares at her! They can't take their eyes off that face! Those eyes! That bloody smile! She's a darling girl but, honestly, I could just murder that Audrey Hepburn!'

When I appeared in my first film only a year later, a downbeat political melodrama written and directed by the distinguished Thorold Dickinson and called *The Secret People*, I wasn't too surprised to find our prancing ectomorph with the magic face was one of its stars.

Denis Goodwin and I had continued to explore our potential as a creative team and the gags I had written for Derek Roy resulted in his asking us to try our hands at rescuing a disastrous series he was doing with Spike Milligan called 'Hip-Hip-Hoo-Roy'. Successful work on this led the producer to send for us again when he had another series in trouble, 'It's a Great Life' starring 'Britain's favourite American', Bonar Colleano. Bonar came from a circus family and I learned a lot of slapstick tricks from him which I later put to effective use on TV and in pantomimes.

He was also a violently self-destructive man who killed himself in a suicidal car crash at the age of thirty-five. Throughout the 1950s, radio comedy held its own against TV's encroachment and we were two of its keenest exponents. We scripted and appeared in literally thousands of shows, among them 'The Show Band Show' with its star guests from the USA, enabling me to write and perform comedy with Frank Sinatra, Rosemary Clooney, Billy Eckstine, Bing Crosby, Nat 'King' Cole, Jimmy Durante, Johnnie Ray, Dolores Gray and Tony Martin. One of our series, 'Hallo, Playmates!' starring Arthur Askey, David Nixon, Irene Handl and Pat Coombs as 'Mrs. Purvis and her daughter, Nola' and ourselves, won the 1953 *Daily Mail* Radio Award. Another, 'Mixed Doubles', about warring neighbours played by Cyril Fletcher and Betty Astell versus Michael Denison and Dulcie Gray, won the *London Evening News* Best Comedy Award.

But rather than bore you with any more names and titles, let me tell you about one rather exciting series that introduced me to one rather exciting star.

10

RADIO FUN

– Act Two –

*Calling all forces, we find both success and a heroine,
only to have the air turn blue. Reprieved, we still feel like
throwing it all up*

It was her energy that first attracted me. The film was really bad,
a low budget black-and-white 1948 B movie called *Penny and the
Pownall Case*. She was billed fourth after Peggy Evans, Ralph
Michael and Christopher Lee. Her acting was raw but promising
and her vitality made me remember her afterwards as if her part
of the screen had been in colour. I walked out of the Essoldo
Cinema, Penge, a fan of Diana Dors.

Other, more experienced eyes than mine saw her potential and
within two years Diana had been successfully promoted as
Britain's brightest new pin-up girl. Her hair was bleached to a
sunny blonde, patterned one-piece swimsuits showed her lovely
legs and figure while concealing the puppy fat, and she gave the
camera the same amused gaze that she gave everything for the
rest of her life, a bravely lived life that was to be cruelly cut short
when cancer killed her on 4 May 1984. She was fifty-two years
old.

When we met for the very first time, it was obvious we were both
deeply in love – she with her first husband and me with my new
wife. That didn't stop us taking a strong and immediate liking to
one another, a mutual affection that lasted over thirty years and
which was to become briefly supercharged on a wet October
Sunday afternoon in 1953 that neither of us ever forgot.

Three years before that very physical encounter took place,
Denis Goodwin and I were writing funny stuff for our customers

in a grim little office which we rented from the grumpy Marvelman Comics cartoonist, Mick Anglo, on the third floor of 164 Gower Street, London, NW1. We paid him four pounds a week for the room and if you think that was small money, you should've seen what we paid our secretary. She was a good-looking girl named Pam whom neither of us fancied because of her daily habit of handing us pages packed with typographical errors and then, when we looked up reproachfully, saying in excruciating cockney, 'Wha' I dun? Wha' I dun?'

The oddest things can put you off a girl, even when you're a carnal-minded twenty-two-year-old ready to jump on almost anything with a pulse.

There came a phone call on that Thursday morning from the BBC that made us wide-eyed with hope. We abandoned an eight-minute patter spot ordered by the multi-accented comedian Harold Berens for his appearance on 'Workers' Playtime' the following Monday. We knew he'd only jam in three of his own old Jewish jokes and pay us half the promised ten pounds anyway. We loved him but when we wrote Harold one-liners like, 'I won't eat asparagus in a restaurant in case I accidentally leave a tip', it was based on real-life observation.

Thirty minutes later we were in Leslie Bridgmont's office at Aeolian Hall, Bond Street. We knew he had liked the thirty-minute comedy scripts we had written for his Derek Roy series 'Hip, Hip, Hoo-Roy!' and his Bonar Colleano series, 'It's a Great Life'. His phone call had hinted at something bigger.

'*Mucho* bigger, boysies,' said Bridgie (radio was a breeding ground for such affectionate diminutives), 'the biggest show the Corpse has done for yonks! It'll have everything our boys in uniform want. Beautiful girls, Geraldo's big orchestra, sports stars, the George Mitchell Singers, Petula Clark as the Sweetheart of the Forces, the Stargazers, Leslie 'The Memory Man' Welch, Ted Ray as the host, the top comedy guests, film stars . . .'

He paused for breath and wiped his sweating forehead and moustache. Bridgie was a corpulent old boy with a terrific track record of comedy successes to his credit and a heart condition to show for it.

'It'll be the making of you, lads. Now, I want a four-minute patter spot for Ted to kick off the hour, a clever link to the troops' requests . . .'

The series was titled 'Calling All Forces' and it was just as big a hit as he'd predicted. As for it being the making of us, within a few weeks the *Daily Mail* was running an article by Robert Cannell about 'radio's youngest masters of mirth' headlined '22 AND 21 GET LAUGHS IN HOMES OF 11,000,000'. That kind of praise put me in just the cocky frame of mind to meet our special guest star for the following week's show, Diana Dors.

Denis and I arrived at our usual time of nine-thirty a.m. that Saturday at the Playhouse Theatre on the corner of Northumberland Avenue. The rehearsals ran from ten till three-thirty p.m. and the sixty-minute show was performed between four and five-thirty, recorded on discs for broadcasting on the Light Programme next day at nine p.m. Diana was due to arrive at ten thirty but, already the total professional, she made her entrance at ten thirty-one, giving one minute for Rank's Public Relations maestro, Theo Cowan, to announce her arrival. Geraldo silenced his forty-piece orchestra, Ted Ray straightened his tie, Bridgie wiped the sweat off his face, Denis got a fit of the giggles and I decided to be the greeter.

As I walked up the aisle, Diana appeared through the plush curtains from the foyer. Her golden mane fell over one eye in a soft, sweeping wave, her full lips were painted in what was then called shocking pink, perfectly matching her elegant Schiaparelli silk suit, low at the neckline to show a little creamy cleavage and a silvery camisole. She had a ring on her right hand that could have been used as a blunt weapon, her nylons were extra sheer and her pink-and-silver shoes from Anello and Davide had heels long enough to spear salmon. She was the vibrant incarnation of every Hollywood fantasy of my adolescence and I was dumbstruck – rare for me.

'Hello,' she said eagerly, 'are you the producer?'

From behind me Theo said, 'He's just one of the writers, Diana. Follow me.' He began to lead her to the stage but Diana didn't move.

'Are you Denis or Bob?'

I told her who I was and introduced my partner, who was lurking nearby.

'Very funny script, very clever. I just hope I can do it justice, that's all.'

This time Theo succeeded in taking her away to meet more important people and we were left marvelling at the young star taking the trouble to memorise our names. It beat a dozen articles in the *Daily Mail*.

She was a delight in rehearsal, cracking up the musicians by finding sexy double meanings in the script without once stepping on the comedy toes of Ted Ray and guest comic, Max Wall. Every time she got a laugh, she looked over and caught my eye, sharing the moment. Denis noticed this eye contact happening and his giggling was over for the day. He went into a sulk and retired to the back of the stalls to glower at us.

A uniformed audience with free tickets began queuing outside for the show at four o'clock, entered the theatre at quarter past, and laughed cheerily at Bridgie's warm-up. Bridgie finished his little chat to the audience with two minutes to go before the red light went on. He was about to leave the stage to go to the control booth when a last minute thought struck him.

'We've got a smashing mystery glamour star on the show today, boys and girls, who deserves your applause, so please give her a big warm round.'

Ted adlibbed from his chair onstage, 'Why not? Everything else she's got is big and warm and round.' The crowd roared but I didn't. I was too busy making a note of the line for future use. Ted got it back in one of our later scripts for the series and never even recognised it as his.

The show that followed was going well enough right up to Diana's entrance. Then it became what the flower children of the next decade would call a happening. Though I'll try to explain in some detail the unique hysteria of the next forty minutes, I don't think I'll ever find a more apposite use for the cliché, 'You just had to be there.'

None of us had quite appreciated what an impact Diana would have on a predominantly male services audience. They cheered and whistled and applauded her first appearance for so long, Ted had to quell it by holding his hands up and yelling, 'Stop it or I'll send her home! Stop it or I'll send her home!' They subsided but only with suppressed excitement waiting to explode again.

From then on, every line she spoke was greeted with joyful whoops and more applause. When Ted's W.C. Fields put his arm around her and said, 'I'm groping for words to express my love', Diana's Mae West replied, 'Well, move your hands, sonny, I ain't got no dictionary there', and the old theatre shook with the crowd's approval far beyond the worth of the joke. That was followed by a second and third wave of laughter as different sections of the audience found extra meanings and both Ted and Diana milked it as instinctively as natural performers always do.

Still recording and oblivious of the effect Diana and the happy audience were likely to have upon the delicate ears of our eleven million listeners in Britain alone, we were more worried about the show overrunning than anything else. Editable tape recording lay in the future: our shows had the same discipline as a live broadcast and had to keep exactly to time. The excessive laughter and applause had already spread the programme length by two minutes. Denis and I were hard at work with the cast backstage, agreeing upon and making cuts in the final comedy sketch. I tried to slice out complete gags that could be re-used in other situations. After all, the way things were turning out, this particular show didn't need great gags; the troops were so excited by Diana that they'd have laughed at a gale warning. Bridgie had quit the control booth and was re-arranging Pet Clark's request spot to cut out a three-minute song.

Everyone was concentrating so much on squeezing the remaining material into the available time that we failed to see disaster in the making.

Our big closing sketch was a film burlesque, a type of comedy made popular on American radio by Bob Hope. We had based this one on *White Cargo*, a steamy 1942 movie starring Hedy Lamarr and Walter Pidgeon, in which Hedy played her best-known role of the seductive Tondelayo, entrancing all at a British plantation post in Africa; just the part for Diana. Ted played the expeditionist who loved her and Max Wall was an alcoholic doctor. It was a corny plot and we'd provided a sketch to match. But in summarily cutting it down to fit, we had overlooked a time bomb. Here's how the dialogue ran on the page as we wrote it.

MAX: *Tondelayo, I'm trembling at your touch.*
DIANA: *Ahah, Tondelayo she make you come over all weak.*

MAX: *Okeydokey, and I'll come over all next week too.*

DIANA: *How long is it since you kissed a woman?*

MAX: *Not since I came out of the hospital.*

DIANA: *You were being ill?*

MAX: *I was being born.*

DIANA: *Kiss me, bwana.*

FIX: *LOUD AND LENGTHY KISSING NOISE.*

DIANA: *(GASPING) Where did you learn to kiss like that?*

MAX: *I played the trumpet for five years before I found out I should've been blowing the small end, not sucking the big end.*

FIX: *DOOR OPENS*

TED: *Tondelayo! Doctor Wall! I can't believe this has been going on behind my back under my very nose.*

MAX: *I can explain.*

TED: *Silence! I'm going to beat you within an inch of your life!*

FIX: *SERIES OF FOUR VIOLENT WHACKS UNDER MAX YELLING:*

MAX: *(OVER WHACKING NOISE) Ow! Ow! Ow! Ow!*

TED: *How much further to go?*

MAX: *About five inches.*

And so on. Such dialogue was never meant to be read in a book, you'll agree. We wrote for our performers, knowing what they could best exploit.

By the time the sketch had reached this particular page, the audience had become almost delirious with laughter at Max's lecherous mugging, Diana's mock sexiness and Ted's hammy version of a great lover. Everyone was having good, clean fun. What no one knew was that, in the confusion of marking the cuts in their separate scripts, the three players had made quite different deletions in this next section of dialogue.

Diana herself was laughing as they all three turned to the next page, which is probably why she got a frog in her throat on the second line. What everyone heard was:

'*Ahah, Tondelayo, she make you come –* '

88

There was a little pause as Diana cleared her throat, then she began the line again but it was too late. The boys in blue and khaki knew a mucky mistake when they heard one and they let out a rugby match roar.

Diana blushed, which only added to their joy, and they didn't hear Max say his next line – 'Okeydokey, and I'll come over all next week too' – so that that little joke, drowned by audience noise, failed to score a laugh. Diana, however, heard the line clearly – after all, Max was standing beside her – so, as the rowdiness subsided, she carried on in a loud voice:

'How long is it since you kissed a woman?'

Max had cut this line out of his script, deleting everything down to the Effects Man opening the door and Ted's first line of the page. As far as Max was concerned, the cut was logical, since he had been expecting to get a laugh with 'Okeydokey, and I'll come over all next week too.' Now the little man was utterly perplexed and so he looked around hopefully for help. As you will have anticipated, this long pause gave ample time for the psyched-up mob to see a dirty meaning in Diana's question.

'How long is *what*?' was the answer they inferred, so once again they howled with the release of uninhibited emotion. Covered by the audience's racket, Ted cued the Effects Man to open the door. But the technician had marked cuts on *his* page incorrectly and took Ted's signal as a cue for the four violent whacks.

The noise woke Max up from his bewildered trance and he immediately began shouting, 'Ow! Ow! Ow! Ow!', in time with the whacking noise as he had done in rehearsal. To the audience, this lunatic behaviour was wonderfully silly. Diana, happily believing that all she had to do to save the situation was to pick up her next line, said,

'Were you being ill?'

Max gave up. 'This is enough to make anybody ill!' he confided to Geraldo, who was doubled up with laughter on his conductor's podium.

In a misguided move, considering how fast we were running

out of time, Ted appealed to the crowd, crying out, 'Let's do this page again from the top, folks – what do you say?'

'Yes! shouted the crowd, but by this time Max Wall was getting his own laughs, plucking the pages out of his script like the leaves of a daisy and tossing them around the stage as he skipped about.

'She loves me, she loves me not . . . ' he chanted.

Ted was still trying to get the sketch back on track.

'Maxie, Maxie!' he called out, as if he were a Yiddisher Mama calling to her naughty child. 'Come on, be a good boy, already. Read the words, already.'

He shared his script with Max, pointing, showing him the words.

Max poked his head backward and forward like some weird tropical bird.

In a strangulated schoolboy voice he pretended to find it difficult to read out loud: 'Hi . . .woz . . . beein' . . . born.'

Ted threw his script in the air and mimed despair. Meanwhile Diana had recognised a cue line. Still laughing along with the audience, musicians and cast, she plunged in with the next line as scripted.

> *'Kiss me, Bwana!'*

Ted couldn't help himself. Without missing a beat, he came back with:

> *'So I kissed her Bwana . . .'*

Over his headphones Geraldo finally got what he'd been expecting, the voice of the producer. The message from the control booth was: 'Play the finale and may God have mercy on our souls.'

The orchestra and singers struck up our closing signature tune and the applause was like thunder. So were the faces of our BBC bosses on Monday morning. Bridgie had allowed the recording to be broadcast without a word of warning to anyone. Halfway through the transmission on Sunday evening the BBC's understaffed switchboards had been jammed with calls from listeners demanding to know what was going on to cause such a furore. Was Miss Dors improperly dressed? Was she stripteasing one garment after each of her lines? The public was much more easily outraged in those stricter times and Sunday was still under the severe surveillance of the Lord's Day Observance Society.

Bridgie was on the carpet first, while Denis and I waited outside the office of Pat Hilliard, Head of Variety, much as we had as schoolboys at Dulwich College, waiting outside the Master's study for a beating. Finally, we were summoned.

'These are my boys,' said Bridgie, 'they've never been in trouble before.'

My God, I thought, it *is* Dulwich College.

No fewer than six senior officials of the Corporation flanked Pat Hilliard, a sandy-haired Irishman who had once been a Broadway producer of musical comedies, despite having little enthusiasm for either comedy or music. He gave us a curt nod and said, 'You can consider yourselves on probation. Most of the hysteria appears to have been caused by the Dors girl so we won't be hearing any more of *her* in this Department. Leslie here says you've been getting the scripts in as late as Friday morning. In future they will be submitted in full on Wednesday at noon for censorship. That's all.'

We traipsed out and walked back to our new office, a converted dairy shop at 52 Upper Montague Street, Marylebone, W1. The prospect of completing our scripts by Wednesday was daunting but that of their perusal by an appointed censor was worse.

As we beavered away to get our next script delivered on time, Denis suddenly stopped and walked over to the wall where he had pinned the page of dialogue which had caused so much trouble. He laughed and said, 'It could have been worse, you know, Bob.'

'Tell me how.'

'Just imagine, if Diana had said, "How long is it since you kissed a woman?" and Max had skipped to the last line and answered, "About five inches!"'

Then we collapsed in hysterics as we considered the interpretations our boisterous audience might have derived from 'I should've been blowing the small end, not sucking the big end.'

On the next Wednesday at noon, our script, cleaner than clean, was in the hands of Frank Hooper, now Bridgie's co-producer and our resident Bowdler. By one o'clock he had put a blue pencil through nearly half of it.

We sat in a spare office at Aeolian Hall on Thursday and Friday, frantically replacing the material Frank had cut and taking the script to his desk, page by page. Then at four o'clock on Friday afternoon, Bridgie's twinkling eyes peeped round the door. He held out his hand and rattled some sheets of paper.

'Fancy some statistics, boysies? Complaints about the show last Sunday: thirty-three by phone, five by post. Listening figure: up by half a million. Reaction from the two General Overseas repeats: our best show yet. Wait till we get the letters in from the troops! Complaints about the cancellation of our Home Service repeat: forty-nine by phone, fifty-five by post. And finally, the Appreciation Index . . .'

This was the all-important measurement of the listeners' enjoyment of each show, taken by national survey. All editions of 'Calling All Forces' that had been broadcast had registered well, with a A.I. of between sixty-eight to seventy-four per cent. Only the BBC's most popular show, 'Take It From Here' did better with an A.I. in the upper seventies. Bridgie paused, closed his eyes with bliss and purred his next words.

'Appreciation Index, eighty-four!'

We whooped louder than the audience had done.

'I've taken Frankieboy off his Mrs Grundy duties for the time being, so the script can return to being funny again. Oh, yes, and I'm booking Dorsie back as our glamour guest the week after next. Everyone out there loved her!'

Diana returned to us again and again, her comedy skills improving with each show. Ours were not. After seventy-nine consecutive weekly hours, comic invention was flagging. A memo came from a senior BBC executive named Con Mahoney: 'Dear Bridgmont, Re. *Calling All Forces* – Your scriptwriters have set themselves extremely low standards which they are failing to live up to. Do something.'

'Change of plan,' announced Bridgie. 'We'll take the show abroad. How do you boysies fancy taking Dorsie to Hamburg?'

The army and RAF had been begging the BBC to bring our show to Germany. Morale was low among the troops stationed at Bielefeld and Lüneburg and it seemed that we were just the tonic they needed. It turned out that they were just the tonic we needed.

Most of the company went by air. Denis and I were given less costly boat and train tickets, although we weren't alone on the voyage. Our most popular comedy guest throughout the series had been Cyril Fletcher and air pressure affected his mastoid ear. Diana was still filming when the plane departed so she was also with us on the following day. The four of us gathered on a Royal Navy wharf on a March evening cold enough to freeze the baubles off a Christmas tree. We were told that the sea was 'very unfriendly' and that no civilian ships would be sailing to The Hague that night. It was explained that our naval vessel was an old ice-breaker and could survive anything the cruel sea might inflict. We smiled and said we'd be all right. I said, 'If it gets too rough, I'll just lash myself to Diana.' No one laughed.

We learned later that it was the roughest crossing since 1880. Throughout the night the ship was lifted twenty feet in the air and then dropped into space. The Captain was sick, an Admiral on board was sick, Cyril was sick, Denis was sick, and I was bringing up meals I'd eaten at school. Only one passenger was not sick. She greeted us at the gangplank, beaming and immaculate in the cold morning sun: 'Can some strong man help me with my luggage and point me at some breakfast?' Diana's luggage consisted of eleven cases, three of which were empty to contain the purchases she planned to make in Hamburg. She wore an A-shaped suede top coat in a shade they called powder blue, trimmed with mink at the collar, wrists and bottom edge, topped off by a matching Hussar hat. Her shoes were dark-blue snake-skin and around her neck was a Chanel scarf, a parting gift from her husband, Denis Hamilton. Knowing Hamilton, he'd probably shoplifted it.

We travelled across Holland and into Germany by train, amazed at the lack of damage to be seen. We'd left a Britain still full of shattered buildings six years after the Nazi surrender but the industrious Germans had lost no time in tidying up the ravages of war. Denis and I used the journey to make up unusable jokes about Germany, a deliberately silly exercise of the kind that comedy writers often use to tone up their funny muscles. At one point we had Diana saying, 'My husband's German – I have to dress up as Poland before he'll invade me.'

We imagined Ted Ray telling the hotel porter, 'My room is cold. Could you throw some more books on the fire?' We arrived in Hamburg, giggling and excited.

11

RADIO FUN

– Act Three –

No sooner back from German victory to home defeat, I am almost trapped into being the life and soul of the party. Jack Buchanan plays the lead, Charlie Chester plays Cupid, and I play l'Après-midi d'un Fornication

We were quartered at Streit's Hotel on the Junfenstieg, where Bridgie installed himself in the suite once regularly occupied by Hitler's deputy, Field-Marshal Herman Goering. Denis and I found a shop that sold cheap medals, bought a dozen, persuaded a chambermaid to let us into Bridgie's bedroom and pinned them to his pyjamas. He didn't say anything to us about them but two days later, when we recorded the first show in the cinema at Bielefeld, he sat in the makeshift control room wearing all of them. The German radio engineers were deeply impressed.

The shopping was a revelation to us all after five years of war and six more of peacetime austerity and rationing. Nothing was unobtainable in Hamburg in 1951. Within the first day Diana had filled her three empty cases with lacy underwear and French designer clothes, and sent out for three more. Ted bought nylons and perfume, both very scarce in Britain, while Carole Carr, our new 'Forces' sweetheart, and Cyril showed their more practical natures and raided the food shops for tinned steak and pork. Leslie Welch, our mild-mannered Memory Man, came into the hotel with his arms full of whisky and brandy in fancy bottles. He disappeared up the stairs, uncorking one of them as he went. 'That'll bugger his memory,' said Diana.

The shows were an extraordinary success. Our scripts were quite inspired and the audiences enthusiastic to the point of mania. For the first time we were able to let the shows overrun and edit them for transmission, cutting out any mistakes, trimming pauses, keeping in only the best parts. This novel luxury was due to the German engineers having abandoned disc recording in favour of tape, something the BBC was yet to consider, reject and then accept reluctantly. Denis said, 'If we'd had this for the Tondelayo sketch, we'd never have been in trouble.'

'And we'd never have got an A.I. of eighty-four,' said Bridgie, who tended to see the sunny side of things.

After each radio show had been taped, the cast put on an impromptu concert for the forces audience that lasted another ninety minutes or so.

Diana's performance in this part of the entertainment was a bigger revelation than the Hamburg shopping. She'd brought two fantastic gowns for the recordings, one a strapless, sleeveless, calf-length number in glittering green and the other a canary yellow organdie creation with puff sleeves and flounces and a skirt that ended above the knee. But in the less formal second half of the evening, she let her hair down, tied an army shirt round her top, leaving her midriff bare, and wore army shorts and tennis shoes. Two nights later at Lüneburg, she did the same thing with RAF issue. The effect was enchanting and so, to everyone's surprise, was her singing.

She and Bridgie had prepared in secret. He sat at the piano and accompanied her first song, 'I Wanna Be Loved By You, Just You, And Nobody Else But You', a 1920s number made famous by the American Helen Kane, 'The Boop-a-Doop Girl', and later by Marilyn Monroe. Diana included the first two 'Oop Boop-a-Doops', then paused to ask nine hundred servicemen, 'What do you think of my two nice Boop-a-Doops?' They let her know exactly what they thought of her two nice Boop-a-Doops.

Geraldo's pianist, bassist and drummer then accompanied her for the Gershwins' 'Embraceable You' and her final medley of sing-along, clap-along songs went over so well, it quite shook Ted Ray, due on next and standing in the wings watching.

'I need a good line to follow this, Bob, think fast.'

I invented a line on the spot, one that subsequently went all round show business to be used by comedians everywhere.

'Say, "Thank you, Diana, you may go to my room and lie down. And if I'm not there in twenty minutes, start without me."'

(Only two years later I offered the same gag to Bob Hope. 'But I know that line,' he said, as if I were trying to sell him a stolen watch, 'Jerry Desmonde uses it every night after Gloria De Haven's act.')

Meanwhile I had learned a valuable lesson – that I thought up my very best lines when I was under pressure. The lesson was to pay off sooner than I knew.

As Diana came offstage to a wild ovation, my eyes must have been shining with admiration for her. I said, 'You were fantastic!'

She just kissed me a thank-you and went. And I thought, 'If she weren't married and I weren't married, I think I might have proposed just then.'

Our attempts to make a second smash series out of 'Calling All Forces' led to only a moderate success with 'The Forces Show' starring Richard Murdoch, Kenneth Horne and Sam Costa. We got one series of twenty-six hours out of that. Another version hosted by Cheerful Charlie Chester and Tony Hancock defeated us. We could write funny stuff for Charlie but Tony hated everything we gave him.

'This,' he shouted during the read-through on the stage of the Garrick Theatre, 'is shit! And it's written on shit paper so I'll take it away and have a shit and wipe my arse with it!' And he actually did just that; please don't ask me how I know.

Denis and I surrendered the script-writing job to two new kids on the block, Ray Galton and Alan Simpson. The show still didn't work very well but the team of Tony, Ray and Alan did. The rest is the Hancock Story and enough people have written that.

Meanwhile, my fondness for Diana had not abated. One November night in 1952 I attended one of her famous parties for the first time. My wife was away visiting her family in Northern Ireland so I was alone. As it turned out, I didn't have to remain alone if I didn't want to. Hamilton had provided a number of obliging girls for single gentlemen to enjoy. One pretty youngster in particular seemed to like me very much and, as we ate the buffet and tried to drink the wine cellar dry, Hamilton murmured in my ear. 'You can take Anita to bed in about an hour.'

The lights were kept dim for the continuous showing of blue

movies on a big screen. I knew when Diana was somewhere in the room only by the occasional glimpse of her bouncing blonde tresses and her wonderfully dirty laugh. Keeping a watch on events as best I could, I gradually became aware of a pattern of behaviour.

An amorous couple would get the nod from Hamilton and follow him out of the room. He'd come back alone and then leave again with Diana. After fifteen minutes they'd both return for more food and drink, then the same routine was repeated. But the amorous couples weren't rejoining the big party with its nonstop porno movie show. Why not? Where were they going? How could they bear to miss the flickering festival of naked men in false moustaches and black socks bouncing up and down on matrons with tattoos?

Sure enough, my turn came. I was on one of the many couches with Anita, giving her an Ear, Nose and Throat examination with my tongue, when Hamilton softly called my name, winked and signalled for us both to follow him. We walked through a hall full of enormous houseplants, along a corridor decorated with nude drawings and 'art photos', and up to a dark panelled door. Hamilton opened it and made a grand gesture towards a very large legless bed, lying flat on the floor in the centre of the room. It was draped about in scarlet and purple silks in the style of the Arabian Nights and half-a-dozen small spotlights glowed down from the dark walls to illuminate it. Add the smell of camel dung and you'd have had a knocking shop in Marrakesh.

As I moved forward with the girl, something flashed and I looked up. I caught a reflection from the ceiling. Fixed to it and almost covering it was a mirror. 'I'll lock the door so that no one can interupt you,' murmured Hamilton. 'You've got about a quarter of an hour so make the most of it.'

He closed the door, turned the key and as I was wondering why I couldn't have locked it myself on my side, Anita was already half naked.

'Hurry up, he said we've only got fifteen minutes!'

I was slightly drunk and she was quite beautiful, with a dancer's body; lithe legs, flat stomach, breasts like the tops of minarets. I stripped off my clothes, knelt on the bed in only my underpants and groped around.

'Bob! Come on! What are you looking for?'

'The top bedsheet, I can't find the top bedsheet.'

From far away, I heard someone at the party give a stifled squeal of laughter.

Anita laughed too and, admiring her reflection in the ceiling, cried, 'Don't be so silly, darling, there are no sheets or blankets on *this* bed. Come *on*!'

She reached out and yanked. My underwear stayed with her, but now I was busy searching the wall by the door.

'What the hell are you doing now?'

'Looking for the switch, I want to turn some of these lights off.'

Another stifled squeal came from the distance. This time it seemed to come from somewhere above us. Had the party spread to the upper rooms? Was that where the disappearing couples had gone?

'Bob, you come to me at once, d'you hear? That's an order!' It occurred to me that Anita was showing off to the mirror, performing for an unseen audience.

The penny, by this time suspended long enough to rust, dropped.

'Sweet Jesus! They're watching us! You creepy bastard, Hamilton!' I was simultaneously yelling at the ceiling and pulling my underpants on. Anita snatched them down again and grabbed at the only part of me which appeared keen to do business.

'Don't be so bloody daft, Bob! You've got to let me take care of that!'

Now I was on my back on the bed, pushing Anita off me and trying to drag my trousers over my feet.

'Forget it, it's over, I'm no bloody peepshow, get off! *Hamilton! Open that bleeding door!*'

Anita fell back, angry and defeated. 'He's a homo!' she offered the ceiling.

I didn't think that was at all logical so I ignored it. I finished dressing, shouting out my fury all the while, and as I tied my second shoelace, the key turned in the lock and Diana opened the door.

'What a waste,' she said, tilting her head in sorrow, 'what a wicked, wicked, waste. Still . . .' she brightened, 'the night's still young and Hamilton's got a cracker lined up next. Come on, you squeamish boy you, come upstairs and join us.'

We left a sulky Anita pulling on her clothes and I followed

Diana in silence while she chattered merrily. 'Some people absolutely adore putting on a show, they come back to my parties just to do that. Paul said you might guess or that you might've even heard about our one-way mirror but he thought you'd go through with it if we got you someone as lovely as Anita.'

Paul was Paul Carpenter, the Canadian B-movie star and compère of the Ted Heath Band Shows. Along with Bonar Colleano, Harry Fowler, Michael Balfour, 'Dandy Kim' Waterford and others, Paul moved in hell-raising circles, circles which frequently revolved around Diana.

We reached the large upper room above the lurid bedchamber. It was filled with whispering, laughing couples, mostly in varying stages of undress. The lighting was dim and most of the illumination came from below, shining up through the grey-tinted glass of the Alba mirror set in the floor.

'Here's our reluctant Romeo,' announced Diana, and there was a low sound of hissing and booing. Someone called out, 'Shrinking violet!'

'I didn't see anything shrinking,' laughed Diana. Then, seeing my unsmiling face, she gave me a squeeze and pointed to some unoccupied cushions fringing the glass on the floor. 'Lie there, you'll have a great view of everything that happens.' She turned and left.

The bedroom beneath went dark and there were sighs and sniggers of anticipation all around me in the gloom as the couples gathered around the rim of the mirror, like nocturnal creatures come to drink at a black pool.

Suddenly the lights below shone brightly again and, judging from the approving sounds coming from the voyeurs, the woman on view was a well-known favourite with them. She was spreadeagled alone on the bed and, as she began to undress, from somewhere came the music of Mantovani. The tune was 'I Could Write a Book'. I thought, 'Some day I will and this has got to be part of it.'

'She's Carla,' said a familiar female voice in my ear. 'She's incredible.'

I turned to see who had spoken and recognised a graduate of the J. Arthur Rank Charm School who had appeared on 'Calling All Forces'.

'What's incredible about her, Sandra?'

She mentioned a free-thinking journalist on a national newspaper.

'He's brought his boxer dog. Carla can make the dog keep it up for ages. I don't now how she can take it, I couldn't.'

Neither could I.

No one tried to stop me leaving although I was ready to plead my need for a loo. I found one but it was engaged. Judging from the gasps coming from the couple inside, they were equally engaged. I thought, 'Well, there are at least two people here besides me who prefer privacy.'

I left the house by the back door and ended up wandering round Marble Arch, looking for a taxi at three o'clock in the morning. It wasn't a particularly cold morning for November but I found myself shivering.

★ ★ ★ ★ ★

Ten months later I was shivering again and once more the cause was Diana, but this time it was a shiver of desire. We had been brought together again on the stage at the Scala Theatre, Charlotte Street, rehearsing a show that included quizmaster Michael Miles with 'I Want To Be a Conductor', Humphrey Lyttleton, Max Jaffa, comedy guest Ted Ray, the Hedley Ward Trio and, as the host, the most debonair entertainer ever to park his top hat on top of one of our scripts.

Jack Buchanan had become an international star in the 1920s; dashing, long-legged, the paradigm of elegant song-and-dance for Charlot and Cochran. His latest triumph was in the cinemas, *The Band Wagon*, in which he co-starred with Fred Astaire.

Denis and I had been called in to attend a creative conference at the BBC by Bill Worsley, the producer who'd booked me for my first broadcast as comedy compère of 'Works Wonders'. He told us that he'd had instructions from Pat Hilliard to come up with a big series of shows for Sunday evenings 'that would bring listeners back from their TV sets to their wireless sets'. Acting as radio's friendly broker, the songwriter and sometime BBC executive, Eric Maschwitz, had approached Buchanan to head the cast. Only weeks before, Jack had been the star guest in an extravagant radio production in the USA called 'The Big Show' with Tallulah Bankhead, where he'd been fêted and loved. He was in the mood to accept.

Bill had received a strict briefing from the star. 'He wants two leading ladies, a sweet English rose who can sing and a translatlantic glamour star, what Jack described as a sexy bombshell sort of piece who can handle wisecracks.'

Guess who sprang to mind for the sexy bombshell sort of piece.

From our very first transmission we knew we had a winner. Jack's gift for expressing charm and self-mockery came across on radio just as well as on stage and film. He was in his sixties, yet so youthful in manner and appearance that his comedy flirtations with Diana were perfectly acceptable. Lizbeth Webb, star of *Guys and Dolls* on the London stage, sang mighty like a rose and was grateful to leave the comedy to Diana. Comedy guest stars were to include all our usual favourites, strong comedians for whom we knew we could write funny routines – Ted, Max Wall, Murdoch and Horne, Cyril Fletcher, Askey, Benny Hill, Max Bygraves, Dickie Henderson, Irene Handl, Pat Coombs, even Hancock, who had relented enough to let us write for him once more. It turned out very satisfactorily now that we were able to imitate the style that had been created for him by Galton and Simpson.

Jack's international standing attracted American stars to our show and my partner and I were thrilled to be writing the words for our personal pantheon of comedy gods like Bob Hope, Bing Crosby, Jack Benny, and Phil Silvers.

The series had only been running a couple of weeks when Cheerful Charlie Chester was booked to appear on show number five, 11 October. He decided to pop into the Scala Theatre on the two previous Sundays to watch the recordings and get the feel of the show. 'Never worked with Jack before, man's a legend, just want to see what's going on.' What he saw going on was a romance rapidly coming to the boil.

Diana and I had met again at the rehearsal on 13 September and began by concealing our mounting hunger, if you'll overlook the expression, with jokes and horseplay. By week two, we were kidding the cast and ouselves by pretending to be in the throes of a bogus passion. Behind the juvenile posturing and laughter was a slowly increasing seriousness that no one else seemed to notice.

But when week three came along, so did Charlie and, not having endured two Sundays of our coy theatrics to lull his suspicions, he knew at once.

'She's in love with you, you berk,' he whispered. Dear Charlie always spoke and still speaks in a furtive, high-speed manner as if planning a jail break.

'You're wasting your time, playing the fool. Listen to Charlie, you wanna get in there, my son, best chance you'll ever have.'

'Best chance?'

'Today fortnight, the week I'm on, read-through's been called for ten in the morning, music at eleven, finish by twelve, not wanted back till five! Love in the afternoon! Who's a lucky boy then?'

Charlie was right. Due to a clash in the booking of the Scala Theatre, our usual afternoon rehearsal was to be moved forward on the day of our fifth show to make way for a charity matinée. My throat went dry at the mere idea of what he was suggesting. But I decided to approach Diana and make a joke with a subtext, just to see how she'd react.

That evening's show completed, I followed Diana to the dressing room she shared with Lizbeth and waited nervously in the corridor. Musicians and technicians passed, calling their goodnights. Moments later she came out with her coat and handbag. I'd worked out what I was going to say; I'd tell her about the unexpected free afternoon and pretend it was going to be our big chance to run away together and hide in Battersea Funfair.

We walked down the stone steps to the stage door, me talking as we descended. Only the first part of my little speech had been spoken, the plain facts about the early rehearsal ending at noon and the five-hour wait before we'd be needed again. At that point, almost at the stage door, Diana stopped and turned sharply. She was staring at me, face blank, eyes wide, lips parted.

She said, 'Oh, my God!' so huskily it startled me.

The shadow on the wire-meshed glass panel of the stage door pushed it open. Denis Hamilton had come to collect his wife.

Hamilton was a frightening man, known to the police, three times arrested in association with crimes of violence but never convicted. He wasn't one's best choice of enemy. He stood in the doorway and looked at us.

Diana, still facing me, flashed a fierce signal of warning with her eyes, recomposed her expression and turned to her husband.

'About time, Hamilton, I was having to pass time with the staff.'

Hamilton gave me an unfriendly nod and they were gone.

Came the next Sunday and with it, naughty Charlie.

'Petty crook, Hamilton, all bluff and no balls, you can't put your hands up because of that git. Makes it more exciting anyway, double-crossing the seedy little sod. Look, Roberto, how many millions of men would give their right bollock to be in your position? The most gorgeous gal in Britain, crazy about you! And you're going to pass it up? Impossible!'

Throughout the rehearsals, the tea breaks and the recording, Diana avoided me. She stuck close to other cast members, making it impossible for me to reopen the subject that was becoming an obsession with me, fired by my mischievous friend, Charlie. She even brought her coat and handbag to the wings so that there was no need for her to go up to her dressing room after the show, thus preventing a repetition of my manoeuvre of the previous Sunday.

After the recording, I stood talking to one of the stagehands when Diana suddenly appeared beside us. 'Excuse me, Bob. Gerry, do you know of a good hotel in New York? No? Oh, it's just that my husband has to go over there next Thursday for about eight days and . . . oh, never mind. Goodnight!'

Gerry looked at me. 'Why didn't she ask you?'

'She probably knows I've never been to New York.' My pulse was trying to imitate Buddy Rich.

'And she thinks I *have*?' Gerry was just seventeen.

I was unable to think about anything else that week. The extraordinary coincidence of Hamilton's absence from London the following weekend seemed heaven-sent. And Diana had delivered the news, perhaps on the spur of the moment after a day of evasion, but clearly intended as a message. Had she even arranged his departure? No, come off it, Bob, you're flattering yourself too much. Should I phone her? Not until her husband had left for New York. On Thursday Denis Goodwin looked across our two desks which faced each other in the inner sanctum of our office and said, 'Are you a writer on this show or the retired owner of a Jewish slave?'

On Friday I seized upon a few minutes on my own to phone Diana but her housekeeper said she was filming somewhere on location.

The American comedian Jack Durant had spoken highly of the privacy and discretion at a block of furnished apartments off Oxford Street called Stratford Court where he'd romanced another highly recognisable blonde star, Frances Day. So I booked one of their flats over the phone, using my partner's name. In those early years of our collaboration people never knew which of us was Denis and which Bob. And Denis was single.

On Saturday I drove to my intended love nest, registered under my assumed identity, paid fifteen guineas for a weekend stay – that would be fifteen pounds 75p today – went up to the luxurious little flat and tried phoning Diana again but this time no one answered.

Standing at the window I saw that there was a pavement flower stall nearby, so I bought a lot of pink carnations from what used to be called a spiv or a wide boy. He overcharged me, winked and said, 'Was she worth it?' I winked back conspiratorially, man to man, but I couldn't think of a reply.

Back in the flat I put the flowers around the place, ran out of vases and improvised with pots and pans from the tiny kitchen. Then I lay on the bed and thought about the following day, trying to imagine what it was going to be like. By this time I was almost idiotic with apprehension. Here I was, 'one of radio's youngest masters of mirth', so mentally paralysed by adulterous craving, deception, risk and excitement that I couldn't answer a barrowboy's crack.

The rehearsal on Sunday morning had me drawing in great gulps of air to calm my nerves as our script was read aloud by Jack and the cast, seated at random around the stage. Diana had never looked more desirable. She wore a soft beige suit by Yves St Laurent, a high-collared chocolate-coloured blouse, a little plain gold jewellery and an air of womanly composure that had me in awe.

Charlie Chester winked at me so often it could have been taken for St Vitus Dance.

The musicians arrived and Geraldo took each musical item in turn. It seemed to me he'd never been slower.

As I waited for the final song medley to be rehearsed – one that included a chorus sung by Diana – I reviewed my strategy: let's see now, my Austin Hereford is parked in St Martin's Lane. I'll offer Diana a lift home, she'll cancel any request she may have made for a taxi, we'll walk round to my car, I'll drive to Stratford Court, give her the key to the flat, she'll go up alone while I park the car in a small side street where it will be unlikely to be identified, then I'll make my way to the East Side of Heaven Where An Angel Waits For Me. Jack Buchanan's song in the medley was invading my plans, but it almost fitted.

'Want to come back with me for the afternoon?' Denis Goodwin's voice fetched me up with a start. He'd bought a flat in Cleveland Square from Anthony Newley's first wife, the actress Ann Lynn.

'Ah, thanks but no, I'm going to the pictures.'

'I'll come with you. What are you going to see?'

'*Monsieur Hulot's Holiday*.'

'Oh, never mind then, I've already seen it.'

I knew Denis had seen it, that's why I'd chosen it. Bill Worsley was raising his voice, 'That's it then, thank you, everybody! See you back here at five!'

Charlie gave me stealthy thumbs up and then hugged himself and made little kisses to the air. Dear Charlie, I loved him, he'd played midwife to my unborn dream. Trying to look casual I sauntered over to Diana. 'Can I give you a lift?'

'No thanks, Bob, I've got a chauffered car to take me home.'

My heart sank but my nerves calmed. So the whole thing was off then.

'Why not leave your car where it is and come and spend the afternoon with me?'

So it wasn't off. Denis Goodwin was listening.

'I was going to the cinema, *Monsieur Hulot's Holiday*, Jacques Tati.'

'Wonderful, that's at Studio One, Oxford Street, I'll drop you off.'

Diana and I walked out of the stage door, past the spot where

Hamilton had loomed only two weeks before, and ran through the rain to where a uniformed driver was holding open the door of a white Rolls-Royce. In the back of the limousine was a row of crystal tumblers and matching decanters with ceramic labels describing their contents in an unfamiliar language.

'Where to, Miss Dors?' said the driver. His accent was foreign.

Diana turned her enquiring gaze to me.

Softly I asked, 'Do I tell him where?'

'Well, dear, if you don't we'll never get there.'

'Can you trust this bloke?'

'No idea, I've never met him before. Relax, darling, I'm not paying for this. I told my friend what we were up to and she lent me her car and her driver for the day. She'll be taking them both back to Italy tomorrow.'

Her friend turned out to be Valentina Cortese, the beautiful Italian actress who had been one of the stars of the 1951 film *The Secret People* in which I had played a small role as a barber.

We arrived at Stratford Court as discreetly as a brass band.

We got to the door of the flat. Diana said, 'What time is it? Exactly?'

'Twelve twenty.'

'Race you!'

We were both undressed and in bed by twelve twenty two, a dead heat.

I've been very fortunate throughout my life with sexual liaisons, at least as regards my physical ability to do my part. Only twice have I failed to rise to the occasion. The second time was in a Norfolk nightclub called the Sunset Strip, but that deflation was due to what was to me a unique experience described elsewhere in this book.

The first time my manhood remained in its childhood was in Apartment Eleven at the Stratford Court on that Sunday afternoon with the woman whose body I most coveted.

At first I concealed my shameful condition through foreplay, caressing and kissing everything and anything on Diana that presented itself. While she seemed overwhelmed by my ardour, it was animated as much by panic as by passion. The waiting for a response from the most needed part of my anatomy seemed endless. Never having had this problem before, I was becoming more and more desperate. And, of course, the more desperate I was, the less likely it became that anything would develop.

Miraculously, and due largely to the enthusiasm of my love-making with everything I had except for the one essential asset, Diana continued to be unaware of the major absentee. Indeed, she appeared to be tossed adrift on the high seas of ecstasy. She trembled, she shook, she made a tremendous amount of noise. But, even as I laboured to postpone the inevitable discovery of my shame, I knew that the situation couldn't last. There was no way I could entertain her in bed for four hours without bringing on my star turn.

Suddenly the amazing sounds emanating from her lovely throat reached a peak, ceased and subsided. She shook herself and then surfaced very slowly as if coming out of a pleasurable seizure. Her blue misty gaze focused on me through blonde disarray. She blew out her cheeks with a big puff of relief, snuggled and blinked like a cat.

'My God, I was so nervous all week! I nearly ducked out of this on Friday when you phoned. I put on my housekeeper voice and you didn't recognise me.'

'I didn't realise . . .'

'No, that was me. I told you a lie about me being on location.'

That wasn't what I'd meant. I was going to say I didn't realise that she had been as terrified as I had. This information immediately began to have a palpable effect on me.

'I believe I had too long to think about how much I wanted you and how this would be. You always seem so unavailable, Bob, so near and yet so far. That affair at my party, I was so afraid you'd never speak to me again. Then all those jokes, you kept me at bay with them. I couldn't credit it when you came up with this idea. I absolutely flipped, didn't I?'

'When you saw Hamilton at the stage door, you mean?'

'No, when you said we'd have a five-hour wait. *Five hours!* The men I've known have all been in such a goddam hurry.'

This completed the repair of the temporary breakdown of communication between my mental demands and my corporeal reaction. Like the other men she'd known, I too was now in a goddam hurry. But I now knew more about the lady's tastes. I silently told my loins, 'You made me wait, now it's your turn.'

The tense expectancy which I now knew we had shared, the

same anxious anticipation which had so alarmingly robbed me of my potency, all of it now was transformed into the most ardent emotion. I felt myself suffused by waves of sentiment, adoring Diana, sustaining my capability as a lover with this heightened affection. We were both young, strong and healthy, and we spent that happy afternoon forty years ago exploiting the fact.

The white Rolls-Royce was patiently waiting for us, but even so we were late in travelling back to the Garrick. On the short return drive we talked with contented exhaustion. Then, as the car turned into Charing Cross Road, I asked, 'When can we do this again?'

'I don't think we dare, darling. If Hamilton found out . . .'

'What's the worst that could happen?'

'He'd kill you. First he'd kill you, then he'd kill me. He's got two handguns he plays with all the time, a Browning and a Mauser . . .' – she pronounced it Mouser – ' . . . and he told me he did kill somone once, someone who cheated him. I believe him, Bob.'

'I wish he'd never come back from New York.'

'He never went.'

'What?'

'He never was going to go to New York. I made that up. I figured you were so scared of him, you'd never go to bed with me while he was around. So I sort of put him out of your mind, a few thousand miles away.'

'Then where the hell is he really?'

Diana smiled brightly. 'He's at home in bed with the flu.'

Now I had influenza bugs to thank for my rapture. But something had alerted Hamilton's suspicion, however faintly. Each successive Sunday in that series he brought Diana to the theatre; either he sat quietly at the rear of the stalls or he walked around the area, attended the recording and took her home immediately afterwards. All I could get from Diana was an occasional wistful smile and a look I liked to believe was one of yearning.

How Hamilton actually found out about my wanton rendezvous with his wife I still don't know and, after so long, I'm certain I never will. What is certain is that his discovery of our secret prompted one of the very few acts of violence I've ever perpetrated, albeit in self defence.

12

RADIO FUN

– Act Four –

*Another party, another escape, waiting under the Sword
of Damocles and so towards closing Dors*

On a warm summer evening in 1956 my wife and I dressed for a
party at the home of the greatest of all harmonica players, Larry
Adler. That isn't just my opinion, it's his. Larry's idea of being
unfaithful is turning away from a mirror. Once at a party given by
the brilliantly funny Canadian singer Libby Morris and her actor
husband Murray Cash, I told a Jewish joke. After everyone had
laughed except Larry, he snapped his fingers for general
attention and spoke reprovingly.

'Bob, you must read my book, *How to tell a Jewish Joke.*'

I replied, 'Larry, you must read *my* book, *How to Shove a
Harmonica up Your Arse.*'

Anyhow, that's what Libby insists I said. I believe it was Libby
who said it; I couldn't possibly be that rude, even to Larry.

When my wife and I arrived at Larry's front gate, moved
through his small front garden and mounted the steps leading up
to the open front door, the rattling chorus of laughter from inside
the house told us that the party had started. She walked straight
through the darkened lobby and on into the brightly lit hall,
exchanging greetings with friends. I stopped in the lobby.

I didn't want to stop in the lobby. Denis Hamilton had been
waiting for me in the shadows of the porch and, as my wife had
walked past him, he had stepped forward behind her, put his
open hand on my chest and brought me to a halt.

'A private word.'

He jerked his head towards the front garden and, gripping my
lapels, propelled me backwards down the steps and into the

111

shrubbery. I was too surprised to speak. Hamilton was growling and tossing his head as if in an effort to suppress violent emotion. We stood facing each other long enough for him to gain self-control and for me to start losing mine.

'No one, *no one*, fucks about with me and lives to laugh about it.'

'What are you talking about? What's wrong? I haven't – ah – I mean, my God, if someone's told you. . . .'

'Someone's told me all right, you shit, oh yes, someone's told me!' He glanced quickly around and so did I. Not a soul in sight. Just louder laughter from inside the house and car hissing past on the far side of the road. He changed hands, still gripping my jacket and fumbling in the pocket of his own.

When he brought his hand out it was holding a barber's razor, the old cut-throat kind. He then said a sentence I could never forget:

'I'm going to slit your eyeballs.'

He steadied himself with his legs apart and, as he raised his right elbow and tilted the blade towards my face, I brought my knee up into his crotch with all the strength I possessed, lifting him off the ground. All the breath came out of him in a single bellow and he fell sideways into the shrubby shadows.

Moving very rapidly, I ran up the steps into the crowded party where the chattering guests were oblivious to the confrontation that had just taken place only a few yards away. My one priority was to get myself and my wife away from the scene, away from Hamilton, away from his accusations and his revenge. Never one to tell the truth where a lie would serve, I told her our babysitter had phoned with an urgent message: 'We've got burglars!'

I hurried her to the front gate. Hamilton was on his knees in the shrubbery, throwing up.

'Bob, who's that? Is he ill?'

'No, just some drunk.'

When we got home I blamed the babysitter's phonecall about nonexistent burglars on a hoaxer and rang Larry to apologise for our hasty exit.

'That's OK, Bobby boy – why don't you come on back? Someone's been asking for you.'

I could imagine who. I made an excuse about my having to drive our babysitter home, then went upstairs to the bathroom to examine my right knee. It was beginning to hurt me severely and an angry bruise was forming. If I'd done that to my knee, what had I done to Hamilton's testicles?

From that night on, I lived in fear of Hamilton's vengeance. If he had been prepared to blind me and suffer the consequences just because I had made merry with his missus, it followed that his retaliation to being kneed in the balls as well would be even worse.

In the following spring I had a phonecall from the boxing promoter, Jack Solomons. I'd done a few charity appearances for Jack and he regarded me fondly.

'Just to mark your card, my son, strictly *unter em tisch*, some bugger's out to do you a mischief. You know I've got one or two naughty lads fighting for me, not above upsetting the law, you follow. Well, one of 'em's been offered a pony to duff you up, hospital job, and he might've taken the job too, but for this customer saying he'd cough up a monkey to see you finished. Yeah. A beating's one thing but snuffing's another, so the lad came to me, and I've come to you. Are you still there, my son?'

This information made me paranoid. I began to take all the textbook precautions of varying my timetable, arriving at engagements and leaving them in the company of friends, even checking underneath my car to detect any interference, all the time feeling embarrassed at playing the marked man in a bad gangster movie. Autumn came and so did another warning phonecall, this time from the boxer Freddie Mills, a friend of mine since he'd appeared on 'The Forces Show' as our sporting guest star.

'I saw Hamilton at the Astor, pissed as a fart but bloody dangerous. He's round the twist and that, I know, a nutter – but he's got it in for you, I mean really got it in, no error. So watch your back, all right?'

I knew I'd been a promiscuous fool but this retribution seemed excessive.

Every day I lived with the possibility of Hamilton or his hired muscle waiting for me in each carpark, each alley, each doorway, perhaps even my own. I considered approaching him directly with an apology, sending him a solicitor's letter threatening action, reporting him to the police – all ideas that withered in their own absurdity. The seasons passed without bringing relief from suspense. Occasional rumours reached me that my nemesis was showing signs of mental instability. Some surprise that was.

I knew adultery was wrong and I tried to regret it. Well, I did regret it but only because of my cowardice, my dread of a vicious husband's mad vendetta. But then I did something that was even more sinful. I rejoiced at the death of a fellow man.

It was a Sunday morning in January 1959. I was in bed reading the *Sunday Despatch*. A small headline read 'MISTER DIANA DORS DIES', with a short report beneath of Hamilton's death from heart failure. This was a more discreet age for newspaper reporting and it later transpired that Denis Hamilton had actually died from tertiary syphilis, two words that a respectable family newspaper preferred not to print.

'Why are you smiling?' asked my wife.

'It's better than crying,' I said.

I might well have cried with relief but, looking back across the years, I think I should have cried with shame. God forgive me, I swear I felt like Atlas, the world lifted from him; Jean Valjean, set free of Javert.

It was a mean victory but it was the only one I had, so I was grateful. I've often been grateful for things I haven't deserved.

And I can't pretend to you that I look back in guilt. I don't look back with much pride either. Just a sense of discomfort because I think I should feel some guilt. Is that the voice of conscience clearing its throat?

Over the subsequent years of my friendship with Diana I did manage to ask her more than once how she thought her first husband had learned the truth about our clandestine rendezvous, but she was awfully good at changing the subject.

I lost touch with her during her marriage to the impressionist Dickie Dawson, father of her first two sons and, as Richard Dawson, a very successful game show host in the USA. I found him as lovable as a piranha in a bidet.

Occasionally we met and worked together again while Di was having a close relationship with the muscular Tommy Yeardye, proprietor of The Paint Box in Queensway, which got around the law forbidding nude floorshows by having naked models sit around the joint, posing for the customers to paint their portraits.

Maybe I turned up there once or twice, just to check on the artwork.

Then Di met and married the love of her life, a violent but gifted gypsy actor named Alan Lake. Their devotion to one another was profound, and after she had died in his arms, Alan's huge grief blinded him to the needs of their young son Jason and he shot himself to death.

Di and Alan often came to dinner parties arranged by Jackie throughout the 1970s. Jac loved spotting her occasional conspiratorial wink at me. One evening Di asked her, 'Do you know I was crazy about your old man years ago?'

'He says he felt the same about you.'

Di gave her an affectionate little hug and said, 'He was the best.'

Later that night, the last guest gone, Jac said, 'Di seems to remember you as a Great Lover. You've always said you didn't think you'd acquitted yourself very well.'

'There you are then. Women do have better memories.'

13

TV TIMES

First – Fast and Loose

In which a series is modestly titled, real ineptitude is covered up with false unconsciousness for which there can be no faint praise, a wee clown is punctured and shows what he's made of, and an athletic trick fails to make the big break

'I want six forty-five minute comedy programmes starring you and we'll call them "The Bob Monkhouse Show",' said Ronnie Waldman, Head of BBC TV Variety, and beamed expectantly. I replied, 'How wonderful! Thank you! But please could we call it something else?'

It seems an unlikely exchange, I know, but this was December 1953, and I didn't think I'd earned the right to enjoy the American habit of naming every radio and TV show after its star. I'd only popped up on the small screen a couple of dozen times, guest spots on such shows as Geraldo's Band Show, 'Rooftop Rendezvous', 'Variety Parade', Vic Oliver's 'This Is Show Business', 'Garrison Theatre' and the popular 'Café Continental', although the impact of these appearances was much greater in those days because there was so little comedy on television. In fact, there was so little television altogether, just a few hours a day with a shutdown just after ten o'clock each evening. I'd had some favourable press but even so I couldn't expect Denis Goodwin to enthuse over the title Waldman was suggesting. We settled for calling it 'Fast and Loose' and planned it as a sketch show with musical breaks to cover the shifting of scenery.

As our producer we were threatened with Richard Afton, an arrogant Irish disciplinarian whose bed had four wrong sides to get out of. At the BBC's Lime Grove Studios, you could count his friends on the fingers of Captain Hook's bad hand. Luckily, a booking on one of his shows the previous year had already alerted me to his short temper. At our very first meeting, we managed to irritate him just enough to make him blow up and tell Waldman he couldn't work with us. In his place came mild Ken Carter, the man who would also guide Benny Hill's early TV career to success, a gentle and dependable man; 'just the sort,' said Denis, 'that you can turn on in a crisis.'

We worked almost nonstop on the script of the first show, scheduled for its live transmission on the second Tuesday in May. Other obligations for radio scripts and performances ate into our time and as the starting date approached we began to panic, realising that Denis's wry line about a crisis was rapidly coming true. We'd never keep up the high standard we were setting in show number one without landing in the number two. Denis came up with a desperate idea.

'As you step through the curtains to say goodnight, the audience will be applauding and the credits rolling over you. You start to wave, you stumble, your eyes flutter, your legs give way, you fall down in a dead faint and stay that way for about five minutes. You'll make all the papers and we'll get some sympathy and breathing space.'

'At last! My chance as a dramatic actor!'

The plan depended on perfect timing. If the show overran, we'd be faded out before I could throw my wobbly. As it turned out, the God of Comedy was smiling on us. The day of the show was the hottest May weather ever, lending extra conviction to my curtain call collapse. The show was a high-speed smash, every gag worked, my farewell wave and crumple to the stage happening exactly before our final credit. Startled viewers saw an equally startled Sylvia Peters, one of the regular on-screen announcers at that time.

'Gracious!' she was reported to have said. 'Did you see that?'

The press reviews were unanimously enthusiastic (my last good ones for a very long time) and the publicity even better than Denis had predicted. Waldman brought forward a Fred Emney show to replace us while I 'recovered my strength', prepared future material and reflected upon the fact that no aspect of my career so far had been untouched by flimflam, even fraud. The devil of it was, no one ever guessed the truth about my fake prostration and I couldn't boast about my acting.

Charlie Drake still bears the scars of 'Fast and Loose' to this day. On one show, I blew half of Charlie's left ear off. It was during our send-up of a wartime spy thriller with Irene Handl as the beautiful Nazi spy, equipped with feed lines for excruciating jokes –

> *'Meine name ist Gerda.'*
> *'It suits you, you're built like one.'*

– and Charlie had to hide in one of her six connecting bedroom cupboards. The frantic plotline called for me to fire my revolver into each cupboard in turn while Charlie played Russian roulette, scurrying from one cupboard to the next, trying to avoid the bullets. On the sixth shot the wadding blew out of the gun's cylinder and blasted a hole in the flimsy door. When Charlie came out, he kept his right side to the audience. The left side of his face was peppered black and wetly red and his eyes were wide with shock.

We were under two minutes from the end of the sketch. Heaven knows how courageous little Charlie kept going but he did, getting every one of his laughs and all in profile. I was cold with horror as I watched his left side becoming bloodier with each second. We finally got to the last punchline and the BBC's Hammersmith Theatre's curtains closed to conceal Charlie's genuine collapse much as they had failed to hide my phony faint. I walked out on to the apron of the stage to announce a song from the Tanner Sisters and then rushed back to the wings where a St John's Ambulance volunteer was mopping up the gore and a doctor was preparing to stitch Charlie's ear up. Believe it or not, fifteen minutes later Charlie came on for the finale and did the walkdown wearing a hat at a rakish angle to cover his wound.

When I told this story to Eamonn Andrews years later on Charlie's 'This Is Your Life', Charlie fingered his left ear wonderingly. Afterwards he said to me, 'Do you know something? I thought that was a dream, me getting shot on your show. I often dream about it but I didn't think it ever really happened. I must've blocked it out of my mind.'

Live TV was always an accident zone but it was great fun for the audience when things went wrong. One of the biggest roars I ever heard came as the result of a glass door that wouldn't break.

In each edition of 'Fast and Loose', I appeared in a slapstick sketch as Osbert the Suitor. He was always trying to ask for the hand in marriage of his beloved, played by Sheila Sweet or June Whitfield. Her mother was Irene Handl and the Victorian father was the stern and massive Alexander Gauge, later famous as Friar Tuck in the ITV series that starred Richard Greene as Robin Hood. Osbert's efforts to please his intended in-laws were always doomed to failure due to his destructive clumsiness – all these sketches ended in my leaving a stage full of wrecked furniture, busted vases, ripped clothing, total mayhem, while Gauge's towering rage would give way to an unexpected punchline: 'I *like* that boy!'

One week Osbert was on trial as a junior clerk, working in Gauge's family business. At the very start, a glazier was completing the installation of a new glass door to the boss's office. 'Magnificent!' boomed Gauge to his daughter. 'Apart from you and your dear mama, this new glass door is my greatest pride and joy.' So the audience knew what to expect.

Throughout the sketch, in which my clumsiness steadily destroyed everything in the office, Gauge controlled his fury to sing the praises of his new glass door. It all ended in a complicated acrobatic trick from me: dismissed, I snatch my coat from the upright Victorian hat-stand, fall back holding the stand tight against my body, keep rolling over in a backward somersault with the heavy base of the hat-stand held between my feet, then kick it free so that it lands smack in the centre of the glass door and shatters it. It's an even harder trick than it sounds. It's necessary to snatch and fall with great force so as to have the momentum to pull the hat-stand upside down on to its top and aim the base as it passes overhead. I acquired the knack of it, and countless bruises besides, watching and imitating cross-eyed Ben Turpin in a 1918 silent one-reel movie in which he too played a clerk who knocked out a bankrobber with this same piece of business.

It worked perfectly in rehearsals and I had no fear as the moment approached in the live performance that evening. The audience knew the glass door was going to be broken and they couldn't wait to see *how*. I went into the gag, snatch, hug and fall, roll over, tip the hat-stand over on its head and watch its bottom hit the glass dead centre . . . and simply bounce off it. There was a moment of silence. Then the audience set up a howl of good-natured derision and joy such as I've never heard before or since. So I rose, picked up this six-foot hat-stand and swung it at the damn door. Still it didn't break. I did it again. Nope. Third time lucky? I used every ounce of strength and, hallelujah, the glass splintered into shards. What a cheer went up! I waited till it subsided and announced, 'I learned it all, beating the gong for Rank films!'

As I came off, I said to Bill King, who was in charge of props, 'What happened to that door?'

He said, 'I know, I know. But when I saw it break this afternoon in rehearsals, I thought, "Now that's dangerous." So I put in shatter-proof glass to make sure it didn't happen again.'

I stared at him.

He nodded and sniffed and added, 'Mind you, you did hit it bloody hard, mate!'

Bill was a great bloke but he never could see the point of a joke.

14

TV TIMES

Second – 'What's My Line?'

*Wherein we confirm the correctness of Congreve, cross
swords with a cross man and sit out a sit-com; followed
by a flop in New York, a stratagem in Maida Vale, a
première in Birmingham and a Power failure*

I hoped my parents would see these early TV shows of mine,
perhaps even be a little bit proud of me, and that my mother
would relent – she'd been cool and distant right after my
marriage. My bride felt hurt at such offhand treatment, and
wanted to write a letter to express her grievances but couldn't
find the words. Foolishly, I offered to rough out such a letter and
she copied it very closely. Of course, I should have known my
mother would recognise the true authorship. An envelope came
in reply but all it contained were the torn fragments of that
farmyard painting I had done under my mother's instruction as a
tiny boy. The rift was now official. When my Aunt Eckie asked
my mother about me she was told, 'I don't wish to hear that name
spoken under my roof.' We'd done *Love for Love* at school and I
felt haunted by William Congreve's often misquoted line:

> *Heav'n has no rage, like love to hatred turn'd,*
> *Nor Hell a fury, like a woman scorn'd.*

Not a big laugh but pretty good for a civil servant. Gary's birth in
1951 gave me a good reason to attempt a reconciliation with my
mother and, after being at first unresponsive, she paid a very
brief visit to my house in Greenways, Beckenham. She was very
reserved, her speech was clipped and she didn't meet my eyes.

After looking at Gary, she left and later sent a blue matinée jacket in the post. And that was that.

One of television's most popular shows began in Britain in 1951, the invention of two Americans, Mark Goodson and Bill Todman. A panel of four personalities tried to guess the unusual occupation or product of guest contestants, who were restricted to answering only yes or no to their questions. After ten negative answers, the panel was defeated. Regular panellists included Barbara Kelly, famous for her ear-rings; Jerry Desmonde, straight-man to Hope, Wisdom and Sid Field; Ben Lyon, a Hollywood star who'd become head of Britain's favourite comic family in 'Life with the Lyons'; David Nixon, the gentle comedy magician; and, of course, the ferocious Gilbert Harding. Of this last gent, Waldman enquired, 'Bob, do you think you can give him as good as you get?'

Gilbert had become legendary for his rudeness and impatience, so very famous that comedians scored easy laughs with his name, me included:

> *Gilbert will live forever.*
> *Heaven won't have him and Hell's afraid he'll take charge.*

When Gilbert heard I was joining the panel, he felt much the same about me; unwilling to have me and afraid I'd take charge. He picked on me from the very first show, ridiculing my questions, jeering at my guesses, handing me the audience's sympathy on a plate. On Waldman's instructions I was to provoke Gilbert's famous temper to produce 'exciting television', but no such provocation was necessary. Within three weeks, our Sunday evening exchanges were being reported in Monday's papers. Everything that happened on that series was treated as news, often front-page stuff. When Australian film actor Ron Randell bussed female guests, a headline screamed: 'Distasteful Kisses Could Kill "What's My Line?"' When I produced a swear-box for Gilbert, a picture of it made the *Daily Mirror*'s front page under: 'What's My Fine?' Gilbert's angry outbursts at me – 'Oh, do shut up, you dreadful young fool!' – and my good-natured reactions – 'I like doing this show, it stops me getting big-headed' – were doing just what Waldman wanted. The old Harding reputation was sustained and the new Monkhouse reputation was advanced.

Of course, Gilbert knew what was happening but, though he made no attempt to curb his peevishness, it was never faked. He wasn't that good an actor. I grew to love his honesty and eventually we became friends. When he was taken ill with the effects of diabetes and self-loathing, I visited him in his Brighton home for long talks. I was driving my car there in 1960 when the news of his death came on the radio and I pulled into a lay-by and wept. He was tortured by his alcoholism, his uncontrollable fits of fury, his repressed homosexuality and a painful religious ambivalence in which his much-needed Roman Catholic faith was constantly undermined by cynical atheism. Once represented in Madame Tussaud's waxworks, his likeness needed no name tag, just a plaque that said: 'The Most Famous Man in Britain'. A few years later I read that it had been melted down to make Christine Keeler.

Mark Goodson came across the Atlantic to see how we were treating his creation and liked what he saw of my verbal sword-play with guest celebrities, especially with Zsa Zsa Gabor –

What is your line, Miss Gabor – doing social work among the rich?

As a result, I was invited to fly to New York and take the seat on the panel usually occupied by humourist Bennett Cerf. How much I impressed the TV critic of the *Daily News* can be judged from a single quote: 'Mister Cerf's chair was empty but for a British grin.'

Back home for my second series, the BBC moved us for a six-week run to the Carlton Rooms in Maida Vale, home to many editions of 'Come Dancing'. The first five weeks there were remarkable for only one thing: Lady Isobel Barnett correctly guessed every single challenger's line. It became hysterically monotonous. Chairman Eamonn Andrews' expression as Isobel piped up with yet another right answer was gloriously chopfallen. Then, in our sixth and final week at that venue, Isobel didn't guess them all correctly, but I did. I'd discovered her secret.

Over her persistent objections, the producer had decreed that I should move to Isobel's seat at the left end of the panel, next to Barbara Kelly, while Isobel would take my seat at the other end next to Gilbert. 'No more arguments, Isobel dear, it's a better balance for cameras.'

That evening my questions were unnaturally comical. Of a man who made chamber-pots I asked, 'Is there an end product?' and 'What would I find inside it?' My questions to a professional nude model were 'Does your job require any kind of suit?' and 'Would I enjoy watching you work?' The studio audience laughed because they knew what the contestant's line was. They were shown the occupation of each guest on a large card held up high by a studio attendant with his back to us. From Isobel's seat the reflection of the card could be read clearly in the glass window of the technical control booth. All I had to do was glance across the hall and mentally reverse the writing in the reflection. Once I knew the answer, it was easy to make up loaded questions for a while before coming up with the solution. After the show, Isobel looked at me so imploringly that I had to wink my reassurance that her secret was safe.

The wife of Leicester's Lord Mayor, Lady Barnett was a witty woman who sadly committed suicide in 1980 after a conviction for shoplifting goods valued at just 87p.

Waldman's next plan for me was a situation comedy about a TV comedian and his homelife. Billie Whitelaw played my wife and Terence Alexander our drunken neighbour in a six-week run of 'My Pal Bob', with Denis Goodwin as narrator, popping up in a starburst at the corner of the frame to tell the story and so circumventing the problem of his bodily stiffness.

The series did well enough for a second run to be commissioned and Denis and I, having set up our own agency under the genial management of Dabber Davis, suggested a change of plan. We would package the whole series on film, script it, cast it, make it and lease it to the BBC for one showing. The Corporation would then give us back the prints together with world rights. Incredibly, we got the deal. The results are still in my film library, half a dozen half-hours of domestic nonsense that not even the tender mercies of rosy nostalgia can render watchable.

By some inexplicable quirk, Val Parnell saw one of the shows and liked it. The self-appointed King of Show Business, Val's castle was the London Palladium and his Chancellors were the agents, Lew and Leslie Grade. We were summoned to attend his court at the HQ of the newly launched ATV, London weekend and Midlands franchisee of Independent Television, and we went gladly.

'Lads, I want to talk about Friday, February 17th, 1956, the day of days,' said this son of a ventriloquist. 'Picture this: the Birmingham Town Hall, all the bigwigs there, free orchids for their wives, Sir Kenneth Clark for openers – do you know Ken?'

No, but we knew he was Chairman of the Independent Television Authority.

'He does ten minutes, no more. Now we hit them hard with the biggest, fastest, most colourful variety show the region's ever seen! And who's going to be the host?'

Val pointed at Denis.

'You are, my lad.'

'I am?' said Denis, as surprised as I was.

'Yes, you, Bob Monkhouse.'

'I'm not Bob Monkhouse, I'm Denis Goodwin.'

'Let's not get bogged down with details,' said Val, 'Alec, who else have we booked for definite so far?'

Alec Fine, a shrewd and honest theatrical agent, had lined up a wonderful bill of star names including Richard Hearne (famous as the white-wigged knockabout 'Mr Pastry'), and Hollywood's most dashing hero, Tyrone Power.

'What do you want us to do with Mr Power?' I asked.

'Whatever he wants you to do,' answered Val. As it turned out, I wasn't entirely able to oblige.

The London opening of commercial TV had been disappointingly received, but this Midlands debut was destined to shake the BBC's haughty confidence. An estimated one and a half million Midland viewers alone would forsake the BBC's 'Burns and Allen Show' to turn to ATV's opening transmission, a staggering figure when it's remembered that most of the six million viewers in the ATV region still had single channel sets, purchased when the BBC arrived in the central area of England only four years earlier. Two-channel TV sets that could pick up the new service were not cheap at between £70 and £110, in times when most viewers sat in semi-detached houses that cost them £2,500.

Denis and I wrote a very brisk, punchy script with a terrific opening line for me: 'Hello, traitors!' Everyone had guilty feelings about deserting the BBC and the line had such impact it was widely quoted. For ourselves, we had a fast crosstalk piece, a song parody routine and for Tyrone Power, two comedy scenes, one a rhyming monologue about Hollywood and the other an extravagant costume sketch burlesquing his swashbuckling movie success of 1940, *The Mark of Zorro*.

We checked into the Midland Hotel, Birmingham, two days early for rehearsals. Power had left his film actress wife Linda Christian in America with their two daughters; they were to divorce the following August. He arrived with the theatrical impresario, 'Binkie' Beaumont, who'd persuaded him to play in a stage production of Shaw's *The Devil's Disciple* at the Manchester Opera House, a venture doomed to disaster. Gossip linked the star with the Swedish actress Mai Zetterling and, sure enough, she turned up too. I had no idea that Power was bisexual and so was quite unprepared for his flattering interest in me.

On the morning of the show, Beaumont phoned my hotel room and told me Power wanted to see me. I went to his suite with my copy of the Zorro sketch where Beaumont admitted me and said, 'I'm hearing Ty's lines for him, come on.'

I followed him into the bathroom, where Power was lying in the bath with the script in his hand. For a naked man of forty-two, he looked quite beautiful and I was both impressed and embarrassed.

'Don't be nervous, sit down,' said Power and patted the edge of the bath.

The only other place to sit was on the toilet and Beaumont had perched there.

'This stuff is really funny, Bob. Let's run through it together.'

We began to read the dialogue and Beaumont suddenly rose, excused himself and went out. The reading continued for a minute and then Power tossed his script on the floor.

'This is a big bath. You want to get in with me?'

I gave a very awkward laugh and said something stupid about having had a bath already. Power said, 'Aw, come on, take your clothes off and climb in. We'll fool around. Come on, Bob, cure my headache for me.'

All my life I've been a film fan and I grew up regarding the stars as demigods. Tyrone Power had first become a hero of mine in 1936 when I was eight and saw him in *Lloyds Of London*. I'd rushed to see all his movies as they came out, from *Alexander's Ragtime Band* and *Blood and Sand* to *Suez* and *Jesse James* – and, oh yes, *Son of Fury*. Now, there's a coincidence. My only previous homosexual come-on, described elsewhere in this book, had been in the stalls of a stifling cinema thirteen years earlier, watching the same Son of Fury who now lay nude before me, his dark eyes shining with invitation and his right hand gently moving around his groin. I didn't know what to say so I said it.

'I don't know what to say. I'm sure you're joking.'

'No, I don't kid about things like this. Come on, do like I say.'

'I'm a married man.' I stood up.

'So am I, Bob, twice so far. But that needn't make any difference to us. Stop wasting time and that's an order. Get undressed.'

Now Power was becoming visibly aroused and I was sweating with anxiety. My throat had dried up and I croaked, 'I'm sorry, I just can't do that.'

Suddenly he rose to his feet in one smooth movement, standing up in the bath. I flinched and stepped towards the door.

'Don't panic. You blew it.' He reached for a towel. 'Forget it.'

'Right you are, sorry, I'll see you at rehearsal then.'

As I hurried out and back to my room, I thought to myself, 'I blew it, did I? Oh, no, I didn't.'

After the success of the ATV launch show (in which Power was relaxed and very courteous to me), the company started to book me for all their light entertainment shows, sometimes solo and sometimes with Denis. We shared the fees equally and Dabber Davis made sure there were jobs in our shows for all the performers our office represented: Cyril Fletcher, Pat Coombs, Hugh Lloyd, Cardew Robinson, Sheila Buxton, Barbara Law, Derek Roy and others had become part of our TV and radio repertory company.

Everything in my partnership with Denis Goodwin appeared harmonious but the weight of the problems that would soon bend and break it was increasing invisibly. Invisibly, that is, to someone as inherently *poco curante* about others' sensibilities as myself.

15

DENIS GOODWIN

My best friend, his own worst enemy

He once silenced the great ad lib *comedian Tommy Trinder who was in the middle of describing his career. During Trinder's pause for breath, Denis said, 'Tommy, failure has gone to your head.' It was a joke that backfired when it came true for its author.*

Denis had large brown eyes, thick dark hair in large waves, a slightly bulbous nose and full lips. His body was stocky and strong, not very hairy, with heavy legs, unsuited to any athletic activity. He had small, white, well-manicured hands which he handled awkwardly, often unintentionally hitting them against a wall or furniture when making a descriptive gesture. Shaking hands with Denis was not pleasant. He squeezed your hand in his with rigid fingers and thumb, folding them like a closing book.

When I first knew him, his disposition presented a start-and-stop medley of nervous inadequacy, sulky arrogance and impulsive kindness. His likes and dislikes were formed instantly and seldom revised. Possessive with his friends, envious of success in all but the very greatest, spiteful in mockery of those he hated, he would argue for hours, even days, over a small discount on a purchase from a shopkeeper and then, upon a whim, spend a bundle on some gratuitous gift or pay for a meal he hadn't instigated. He didn't smoke or gamble and – as became clear in later alcoholic years – he couldn't drink. All of these qualities in Denis were subject to one principal, overriding force which rendered them generally lovable – his all-encompassing sense of humour. He didn't take himself, or anyone, seriously.

What we shared then was this abiding humour. We may have had scant time for the seriousness of adulthood, for law and order, for the useful, the meditative, the sublime, the intellectual or the spiritual. Instead we worked through our jointly spent days and nights totally occupied by our enjoyment of the incongruous, the nonsensical, the illusive and the unexpected. Let religious and artistic sensibility glory in the perfect; we found our greatest satisfaction in the imperfect.

With the dwindling of Denis's humour in his latter years came the encroachment within him of human frailties we had once joked about with the invulnerability of youthful certainty. Replacing his sense of fun and his once playful dismissal of such corrosive emotions, he fell victim to his self-pity, his bitterness and his scorn of life itself. As a result, while I still loved him with my heart and in my memories, I grew to resent him quite as much with my mind and in my adjusted critical estimation. In the end, if I disappointed Denis, he disappointed both of us.

His drollery was sometimes facetious, often expressed for its own sake rather than to amuse others. In our very first office, the rented front parlour of a private terraced house in Kent House near Penge, Denis hung a woodcut picture of Chaucer on the wall. It was inscribed: 'To Denis and Bob, Thanks for the tales! Yours, Geoff.' In the drawer of his desk he kept a dog whistle with the declared intention of taking it to a circus some day and screwing up the performing poodle act.

Once, on one of our long 'talk walks' around our second office in Gower Street, he saw a sign outside a builders' merchants that said 'STAINLESS STEEL SINKS'. Denis came back in the dead of night with paint and a brush to write underneath: 'OF COURSE IT DOES.' If these simple eruptions of schoolboyish humour seem oddly self-indulgent, so much more was Denis's 'secret joke book'. I doubt that anyone else but me knew of its existence. I found it quite by accident after a long night's work at Denis's flat in Cleveland Square, writing scripts for our Radio Luxembourg show 'Smash Hits', in which we pretended to destroy the records most hated by our listeners. Denis went to have a bath and I was preparing a makeshift breakfast in his kitchen. Moving some packets of sugar and coffee in a wall cabinet, I noticed a rather battered old box of washing powder called Rinso. I picked it up and shook it to see how much it still contained. Something rattled flatly so I prized open the top very gently and took out a thin red notebook, dog-eared with use.

Denis's spidery handwriting was more illegible than usual and, on the first dozen pages, adolescently unformed. The more recent entries toward the middle of the book were written with his new and expensive Biro ballpoint. I guessed that the notes had been made irregularly over the previous eight years or so. The feeling of prying into his hidden thoughts made me hot with embarrassment but my curiosity was overwhelming. As I skimmed the pages I slowly became aware of what I was reading. These were my friend's private jokes, comic notions never intended for anyone's amusement but his own. Some were so cryptic and obscure that I couldn't puzzle out their meanings but others seemed less enigmatic. I could hear Denis singing and splashing in the bathroom so I went quickly into the living room, returning to the kitchen with pen and paper. Within a few minutes I'd copied a selection of extracts from his book, then restored it to its hiding place. I never mentioned the discovery to him and he never revealed its existence to me. My creased pages are still among my older possessions. These lines are six of the less arcane that Denis composed for himself alone:

> *All the coffee I drink will kill me and when I'm dead I'll*
> *be awake.*
> *There's only one thing I'm not sure of but I'm not sure what*
> *it is.*
> *I will go to evening classes and learn to be an evening.*
> *Since I like dry humour I must never laugh when it is raining.*
> *Just because I have been here before does not mean that I am*
> *not lost again.*
> *To thine own self be false because who else will know?*

His stepfather, whom he despised, was the glass manufacturer Albert Gee, a hugely successful man of little education. Denis delighted in A.G.'s syntactic bloopers and malapropisms. In a cruel imitation of the old man's East End accent, he'd repeat them over and over until they became our private catchphrases: 'It's half of one and six dozen of the other' . . . 'Noisy? It was worse than Alexander's Eggtime Band' . . . 'Time you was going up the apples and stairs.' Of Denis's sister Ruth, he'd quote A.G.'s curiously mangled maxim, 'There's no making 'er out, that girl, it's like the Bible says: Ruth is stranger than fiction.'

At Denis's wedding to our pretty secretary Barbara, a semi-orthodox affair at St John's Wood Synagogue, I acted as joint best man with his oldest friend, Paul Mendel. Paul asked him if there was any pious text he'd like to have read out and Denis soberly handed him a page bearing a passage from William Butler Yeats: 'I have known more men destroyed by the desire to have a wife and child and to keep them in comfort than I have seen destroyed by drink and harlots.' Paul's uncertain expression while he read it and looked up to see if Denis was serious had my partner in outbursts of giggles for days.

I'm not sure when the deep change in Denis's demeanour began. Initially we wrote and performed – together or singly – as equals. Our scripts came out quite naturally as fifty–fifty efforts, and in our many broadcasts as a double act, the laughs were evenly distributed; neither was the straight man.

It was inevitable that the inequality in our facility for performing on television and stage would unbalance that arrangement. Where I was quick to memorise lines and physically adept, Denis was a slow learner and ungainly. Because of these difficulties he always favoured radio work over TV and tried to persuade me to agree with his choice. We were partners so I gave in again and again, passing up some good opportunities to perform in various TV plays and shows in preference for labouring on radio scripts for others to perform. If I was aware of some small sacrifice in doing this, it seemed worth it for the sake of such a productive alliance.

As I've said, we'd moved to a converted dairy in Upper Montague Street in Marylebone where Dabber Davis ran the front office, managing our business and building up our theatrical agency. Dabber was – still is – a wildly enthusiastic zany with a mane of dense brown (now greying) hair swept back from his forehead as if he were emerging from a pool. Bright eyed and excitable, with a thrusting nose and wide nostrils, he didn't hold conversations on the phone, just monologues in the presence of witnesses, their prime purpose being the prevention of interruption. I observed, 'He's always got something to say.' Denis corrected me. 'No, he's always got to say something.'

Thanks to Dabber's indefatigable industry, we were free to sit in our cramped backroom, with just space enough for us to squeeze behind our facing desks, and apply all our working energy to churning out a nimiety of handwritten pages which he'd scoop up periodically and take away for typing. Throughout this period, my growing ability as a solo comedian had not gone unnoticed by BBC producers and theatrical bookers. This had a divisive effect on Denis's feelings. He was both pleased for me and yet begrudging; supportive of my success while demanding his share of it.

Our secretary, Barbara Goodman, had become engaged to marry Denis and quit her job to be replaced by her equally lovely schoolfriend, Jackie Harding. Jackie remembers how often Dabber had to say to bookers, 'If you want Bob, you've got to take Denis.' However much Denis affected ignorance of this, it must have been very humiliating. You might suppose that the simplest way out of his dilemma would have been to accept reality. We were a prolific writing team but one of us was the more able performer, ergo: go with the flow, put the comedian in the spotlight and write for him. We'd still have shared the income equally. Denis would surely have been perceived as the brains of the outfit with a consequently soothing effect on his hurt ego, and I'd be free to strut my stuff without feeling guilty. Yes, that scenario could have worked, I'm sure it could, except it didn't take into consideration Denis's blind, imperative need to compete; not necessarily to win, but to not to lose either. He wanted what I'd got and he just couldn't settle for less.

A lovely twenty-two-year-old girl called Billie worked for us once. We both flirted with her flagrantly and, one Monday while Denis was occupied on the phone, she took the opportunity to speak to me alone. She was still a virgin. She felt ready to quit this estate but was anxious to have it done as painlessly as possible. Could I help?

It was a male fantasy come true and, even as I relate it, I find it just as incredible in the telling as you must find it in the reading. Nevertheless, every word is true except for the girl's name.

I booked a room for the weekend at the Grand Hotel, Brighton that same Monday. Brighton was the traditional location for clandestine couplings and I was too naive to be more imaginative. We were both too naive to realise how apparent our rising excitement would be as the weekend approached. Denis was very sensitive to secrecy so he'd got us pegged as prospective fornicators by the Wednesday. His manner became distant, even mildly bellicose. By the time Billie quit work on the Friday his

Wammy (my father's nickname) at a 1938 Sunday picnic near Arundel, his old tweed jacket smelling of the tobacco in his second-best pipe. *(Author's collection)*

Buddy (my mother's nickname) posed for this studio portrait on her 50th birthday. It was the only photo of herself she really liked. *(Author's collection)*

My aunt Eckie snapped me floating off Littlehampton, aged nine and praying that my rubber tyre won't burst. I remain hydrophobic to this day.

Enduring the pebbles of Worthing beach with a patient smile, my mother relaxes uneasily in the summer of 1936. The costume was considered very daring and she was already nervous enough about her short haircut. *(Author's collection)*

Left: In 1952 Dabber Davis snapped Denis Goodwin and me on our first day at our new office in Upper Montague Street. Where better to say "Cheese" than outside a converted dairy?

Below: July 1953, and the dynamic duo of Monkhouse and Goodwin has delivered a rewritten, Anglicised version of the comedy material used at the London Palladium by Dean Martin and Jerry Lewis. You see how grateful they are. *(Author's collection)*

Top left: My 10-month-old daughter, Abigail, regarding me as an infant. She still does. *(Author's collection)*

Left: A smiling contest at Waterloo Station as I welcome Liberace and his mom back to London to sue the Daily Mirror in 1959. A columnist had implied that he was effeminate. Liberace won the case. *(Associated Press)*

Above: In the 1960 film with Peggy Cummins, Kenneth Connor and Ronnie Stevens, I played the 'Dentist in the Chair'. I was about as funny as the real thing.

Right: Writing and presenting thirty-nine editions of 'Mad Movies' in the mid-60s was a labour of love that became a profitable pursuit. It was still showing somewhere in the world until 1980. *(Author's collection)*

Readers of 'TV World' voted me 'King of Comedy' in 1962.
The 'Queen' was Hylda Baker. There were no children. (ABC TV)

Left: This is me in 1956 (aged 28) – a portrait for a romantic role in a
BBC TV play, 'Fool For Love'.

In Reuben Shipp's drama for Associated Rediffusion TV, 'The Taxman Cometh' (1965), I played a two-faced tax cheat who slept around. This is called 'casting against type'.

gaze was openly hostile but still nothing was said between us. I sensed his anger but balked at giving it open recognition for fear of causing some irreparable rift between us. Having invented some story about attending a weekend charity function in the country, I left him sitting alone in the office, tight-lipped and seemingly lost in thought.

Billie and I made our *rendezvous* at the Empire Café opposite Victoria Station. I had tickets for the 'Brighton Belle' and, after leaving two coffees untasted, we walked to the platform, laughing and chattering in anticipation. Then, as we sat in the stationary train waiting for our imminent departure, I glanced out of the window and my face froze.

'What's wrong?'

'I don't believe it.'

'Have you seen someone?'

'Yes, but don't turn round, don't look. It's Denis, he's standing on the platform about twenty-five yards away. Just staring.'

A whistle blew, the train shuddered and slid out of the station, and we tried not to let the feeling of being observed cast a cloud over our eagerness. An hour and a half later we were embracing in our hotel room. Billie decided to have a shower while I was ordering our room service dinner. The meal – smoked salmon, lobster salad, fresh fruit, with a bottle of dry champagne – was a deliciously suspenseful preliminary, blunting one appetite while sharpening another. As Billie sat there, wrapped in a white bathrobe and a towel turban, eating urgently, eyes fixed brightly on mine, her yearning was overcoming her fears, while the appeal to my own masculinity as the chosen instrument of defloration had got me as concupiscent as a sperm whale. When we finally undressed each other and hit the mattress, bedsheets hit the ceiling and all heaven broke out.

Some time later, watching lazy spirals of smoke intertwine as they rose from our cigarettes, both knowing we were resting in a tender clinch between the first exploratory round and the slower main event to come, Billie said, 'I haven't been to the seaside since I was a little girl. It's nicer than I remember.'

She went to the bathroom and, returning, gazed out of the window into the night. It was her turn to freeze.

'Bob, he's here, he followed us!'

I jumped off the bed and joined her as she pulled the curtain across her to cover her nakedness. We looked down from our fourth floor window and saw Denis. He was standing under a streetlamp and staring up at the hotel, so his face was clearly lit. It was an upturned, expressionless mask.

We looked at each other incredulously, forcing a little laughter without much conviction. Neither of us wanted to speculate on Denis's actions, they seemed too pointless and depressing. We returned to bed and once more strove to put this haunting out of our minds but, despite the pleasures of our congress, the distraction was impossible to ignore. We just had to sneak back to the window to see, the two of us standing there, my arms around Billie's neat nudity, peering down through curtains now drawn against the night, speaking in whispers as if he might hear us. The motionless sentry was still keeping watch up to an hour later but, when I looked again at midnight, he was gone.

After an indulgent breakfast in our room, Billie and I walked along the Brighton front on that warm, showery April morning, thinking we saw Denis spying on us from every corner and doorway. We could talk of little else:

'What would make him want to follow us? Did he want us to see him? How did he find the right hotel? How should we deal with this in the office tomorrow?'

Then we remembered we were lovers and went back to the hotel, determined to test the mattress to destruction. The room had been cleaned, fresh towels and soap provided, the bed made with clean sheets, and a bunch of twelve red roses was arranged in a glass vase on the dressing table. I looked for a note or card beside the flowers – 'With the compliments of the General Manager' perhaps – but there was none. I picked up the phone and called the reception desk.

'The flowers were delivered while you were out, sir. No, there wasn't any message with them. A dark young man, well dressed, he didn't leave his name. He just said to put them in water and leave them in your room.'

Billie, angry and now close to tears, stuffed the wet roses into the room's wastepaper basket, crushing and breaking them and scratching her hands on the thorns.

'He's done what he wanted,' she said. 'He's spoiled everything.'

'How?'

'I don't know how, but he has!'

And he had. We returned to London, thrown off balance, uneasy, feeling diminished without knowing quite why.

On Monday morning I drove to Denis's flat, quite determined to face him with my demand for an explanation, but he wasn't there. When I got to the office, Dabber and Billie were full of the news that Bernard Delfont was suing us for infringement of copyright and that Denis had rushed over to his Coventry Street offices to placate him. I followed by cab to join Denis in persuading Bernie that the sketch we'd done on TV the previous week was our own original work and only coincidentally similar to one he had bought from an American revue for his next stage show at the Prince of Wales.

Leaving his building, we both sighed with relief, checked our watches and realised that we were two hours behind in writing a routine for Peter Sellers. In the taxi back to Marylebone there was no time to discuss personal matters, only to map out the work ahead. And so it continued, the confrontation postponed day by day, my resolve to have things out with him weakening with the passage of time. It must have been more than a year later that Dabber came into our constricted inner office to announce an engagement for me at the Dome, Brighton.

'Where do you want me to book you overnight, the Grand?'

I said that the Grand Hotel would be fine and, as Dabber went out, I tried to return to the job in hand, a song parody for Dick Emery, but Denis was looking at me with an expectant expression. I looked back in silent enquiry. Neither of us could prevent the slow spread across our faces of stupid grins. We both knew what we were thinking. We both knew we wanted it to remain unspoken.

'Come on,' I said, thinking of Emery, 'let's keep our minds on Dick'

Denis laughed so violently he had to go out to the bathroom to recover.

Billie left us for a job on the other side of the Atlantic and I only saw her again once, many years later, just a brief encounter at a crowded party, a shrug, an exchange of rueful smiles and, for me, a sentimental pang not untinged with guilt. It was as if I had failed to repay a debt or to appreciate the deeper reasons for a gift. I have to put up with a great many weaknesses in myself – vanity, untidiness, irresponsibility, unpunctuality, many more – but I really fear my lack of loyalty. It didn't come with my bag and baggage when I was born.

We are many of us foxes in youth, initially loyal only to self. We must be taught humility, consideration for others, the constant business of fair exchange, the development of such innate human qualities as modesty, honesty and fidelity. It's the last of these, faithfulness to family and colleagues, allegiance to those who require it of me, that I've had the greatest difficulty in cultivating and which has consequently become as paramount to me as the display of his sense of humour is to the person who has none. I had to invent, or perhaps manufacture, my own scruples. They were never built in when I was originally delivered. You, who may have a natural trueness that cannot be deflected, please spare some understanding for a person who lacks such involuntary integrity and so, aspiring to it, must be forever checking his behaviour to see that it complies with the standards you set so intuitively. I have been so grateful to discover that, as one grows older, artificially assumed characteristics become real. With any luck I'll have become the man I really want to be by the time I'm dead.

It was this fear of my own inconstancy, exacerbated by the breach with my parents, that bound me so tightly to Denis long after it had become clear that our compatibility was exhausted. Disloyal or not, by the end of the 1950s I knew that I had to break free of our restrictive partnership. Denis had insisted on appearing onstage with me in summer season and pantomime and the result had been a nightly embarrassment for everyone. Despite his most determined endeavours, he could no more move across a stage with ease than an eel could juggle. His comic timing, superb on radio, was lost in his doomed attempts to master the gestures and grimaces he felt were *de rigueur* for stagework. The effect was closer to *de rigueur mortis*. The *Daily Mail*, reviewing our respective performances as Buttons and the Major Domo in *Cinderella* compared us with Sinbad and the Old Man of the Sea. I was glad that Denis failed to understand this allusion to the strangling human burden who'd climbed on to the sailor's back and would not be dismounted. Even so, anxious to shield my friend from such pain, I had to find a way to cut loose. Once my novelty value lost its public appeal, I knew I simply hadn't got enough talent to carry a partner who was contributing less and less to our undertakings.

Cinderella had hardly begun its record-breaking run at the Manchester Palace and my wife only just returned to London and our small sons, when I fell madly in love with a beautiful young woman in one of the principal roles. I hope you'll excuse my specifying neither. She is now a still beautiful widow who will expect me to have loved her enough then to be discreet now. She had a sweet and reckless spirit and demanded nothing of me while giving me her abundant affection. If I felt a little ashamed, Ugly Sister Danny La Rue, who adored both my wife and my new lover, would lift the guilt from me by gurgling, 'Get your fun where you can find it!' sometimes adding, 'but you mustn't mind what your wife may be getting.' One of the things my wife was getting was a phone call.

According to her understandably indignant report, she had received an anonymous tip-off from a man with an Italian accent who said he worked as a part-time waiter at the Milverton Lodge. This was the private hotel in the Dickenson Road where I was staying for the run. He told her that he was a good Catholic and did not approve of my bringing my 'paramour' (he actually used that word) back to my suite every night. When he named the lady involved, my wife became very upset. She had met her at the opening night party and detested her on sight. I denied everything. She came up to Manchester to see for herself and left a few days later, grudgingly mollified by my show of innocence and my 'paramour's' apparent infatuation with one of the George Mitchell Singers, a pimpled lad named Mike Sarne, later to achieve some fame with a pop record called 'Come Outside' and as a film director. The poor boy must have wondered what hit him. Here was one of the pantomime principals suddenly making such a passionate show of interest in him for half a week and then ignoring him completely thereafter. Sex can be hard on innocent bystanders.

The lady and I resumed our illicit affair but it didn't survive much beyond the end of the panto and our departure for distant employments, she on tour and I to another summer season. We met from time to time until she found the man she would marry and care for so well for the rest of his life. It was two years after the panto that I had an urgent late-evening phone call from Benny Hill. Denis Goodwin had called on him at his Maida Vale flat, unexpected and inebriated, planting himself immovably in the kitchen.

Benny only had one bottle of British sherry in the place. Denis had downed it and was now too drunk to be put in a taxi and sent home. I drove over at once and somehow Benny and I manhandled Denis out into the night where he threw up in a gutter. When I got him back to his new house in Bayswater, Barbara Goodwin wasn't there. I had some difficulty finding his latchkey and getting him up the stairs to his sitting room. While I was using the toilet, Denis recovered his wits enough to find some vodka in the sideboard and was drinking it when I came back. He was very emotional and didn't want me to leave him there alone. I decided to sit with him for awhile in the hope that Barbara would soon come home. Denis was sobbing. 'What's wrong with me? Why does everything happen to me? It's always going wrong. Sometimes I do things I can't help. It's not my fault, it just happens, you know what I mean?' He looked at me slyly. 'Like that fucking phone call.'

'Which one?'

'You know which one. From Manchester. It was me.'

'What was you?'

'The waiter. I pretended to be Italian. Fooled her. Dropped you in it.'

'I don't believe you.'

'It's true.'

'If it was you, tell me what word you used to describe my friend.'

'What word? What do you mean, what word? Oh, I see. *Paramour*. I said she was your paramour, Italian word for mistress.'

'It's French.'

'Is it? Never mind, your wife wouldn't know the difference.'

He giggled but it turned into a fresh outbreak of sobbing. I consoled him, told him I understood, knew that he couldn't help himself, and said that I forgave him. I really thought that I had forgiven him but, deep inside me, it seemed otherwise. Only twenty-four hours later, the treachery of my best friend had worked its effect on my inner feelings and a rash of eczema spread through my eyebrows and over the bridge of my nose. Now, more than ever, I had to find a way to separate us without further damage to his hypersensitive ego. As I fretted, fate was conjuring up a chain of events that would reach from California to Bayswater with the solution.

The sequence goes like this: Bob Hope comes to London in 1961 on one of his regular visits. We're commissioned to write a BBC radio show for him with guest stars Boris Karloff and Peter Sellers. I'm working nightly on the coast all summer so the greater part of the writing has to be done by Denis in his Bayswater home. Not having written much of worth in recent months, he amazes himself by turning out an inspired script. (I listened to my tape of the show just recently and it's still wonderfully funny.) Hope now goes home and a blood vessel bursts in his eye. He's advised to rest, so he announces his semi-retirement and lays off some of his writing team, keeping only the top men on salary. Meanwhile, Denis's wife is falling out of love with him and in love with her hairdresser. I receive the script of Neil Simon's first play, *Come Blow Your Horn* with an invitation to play the leading role and the offer is irresistible. While Hope is recovering, his chief writers take a break, one of them coming to London to visit with his East End relatives. He finds he's related to Denis by marriage and they meet. In conversation, he learns that Denis did the main job of writing on the Hope show with Karloff and Sellers. He tells Denis that Hope had considered making an offer for the Monkhouse-Goodwin team to join his writing staff in Los Angeles but was advised that hiring both of us would be too costly. Meanwhile in Palm Springs, Hope cancels his retirement and summons his writers back to work. I open in the West End play and it's a hit. Denis is unhappy. His partner is doing all this solo work, his wife is involved with another man, his writing standards are dropping again. Then comes the offer – come to LA and work for Hope, replacing one of the men previously laid off and now unavailable. Denis says, 'Bob, I'm splitting up with you. I think I stand a better chance of success in Hollywood on my own. We know one another too well to mince words. The fact is . . .'

Then he says the line that gladdens my heart. I can see him now, leaning with uncharacteristic informality against my dressing room wall in the Prince of Wales Theatre, holding a rare glass of the vodka that was to become all too common. He has a relaxed air of autarky about him. And he says this marvellous line:

'The fact is, I think you've been holding me back.'

By 1963, Denis told me he was earning about five hundred pounds a week working for Hope, but that double taxation cut it to a hundred and fifty. His letters complained that he was kept away from Hope by the more established writers and received little credit for his best work. In the grip of homesickness, he came back to London. His wife and children moved out of their home and, workless, Denis returned to the States where he picked up sporadic assignments from Hope, Jack Benny and a few Las Vegas comedians. In Nevada, he was having a rather boozy affair with a striking British showgirl when, after two years' separation, his divorce came through. Back in London and in debt, he did unreliable work for David Frost and Eamonn Andrews, blaming his lapses on a sleeping draught recommended to him fifteen years earlier by the producer, Leslie Bridgmont, and taken by Denis every night since then. It was a bromide which he claimed had built up in his system and slowly poisoned him. Unwell mentally and physically, his hospital treatment included the fast blossoming love of a twenty-three-year-old nurse named Jane Cappleman. They set up home in Campden Hill Towers, Notting Hill, and after surviving the odium arising from a shoplifting incident in 1968, they married.

I had come to dread Denis's late-night phonecalls but sat through their lengthy and incoherent repetition for what I liked to think as 'old times' sake'. He was hounded by creditors and living from hand to mouth on loans from old friends and family. I felt wretched for him but also fearful for myself, of the dangers of getting involved once more in a working relationship which would be less symbiotic than parasitic. Denis had become stuck in his own version of Catch 22: he hated to sponge and he hated those on whom he sponged, but most of all he hated himself for sponging. He wanted work but, when offered it, he ducked the responsibility of doing it and, in detesting himself for this, rendered himself less capable of working the next time. Vodka kept his demons at bay but fuelled the incessant phonecalls throughout the night which estranged even those who had previously wanted to help. On a cold March morning in 1975, he had one of his more frightening fights with Jane and she walked out. Denis took an overdose of sleeping pills and swallowed them with vodka. His suicide note was illegible. He was forty-five.

If you were to ask me whether or not I could have done something more to help Denis, my answer must be yes. I could have done more than listen to his rambling grievances and offer my sympathy, both sincere and insincere, through the small hours. God knows I tried to keep it sincere. Even fried to his tonsils, Denis could still detect any false note in my condolence, whereupon I would become the target of his disapproval, the very act of indulging him in his telephoned jeremiads condemned as mere condescension. Offers of money were met with either, 'You can lend whatever you like to Jane, that's up to you,' or an outraged, 'Don't patronise me!'

Yes, I could have made greater efforts to make a place for him in the TV work I was doing, but I didn't try very hard, unwilling to risk harming my career any further with my insistence that he be employed. Perhaps I might have cut down my own fees, so that the spare cash could have been used to pay Denis without his knowing. But what if he'd found out? And what of his incapacity for coming up with new ideas? He'd only suffer further loss of face in the presence of my new, younger writing colleagues, Tony Hawes and Wally Malston. I'd made him a gift of my half of all the material we'd ever written together, filing cabinets crammed with monologues, sketches, sitcoms and comedy dialogue, all of it with some potential for recycling and resale. I hoped it would be enough to keep him going.

Easier to answer if you asked me whether or not I could have prevented his suicide. No, I could only have postponed it. His attempts to end his life had continued on and off throughout the years since we first met. It was only through constant vigilance during his bouts of depression that he had been saved from himself again and again. We all knew the tell-tale signs: long silences, lethargy, sudden bursts of ill-temper, paranoid accusations, everything that was antithetical to the positive side of his nature. Dabber, Barbara, all his family and close friends, kept alert eyes on him during these phases. It was inevitable that one day he'd defy us all and make his pitiable escape.

Lastly you might ask me, 'Do you feel guilty about what became of Denis?' My answer is, 'Are you kidding?' Just go back over the last page and count the cop-outs and excuses I've offered to accommodate my conscience.

Yes, I feel guilty, but I forgive myself. I know now that you can't live another man's life for him. I also know that the self-hatred which destroyed Denis can all too easily become infectious. Accepting blame for what you are intrinsically unable to give another person is to curse yourself for being you. You can give no more than your best, and agonising over your natural inability to do better is destructively futile. If you won't accept unfair criticism from other people, why should you accept it from yourself? It took a Saint, one Bernard of Clairvaux, to write, 'First learn to love yourself, and then you can love me.'

Well, I've learned to forgive myself, so now I can forgive Denis.

★ ★ ★ ★ ★

Meanwhile, Lew Grade bought an American gameshow hosted by ventriloquist Edgar Bergen and boasting the sexist title 'Do You Trust Your Wife?' On the US original, later hosted by Johnnie Carson, married couples could win one hundred dollars a week for life. On the British version which Denis and I presented, we could award the maximum lifetime income per week of two quid. Producer John Irwin added a celebrity couple to the US format and after a few weeks we stuck our necks out and insisted on Max Wall and Jennifer Chimes. Against Lew's wishes, we got them and our rating went sky-high that week as we believed it would, relying on Britain's insatiable curiosity about figures of scandal. You had to have been around in those times of harsh moralistic judgement to appreciate how cruelly Max became rejected by the public and show business in general. He had left his wife and five children for a Beauty Contest winner and so was considered a wicked man. Both Denis and I had adored the comic genius since childhood and begged to have him as a guest star on every radio series we'd done. I also knew how miserable his first marriage had been until Jennifer had transformed his existence from the depths of misery to a seventh heaven. For the next few years I did my best to keep Max's career alive in what was otherwise for him a professional wilderness and he was gracious enough to say just that when he appeared on my edition of 'This Is Your Life' in 1982.

At the party afterwards, I reminded him of our first meeting on 'Calling All Forces'. I'd shown him a review of his act clipped from the *Beckenham and Penge Advertiser* in the late 1930s and among my souvenirs to this day. The report said, 'Mr Max Wall exploded on to the stage.'

'Ah yes,' said the Great Clown, 'it was something they put in the bread in those days.' He sucked a tooth and rolled his eyes and suddenly shouted, 'Show business is very hard on clothes!'

I laughed a lot, Max always made me laugh a lot, but the eccentric statement triggered another memory. I agreed, 'Show business is terribly hard on clothes, Max. I once exploded on to the stage too.'

My considerable exposure on ITV had consolidated my drawing power and 1957 was the lucky year I found myself regarded in the business as a bright new star. The bookers of cabaret attractions for the River Room of the Savoy Hotel in London saw me on TV while I was imitating a much bigger star and invited me to repeat the impression in their floorshow. I thanked my own stars for Liberace.

16

TV TIMES

Third – The Liberace Show

'Show business is very hard on clothes' – Max Wall, 1982. *Tails and tales of a glittering star are illuminated and exploded*

'The Liberace Show' had numbed Britain with disbelief. In an austere decade, his flamboyant costumes, ingratiating winks and kisses to camera during flashy flourishes on a gem-studded piano, well, it was all just too much for a respectable Sunday afternoon's viewing. It was also a free gift for me that I bore a strong facial resemblance, so into my act he went.

I had a black tail-suit made with glittery tinsel fringed round the edges, scrolls of sequins along the arms and white fur epaulettes and cuffs. The facing of the lapels and pockets was black gauze beneath which were hidden dozens of little coloured bulbs. These were wired to heavy acid batteries in the tails, ready to be switched on for my big finish. On my head was a wavy matching wig frosted with glitter and I sat at a grand piano as the lighting came up slowly, revealing only my silhouette as I mimed the Liberace opening theme to a tape recording played through a speaker attached to the underneath of the Savoy's Steinway. The audience hooted and applauded.

When the pin-spot lit my grinning head, the clapping and laughter became uncontrolled. I had to wait for it to subside before embarking on my parody of 'I'll Be Seeing You', Liberace's regular song. Some satirical patter followed, then came the introduction of 'my mom' (played by a sexy little blonde actress named Carole Lesley who, I explained, was a walking miracle of cosmetic surgery), and finally the closing song, ending tastefully with the climax of what was a pretty cruel lampoon – a stage blackout and the illumination of my jacket into a blaze of fairylights. Boy, did I love that jacket! It was the biggest laugh of all.

I had been playing to very good business and my booking had been extended by two weeks on the night it happened. No one warned me because no one knew. The first I knew about it myself wsa during the first song. I'd reached the middle eight bars of 'I'll Be Seeing You' when a section of the audience near the entrance to the big room broke into puzzling applause. Apparently a celebrity had entered but I couldn't make out who it was. As I continued with the act, the laughter took on an oddly excited note and a buzz of delighted chatter spread rapidly. It wasn't until the introduction of 'mom', when the spotlight had to follow her wiggling walk around the perimeter of the stage, that I saw him in a passing flash, sitting ringside. Yes, you're right. It was Liberace, in London on an unannounced visit.

I suppose I could have fled or died on the spot or changed my name or lost my mind or denied everything or blamed my parents or sacrificed my children. Instead, I finished the act as if in a trance.

Moments later I was slumped in my dressing room as one transfixed by the enormity of his transgression, wondering whether Liberace was powerful enough to have me feeding the fishes in the Thames before dawn, when Ethel Levy, the Savoy's cabaret booker, came in looking flustered.

'No time to change. Mr Liberace wants to see you at once.'

It was the walk to the scaffold. I had been warned that my mordacious travesty might be actionable if reported to Liberace's agents. Still wearing my guilt, the sleazy tail-suit, I was shown into Liberace's suite. He was seated at the grand piano with a small entourage around him. I stood there in silence until presently all heads turned towards me.

'There he is,' said somebody.

The Magnificent Showman rose and walked across the room, his arms extended. He hugged me warmly and said, 'Oh, you were *wunnerful*, Bob, just *wunnerful*!' With his arm round the shoulders of my vulgar jacket, he waved everyone aside and gestured at the piano. 'But come on, come on over here to the keyboard, let's open some more champagne, and let's get to work on this! You gotta make the whole thing more *evil*, camp it up! Put in a big gaudy handbag, smothered in multi-coloured sequins! Look, I'll show you, Bob, I'll show you how to do Liberace so swell you'll make me *hate* you!' And for the next hour and a half, he showed me and I learned.

My Liberace impression became standard fare for me on TV and a must for my summer seasons. My jacket was rewired and mended and hand-cleaned again and again. I could have had a new one made but this was the magic garment to me now, the one that Lee himself had embraced. I tell you again, I loved that jacket. I suppose a love affair like that isn't meant to last.

Nothing had gone right with the preparation of the show. There were arguments, disagreement over music, in fact I was sorry I'd taken the booking. Most comedians are wary of playing the Albert Hall anyway. It's too big for the use of any but the broadest grimaces and gestures and in 1962 the sound system was unsuitable for fast patter.

Still, it was the right venue for the occasion, the launch of a new car to the motor trade. They'd engaged me to compère the first part and then, while a promotional film was shown, change into Liberace and drive the new car on to the stage from where it was hidden behind a huge cerise curtain. It was to be edged in light bulbs but the electrical problems were a nightmare. So was the last-minute decision to turn me into a Christmas tree.

'Your jacket won't stand out next to the car, Bob, not when we blackout the hall and switch the bulbs on,' they told me. 'We'll have to fit you up with equally bright bulbs. You're not to worry, we know what we're doing.'

I looked like the Blackpool Tower in October by the time they'd finished with me, with two dozen light bulbs sprouting all over and two long black cables snaking out of my trousers at each ankle. All possibility of comic effect was gone. I was a serious safety hazard. But I was not to worry, they knew what they were doing.

That night the presentation was going smoothly enough, the audience of car dealers seemed pleased, and I completed my first-half duties feeling reasonably confident. Even as I was strapped and plugged and bound into my now unrecognisable tail-suit, I thought everything might be all right. I climbed into the small car with some difficulty, listened for my announcement and the Liberace theme, drove off a ramp and out through the curtains into the centre of the auditorium, halted, climbed out as best I could, trying to drag my cables with me as surreptitiously as possible, and finally took my place beside the motor, waving my arm in greeting and grinning the Liberace grin all around. On that cue, the Albert Hall darkened and all the bulbs came on.

The car was OK.

Me, I did what Max Wall was said to have done in the variety theatre.

I exploded on to the stage.

Those who were there that evening still speak of it. They tell me they saw the car's outlines etched in chains of brightly shining bulbs just for a moment. Then its brilliance was completely outshone as its driver blew up. What had been my smiling and waving figure a moment earlier now blazed into a white-hot starburst. A plume of heat and smoke and fizzing electrical fire streamed up from my body, shooting from my ankles to my scorching wig and upwards. I must have looked like Joan of Arc in formal wear.

The full stage lighting was brought up and there I stood, my clothes smoking and sputtering with the last odd spark or two, the stage around me strewn with glass and twists of wire. If I'd had a decent *ad lib*, no one would have been able to hear it bcause my radio mike had blown as well. I made an unsteady exit to sporadic, uncertain applause.

Later, as two St John's Ambulance volunteers applied ointment to my singed bits and repeated things like, 'You were really very lucky, you know,' and 'Why on earth did you agree to do it?', I saw my Liberace jacket for the last time. It had been peeled off me and dropped on the floor. It was scorched and torn beyond repair, its skeleton of burnt wiring exposed, all its dozens of sockets fused and choked, its tinsel dangling forlornly. I watched a cleaner pick it up and stuff it into a bin.

It's just as the blessed Max Wall said. Show business is very hard on clothes.

17

TV TIMES

Fourth – A series, a special, a commercial

No laughs in LA, a most happy meeting in NYC, and a song title for AJL. Then, after meeting a hero in a snowbound diner, comes a candid view of Britain.

It was through another American musician that I came to trade sneezes in a snowstorm with Buster Keaton, and search for myself on Blackpool front. These peculiar memories would never have been mine but for the composer/lyricist Frank Loesser.

Our first brief encounter was in 1958 when I was in the USA to appear on ABC's 'Make Me Laugh'. One of this show's star panellists was the 'King of the One-liners' Henny Youngman, who'd befriended me after I'd introduced him on one of the London Palladium shows as 'a rumour in his own lifetime' and followed his act with 'what a comedian – he has such an original memory'. Henny enjoyed these insults and, as soon as he got back to the States, he recommended me to executive producer Mort Green, who booked me as one of three guest comedians who took turns at trying to make a blank-faced contestant laugh within one minute. For every second the punter didn't laugh, he or she won a dollar. I took part in three shows in one evening and, during each of my twelve one-minute efforts to crack their resolve, my contestants won their full money. As I was leaving the studios to crawl in shame back to my hotel, Green stopped me and said, 'I knew you still had shortages in Britain but I never figured you were all out of funny.'

In New York's Stage Door Delicatessen, I ran into Kenneth Alwyn, who took me with him to see *The Most Happy Fella*, an unjustly neglected musical today, just about to close after a fine two-year run at the Imperial Theatre. Alwyn was to be the show's musical director when it opened at the London Coliseum and we went backstage to meet Art Lund, the leading hunk who was set to repeat his role in the British production. Frank Loesser, who'd created the music, lyrics and book, was in Lund's dressing room having a screaming match with his wife, Lynn Loesser, co-presenter of the show and victim of humourist Harry Kurnitz's infamous remark as she passed his table in Sardi's: 'There goes the evil of two Loessers.'

She stormed off and Frank said, 'Come on, you guys, let's go eat.' Half an hour later I was in a club called The Gaslight sharing a meal with a group of Frank's friends including Lee Remick, Moss Hart and Alan Jay Lerner. Lerner was seated beside me and, perhaps because of his mild Anglomania, was charmingly chatty with me. He pointed out Paulette Goddard at another table and told me that, after years of handling the men in her life like children, she had finally met her match in her third husband, the German journalist and novelist, Erich Maria Remarque.

'Paulette's temperament is sunny with sudden squalls. Erich avoids all confrontations with her anger by interrupting it with admiration. No sooner does she burst into the room screaming with rage about his untidiness or his forgetfulness than Erich produces a gasp of amazement and says something like, "My God, what have you done with your hair? It looks fantastic!" She's instantly diverted and makes straight for the nearest mirror saying, "Do you really like it?" while he piles on the flattering attention until all memory of her fury has passed away.'

I said, 'He should write a book on how to handle a woman.'

Frank overheard me. 'I'll subscribe to that. What's the secret?'

'You just tell her she's wonderful all the time, simply blind her with love. Isn't that right, Alan? How to handle a woman – in one lesson.'

'Alan, I think Bob's a lyricist. How to handle a woman. Simply love her. You want to write it or shall I?'

A year later in London I got a message that Frank wanted me so I phoned New York. He asked if I remembered our conversation with Lerner.

'You had a title for a song, Bob, "How To Handle a Woman". Alan's writing a musical called *The Once and Future King* and he can use the title in the show. What do you say?'

149

I said that I was very flattered and that he was welcome to what had been more a passing comment than a serious suggestion.

'Bob, song titles are gold dust. When you do Alan a favour, you do me a favour. I owe you. Pick up the marker some time.'

As it turned out, I picked up three markers: a series, a special and a commercial. I'd been after the series for some time, having seen Allen Funt's 'Candid Camera' shorts for Columbia in the newsreel cinemas and heard Pete Murray and Jonathan Routh doing Funt's 'Candid Microphone' on Radio Luxembourg. ABC TV, the Teddington-based franchisee that eventually merged with Associated Rediffusion to become Thames TV, was happy with the success of a game show I was presenting for them, 'For Love or Money'. Three contestants opted for a visible prize like a washing machine or small refrigerator ('Love') or gambled on an unknown amount ('Money') which varied between nine shillings (45p) and nine thousand, nine hundred and ninety-nine shillings (£500), the 'Flying Shilling Sign' flickering to and fro as I read the question and halted by the first player to buzz in with an answer. So if anyone ever comes up with the Dancing Decimal Point, you'll know where they got the idea.

ABC TV had expressed some interest in making the hidden camera show if I could set it up, as they could get nowhere with the show's leery American creator. A personal approach was needed. One phonecall to Frank Loesser and I was furnished with an introduction to the ape-like Funt. I flew to a frozen New York to secure my place as the host and writer of the first British version of 'Candid Camera', co-producing with Routh and Ronnie Taylor. 'We're shooting from seven tomorrow morning,' Funt told me. 'You wanna string along, see how we do it?'

The leaden early morning sky was pregnant with snow as I made my way through hunched workers from the Algonquin Hotel to a diner on Eighth Avenue and Forty-second Street, an area later to become a haunt for pornographers and full-moon weirdos. The camera crew had set up behind a see-through mirror so as to face unsuspecting customers seated along the counter. The gag was to observe people's reactions to the embarrassment of being in the same joint as a crazy man, a bleak-eyed nut who'd behave in a very anti-social way. The old actor who'd been hired for this stunt was introduced to me. He was Buster Keaton. I stood rooted to the spot, speechless, popeyed, totally starstruck.

My personal love affair with Keaton began in my childhood, endlessly cranking the 9.5mm Ace projector in my Beckenham bedroom to watch his athletic antics in three minute clips from *The Balloonatic* and *Cops*. Over the ensuing years I learned that The Great Stone Face had become one of the top three champions of silent comedy during the decade before my birth, five of his dozen feature films being among the best and funniest ever made; indeed, 16mm copies of them remain the most precious in my collection. Keaton didn't easily survive sound and his tragic alcoholism reduced him to sleepwalking through dreadful two-reelers for poverty row studios, gagwriting for newer stars and playing small supporting roles.

Nevertheless, he ranked alongside Charlie Chaplin and Harold Lloyd as a comic genius and I found him far and away the funniest. Now he wasn't far and away but standing there in front of me, holding out his hand to shake mine. I snapped out of my trance and said the first thing that came into my head: 'I had you in my bedroom all the time when I was a little boy.'

A copy of the film that was shot that morning is on the shelf beside my other Keaton treasures. Watching the unceasing flow of invention as he created funny business with extraordinary dexterity and cunning was a masterclass in visual comedy. The reels ran for ten minutes, then the cameras were reloaded and I had my chances at conversation with him. I could hardly believe that he was consulting me about how best to do the sight gags he was devising. 'Whadya think? Do the pepper pot first? Or eat the guy's food first? Whadya say?'

Once the unexposed film was loaded for the next take, everyone dived back into the kitchen, the entrance door was unlocked and we waited for enough customers to sit on the stools beside Buster, order their meals and get served. Then he went to work: dipping his finger in a man's ketchup and checking the flavour; removing the flower from his buttonhole and standing it upright in a woman's glass of water; asking a couple to pass the pepper pot, its top already unscrewed in preparation, then shaking pepper into his minestrone until the loose top fell in the soup with all the contents of the shaker; sneezing so hard that his ginger toupé flew into the soup, fishing the hair piece out, removing pieces of spaghetti from it and pasting it back on his scalp; these and dozens of other deftly executed tricks, while the concealed lens recorded public reaction ranging from scowling disbelief and restrained tittering to outright disgust and helpless hooting.

Snow was falling very fast and the flow of customers dried up. Buster's driver advised him to leave and, sorry as I was to see him go, I felt I'd been sufficiently privileged that morning. Funt wanted to shoot another stunt involving a prop flower that would dip its head into the customer's coffee and drink it. 'We'll stick it out till the snow quits,' he announced. The snow didn't quit. Within the next few hours a record eleven-and-a-half inches of snow fell on New York City. We were trapped in that diner from mid-morning till early evening when snow ploughs cleared a passable path. I never want to smell another hamburger as long as I live. On my way back to the hotel I sneezed so hard my hat flew off. It was my involuntary tribute to Buster Keaton.

In the very first British edition of 'Candid Camera' I introduced our most famous spoof, 'the car with no engine'. Jonathan Routh and Arthur Atkins ran a car downhill on to a garage forecourt and asked the attendant to change the oil. When he opened the bonnet, the engine was missing. He lay down and looked under the car, in the boot, even peered in the rear windows.

His bewilderment was not only funny, it was a revelation in TV comedy. Everyone wanted to see it again so we repeated it once immediately and then shelved it for two years. The demand for its repetition grew so great that we screened it once more. There were howls of protest. Why had we cut it? Where was the part where the garage attendant lost his temper? What had we done with the bit when the mechanic said, 'Have you come far?' to which Routh replied, 'Yes, but running very quietly for the last twenty miles'? Quite amazingly, public imagination had added comic chapter and verse to the memory of the original stunt, expanding it in the telling and re-telling until it became far funnier than it already was.

Lerner and Loewe's *The Once and Future King*, renamed *Camelot*, opened at New York's Majestic Theatre in December, 1960, and I confess to feeling a glow of pride when I heard the album track of Richard Burton singing the delightful song for which I'd coined the title. In view of the state of my marriage at this time, I wished I'd known better 'how to handle a woman.'

Rather more modestly, I had opened at the Wintergardens, Blackpool, and the popularity of 'Candid Camera' ensured twice-nightly full houses for seven months. We were filming sequences for TV during the day and one stunt had me searching for myself along the promenade. Dressed as a police constable, I showed my photograph to passers-by and asked if they had seen anyone resembling this wanted man. Responses included, 'No, officer, but you could look in the (name of hotel), it's full of nancy boys like that, and 'I seen 'im on the telly and I just knew 'e was bent.' Not one person out of fifty recognised me in my uniform and helmet. I tried selling five-pound notes for four pounds, ten shillings (£4.50), believing that the holidaymakers would be too suspicious of trickery or counterfeit notes to buy them. My co-producer Ronnie Taylor was less confident and insisted I use my own money. To my dismay, I did a roaring trade and in under half an hour was sold out and fifty quid poorer. Classic hoaxes included selling left-handed teapots; posing as a Serbian tourist asking the way to 'Kee-app-siddee' while flourishing a map of Cheapside; speeding up the conveyor belt in the packing department of a cake factory; paying taxi-drivers with wet money from a clothesline hanging over a printing press; and having Professor Stanley Unwin burbling his double-talk to a job applicant ('I think I get your drift' the man answered and, when given an even more incomprehensible blast of scrambled nonsense, 'Oh, boy, now you're talking!').

If our pioneering practical jokes seem lightweight stuff in comparison with the spectacular vigour of today's TV japesters, the continuing success of the technique is justified by its popularity. In entertainment as in any other commerce, demand dictates the nature and quality of supply. *Vivat, vivat* Jeremy Beadle!

18

ANIMAL CRACKERS

Losing a poodle in Bournemouth, losing a Basenji in Golders Green, losing a chihuahua in St John's Wood and very nearly losing a cat in Worthing

I can't remember any great length of time when I didn't belong to a cat. Oh, yes, there was a brief period when my children were young and wanted a dog to play with. We gave a home to three dogs in succession, all disastrous.

The first was an irritable poodle which my younger, four-year-old son named 'Stamp' because he couldn't say 'Tramp' very well. We took the noisy creature to Bournemouth, where I was appearing in the 1958 Pavilion summer season with the Beverley Sisters. The girls were very popular on TV so I had to share top-billing with them, although I made sure my name appeared on the left. That's the side people read first unless they're Arabs.

I hired a big house in Branksome Chine for the summer, not so big that we couldn't fill it in with noise. My little lad ran around it and shouted like any normal kid and my seven-year-old son Gary cried piteously much of the time, going through a long and painful adjustment to his disability. He would weep and struggle with me for half an hour each day as I sat behind him on the lavatory seat, holding his wrists to prevent them flailing, and praying for his early bowel movement. Add to this racket the perpetual yapping of Stamp as his toenails rattled on the parquet flooring and you have some idea of how grateful I was to go to work every evening.

Denis Goodwin appeared beside me in only two stage shows and this was the first of them. He had married our secretary Barbara two years earlier; now she was pregnant with their first son, Jeremy, and living in another rented house around the corner from ours. There was tension between our wives, who had stopped speaking to one another, and this made it a little difficult for us to write our radio and TV scripts during the day. Stamp didn't make it any easier. The dog had taken an instant hatred to Denis and barked at him harshly and continuously.

'There's nothing wrong with that dog a Filipino chef couldn't fix,' said Denis.

Having taken the boys and their dog to the beach on one of the few sunny days that long summer, my wife called at the stage door while a matinée performance was taking place. Gary's wheelchair got stuck on the step and in the effort to free it, Stamp got loose.

The dog ran backstage and spotted Denis standing in the wings, just about to walk on to introduce the whistling Arnaut Brothers. Barking mad, its woolly body shaking with fury, the dog pursued Denis across the stage and bit him on the ankle. The audience loved it.

Denis shouted the name of the next act and ran off, dodging Stamp's attempts to get in his second bite, reaching his dressing room and just managing to close the door before the dog could follow him. Stamp went into a fit of madness, scooted around the backstage area and out of the stage door where he stopped in the middle of the car park and literally barked himself to death.

He just gave one last fusillade of barks at the sky, railing at the doggy gods, and keeled over. A heart attack, according to the vet. 'Wish fulfilment', according to Denis.

My younger son began pining for another dog but this time I played it smart. I contacted a dog breeder and told him my mission – to find a dog that didn't bark.

'You want a Basenji,' he told me. 'Oldest breed of dog known to man, there are drawings of the breed in the tombs of Egyptian Pharoahs. I could find you one but it'll cost you.'

'You're absolutely sure it doesn't bark?'

'That's the chief characteristic of the breed, not barking. If it's happy, it laughs – hur, hur, hur – and if it's unhappy, it cries. But it never barks.'

'That's the dog for me,' I said.

The Bournemouth season over, we moved back to 87 Hodford Road, Golders Green, London NW11, where our one-year-old Basenji was delivered and I forked out a small fortune for it, along with a pedigree and ownership papers. A Basenji is not cheap.

Within the day I had discovered two more facts about a Basenji. First, it has very high sexual motivation. This animal would screw anything, all the time and everywhere. It had my leg, then the sofa, then my wife's leg, then the cushion in its basket, my leg again, the kitchen swing-bin, the umbrella stand in the hall, my leg again – if that dog had lost its own legs, it would have heaved itself over to the wall and screwed the electricity outlets.

The second thing I found out about a Basenji was that, although it doesn't bark, and it really does laugh when it's happy and cry when it's sad, this laughing and crying *sound exactly like barking*.

Before we could get fond of it and before it could get much too fond of us, I found another home for our canine rapist. The only person I could find to take the dog off my hands quickly and as a gift was a sheep farmer in Buckinghamshire who came and collected it in his truck.

'It's a working dog, your Basenji,' he explained. 'He's not too old for me to train as a sheepdog.'

'Is that right? Well, goodbye.'

'We'll make him happy.'

As the truck drove off with the four-legged sex machine on board, I thought, 'He'll make your sheep happy and all, chum. And then keep you up all night with his laughing.'

We remained dogless in 1959 while my adopted daughter Abigail joined the family and we moved to 7 Loudoun Road, St John's Wood, London NW8.

The cry went up again in favour of getting a dog for the children to play with and again I got smart. I decided that if dogs had to bark, at least a smaller dog ought to make a smaller noise. Also, the smaller the dog, the less exercise it would need, ergo: no walkies. Besides which, a very short dog meant humping my leg would be physically impossible. And getting smarter by the moment, I figured that if I bought two such dogs instead of one, they would keep each other company and not bother me. I had the whole thing figured out.

I came home with two tiny chihuahuas. They looked like abortions, but the chap who sold them to me said emphatically that these very young animals were perfect. Never buy dogs from a man you've met in a pub.

Our children named them Romeo and Juliet. In the best Shakespearean tradition, Juliet died. Romeo, however, thrived and swiftly grew to fulfil his mission in life – to take dog revenge on my household on behalf of Stamp and the Basenji.

Instead of barking like the poodle, or making emotional noises that resembled barking like the Basenji, Romeo just whined. No, he didn't just whine. He whined and whined and whined. Instead of coitus with my shin, Romeo spread his back legs like a spatchcock, paddled his front legs and dragged his genitals across the white Indian carpet in our living room.

As for being nervous, none of us could so much as turn over in bed without hearing Romeo wake in terror and begin whining again. If any of us even began to move or speak, however gently, he would quiver, shiver, shake and quake in no particular order. In desperation I phoned my friend, Barbara Woodhouse, who had provided dogs for my 1950s sitcom, 'My Pal Bob'.

Barbara suggested that the young dog missed its mother and that we should wrap it up in a soft blanket at night with a ticking clock, the sound of which would simulate the mother's heartbeat.

I sat up and waited for the agitated little beast to become sufficiently exhausted by its own jumpiness to fall asleep. Then I carefully wrapped an old wind-up clock in one of my wife's unwanted jumpers and gently tucked the sleeves around his twitching body. For once, the tiny monster seemed to relax. He actually snuggled closer to the ticking clock. Wearily, I went upstairs to bed with only the faintest feeling that I'd forgotten something.

What I'd forgotten was that I had wrapped up the chihuahua next to an alarm clock that was set for six o'clock in the morning.

When we came down to breakfast, the dog had to be scraped off the ceiling.

My small son finally said it. 'Mummy, could Romeo live somewhere else for a while, somewhere near where we could visit him sometimes? He's giving me headaches.'

He went to a woman with six chihuahuas of her own somewhere off Acacia Avenue. We never did visit him.

I grew up with a cat and I'm growing old with a cat. Jackie and I love cats. To be more exact, I just like cats very much and Jackie is dangerously dotty about them.

The year after I was born, my parents acquired a jet black cat called Sam. I was quite small when Sam adopted me and moved into my bed. Although my mother was hot on hygiene, for some reason she never objected to my cohabitation with our cat. I would wake in the mornings on my back to find Sam sitting on my chest, regarding me mildly. Sam and I held staring contests which he always won.

Apart from two summer holidays on the Isle of Wight (where I saw two rising comedians in concert party, Eric Barker at Sandown and Arthur Askey at Shanklin, and worshipped them both), we took our fortnight's holiday throughout the 1930s at the Eardley House Hotel, Worthing, Sussex.

In the summer of 1935 my parents couldn't find anyone to look after Sam while we went away; my paternal grandmother was too ill, my mother's parents didn't like pets, neighbours had dogs, and so forth. So I held Sam on my lap in the back of father's black Vauxhall 8 and we drove the sixty or so miles to Worthing. He'd travelled by car before and liked to look out of the window. We stopped halfway for tea, as we always did, at ·Clematis Cottage, outside Horsham. Sam had a saucer of their milk and inspected the garden. The kindly old lady who owned the place remarked on how handsome she thought Sam and made friends with him. Bear with me, there is some small point to this.

At the Worthing hotel, Sam stayed in the room with me and my brother, venturing out on the balcony and into the garden at irregular intervals. He was never far away and came enquiringly when called. That's what made his disappearance so bewildering. It was our last day and my father delayed an intended departure time of two p.m. until early evening while we all searched and called for Sam. Despite my tears, we had to leave without him.

Over the next few months I missed Sam most miserably. I thought about him all the time and wondered where he was and who was feeding him. My parents must have talked it over because they chose a moment to sit me down in the front room, the one my mother called the drawing room, and tell me to stop fretting about the cat.

'Your father and I believe he must have been killed by a car. But, listen, Robert, we're going to get another cat. Your aunt Muriel's cat just had kittens and she says we can drive over to Sydenham next Saturday and choose one. What do you say?'

I had nothing to say. Killed by a car? I could see Sam in my head, being squashed under a wheel. It was too much to bear. I ran into the dining room, opened the sideboard drawer, pulled out our holiday snaps of Worthing and began to tear them into pieces.

The next day Sam showed up.

It was an early morning in late October and at first I thought it was a shadow in the rockery. I rubbed my bedroom window and looked again. No, it was a black cat that looked like Sam but much thinner. Painfully thin, in fact. It needed feeding.

I ran downstairs and got Sam's dish, a bottle of milk and some slices of luncheon meat in greaseproof paper. I unlocked the back door and walked round to the garden. The strange cat was lying among the rockery plants, too weak to look up. I arranged the meat on the paper in front of its face and poured some milk into the dish beside the food. Then I took a closer look, bending low. The cat looked into my eyes and my heart jumped. I must have gasped his name because Sam miaowed.

The reporter who called from the *Beckenham Journal* said this kind of thing had often happened. Not to me and Sam it hadn't. As far as I was concerned, Sam had come back because I had kept faith and somewhere in his pussy mind he had known that. Within ten days or so Sam was almost his old self again, his coat a bit raggedy, his paws healing well.

The next year we went back to Worthing. This time Sam stayed with cat-loving neighbours. As usual, we stopped at Clematis Cottage for tea. The proprietor recognised us, as she did every year, and asked me, 'How is that handsome cat of yours?'

I said he was fine, thank you.

'He passed through here last autumn,' she said. 'I gave him some fish and a little milk and then he was gone again.'

19

TRUE ROMANCES

Awakened to sex, then awoken by it, the animator attempts it without awakening others. Two lost lady loves are remembered and another who was certainly no lady

Kiss-and-tell confessions bother me. Their only motivations seem to be greed, boastfulness or vengeance. My dilemma arises from the conflict of honesty and indiscretion. I began by promising you the truth, warts and all, and here I am, waxing shy about my occasional sexual adventure. Oh, I've made an exception in the case of my brief conjunction with Diana Dors but only because she kiss-and-told first. Second as well. I rated fairly explicit mentions in *two* of Di's books and I hope you'll agree that this gives a gent the licence to give his version of events, as I do elsewhere in this one volume. As for more of the important romances in my life, most of the laughing girls I was lucky enough to sport with in my teens are now respectable matrons and grandmothers. Some of them are still laughing. But I hope you'll agree they have a right to expect some secrecy about their flaming youth.

My very first sexual experience involved a mature lady related to me. Since I was just fifteen years old at the time, you may guess that she is no longer with us, but she had children about my age who are still living and certainly won't want to read about their late mother instructing a grateful adolescent as to the way of all flesh in a sweaty family bathroom fifty years ago. Preserving her anonymity then, I can at least explain that this revelatory experience took place during a young relative's July birthday party where the grown-ups had been tippling since lunch. As soon as I arrived at the house, this pretty fortyish woman had expressed an amazed interest in my sudden development from tubby boy to blooming youth. She began to display family affection for me with kisses and fondling, provoking the other adults to tipsy laughter, while the youngsters ignored it. I drank two glasses of 'champagne cider' but couldn't relax, feeling smothered by her fond attentions. When everyone went into the garden to eat from cold dishes on trestle tables, I slipped upstairs to use the toilet. As I unlocked the door to return to the party outside, I was startled to see her bright-eyed face peer through the crack. She hushed me with a finger to her full scarlet lips, slid into the bathroom and turned the key. Turning, she embraced me in her plump arms, winked and said, 'I need a nice quiet cuddle from a very handsome young man.'

No one had ever called me handsome before and the thrill of it banished any tension I was feeling. No one but me had ever put their hand on my crotch before either and that was an even giddier thrill. There was never any question of my non-cooperation in what followed. My belt was deftly undone and my trousers and underpants around my knees in the same brisk moments employed in snatching some paper off the toilet roll and wiping telltale lipstick from a mouth that now consumed mine. The nimble fingers that manoeuvred me into position as I first knelt, then lay supine over the candlewick mat that softened the lino, were lightly and expertly applied so as not to precipitate the premature denouement of my galvanised condition. Then thighs were astride me and a silky warm grip had eased on to my tumescence. I knew that if I even brushed my hands against the ample breasts that hung above me in their floral blouse, I would explode too soon in a terrible mixture of ecstasy and despair. Straining for self-control, I concentrated hard on my most recently studied pages of *Deutsches Leben*, the College textbook on German grammar. Then I heard her gasp of pleasure and gone were all thoughts of nominative, genitive, dative and accusative.

Ich bin heiss, ich bin kalt – was schönes Wetter!

Dazed and uncertain but utterly intoxicated with my astonished elation, I was kissed, cleaned up and dressed as rapidly as I'd been manipulated into our coupling. She glanced out of the partly open window at the crowd in the garden and smiled in satisfaction, turned to the mirror, applied fresh lipstick from a handbag I'd never noticed, turned to me to pinch my cheek and said, 'Stay up here a few mintues longer. If anyone asks where you've been, you've got a gippy tummy.'

When I finally rejoined the party I was quite certain that everyone there knew exactly what we'd been doing upstairs. If anyone guessed, if my amorous relative had a reputation for the seduction of unfledged lads, I had no idea but it appeared that our absence hadn't even been noticed. As the party ended, I said my thank yous and goodbyes. She was in laughing conversation with a group on the far side of the room but she broke off to wave me a brief but cheery goodnight. I cycled home wondering if I looked different now. Back home in my bedroom, I searched my reflection for some sign of change and was sure I detected newly acquired wisdom in my eyes.

My second sexual experience was only a week later, sitting in the King's Hall Cinema, Penge, watching Tyrone Power in *Son of Fury*. It was hot, an early August weekday afternoon, and the stalls were empty but for me and an old man who was seated in the row behind me. What with the heat and my fatigue after a late night completing strip cartoons for the *South London Advertiser*, I dozed off. When I woke up a few minutes later, the old man had moved into the seat on my left, my flies were open and he was slyly groping through my underpants, introducing his right hand to my very recently initiated male parts. I froze. For a deranged moment I thought I was still asleep and dreaming. Taking in the situation through half-closed eyes and trying not to panic, I could see the old man's profile, his unfocused gaze fixed upon the screen. His hand continued its gentle exploration. Foremost in my mind was one thought: I didn't want to offend him.

Can you believe that? Instead of outrage, instead of physical resistance, indignant accusation, hysteria, contemptuous withdrawal or shocked collapse, I was so paralysed by the fear of upsetting the finer feelings of a stranger, busy exploring my no-go area without permission of the proprietor, that my first thought was how to avoid hurting his feelings.

What I did was clear my throat and murmur huskily, 'Excuse me, I think there's some mistake.'

Taking this as some kind of encouragement, the man leaned his whiskery chin towards me and rasped with beery breath, 'Can I kiss it?'

I heard myself answer, 'I'm afraid that's not convenient at present.' Then I was gone, wrenched clear and trotting breathlessly toward the exit, clattering through the fire doors, blinking in the sunlit street outside, hastily adjusting my dress, running for the 227 bus, throat dry and hot with shame. That was the last I saw of Tyrone Power in the original sepia-tone south London release of *Son of Fury* and my last homosexual encounter until I met Tyrone Power himself thirteen years later, as I've previously related.

What sort of schoolboy ninny tells the molester of his underage anatomy, 'I'm afraid that's not convenient at present'? The words went round and round in my head like a stupid song lyric that wouldn't leave me alone. How polite could I be? I couldn't meet my own eyes in the mirror, this timid wretch of a boy who hadn't the guts to react angrily to an uninvited intrusion into his trousers. The self-disgust numbed my adolescent sex-drive and stayed with me until the following Christmas when I went to a party at a friend's house and was cured of it by a fat girl with no knickers.

Thereafter my teenage passions were a blend of my own compulsion to adore the current object of my affection with uncritical devotion and the kind of Hollywood behaviour I'd absorbed from the movies. While making time for my schoolwork at Dulwich College, my cartooning and writing for comic weeklies and my amateur performing for any youth club or charity that would let me unleash my jokes in public, I began an optimistic pursuit of admirable girls that was quite at odds with my fear of rejection.

Having passed my Higher Schools Certificate exam, I left school six months before my eighteenth birthday and got myself a job with a new enterprise by the flour magnate turned movie mogul, J. Arthur Rank. He was setting up a cartoon film studio intended to rival Disney and had poached one of their top executives to run it, a steely-eyed Californian named David Hand. With him from Hollywood came legendary storyboard creator, Ralph Wright, and one of Tom-and-Jerry's principal animators, Ray Patterson. From these men I, and forty others, were to learn the wonders of Walt.

The studio was named Gaumont-British Animation Ltd and

located in a rambling mansion, Moor Hall in Cookham, Berkshire. My salary was five pounds a week, all found, and my quarters were in hastily knocked-up out-buildings behind the stables. With a dozen other trainees I sat over a frosted glass panel, set in a sloping desk and illuminated from below. Large sheets of paper, fixed in place by a clamp along the bottom, were interleaved with my fingers so that I could fan them back and forth, checking on the illusion of motion produced by my drawings on each page. In an article I wrote at the time for the May 1947 issue of *Movie Mag*, 'We spent our first weeks making a flag wave and a tap drip. When you're used to drawing a single cartoon and seeing it reproduced in a magazine like the one you are holding for a hundred thousand readers to see, this film animation is tough art. We must draw twenty-four separate pictures for every second that's flashed before your eyes. A ten-minute movie requires 14,400 drawings. At the end of a ten-hour day, I'm what you might call "drawn out".'

With sixty young women resident in the studio dormitories, I wasn't too drawn out to be animated. Once I went sleep-walking. I knew I'd been sleep-walking because I woke up in my own bed.

These adventures involved me in occasional danger of punishment from the girl's boyfriend or father or even the girl herself when she found my declarations of undying love were on general offer. One Saturday afternoon I took a flirtatious cleaner named Molly to the cinema in Maidenhead. While entwined in the back row, we watched one of my heroes, Sid Field, in *London Town*, a truly terrible musical but a record for posterity of four of the great comedian's sketches. By the time we came out it was dark.

She told me her parents were planning to have their tea at the Aerated Bread Company Tea Rooms in the High Street and then come to see the same film we had just seen. It was a three-hour show including the supporting feature, newsreel and trailers so, she said, we could have a bit of time to ourselves back at her house. This turned out to be one of those tiny prefabricated wooden homes that were assembled wherever bombing had destroyed the original houses. The front door let directly on to a tiny sitting room, kitchen and toilet. Her parents' bedroom was on the right and hers, I discovered at once, on the left. It was the size of an airing cupboard with a bed as wide as a plank and a window no bigger than my head. That it was no fit site for sexual callisthenics didn't discourage us in the least, however.

Resting after the preliminary bout, we were whispering endearments when we heard her parents returning. They had walked out of the pictures because of a rowdy element in the audience. Molly pushed me under the blanket as her father tapped on the flimsy door and asked if she was all right, not like her to turn in so early, had she had something to eat? Her reply was that she was OK, ta, was taken as an invitation to open the door and come in. Her dad eased his body into the little chamber and sat on the edge of the bed, trapping my left hand under his bottom. I half suffocated under the blanket as my hand slowly died, crushed under his shifting weight. He chatted to his daughter for what seemed like the entire weekend but was actually about ten minutes. After the third time she had turned down the invitation to join her parents in listening to John Sharman's 'Music Hall' on the Home Service, he kissed her goodnight and withdrew. We then lay there, Molly shaking with suppressed giggles, me examining my left hand for fractures, while her mum and dad chuckled at Stainless Stephen and sang along with Pat Kirkwood. We heard the wireless switched off at nine, every syllable of conversation as the day's events were picked over and every sound as the evening in this shed of a home closed down: cups of tea were made and drunk, washing up was done, clothes were removed, ablutions were completed, the light clicked off and the bed occupied. Mum and dad then embarked upon their Saturday night ritual of passion. After two hours of naked juxtaposition, Molly and I were more than ready to match their tempo instantly and, covered by the noises of their pleasure, find our own.

If you have never had sex while copying the changing rhythms of another and older couple, keeping pace by sound alone so as to remain inaudible to the pair whose activity you are striving to imitate, you might not suppose it to be all that difficult. You'd be wrong. It's hellishly tricky, especially when the bloke you're trying to follow is an old married man in his forties and you're seventeen. I can't tell you how deeply I sympathised when, a dozen years later, I saw Curt Jurgens in a German submarine trying to remain undetected by Robert Mitchum's Yank destroyer above by duplicating his movements. The film was *The Enemy Below* and I writhed in my seat all through that bit.

Having reached our mutual conclusion to my double relief, Molly's dad and I subsided. Within moments he was snoring and I began to plan my escape. Getting dressed in such a cramped cubicle as Molly's bedroom with all the attendant creaks and rustles was out of the question. All I could do was slip on my socks, roll my clothes up into a ball around my shoes and creep as softly as possible from the bed, across the sitting room and out of the front door, praying for an empty street. There had been some bushes beside the pre-fab and perhaps I could dress unseen behind them. By the time I'd figured this out, Molly was asleep.

Summoning up all my nerve, I slid a foot to the floor and gently rose to a standing position, steadying myself with one hand on the door latch. All was silent but for my lover's deep breathing and her dad's comforting snores. The bedroom door opened quietly enough and I pussyfooted the short distance across the dark sitting room, navigating by the light of a lamppost through a window. Gratefully, I found the front door had no noisy bolt to slide back, just a normal yale lock. Then, just as I had the aperture open wide enough for me to make my exit, I heard Molly's mother say softly but very distinctly, 'Goodnight.' I actually mouthed a silent response as I left.

My nude arrival in the street was the signal for the clouds to burst. The torrential downpour would have helped to hide me from public gaze if there had been any public to do any gazing. But this was eleven thirty at night in 1946 and, Saturday night or no Saturday night, Maidenhead was fast asleep.

Since I was carrying the only clothes I had with me to wear for the week ahead, I hunched over them and loped through the wet night, naked but for shoes and socks, all the way back to Moor Hall, sticking to the shadows on the two or three occasions when a car whooshed past. Regaining the sanctuary of my room, I looked at myself in the mirror. Bedraggled, mud spattered, my clothes damp and wrinkled, I gave myself a conspiratorial wink and said, 'A regular Casanova!' A Casanova, it turned out, with a terrible but well-deserved cold. I was lucky that a cold was all I caught. The following Wednesday I was hard at work animating a dewdrop falling from a leaf to a puddle when the boss sent for me. David Hand was mercifully brief. 'When you joined our team your father signed a contract with us on your behalf. Here's a copy. It's open at the Morals Clause. Sure evidence has reached me regarding your breach of that clause with a company employee. We're going to release you to find opportunities for your abilities elsewhere. See the wages clerk on your way out. I believe you owe us money.'

I fell in love every time I met a girl who liked me but only set my heart on marriage when I met my first wife in 1947. Only her refusal could have stopped me and there was no likelihood of that. Thereafter my relationships with women have been most agreeable. They're generally much nicer than men, more emotionally genuine, less selfish, and less lazily impatient about life's dull necessities. They cope with the untidiness of human existence. If it had been left to Adam, we'd all still be standing around in the Garden naked. Women's humour is more realistic and honest than ours. They laugh at truth while we laugh at fiction. Only the youngest girls find 'The Three Stooges' remotely funny; ugly men hitting each other with household objects is for male amusement. Likewise, when the National Film Theatre offers a programme of Laurel and Hardy films, the audience is eighty per cent and the laughter closer to one hundred per cent masculine. Women don't want to watch unsexy, middleaged men on the screen behaving like little boys. They see enough of that in real life.

In a cabaret audience, women react more naturally to my comedy if they are together in a group without men. They can relax in the confidence of their true identities and share that self-determination in what they choose to laugh at together. In the presence of even one heterosexual man, they begin to assume a role that is mutually understood by the others. A different process of selection takes over. As I deliver one comic idea after another, it's quite apparent that what's considered funny by a table of women only will register on a different level with women at a table with men. It's nothing so serious as male intimidation, it's simply a social and sexual adjustment that women make and men generally don't. I think it has more to do with female sensitivity and subtlety than anything else.

In comic subject matter, men will go along with fantasy more readily than women. Tell a woman a joke that begins with, 'These three elephants are playing rugby in the jungle . . . ' and watch her eyes glaze over. Start your story with, 'Clint Eastwood was shooting a film in a nunnery . . . ' and you'll probably have her undivided attention. The first is impossible and stupid, the second could be true and therefore interesting.

Men have had the reputation for enjoying blue humour at stag parties ever since the days when coarse jokes were considered unsuitable for a lady's ears. I've found it fascinating to observe the change that has taken place over the years of my career. Today many men flinch at the intimate honesty of some female comedians who have defied convention to deal openly with the comic aspects of childbirth, menstruation, orgasms, premature ejaculation and even mastectomies. Done skilfully, such comedy can dispel inhibition and lighten fear. Women are able to welcome that development much more comfortably than those men who prefer their humour to concern the stupidity of wives, the ignorance of immigrants and the mockery of homosexuals.

The Women's Lib champion Gloria Steinem said that a woman reading *Playboy* feels a little like a Jew reading a Nazi manual. If that's a gross over-reaction from the feminist seventies, my male over-reaction in the forties had been equally, although dissimilarly, gross.

At the age of fourteen or so I had discovered *Health and Efficiency*, an amber-hued magazine for and about nudists. Whether or not the articles were readable, they were never read. All that interested this red-blooded lad were the pictures: half-tone snaps of naked men and women at goose-pimpled play on overcast tennis courts and bleak beaches. In the action shots, taken at naturist clubs from Ormskirk to Oswestry, the bare facts about the British were exposed as fairly unappealing. These were people of average anatomy, some scrawny, some fleshy, all members of the club peculiar only in that they had no members of their own.

Where the photographer had failed to catch his subject with their loins obscured by racquets or medicine balls or picnic baskets, the area where human reproductive organs are located was always a blur of retouched negative. The stimulus this gave to my prurient imagination was far greater than could have been caused by leaving the hairy bits just as they were.

Other photos, more exhaustively examined, were of carefully posed models, gazing gravely into space from some dappled arbour or sandy cover while sporting nothing but a wartime perm and hard-to-get lipstick. These utility sirens, as impenetrable as mermaids, took their place among my unattainable dreams alongside Hollywood pinups of Jane Frazee and Hedy Lamarr. Thus were my sexual ideals shaped in adolescence; no Hitlerite plotting the Holocaust, Ms. Steinem, just a randy youth in awe of beautiful mysteries. And one mysterious beauty became the object of an adolescent fixation.

At first she simply appeared in the magazine more often than the other models, a fresh-faced maiden with a slender form and a curiously shy air. Within a year or two I recognised her nude portraits in the pocket-sized monthlies *Lilliput* and *Men Only*. She was developing a more womanly appearance now, clothed only in shadows by a photographer named Roye. By the time I was seventeen I had managed to collect a scrapbook full of her. I had secretly christened her Laura after the spellbinding character in the 1944 film of that name. Even so, I wrote to one publication, a cheaply produced 'jumble of jokes and girlie pix' called *Prestige*, to ask the name of 'the model holding the anchor in the enclosed picture' but had no reply. I don't think I expected or really wanted one. Distance lent enchantment. And time, of course, lent distance.

The next six or seven years brought manhood, marriage and the foundation of my career. At the age of twenty-four, brimming with confidence and hungry for my share of life, I felt as pleased with myself as Juan Peron: 'If I had not been born me, I would have liked to be me'. Radio and TV scripts were pouring out of our little gag factory and I was sure that the jokes I hadn't yet written were better than the jokes others had. As for romances, they were a necessary demonstration of my new sophistication.

I was dallying with every pretty actress and singer in our shows, flirting indiscriminately and converting enough tries to keep my ego inflated. There was an amazed but immodest feeling of triumph at finding my seductions successful.

Here I was entering the Kensington bed of Fleet Street's most luminously lovely columnist and, if I felt any resentment that it wasn't an exclusive province, there was a compensatory thrill in cuddling in post-coital dampness while she imparted the intimate secrets of famous men with whom I shared her expert charms. So

Peter Finch likes that, does he? And Christopher Plummer does this? Oh, I was up there with the stars all right.

'The Name's the Same' was typical of television's early panel shows. Four celebrities sat behind a table and were allowed one question at a time in their mission to discover the famous name of an otherwise undistinguished challenger. I found myself booked to appear for the regulation fee of ten guineas (ten pounds, 50p) together with film director Walter Forde, actress Patricia Roc, comedian Vic Wise and the host, Peter Martyn. We assembled for a giggly rehearsal, retired to the Green Room for sherry and biscuits, then took our places again for the live transmission before a small audience of women in hats and male pensioners. Together we guessed that a sweaty Frenchman had the same name as the singer Dickie Valentine. Next, we failed to winkle out the truth about a fishmonger called Oscar Wilde. I was quite poised and witty about that. Then the third contestant made her entrance and what wits I had deserted me.

It was Laura. There she was, walking in and sitting and speaking and smiling at the panel – and there I was, transported back to my teenage trance, blushing deeply, hot-eyed and dry-mouthed and terribly guilty. Surely she knew, surely everyone there must know, how my scissors had clipped out her naked poses, my fingers had lovingly applied the glue that fixed her in my private collection, my enraptured gaze had explored every visible inch of her. 'Bob?' said Peter Martyn.

I started and became aware that the programme had been proceeding without me. What had been asked and answered? I had no idea. I cleared my throat raspily and ventured, 'Is your famous namesake alive or dead?"

'Are *you* alive or dead, Bob? Our guest has just told us her illustrious predecessor is no more.'

'Sorry – er – did she pose for – er – that is, are you the Mona Lisa?'

'No, she's not and you're no oil-painting either, Bob. Walter?'

So the questioning continued while I did my best to pull myself together. I just couldn't get over it. I hadn't even thought about Laura for seven years and more. Now my two-dimensional, black-and-white, glossy paper obsession was made flesh before me and I was feeling confused and stupid and entertaining daft, self-important fancies about predestination.

'Well, time's up and you've beaten the panel, madam. Won't you tell us and the viewers at home just what famous name is yours?'

My Laura smiled devastatingly at us and said, 'My name is Mary Celeste.'

One more contestant delayed us while we narrowed his clues down to a successful guess from Pat Roc – 'I think you're Stan Laurel!' – and the show was over.

I ran after the retreating floor manager to ask where our challengers were accommodated and he directed me to the dressing room area but I was too late. Mary Celeste had embarked.

There was no deflecting me. First thing the following morning I was in the producer's office begging his secretary to give me an address and phone number for the woman of my almost forgotten dreams. She found the application form among her files: *Miss – Mary-Ann Celeste – Age: 27 – Occupation: exhibition demonstrator*. Then came her address in Hampstead and her agent's phone number.

The agent stone-walled my enquiries so I wrote her a letter. It wasn't a humble note from a fan, it was a shamefully arrogant letter from a puffed-up catechumen of show biz, an ignorant novice blinded by his first fragment of fame. It told her how enamoured of her I had become in my teens, how I'd accumulated and prized her nude studies and how sure I'd become that fate had led her to me. I offered to meet her anywhere, any time, and promised that she wouldn't be disappointed. As I recall it, I shudder with disgrace.

She replied after about a week, inviting me to come to her flat off Haverstock Hill at six p.m. the following Saturday. I was to confirm by phone to her agent's personal assistant. I confirmed.

The June evening was warm. Despite the cocky tone of my letter, I remember feeling very apprehensive as I mounted a whitened wooden staircase, strewn with honeysuckle, and approached her front door. As soon as I touched her doorbell she appeared, calm and small and wearing a neck-to-floor robe in dark blue velvet. She said, 'Please, let's not talk' and ushered me

171

into her bedroom. The curtains were drawn. I looked around for somewhere to put the flowers I'd brought but she took them and left the room, saying, 'We haven't got very long. Only till seven. Get undressed.' I was numb with bewilderment. It was all going much too fast for comprehension. Had my letter so affected her that she couldn't wait to consummate our foreordained love affair? I took off my smart leisure jacket and tie, slipped out of my shoes and sat on the bed.

She reappeared carrying two glasses of champagne. 'Still dressed? Come along, don't be bashful. Once I unzip this robe, I'll be naked too.'

Attempting what I hoped passed for *savoir-faire*, I offered some urbane wisecrack and stripped off completely. She made some flattering remarks and, skillfully evading my grasp, pulled the topsheets away and pushed me back onto the bed. Then she began to describe the wonderful things she was going to do to me, meanwhile bending to reach under the bed and bring out a shallow box of ropes and handcuffs. I was too anxious to preserve my air of worldly wisdom to protest. 'I know you've done all these things before,' she crooned as she fastened my wrists to the bedhead. 'But I promise you it's never been quite like this.'

Her hands were quick and her voice soothing and within moments I was bound hand and foot, spreadeagled naked on top of the bed. Again she left the room, murmuring 'The oil should be warm by now.'

How long I lay there I'm not sure. Certainly an hour passed, probably more. By that time I'd made myself hoarse from calling her name and sore from jerking uselessly at my bonds. Then the silence of the flat was broken by the same doorbell I had rung what seemed an age ago. I heard excited greetings and laughter as callers were shown into some other room. This was now repeated several times until I estimated that a party of about twenty guests had arrived. I could hear loud conversation with bursts of mirth and the clinking of glasses. Despite the warmth of the evening, I felt a chilly film of sweat upon my supine body.

Suddenly the bedroom door swung open and a throng of chattering, laughing strangers crowded in. They filled the room, some sitting on the bed, others finding perches elsewhere, all noisily busy with one another. They ignored me completely. I was invisible to them. The naked man chained to the bed wasn't there.

After ten minutes or so I tried talking to them but they played deaf. One older woman put her ashtray on my stomach. I heaved it off but she didn't seem to notice. I tried laughing it off, feigning tears, even explaining to all about me that I had a blood condition and needed to take my tablets once an hour or I couldn't be answerable for the consequences. Nothing I said or did had any effect on them. After half an hour had passed they began to drift out of the bedroom in twos and threes. The door closed behind the last of them and I was alone again.

There isn't much more to the story. The party ended some hours later and, about one o'clock in the morning, someone entered the darkened room where I had fallen asleep and opened the handcuffs that held my right hand. Then they were gone and I was hard at work untying the ropes that fastened first my left hand and then my ankles. I gathered up my clothes, dressed and left the quiet flat, pausing only to relieve myself in the bushes. What if someone saw me? My humiliation was already complete.

Over the ensuing years I've been told stories of similar experiences happening to other foolish men, stories with bizarre and sometimes painful embellishments. Of course the same comeuppance may have been visited upon suckers before and after my lesson in female retribution. Then again, these tales may be apocryphal variations on my actual experience. This was simply the way it happened to me. Whenever I hear the story of the ship called *Mary Celeste* and its mysteriously absent crew, I think of my own evening of invisibility and I laugh. Not a lot but I do laugh.

My affinities with women have been deeper, less superficial and more natural than most of the friendships I have shared with men. The failure by observers to appreciate the nature of my cordial relations with certain women during my life has often led to the inevitable conclusion that these companionships had more to do with amour than amity. To deny that sex was involved is as bad as insisting that it was. Such knowledge is the prerogative of the two persons most concerned in the rapport. Three of the most admirable women friends I have ever known were singers. Two of them are dead but I remember our mutual affection with gratitude.

I first saw Doretta Morrow in the 1955 London stage production of *Kismet* at the Stoll Theatre. At the performance I attended she had a slight mishap. When the Wazir's guards seized her and brought her to her knees before him, her bra burst open and her boobs popped out. I instantly fell in love with both of them, although I never dreamed of attaining proximity.

Three years later the London impresario Harold Fielding obtained the rights to a US television spectacular called 'Aladdin' with songs by the great but ailing Cole Porter. It was lavishly mounted at the London Coliseum with a cast of seventy under the direction of Robert Helpmann. Instead of following the British panto tradition of casting a girl as Principal Boy, it was decided to adopt the example of the American production and have the role of Aladdin played by a young man. Despite my shortcomings as a singer and dancer, I had proved vaguely acceptable one year earlier playing Buttons in the Manchester Palace's *Cinderella*, so I was offered the part, vying with Cliff Richard to become the first male to play Aladdin in the history of English pantomime. My mother, the Widow Twankey, was to be played by Ronald Shiner, Abanazar by Alan Wheatley, the Emperor of China by Ian Wallace, but negotiations were still in progress for the casting of the Princess Baroulbedour. Fielding wanted a Broadway star and he was in discussion with the agents of Barbara Cook, Carol Lawrence and Florence Henderson. I asked him if he had considered Doretta Morrow. His eyes lit up. So did mine.

Doretta arrived in London a couple of weeks later and I have good reason to remember the first day she came into the rehearsal room. In preparation for my first meeting with this black-eyed male fantasy, I applied a clear lotion to my face and hands that would make me appear to be lightly but attractively tanned. It was a new idea from New York called ManTan and with it had come an aftershave lotion called Gravel. There was real gravel in the bottle, all the way from Alaska, plus a gold tie pin. I splashed some on but I couldn't smell it due to a headcold. My face hadn't turned the appealing shade of pale amber described on the Mantan label so I put on a second coat. Then I added another dousing of Gravel. During the following hour, I used up the contents of both bottles, still unable to detect any darkening of my complexion or much improvement in my personal odour.

Had I read the ManTan instructions properly I would have known that a single application was quite enough to tint the skin overnight. In my vain and idiotic impatience I had soaked myself with a dozen times too much tanning fluid and, as for the strongly scented Gravel, my blocked up nostrils would have been impervious to a burning rubber moustache. When I walked into the rehearsal room, I attracted alarmed stares and sniffs from everyone in the cast. Helpmann, stylishly ignoring my appearance and effluvium, guided me to the piano where Doretta was setting keys in which to sing.

'Miss Morrow, here is your Aladdin.'

She looked at me and took it all in.

'You're Aladdin?' she said. 'You could have fooled me. You look like Geronimo and you smell like Tinkabell.'

Doretta was direct and funny but, beneath her self-assurance, very fragile. A long and once passionate love affair with the oft-married Alfred Drake, her leading man in *Kismet* both sides of the Atlantic, had been crumbling painfully. She told me he'd once grabbed her long dark hair and swung her head against a wall. 'That's when I realised I was crumbling painfully too.'

The London job had come as a godsend. Along with the job came my infatuation, a reassurance of her attractiveness. Over the following months in the theatre, her natural response to my uncritical regard was to return my affection. We shared a thousand hours of conversation and I was both intoxicated and uplifted by her. My adoration of Doretta continued after the six-month run of *Aladdin* but she ended our friendship for practical reasons: she had an elderly Italian mama to support, her singing voice was losing its quality, her Broadway career was in decline, above all she had been offered marriage by a wealthy London stockbroker who had been wooing her to no avail since *Kismet*. He didn't like me. Before the end of the year she was established in her new role as the glamorous hostess of countless dinner parties in her middle-aged fiancé's handsome Kensington house. I wasn't invited to the wedding.

There's a brief postscript: a few years later Doretta called out of the blue to invite me to lunch. We chatted rather awkwardly over the meal and eventually I asked her why she had contacted me.

She said she wanted to be loved again, loved as totally and as naively as I had loved her before. I found her honesty and vulnerability touching then and, as I type these words, I am touched again by the memory. The hopelessness of trying to relive the past was bleakly apparent to us both as we sat there. Neither of us seemed able to fill the silence with suitable words. The following year Doretta died of a brain tumour.

During the period between the collapse of my first marriage and the romance which led to my second, current and final, I remember no stranger dalliance than my night of passion with an exotic striptease dancer at the Sunset Strip Casino Night Club in Norfolk. The proprietor was a careful man who believed that money was made flat for packing. In fact he kept his packed in a very large concrete safe with a mattress on top where his children slept. His show biz philosophy was simple: 'Give 'em a gamble, bare tits and a laugh and the buggers'll shit money all night.' On this occasion, I was the laugh and the bare tits belonged to a stunning stripper named Mona Maravillosa.

She was there when I arrived at six p.m. for rehearsal with the musicians, smiling a brilliant and vaguely familiar smile, a big girl not unlike Anjelica Huston with the same huskily sexy voice. She fetched me a coffee and then sat watching me run through my songs with rapt attention and illuminated eyes. After I'd finished, she crossed the dance floor, took my arm, kissed my cheek and told me I was unreal, which I hoped was intended kindly. Then she spoke a phrase I've come to dread over the years:

'You don't remember me, do you?'

I hate to hurt anyone's feelings by admitting that meeting them made so little impression on me that I've no recollection of doing so, but lying about it is usually worse, so I smarmed my way out of it by saying, 'I can't believe I could have met a girl like you and forgotten about it.'

'Glasgow, 1963,' she said.

'I did a season in a show called *Five Past Eight* at the Alhambra.'

'And I was one of the dancers.'

'Of course you were, now I remember!' I lied.

'You only had eyes for somebody else then, didn't you?'

It seemed to me I'd had eyes for anything in a skirt at the time, although I had briefly romanced with Yana, the beautiful but rather eccentric singing star of the show. Yana had first got my attention four years earlier by opening my dressing room door and accurately flinging a large jar of cold cream twelve feet through the air to bounce off my skull. We'd been in the middle of the 1959 summer season at the time, in the King's Theatre, Southsea, under the excruciating title *South Sea Bobble*. Her boyfriend then was the popular London tailor Cyril Castle and he apologised for the swelling on my cranium, explaining, 'She's upset with you, Bob, you're the only man in the show who hasn't tried to pull her.'

I knew her reputation as a ball-breaker – she'd once pursued Cyril round every nightclub in London's West End dressed only in slippers and a transparent nightgown and carrying a carving knife with which she planned, she shrieked, 'to cut off his meat and two veg', so she wasn't a lady to annoy twice in a row. Consequently, when we opened in Glasgow I duly pulled her.

Now here I was a couple of years later, not pulling but being pulled. Mona was making it clear that she was set upon my immediate seduction and, presented with such an ample and amorous partner for the evening, it would have taken a much stronger man than me to resist the ineluctable outcome.

Stowing my bag and clothes in my own bedroom, I was sharing a bottle of Krug in Mona's by seven o'clock. We dined together in the club by candlelight and I ordered the best wine on the list in an effort to compensate for the cuisine, all embellished with eye contact and verbal foreplay galore.

Her cabaret was, she explained, a trip round the world. I was alarmed to hear it but her interpretation of the phrase was innocent – she stripped to a tape of exotic melodies and rhythms, matching the music with everything from Turkish bellydancing to the Charleston and stripping all the while. She finished on 'Land of Hope and Glory', posing as a nude Britannia with helmet and Union Jack. I wondered how many men in her audience would be standing to attention.

Watching Mona's performance from the back of the cabaret room, I was struck simultaneously by her endearing attempt to offer a bit of showmanship in her act, all of it wasted on a crowd of good old boys off the East Anglian farms, her fine body and the strong feeling that I had seen her dance before. I wondered how I'd missed her presence backstage in the Glasgow theatre only a couple of years earlier. She finished at ten-thirty, my act went on at eleven and if I had not had strict instructions from the proprietor to work fast and make it short so as not to keep his punters away from the gambling for too long, I would have done so anyway. The night was made for better ways of proving my stamina than a joke marathon. By a quarter past midnight I was in the shower and by half past, knocking on Mona's door. She was very excited and doubled my ardour by saying, 'I've wanted you ever since that first day of rehearsal in the Alhambra.'

Now I come to a conflict of detail and taste. I'll try to explain without offending you. The physical act of having sex with Mona was not unlike plunging your feet into an apple pie bed. You think you're going all the way and you can't. If that's unclear, imagine thrusting your toes into a gumboot only to find the foot of it stuffed with a cushion. Try pulling on gloves that have the fingers sewn closed halfway up. By this time I'm sure I've got through to your imagination.

My frustration must have been obvious. She was so doleful about it, I could have wept for her. I stammered, 'Is there a Dutch cap, er, a diaphragm, some obstruction . . . ?'

'No, that's me,' she said with a sad little laugh. 'The surgeons can't make them any deeper.'

'Surgeons?'

'I had the operation six months ago. You're the first one to try it.'

How long I lay numbed beside her while the facts sank in, I'm not sure. Of course I'd seen her dancing in the Glasgow show, but as a boy dancer. He had fancied me then but it was obvious that I wasn't for turning. Now he was a girl, and a gorgeous one at that, she'd been eager to complete unfinished business with me and I had been given the honour of christening her newly installed anatomical features, from silicone boobs to plastic pudenda. Once again I found one thought was paramount in my mind: how do I avoid hurting Mona's feelings? Fortunately in a way, my own anatomy didn't give a damn about hurting her feelings and gave the answer in the usual unmistakable manner.

'Never mind,' said Mona with cheerful resignation, 'it was pretty good for an out-of-town tryout. And it's not too late for a cup of tea.'

If I reminisce without remorse, it's thanks to the fact that, no matter how necessarily clandestine the conduct of some of my relationships may have been, no one ever made me feel guilty. To any precious women friends in my past who may read these words, thanks for that.

Since I fell in love with Jackie there have been no other deep friendships or romances with other women in my life. She is the dearest friend I have ever had and my very best love affair. If you're lucky enough to find such a companion, the risk of losing her through infidelity is greatly reduced by your own contentment and the consequent lack of temptation. As any gardener knows, it is possible for an old rake to turn over a new leaf.

In 1969 I began proposing and Jackie kept refusing. My anxiety was to protect her financially in the event of my death and hers was a fear of rocking the love boat. In May 1973 we attended a civic function in outer Birmingham where some tinpot councillor kept elbowing her aside to talk to me. She was only my secretary, not my wife. This attitude made me so angry that I insisted that we set a date. She gave in with real trepidation and we consulted our accountant who suggested that the most tax-efficient time to wed would be in October. He jogged our memories again in September and, while Jackie made hurried arrangements with Marylebone Town Hall, I searched Bond Street for a ring that would fit her slender finger.

The only one that came anywhere near the right size cost £7, confirmation that I had found the ideal woman.

My manager Peter Prichard and publicist Tony Barrow arranged for a barrage of photographers and reporters to meet our noon arrival at Marylebone on 4 October. Jackie looked very lovely in a dress I'll never let her give away and we held a jampacked reception at the Churchill Hotel, with her large and loving family easily outnumbering my younger son, daughter and two aunts. It was all very carefree until Prichard reminded us that we were due for TV coverage at the opening night of *Carry On, London* at the Victoria Palace and we rushed off so quickly that we forgot to cut the cake. Our romantic wedding night was spent apart, Jackie at home watching the telly with her mum and my daughter while I drove to Benson, Oxfordshire, to do midnight cabaret at The Chicken in the Basket. When I told the audience that I'd got married that day, they didn't believe it. I didn't quite believe it myself.

20

GOLDEN BOY

1957–1962

*In which our hero is shot in a studio, sued in a theatre,
blinded on a stage and rolled into a pit. After feeling a
little queer at the seaside, there's a little touch of Harry.
Then back to London, where acting on the boards leads
to speaking from the floor, dogs are exercised and a few
pounds are shed*

There's a term I detest although it's hardly likely anyone will ever
apply it to me again. The first time I heard it was from film
producer Peter Rogers in 1957 when he cast me as the juvenile
lead in the very first of his 'Carry On' comedies, *Carry On,
Sergeant*. He came out of the projection room where he'd just
been watching me in that morning's rushes. 'I'm more than
delighted with you, my lad,' he said, slapping me on the back.
'You're going to be my golden boy.' He never hired me again.

On the strength of the film's commercial success, and on the
off-chance that I might have had something to do with it, I was
cast by other producers as the hero in a small handful of slickly
made movies with the same sort of seventy thousand pound
budget as the Carry Ons, some of which I helped to write, among
them *Dentist in the Chair, Dentist on the Job, She'll Have to Go*
and *Weekend with Lulu*. Though they all did moderately well at
the box office, further offers of starring roles in movies never
materialised. No golden boy after all.

Impresario Harold Fielding used the expression next, around
Christmas, 1959. I'd opened as Aladdin in his production at the
London Coliseum and it was doing well. He introduced me to a
journalist: 'Mr Swaffer, meet our golden boy.' Four weeks later
Fielding was suing me for some supposed breaches of contract
and we weren't speaking. Gold had been devalued again.

It was never clear to me why Fielding took against me so fiercely during the run of that lavish pantomime but he did, with a vengeance. His litigation became so hostile that I had to engage the fast rising lawyer, David Jacobs, who disposed of the lawsuits with such serene skill that Fielding afterwards took him on as his own legal adviser.

Meanwhile, the allegations against me had worsened my migraine attacks to the point where they caused temporary blindness, not very convenient in such a physical role. Audiences were treated to some curious variations to the action of the show over the next few months.

They saw the singing, smiling Aladdin dance along the stage, collide with the proscenium arch and crack his head on a gilded pilaster. They witnessed his groping around in the treasure-filled cave, quite unable to find a magic lamp that was in plain view to everyone else. One audience watched as he took up a position three feet too far to the right and rubbed his lamp to summon the genie while standing astride the flash box. Bang! The big laugh made it almost worth having burnt buttocks and toasted testicles. In another scene, Aladdin defies the Emperor's edict forbidding any of his subjects to look upon the Princess as she passes by in a glamorous procession by concealing himself on top of a tall flower stall. From this vantage point, he sees her beautiful face and is smitten. With normal sight I could fling myself across the stage towards the twelve-foot structure, sprinting so fast that it only took me one big leap and two more rapid moves to arrive on the top. After the parade had gone by, with its glittering costumes and jewelled ponies and the princess singing upon her palanquin, I'd drop from my perch to the floor in a forward roll, rising to my feet at the very front edge of the stage and declaim my line, 'I'm in love, I'm in love!', winning a nice little round of applause for not breaking my neck.

My vision went to a milky blur during the song that preceded the procession so that, when the time came for my high-speed rush to the flower stall, I could only fumble my way forward to where I thought it should be. I must have missed it by a couple of feet. The dancers at the forefront of the parade were already on the stage as I stumbled blindly past them to bounce off a piece of scenery in the wings. Realising that I'd come too far, I started picking my way back, negotiating a path through the pageant like a drunk. One bright soul leading the ponies broke away to take my arm and guide me quickly to the stall. The passing spectacle partly screened my unsteady climb up its wooden shafts and I collapsed gratefully into the hammock of sacking on the top, praying that my sight would return before the four-minute cavalcade was concluded. It didn't. As the tail end of the Princess's train departed, I tried to do my usual trick of falling foreward in a roll, tumbling head over heels to the front of the stage and then rising to my feet like a third-rate gymnast to yell my line. I was stupid as well as blind.

I met someone quite recently who was present at this performance of *Aladdin*. She told me, 'It's over thirty years ago and the only thing that I can clearly remember about the show is the moment when you jumped down off a sort of flower shop on wheels, you curled yourself into a ball, and then you rolled over and over towards us until you rolled right off the front of the stage and fell into the orchestra pit. It was so silly I couldn't stop laughing! I'm amazed you didn't kill yourself, doing a stunt like that every night.'

★ ★ ★ ★ ★

Casual sex in the sixties was exactly that. Condoms weren't called condoms, the euphemism was 'something for the weekend' and they were generally used more to prevent pregnancy than infection. Today, before climbing into bed together, people should boil themselves.

If I say my marriage was subjected to the strain of impetuous promiscuity, this should not be taken as a reference to my wife's behaviour since, as I explained at the start, any censure in these memoirs is reserved for me and my conduct. All that concerned me as the decade began was that my wife and three children appeared well cared for and happy, work was plentiful and pleasing, skies were blue and sex was casual. Alas, as in so many things casual, it had its casualties.

If I promised too much and delivered too little in these brisk little trysts, if I disappointed hearts more vulnerable than my own by trotting off to woo the next one, I confess I felt no more guilt than a cockerel. Each *affaire d'amour* was another show, a one-woman audience to be persuaded and entertained and thanked before moving on. On all sides were lovely girls requiring admiration and older actresses in need of fresh reassurance of their charms. I was thirty-something and as surrounded by temptation as an alcoholic in a distillery. Although I loved my wife, I concluded that the difference between love and sex was that love creates stress and sex relieves it. I still loved my mother too, but she would still have nothing to do with me. More emotional stress, more unemotional sex. It all seemed so inconsequential, games for grown-ups, and I gloried immaturely in each girl's regard, believing myself entitled to it; her temporary golden boy.

The show that had brought me back to the Blackpool Wintergardens in 1960 was a lavish musical set in a nightclub called *Don't Stop, You're Killing Me!* Co-starring were America's Peter Sisters, a trio of cheerfully obese ladies led by Mattie, the one who'd say, 'We ain't coloured all the time, folks, we white same as you during the day. This is show business – we just flauntin' our pigment for yo' amusement!' We also paraded a chorus line of happy-go-lucky girls, most of whom could open a jar of Vaseline with their toes. I fell in love with each of them in turn, and every time it was heels over head.

My extra-marital escapades were sharply curtailed by an oriental microbe. The Hong Kong flu epidemic returned to the Fylde Coast, I caught it, ignored it and developed pneumonia with a temperature that hovered over a hundred and three degrees for four days. I knew I was recovering when I heard the doctor telling my wife, 'He must drink plenty of fluids,' and myself croaking, 'It's bloody hard to drink anything else.'

Making low-budget comedy films and 'Candid Camera' occupied me until I opened my 1961 summer season on the Britannia Pier, Great Yarmouth. Today it's hard to believe how many attractions such seaside towns could profitably offer their local residents and holidaymakers. In its five theatres that summer the Norfolk resort had room for Bruce Forsyth, Arthur Haynes, Joe Baker and Jack Douglas, Billy Fury, Arthur Worsley, West Indian recording stars Emile Ford and Jimmy Lloyd, Billy Dainty, Joan Regan, Leslie Crowther, Winifred Atwell, Roy Castle, Val Doonican, Ruby Murray, Tommy Steele, David Whitfield, Lonnie Donegan, Ken Dodd, Russ Conway, Frankie

Howerd, plus all the dancers, musicians and supporting acts that made up the resident shows and Sunday concerts.

While I was by no means the only member of this gallimaufry to be suspected of libertinism, it was widely though secretly supposed that my friendship with a fulgently glamorous singer starring locally was absorbing all my Cyprian energies. Only one of those listed above mistakenly believed that my unquenchable licentiousness would make me fair game for a seductive approach.

As a result, I made my entrance on stage one Friday evening in such a state of nervous astonishment that I completely forgot my words. My opening song went unsung and four minutes of welcoming gags unspoken. I just stood there and stared silently at the audience as if in the grip of catalepsy. It was the reverse of the usual situation on a Friday first house when it's the seaside audiences that tend to be comatose. After the crowd's first nervous laugh and a long and uncomfortable silence, the stage manager lowered the curtain. That gave me a chance to pull myself together while I asked anxious members of our company to remind me of the words I had sung and the patter I had used in every performance for the previous four months. Five minutes later, the curtain rose again and I re-entered to considerably reduced applause, sang my song of greeting and excused myself with some desperate jokes about amnesia.

I'm so absent-minded.
In fact, I attracted quite a crowd at the railway station
when I kissed the train goodbye,
jumped on my wife and went to town.

The reason for my shocked state of mind had occurred an hour or so earlier in the big house I'd hired for the season to accommodate my family and Gary's nurse, Nora. School holidays had ended and my wife had returned to London with the children, leaving me alone in this suddenly empty mansion.

Despite the early September heat, its large rooms were cool with old-fashioned furnishings, dark wood panelling on the walls, heavy brocade curtains and mullioned windows. I was dressed in a beach shirt, blue linen slacks and sandals, having spent the morning on my mail and phonecalls, prepared myself a light lunch and set up my 16mm projector to watch a hired film, a romantic trifle directed in 1935 by a favourite director, William Wyler. For me to have appreciated the irony of its title would have required my prescient awareness of a prolepsis: it was called *The Gay Deception*. In those days, the adjective 'gay' had no homosexual connotation, meaning only merry and sportive, or dissipated and loose living. Perhaps, by those original definitions, I was rather gay myself, although not so sportive or loose living as supposed by the person who phoned as I was changing reels.

'Bob, it's me. Look, could you spare me five minutes of your time? No, listen, listen, it's ever so important or I wouldn't come bothering you, would I? To tell the truth, I'm a bit desperate and I could do with your advice on a personal matter, yes, very personal. Are you alone? Yes? Because I'd like to keep this confidential, d'you see, just between us, yes. Oh, I'm ever so grateful, no, I am. I'll come round now, shall I, and bring a nice bit of Battenberg for our tea? In twenty minutes then. I'm on my way.'

I decided to use the twenty minutes to continue watching the movie and so kept the sitting room darkened with curtains drawn. When my backdoor bell rang, I switched off the projector, clicked on a reading lamp, walked barefoot through the kitchen, turning on the heat to boil the kettle for tea, and opened the door to my caller. He stepped forward on the kitchen mat, pulling apologetic faces, and said, 'Didn't want to use the front door, eyes every-bloody-where, yes, neighbours! No, all that talk, you can hear them, "Ooh, 'allo, what's Frankie Howerd doing round 'ere? Slumming?"'

After making the tea and some small talk, I led Frankie into the sitting room. That ratty wig of his was more than usually askew over the famous horsey face. His pithecoid arms hung from the short sleeves of a mustard sports shirt, streaked with sweat stains and worn loose over wrinkled brown slacks which ended well above hairy ankles, white from lack of sunshine. He shuffled his worn moccasins and peered around the dimly lit interior.

'Ooh, what's all this low lighting in aid of? Seduction fills the air!'

'I'll open the curtains.'

'No, don't, leave them. It makes it easier to talk somehow.'

I put the tray on a low table and perched on the old dark leather settee, indicating the matching armchair nearby for Frankie, but he took his seat next to me. I poured two cups of tea and settled back into my corner of the sofa. 'You sounded very serious on the phone, Frankie. What's the problem?'

'Don't be in such a rush. Let us observe the niceties . . . *and* the nicer teas! There's one! No, let's have a bit of social intercourse before I expose myself to your counsel. Why don't we talk about you for a bit?'

'Well, I . . .'

'That's enough! No sense in overdoing it. On our own, are we?'

'Yes, I told you, my wife has taken the kids back to . . .'

'How long have you been a married man?'

'Um, twelve years come November. Why?'

'It's that experience, you see. I've never been married but now I'm seriously thinking about it. You know Joan.'

I knew the lovely actress Joan Greenwood but had always thought that rumours of a romance between her and Howerd had been the work of a larky publicist. It wasn't that I harboured the slightest suspicion about his real sexual preferences; in fact I assumed he had none. He seemed curiously neuter to me, physically inactive, as epicene as Kenneth Williams. He sipped his tea and changed the subject, assuming a haughty tone of voice as if bored with the new topic. 'What do you think of my position in the business now? What are people saying, you can tell me, Bob, how do they see me? Mmmm? I mean, I don't really give a stuff what they bloody think. "That old has-been", is that what they call me? I couldn't care less, I'll tell you that.'

It was true that Frankie Howerd's career had foundered since his radio fame in the late 1940s and early 1950s. Jack Jay, owner of Yarmouth's tiny Windmill Theatre, had booked him as a support act for his top of the bill draw, another star whose popularity had peaked early and was temporarily waning, Tommy Steele. The rest of the cast was listed underneath Steele, with Howerd's name at the very bottom of the bill, full width but without any face-saving phrase like 'Special Guest Star' or 'Added Attraction'. No one in Great Yarmouth that summer could have predicted Steele's triumphant return to favour in

stage and movie musicals, although Hollywood lay only half a
dozen years ahead for him. But even less likely was the
rediscovery of Howerd's comic brilliance. He was regarded as a
spent force, professionally washed up. Ironically, the opening of
the night club that would revive his fortunes and turn him into
the darling of the satire set was only seven or eight weeks in the
future. The Establishment Club at 18 Greek Street, Soho, would
have its riotous launch on 5 October 1961, and Howerd would
eventually become its overnight sensation.

'Frankie, surely you didn't come round to ask my opinion of
how your ghastly agent is mishandling your business?'

Note my self-assurance at this point. It wasn't destined to last.

He adopted a hushed, confidential manner. 'It's the sex act,
you see. I've got a problem with it. What I want to know from
you is this – can a man perform properly without being fully
erect? D'you follow? I mean, is it natural for a man to ejaculate
while his cock is only half hard? I reckon you'd know, with all
your experience and that. Pour us another cuppa, my throat's
gone all dry.'

Only mildly alarmed, I took his empty cup. 'Wouldn't you be
better off talking to a doctor about this, Frankie?'

'Don't fob me off, Bob. My ego is fragile enough. I've come to
you as a friend. None of my friends are doctors. I'm appealing to
you for help as a man I trust. Look, I didn't want to do this but
the only way you'll ever understand is to look and see what I'm
talking about.'

To my astonishment, he threw himself lengthwise and
alongside me on the dark leather settee while simultaneously
dragging his slacks down and his shirt up. His penis was already
excited and he began to tug at it. 'Look, look, don't turn away,
don't make me ashamed of myself! For Jesus Christ's sake, have
some compassion! Be my friend!'

His left fist gripped my right forearm so fiercely that his empty
cup danced in the saucer I was holding and I had to catch it with
my left hand. I was quite glad of something so mundane to
occupy me.

I balanced the crockery with difficulty, gripped it with my left
fingers and thumb and slowly manoeuvred it over to and down
onto the table, giving the task my total concentration.

'See, it's not getting any stiffer! A man can't penetrate a

woman's whatsit with half a bone, can he? Put your hand on my belly, perhaps that'll do it!'

It's easy to look back and see what I should have done. Whatever that might have been, I couldn't do it. I was petrified with confusion, bowled over by this incredible turn of events. My mixed emotions were a stew of pity, horror, disbelief, suppressed hysteria, including a withdrawal of involvement that placed me entirely outside the scene. My flattened right palm was being held in an iron grip against Howerd's bare belly while his own right hand was a blur of frenzied activity.

I opened my mouth to say something, God knows what it might have been, when he suddenly shouted, 'Yes! Yes!' I jerked my hand free and tried to rise, but Howerd had released my wrist only to grab for my hair and seize it. As he forced my head forward towards his naked lower trunk, he exclaimed, 'Come on! Come on!' I used all my strength to tug my hair free of his grasp with a savage wrench. There was a shock of pain in my scalp as I pushed wildly at him and scrambled clear, knocking the low table awry and scattering some tea things. I stumbled backwards, away from the settee to the door, desperate to get to a tap. In my flight for the kitchen sink I heard his laughter, whinnying and high. Hot water gushed over my hand as I soaped it, then quickly soaked a dish cloth and wiped it vigorously. By the time I'd finished, Howerd was standing in the kitchen doorway, grinning and holding out a soiled napkin from the tea tray.

'Souvenir,' he said.

Getting the beloved family entertainer out of my rented home, locking up, rushing to the theatre, getting made up and dressed, making my entrance through the hoop of paper made to resemble a candid camera lens – all this was done in a daze, a daze that stranded me on the stage without a notion of what I was supposed to be doing there. I decided not to tell anyone about the incident and put my lapse of memory down to mental exhaustion, which wasn't too far from the truth, I suppose. In the end, because I wanted to understand what had happened, I told Harry Butterworth.

Harry was ageless. I never knew how old he was. Even when he died there was no birth date given. When I first saw him, fussing with his arms full of my clothes in the number one dressing room of the Blackpool Wintergardens, I thought he was rather old for a sneak-thief.

'Excuse me, I think this is going to be my room.'

Harry spun round, flinging his hands up in alarm, my costumes falling forgotten to the floor. His pale blue eyes wide with confusion behind his pince-nez, he'd gone a blotchy pink. 'Oh! My stars! It's you, Mr Munt'ouse! I'm every so sorry, I didn't mean to – it's just that – I was stood 'ere waiting for you and I thought I'd tidy up a bit.'

He surveyed the jumble of clothes on the carpet. 'Well,' he said, 'I just 'ope them cleaners 'ave 'oovered. Come on, give us some 'elp at picking up.' I was slow to move and he looked up at me sharply. 'We've to work together if we're to work best. Oh now, 'ark at me! My first day as your dresser and I'm turning into your mum.'

It was May 1957, and my first big show *Startime*. All around the theatre were huge display portraits of my twenty-eight-year-old grin. Having photos of my head blown up to a size of seven or eight feet was having an enlarging effect on the real thing. Now I had been allotted a slave to obey my slightest command. Had it been anyone but Harry my vainglory might have gone unchecked, but the little man was adept at puncturing conceit. He treated me like a star but if I ever started acting like one, he'd bring me down to earth: 'Now, now, Mr Munt'ouse, when a man's wrapped up in 'imself 'e makes a pretty small package.'

Harry had retired from his job in a gents' outfitters. Some trouble with the Blackpool Constabulary, under instructions to make things difficult for anyone showing signs of effeminacy, had prompted Harry to propose to a spinster ten years his senior.

'On the wedding night I thought to meself, "'Arry, you'd best put up a bit of a show." So I got in bed beside Ethel and I put me 'and on it. And Ethel took it off and said, "'Arry, there'll be none of that" and there never 'as been.'

Lack of funds had him applying for a job as dresser in a previous year when he had catered to the professional needs of a young comedy star, newly risen on TV like me. I was told that he'd been badly treated by the comedian, pushed and struck and cursed till he was quite sick at the thought of coming to work. The theatre's burly sceneshifting crew consisted of the sort of masculine giants you might expect to scorn those they call pansies and poofs but, when they saw Harry's terror, three of them called at the star's dressing room after his Saturday night performance and showed him what it was like to be bullied. The comedian didn't have a visible mark on him but he moved through his performances the following week like a man in pain. He never mistreated Harry again.

Harry came with me to every theatre I played for almost ten years. We'd been together for four when the Frankie Howerd encounter took place. He was dropping some laundry off at my Great Yarmouth house when I sat him down and told him what had happened. By the time I'd finished, he was apoplectic with wrath. He ran to and fro in the room, his little body shaking, wringing his hands and exclaiming his despair over such an outrage. ''Ow dare 'e! 'Ow could 'e? The crafty bugger! A man like that brings all the rest of us into disrepute!'

After a while he calmed down a bit and had a cup of tea.

'You see, Mr Munt'ouse, men like Mr 'Owerd, they won't stick to their own. They get a kick out of turning fellows as've never done it before with another man. But 'e's crafty, 'e knows 'e's safe with a gentleman like yourself because you're not violent. If 'e tried that on with some, 'e'd 'ave 'ad 'is 'ead flattened. My advice is this: you've to be Christian about it. You've to forgive 'im because 'e can't 'elp 'isself. But if 'e ever tries it on again, smite 'im 'ip and thigh!'

From then on, Harry never left me alone with anyone he thought might upset me in a similar way. He never really liked my wife for a variety of reasons but he loved Jackie and was blissful when I divorced and remarried shortly before his death. We often speak of him and I can picture him vividly and without effort, his quiff of white hair dyed a peachy orange, a dab of makeup and powder on his knobby nose to hide its redness, scurrying like the White Rabbit on his never-ending errands. His benevolent devotion to me and the discretion with which he conducted his private life would be enough to dispel homophobia in anyone for a lifetime. He spoke of me as Bob to other people but never addressed me as anything but his curiously mispronounced version of my surname. He never called me his golden boy either but I suspect that's how he liked to think of me. I never called him my surrogate mother for that matter, he'd only have chuckled shyly and said his usual, 'Now, now, Mr Munt'ouse!'

★ ★ ★ ★ ★

Nobody called me his golden boy when I came back to the West End in 1961 in *Come Blow Your Horn* so I figured I was safe. The funny first play by Neil Simon had quite a cast in its London production – my dad was played by David Kossoff, my mum by Libby Morris, my girlfriends by Nyree Dawn Porter, Shirley Eaton and Claire Gordon, and my kid brother by Michael Crawford. We ran for nearly two years at the Prince of Wales Theatre for Richard Mills, Freddie Granville and Bernard Delfont. Bernie, now Lord Delfont, is a very amusing man. While we were in the last days of rehearsal, one of the most dishonest agents in the history of show business died. Bernie told me, 'I'm not going to his funeral but I've written a very nice letter explaining that I approve of it.' (Bernie's an admirer of Mark Twain.)

Harry Butterworth had to run my dressing room like a private boozing club, catering to all the friends who found it convenient to drop by. Until then, I didn't know how many friends I had, and that included friends I didn't know I knew and some I knew I didn't know.

One regular visitor was an albino midget named Zazi whom I vaguely knew. I'd met him in what would now be called a gay club, a Soho dive owned by an American puppet act called the Trotter Brothers. Zazi wore a Lucille Ball wig and looked like Harpo Marx. He sang at the club in a sweet soprano voice, very off-colour ballads adapted from their heterosexual originals as sung by the American queen of smut, Ruth Wallis, with lines like:

I call my sugar Candy 'cause he makes my peanut brittle.

He was an admirer of Quentin Crisp's and affected equally bizarre clothes: brocaded waistcoats, checkered motoring knickers, high-button shoes, red leather gloves, once a scarlet circus ringmaster's coat and shiny tophat. He made a living from two magnificently haughty Russian wolfhounds.

The dogs slept wherever Zazi slept during the day. At night, when he emerged in all his weird glory, they emerged too, their glory even greater than his. He'd shampooed them and blow-dried them and combed them until they seemed to move in a golden nimbus. Around their elegant necks were flashing collars encrusted with brilliant gems, all theatrical paste but very dazzling. Holding dog leads made from woven gold strands, Zazi would conduct these supercilious Romanovs past our theatre every evening and then return without them.

I asked Harry, 'Where do they go? Are they performing somewhere?'

'Oh, no, Mr Munt'ouse, they're a bit too grand for that. All they've to do is look down their noses at the punters.'

'Punters? Where, in a photo studio?'

Harry looked sly and touched his finger to the side of his nose. So a few nights later I asked Zazi himself. He was nursing a pink gin and sitting back in a dressing room armchair like a child, his yellow patent shoes sticking straight out. 'How do you make money out of those snooty pooches of yours? What's the big mystery? Are they up-market guard dogs? Do they sit in a window advertising Pedigree Chum?'

The little white face turned as pink as his rouged cheeks and pinker than his gin as he doubled up with high-pitched giggles. Harry gave him a make-up tissue to wipe up the mascara-sooted tears. When he'd recovered some of his composure, he gasped out the secret of his livelihood.

'I went to Paris with a circus act, this was years ago. One night I saw a very aristocratic looking girl, very gorgeous, coming out of the Georges Cinq with a borzoi. The dog had a diamond collar. Talk about class! I thought she was a countess or some international model. Then I saw how she took a roll of francs out of her purse and paid off the concierge or whatever they call the headporter. She was a tart and he'd pimped for her. Well, I never forget the impression she made on me. Then a couple of years back a friend of a friend died very suddenly from having a hole made in him by his other friend and there was no one to take care of his dogs, Prince Mikhail and Prince Igor. One way and another, I got them. All I had to do then was find a couple of girls on the game with imagination. Hounds like mine, they're perfect pick-up material, conversation pieces; you follow?'

I had to go onstage for my next scene but I soon returned for the rest of Zazi's tale. He was into his third gin by then and happy to expand on his business theories. 'It's a question of class, you see, Bob. My girls can pick up good money as ordinary streetwalkers, no worry, but add a bit of breeding, polish up the image, and you multiply the rewards something fantastic. So I rent them what you could call my canine royalty. They work the best neighbourhoods, Park Lane, Bond Street, round Claridge's, the Connaught, and they ain't picked up by sales reps and toe-rags, are they? Punters in Rolls-Royces and such, captains of industry, Arab diplomats, Yank millionaires, they're the sort of rich suckers we pull. Snob appeal, Bob, pays dividends. And . . . this is the best part, Bob . . . and . . . *and* . . .'

The giggles shook his little body again.

'And . . . and . . . I get the buggers walked for nothing!'

Work in the theatre was over by ten-thirty unless the audiences were especially vociferous. At a matinée with an unresponsive crowd, the play ran for two hours. A good-natured, hearty mob on a good evening could add nearly thirty minutes to the show, their laughter spreading our pauses and encouraging extra bits of stage business. Even so, I felt idle after the curtain fell at night and started looking for something to do. A pal of mine who booked musicians into London's fancier nightclubs came up with an idea.

'The Colony Club's looking for a new cabaret policy. You might be able to sell them on a midnight comedy show. A few girls, some sketches, a point number or two – if the price is right and Delfont'll let you do it.'

I asked Bernie.

'Give it a try, Bob, it won't affect our business in the slightest. But I don't think the Colony will pay much. Two hundred a week tops.'

For that, I thought, I'd work it solo. I sat in my dressing room every afternoon for a week and wrote the basis of what would be my staple cabaret act for the next four years. Then I persuaded the owners of the smart club in Berkeley Square to let me give them a demo. At midnight the following Saturday, Ronnie Birch's orchestra played my opening song and I walked on to what was to be a personal revelation. I was a born club comic. Radio and TV and stage were fine but I'd found my real home in cabaret.

Oh, I'd done quite a few floorshows before, private engagements in ballrooms and charity marquees, and I'd learned a bit from working at the Savoy, but this was different. Instead of sticking to a set routine, I allowed mood and reaction to shape my act, constantly adjusting my delivery according to my reading of the audience. All at once it seemed that I had a new authority and freedom to do as I pleased, to manipulate the throng while I was responding to their preferences in comedy. No two audiences will have the same mass disposition. Their group ability to absorb the comedian's words will differ from show to show. Then their process of selection, their comprehension, their capacity for enjoyment, their sensitivity, perception, tolerance, prejudice and affection will dictate the overall temper of each comedy performance. Alert to all these shifting patterns, the man in the spotlight can match them, varying his speed and energy, his subtlety or obviousness, to seize control and keep it until, much like a canoeist riding the rapids, he reaches a satisfactory conclusion. I found my feet at the Colony in 1962, the same feet that have trod countless cabaret floors ever since.

The management at the Colony paid me in cash, two hundred pounds every Friday night. One Saturday afternoon the roll of notes was still in my pocket when I reached the theatre for our matinée. I shoved it into the back of a drawer and forgot about it for the rest of the evening. When I went to collect it, there it was, gone. Poor little Harry went into shock. After wasting time trying to calm him down, I called the cops. Two detectives arrived within minutes, asked a few questions and then let me rush off to my cabaret job, never expecting to see my week's salary again.

On Monday evening the two CID men were waiting for me in my dressing room.

'What's left of your bread, sir,' said one, handing me a plastic evidence bag containing about a hundred and fifty quid, 'Chummy managed to spend the rest before we found him.'

'How on earth did you do that?'

'You said you only had one visitor who was left alone in this room last Saturday evening. Your description was pretty clear. And it's not that hard to find an albino midget with a red wig and a frock coat, even in London.'

The other detective cleared his throat awkwardly. He had a big red face surrounding a thick Stalin moustache and I sensed he was getting at something when he asked, 'Just how well do you know this man who calls himself Zazi, sir?'

'Only casually, I met him at the Pink Elephant in Soho.'

'That's a meeting place for known homosexuals, sir.'

'Yes, I know.'

'Your assistant here in the theatre, sir, your dresser, he's a bit light on his toes as well, isn't he?'

'Harry's past is something I never ask about.'

The first officer silenced his colleague with a raised hand. He lowered it to my shoulder and spoke confidentially. 'Just between us, Mr Monkhouse, if you've something to hide, something personal, it might be as well not to press charges. You wouldn't want your private affairs brought out in court, now would you? You theatricals, what you do in privacy, it's better the public don't know.'

'I'm not sure what you're thinking, but I'm married with three children.'

'All the more reason to keep this side of your life hush-hush, wouldn't you say. We'll pick the little freak up for something else. We can have him for the dogs alone. And the girls. And the pictures.'

'Pictures?'

Stalin pulled out a notebook, opened it and spread a few snapshots for me to see. They were photographs of two naked women having sex with a pair of Russian wolfhounds. Both dogs appeared more disdainful than usual and, looking at the women, you could see why.

21

GOLDEN BOY

1963

In which is learned: how humility helps when following a star, the quixotic nature of auditions, something of backstage camaraderie, Royal use of the lingo, and how to master a taskmaster's task from the master

In 1985, Max Bygraves was my principal guest on my BBC2 chat show. Following my defection from ATV/Central TV two years earlier, Max had taken over as host of 'Family Fortunes' for two seasons. I asked him how he'd liked it and he was ready with a friendly answer: 'Well, I didn't much like having to follow you.'

Twenty-two years before that exchange, I didn't much like having to follow Max. In that same twelve months, Sir Alec Douglas-Home had to follow Harold Macmillan as Prime Minister, a tough act. Harold Wilson had to follow Hugh Gaitskell as Labour leader, no easy task. But I had the toughest succession of all: I had to tread a stage vacated by the most successful English comedian ever to play Scotland. His popularity was immense and his national fame as great as any name in the headlines of 1963.

Valentina Tereshkova was becoming the first woman in space, spy Kim Philby was bolting to Moscow, President Charles de Gaulle was giving us the big 'non' for EEC membership, Screaming Lord Sutch was launching the National Teenage Party, Beatlemania was possessing the nation, Christine Keeler was doing to the Government what she'd previously done to her paying customers, and Bygraves was walking on the water in Glasgow.

When it was announced that I was to replace him at the

Above: It's only a rehearsal, but Ken Dodd's in full regalia, on the brink of soaking me and Anita Harris with a jumbo jet. (The Golden Shot, 1969)

Right: Body building is an art and I was an artist, working on my own body. Unfortunately, I was a surrealist. This was for an edition of 'Mad Movies' (1967) that featured silent film stuntmen and athletes. (ABCTV)

Above: Clubland was the inspiration of the Rev. Butterworth *(left)* and Denis Goodwin and I were proud to raise funds for this Boys' Club project in East London by writing Bob Hope's charity broadcasts. It didn't exactly hurt our careers either. *(Author's collection)*

Below: In 1973 Jackie finally gave in to my marriage proposals. I had her surrounded. *(Author's collection)*

Above: My taste for fast models with sleek lines and great bodywork was limited to cars by the time I posed with the chorus of 'The Golden Shot' outside Scarborough's Floral Hall in 1970. *(The Yorkshire Argus)*

Left: An attempt to turn me into a pop singer in 1969 resulted in two CBS records that sold just enough to go vinyl. (CBS)

Above: Trigger happy about returning to 'The Golden Shot' in 1974, a show remarkable for being fondly remembered by people who hated it at the time. (ATV)

Above: Throughout eleven summers in one a.m. cabarets around eight Butlins holiday camps, I did the work of two men. Here I'm trying to double-up the audience at Filey in 1977. *(Author's collection)*

Below: How funny was the US TV series 'Bonkers' (1978)? Judge from the expressions on the Hudson Brothers, Joan Rivers and yours despairingly. (ITC)

Above: It's 1982 and Eamonn Andrews has just said, "This is your life", to which I've replied, "About bloody time!" I'm looking up at a 35-foot frame filled with famous friends, a reproduction of 'Celebrity Squares', in the heart of London's West End. (Thames TV)

Right: Caught in the act, circa 1983. This was snapped by a member of the audience at a nightspot called 'The Bitter End'. For Britain's cabaret clubs, it soon was.

Left: It's June 1st, 1993, and I'm hugging myself because my bus pass has arrived. (© David Hindley)

Below: Ageing gracefully? No, I don't think so either. But glad to be back in drama, playing a City nasty with Hugh Laurie in LWT's 1993 mini series 'All Or Nothing At All'. (© Tobi Corney/LWT)

Me and my two bosses, Sidney the cat and Jackie the wife.
(Author's collection)

Alhambra, one journalist wrote, 'Impresario Stewart Cruickshank is hoping we will not know the difference between a king and a knave.'

Bless that sour press comment! It inspired my secret anti-Monkhouse campaign.

Under various pseudonyms, I wrote immoderately incensed letters to the Scottish papers praising Bygraves and abusing me. Friends of mine were enlisted to phone Scottish TV and radio stations bewailing the end of Max's reign and the coming of the Pretender. The media response was predictable; interviews with press and radio reporters to ask after my feelings at being damned before I'd even opened. My bewildered dismay at such summary rejection was mingled with a plucky determination to win through. I quoted worse remarks about me than had ever really been said and tried to keep my trembling chin up.

'I never thought it was going to be easy,' I told readers and listeners. 'All I ask is the chance to answer all this derision with the best performances I'm capable of giving. If I know one thing about the people of Scotland, it's this – they have the greatest sense of fair play in the world. I'm putting my trust in that.'

We opened in an atmosphere of great public sympathy and, since the show was very good anyway, the notices bent over backwards to set the record straight and proclaim it a hit. 'Bob Bobs up a Winner' said one; 'Fun to Confound Critics' said another, and the very writer whose king-and-knave crack had provided my afflatus, wrote in hackneyed alliteration, 'Monkhouse's modern maturity as a marvellous master of mirth makes Alhambresque magic.' I had another 'm' for him – muggins.

The show looked gorgeous, staged by Dick Hurran ('Flash Dick' to the ladies of the chorus) and Lionel Blair. It featured Yana, with whose charms I was to be shortly favoured in a manner touched upon elsewhere in this history, the brilliant ventriloquist Dennis Spicer, the battling Shaw Brothers from the USA whose act was a sensational stunt fight, and the darkly handsome Welsh baritone-tenor David Hughes. He and I were surprised to find one another at Glasgow airport early one morning. It appeared we were both paying a flying visit to London for the same purpose, to audition for the leading role in a musical at the Theatre Royal, Drury Lane. If I hadn't already been on board the plane when I learned this, I believe I should have abandoned my trip. David was at the peak of his powers, a commanding figure on the stage with an enthralling voice that could handle everything from pop ballads to grand opera. He was a cert for the role. All I could do was sing on the beat and in my key and hope that the orchestra would drown my vocal shortcomings. Artificial aspersions about my talent in comparison with the departing Bygraves might have swayed the fair-minded Glaswegians in my favour, but in a singing competition with Hughes the invention of such disparagement would be unnecessary. We went to Drury Lane together, Hughes sang 'Falling in Love with Love' like an angel and I sang 'This Can't Be Love' like an idiot. They thanked us and we flew back to Glasgow. A week later I was offered the role of Antipholus of Syracuse in *The Boys from Syracuse*. The first person to congratulate me was David Hughes.

Every day after that I sung under his tuition for two hours, until my range had expanded up and down by a full octave. If you ever listen to the album of the London production, you'll hear a beautiful and rarely played Rodgers and Hart song called 'You Have Cast Your Shadow on the Sea'. Every note is sung exactly as Hughes taught me. As a result, it's the only part of my performance that's any good at all. His patience and generosity were all the more worthy of gratitude when you consider that he had lost the part to me, not because he wasn't ideal for it but because my long run in *Come Blow Your Horn* had classified me as a West End draw. As I later learned, my physiognomy had also affected my selection. When I expressed my sincere regret, Hughes said,

'Listen, if your name sells tickets, that makes you their golden boy.'

'I love you, David, but please, *please*, never call me that.'

The Glasgow run's high point came with a performance for Her Majesty the Queen and HRH the Duke of Edinburgh on 3 July 1963. She particularly enjoyed the sketch in which Hughes and I appeared as Glaswegian policemen. When Welshman Hughes expressed his admiration for my command of local slang, I'd tap my head and say, 'Yes, this is where you want it – up here in your *airchie*!' It was a belting laugh because our audiences knew the word as common vernacular. Mums in the Gorbals would threaten mischievous kids with, 'Away or I'll skelp yer airchie!' meaning 'Be off or I'll smack your arse!' After the show, we were presented to the royal couple and the Duke spoke interestedly of my opening patter song in which I listed all the famous beauty spots in Scotland at tongue-twister speed. 'All those names, all those places, I don't know how you remember them all, how you keep it all up here in your – what's the word for it? Your Archie!' To this day I don't know whether or not he was pulling my pendulum. Over the years I've done more than my fair share of Royal Variety Performances and I've never enjoyed one of them. To me a show with royalty present to inhibit the crowd is the opposite of sex – even when it's good, it's lousy.

The off-Broadway production of *The Boys from Syracuse* turned out to be an intimate affair in a theatre so tiny you could've doubled its size by stripping off the wallpaper. The ecstatic New York press reviews upon rediscovering the wonders of Richard Rodgers' melodies and Lorenz Hart's lyrics had prompted the far more extravagant London version, to be staged regardless of expense. Oh yes, the British currency exchange laws had taken care of that. Richard Rodgers had amassed a sterling fortune with *The Sound of Music* in London and had to reinvest it in the UK or let it lie almost idle at niggardly interest.

As soon as I saw the American actor playing the role I would take, I knew another reason why I'd been chosen. Stuart Damon, later to star in such daft drama series as 'The Champions' and 'The Adventurer', looked like my better-looking kid brother. I'd had the look they associated with success. Rehearsals began under the direction of Christopher Hewitt as soon as I returned to London. My twin brother, Antipholus of Ephesus, was Denis Quilley, my slave Dromio was Ronnie Corbett and my heart's desire, the Australian star Maggie Fitzgibbon. As we approached our first night I found I had a problem. I could easily swagger my way through this rather creaky adaptation of Shakespeare's *A Comedy of Errors*, itself based on a Greek plot old Bill swiped from Plautus's *Menæchmi*. I could even pass muster with all the songs I had to tackle. Well, all but one. My problem with this number, a duet with Corbett, was singing it while executing an agonistically robust dance set by our martinet of a choreographer. Little Ronnie got it right every time. I sighed, 'Size isn't everything, is it?'

He agreed. 'That's right – the whale's endangered but the ant's doing fine.'

One day rehearsals broke for lunch but I stayed in the theatre, practising the song and dance over and over again. Eventually I became aware of an elderly man watching me from the prompt corner so I stopped and said, 'Can I help you?'

'Not really.' He walked towards me. 'But maybe I can help you.'

'Well, if you can tell me how to get this bloody routine right . . .'

'What's the trouble? Talent shortage?'

I laughed. 'That could be it. I've got enough to sing it, I've got enough to dance it, but when I try to do both at the same time, I haven't half enough.'

He pulled a bent-wood chair back from the rehearsal piano and sat down at an angle to the keyboard, his mild, nondescript face lumpy and unsmiling, but his eyes bright with interest. He smoothed his neat thinning hair with a liver-spotted hand and spoke in the measured, pedantic tones of an American lecturer.

'Not even half enough talent, eh? Try this – sing it a little slower, don't dance it – just sing strictly on the beat, hit the rhythm with each word. And as you do that, picture the dance. Just picture it in your mind.'

As he played the opening bars with the heavy left-hand beat of a pub pianist stirring up a singalong, I supposed him to be our orchestral arranger or perhaps the US publisher of the musical. As much to be polite as for any other reason, I did as he suggested.

'That's fine. Now dance it, don't sing it. Concentrate on the beat, use your whole body to express the tempo, don't worry about looking graceful, just hit the rhythm. And while you do it, think of the words, just think of them.'

He struck up the same belaboured cadence and I cantered through the choreography. It was easier to do it in this way, I had to admit.

'OK, that'll work out. Now, keeping it slow, do the whole thing, dance and sing, but like a machine, a robot. No interpretation, no expression, just give all your attention to putting the words and movement together. The glue is the beat. The beat sticks it all together, music, dance, lyric, da-da-diddy-diddy-dum-dum-dum, like rivets! Here we go!'

I sang and danced the number without a hitch:

I wanna go back, go back, to dear old Syracuse!

'That's amazing!' I said. 'That's the first time I've done it right.'

'You've got it now. Once you've got the basis, you can start improving as you go along. From here on in, you'll add the old razz-matazz. Let's lunch.'

'I'm Bob Monkhouse.' I held out my hand and he shook it.

'I'm Richard Rodgers.'

'Oh my God!'

'I know. You thought I was dead.'

'No, well, that is, we heard you had – that you were ill.'

'Cancer of the jaw. Give me your hand again. Stiffen your fingers. Feel this.'

He pushed my straightened fingers into his cheek and they sank in to an alarming depth.

'All built up with tissue from my backside. Kiss my cheek, you kiss my arse. You just showed me how you can do that number with half enough talent. Now I'll take you to the Savoy and show you how I can eat with half enough teeth.'

22

GOLDEN BOY

1963–1964

Tragedy brings tears, friendship brings demands, a Welsh sojourn brings pleasure; parties go with a bang but the big noise ends with a whimper

Where were you when President John F. Kennedy was assassinated? A comedian friend of mine says he hates it when that question comes up at parties because he hasn't got an alibi. I spent that evening with a stunned audience in the Theatre Royal, Drury Lane, people so shattered by the news that they had come to the theatre in a daze and stayed that way. Denis Quilley and I, trying to look as much like identical twins as possible for the sake of the plot, wore patrician make-up: Roman noses, Caesarean wigs and curly, golden beards with sideburns. As we awaited our simultaneous entrances, in which we crossed the stage from opposite sides in agitated conversation with our equally identical twin slaves, neither pair noticing the other, the cast of Roman citizens all around each of us in the opposing wings was unable to control its soft sobbing. It was so infectious that I started weeping too. After a short while, our cue came and we strode onstage. Denis and I looked more alike than ever. We had both been crying and the tears had streaked our makeup and loosened our beards so that both sets of whiskers clung to our faces precariously by a few centimetres of gauze. Under normal circumstances, the sight of twin heroes with false beavers dangling from their necks would surely have brought some reaction from the audience. Not on that night. I'm not sure anyone noticed that we'd come on.

Next May, as soon as it was announced that *Syracuse* was due to close, I heard from Phil Burn, my chum since our very first taste of revue together with Benny Hill in 1947. In those early years, Phil had literally kept me in show business by insisting to the agents that I appear on dates with him. He'd persuaded his manager Rex Leslie to book me again and again until that kindly little man got so used to having me around that he stopped arguing about it. As I became more established, I tried to thank Phil in small ways, writing parts for him to play in my TV shows and so on, but nothing like that could have repaid his kindnesses to me. During the past four or five years we had lost touch. I knew that in 1961 he'd married an appealing singer called Pamela Moon and they both felt that he had expanded his comic miming act about as far as it would go. It depended on very well-known records that lent themselves to energetic lampooning and the supply of ideal material was limited.

Resourcefully, they'd gone into the management of complete shows, packaged under the catchword 'Glam' and staged accordingly as glamorous cabarets in hotel ballrooms all over the country. Now his phone call told me that he was mounting his biggest venture yet, a really swanky extravaganza to reopen the refurbished New Theatre, Cardiff, and run throughout the summer. He had everything except a well-known comedian to lead the company, would I meet with him to discuss the matter. We made a date and I hung up with misgivings.

During the last weeks of *Syracuse* I'd developed a TV situation comedy for myself called 'The Big Noise'. The central figure was a smooth-talking egomaniac whose selfishness and vanity were his constant undoing. I'd made him an obnoxious disc jockey named Bob Mason, 'the guy that you're facin',' and worked out some plots and subsidiary characters. BBC TV had expressed keen interest and the fashionable director Joe McGrath was prepared to work on it. Just about the last thing I needed to do right now was spend my summer months exhausting myself twice nightly in a provincial theatre. I felt dreadful about turning down Phil's invitation, I was still indebted to him, but it was going to take all my mental energies to write six thirty-minute episodes all by myself, ready to shoot by September. He had no real idea of the sort of money I'd been earning in recent years. Substantial as it was, perhaps if I doubled the figure he'd give up the idea of using me. That, for what it was worth, was my game plan as I drove to the offices of the Concert Artistes Association for our meeting.

The plan fell apart as soon as I saw him. The handsome young buck I'd known so well had given way to a man looking at least a decade older than his forty years. His most striking feature, big eyes rimmed with black lashes, were now discoloured and veined. The tousled black curls of only about five years earlier now fell lankly, yellowish white and lifeless, to the collar of his camel-hair coat. His skin looked unhealthy and his considerable extra weight made him short of breath and sweaty. I hid my dismay and, as we sat down to coffee at a quiet corner table, I was relieved that he seemed to have lost none of his geniality and keenness. 'I can't tell you how thrilled I am, Bob! My first whack at a really important theatrical production and my best pal will be topping the bill!'

I looked at him closely. He meant it, he really thought of me as his best pal. He was reddening with enthusiasm now, describing the performers he'd booked, the costumes and scenery he was bringing in from his previous seaside shows, the musical items, the deal he'd struck with the management of the theatre, winking and leaning forward to give me occasional soft punches of conspiratorial warmth. As I listened and realised just how much the whole thing meant to him, I silently revised my position, asking the periodic question only to find the answer digging me in deeper.

'Who else have you considered as your headliner, Phil?'

'Oh, blimey, I've offered those Welsh beggars every sort of star, hit parade singers galore, but no, nothing else will do but a famous funnyman.'

'Which comedians have you tried?'

'Well, I tell you, I've run myself ragged, round all the agents, every decent comic had his summer season fixed up months ago. Not that you weren't my first thought, mate, you were, but I thought that Rodgers and Hart thing would run forever. When I heard it was coming off, oh my God, I said to Pam, our bacon is saved, I said, the fat is out of the fire! I mean, we open in four weeks. The printers are standing over their ruddy presses just waiting to fit the star's name into the posters and programmes. Look, I won't beat about the bush. Friendship is one thing, business is another. What's the damage? Can you tell me or would you rather do it through an agent?'

'How much can you afford to pay and still clear a decent profit?'

Phil beamed at me proudly, pulled out a notebook, removed a page and passed it to me. Written on it was a weekly salary. The figure was about a third less than I had been earning over the previous half dozen years.

'Not bad for a week's work, eh? I know you get top dollar, mate, and I wouldn't insult you by trying to get you cheaper.'

I did some mental arithmetic and knew that he was offering me the very best he could. But I didn't want it and I wasn't going to take it and, even if it were the saving of Phil's professional life, common sense dictated that I must turn it down.

'Lovely,' I said, shaking his hand. 'I'll do it.'

★   ★   ★   ★   ★

Sometimes doing the right thing is the right thing to do. The Cardiff season turned out to be a delight and I enjoyed a blithesome relationship with my leading lady, Lionel's vivaciously witty sister, Joyce Blair. She was foxy and funny and, more than enthusiastic, proceleusmatic about the new TV series. I was carefree and crazy about her. That I was carefree was thanks to Denis Norden who, with his writing partner Frank Muir, had agreed to take up 'The Big Noise' and script the first six editions for me. Put my being crazy about her down to her off-the-wall humour. While we were exploring the South Wales countryside, I fell down a steep incline into a brook and Joyce's helpful admonition was, 'You shouldn't try to disobey gravity, it's the law.' Of the contrasting qualities of Cardiff's Lord Mayor I remarked, 'He's got a heart of gold and feet of clay.' Joyce continued, 'And teeth of pearl, ears of corn and a knob of butter.' Some people believed that my friendship with Joyce was more than just friendship but there you are, some people will believe anything. Today she lives in Hollywood with her handsome movie-producer husband, still foxy, still funny.

I don't know whether Pamela Burn knew how ill Phil was when she married him, I've never asked her. If she did, she was even braver than she had to become during the three years that followed the success of his Cardiff production. His physical condition continued to fail and when he died at the age of forty-four in April, 1967, comedy lost one of its most lovable proponents.

The long runs of the Neil Simon play and the Rodgers and Hart musical had kept me at home in London. Now, after the summer in South Wales, I was back in St John's Wood with my wife and children. Gary was thirteen and attending the special school at Tixover Grange near Stamford. His sister and younger brother were at the King Alfred School in Hampstead. Our garden in Loudoun Road was unusually large for the area and a sunny centre for family activity and play. The four-storey Victorian house was in Georgian style with tall windows and high ceilings. Big wrought-iron gates in the front wall opened on a courtyard with a columned porch atop the steps to the purple front door. My wife had renovated the house before we moved there in the late 1950s and she had done it with entertaining in mind.

Guests for countless dinner parties entered a high, wide hall, its floor checkered with big black and white marble slabs. The long scarlet curtains on the front window matched the carpet on a broad curving staircase with a single piece of polished wood as its handrail, rising out of sight to the upper floors. Turning left through double doors, they'd be served drinks by a white-jacketed barman named Harry in a thirty-five-foot-long living room, L-shaped and furnished in the style that Heal's of Tottenham Court Road used to call 'contemporary'. They'd see original paintings covering the walls and sometimes hear background music provided at the piano by Lennie Felix.

When food was announced, they'd file past the door to my study and walk down two short flights of stone stairs to the lower floor. A cosily lit corridor led past a well-stocked wine cellar and a bar with tall stools on the left, a children's playroom and a bathroom on the right. At the end, they'd reach a pine-panelled dining room with a broad iron fireplace and a table that could seat sixteen or more if they were feeling intimate. Caterers served dinner from the professionally equipped kitchen and Harry poured the wines.

After eating, we'd all go back upstairs to watch the latest goodies from my 16mm film collection: short comedies, adult cartoons, old trailers and other rarities, projected through a double-glazed window from my study on to the white, reflective chimney breast where earlier a large oil painting had hung. Often my daughter and my younger son would wander down in their pyjamas and join the guests. Peter and Mary Noble always seemed to be at our parties and we always seemed to be at theirs, just round the corner in Abbey Road. During these parties: Russ Conway composed a song with Lionel Bart; Peter O'Toole fell asleep at three a.m. and was still out for the count on our couch the following afternoon, watched over by his Arab man-servant from *Lawrence of Arabia*; Harold Pinter, during a tale-telling contest, invented a story on the spur of the moment which he later developed as a play; Peter and Mary Noble brought Joan Crawford and her new husband, Pepsi boss Alfred Steele, who poured her ice-cold vodkas from her own jewelled thermos flask until she hooted with laughter and passed out; Topol had an argument with National Theatre actor Colin Blakeley and knocked him down, all because they couldn't agree what 'feeze' meant (don't bother looking it up, it means both 'to drive off' and 'to perturb'); Lana Turner did a jig; Vincent Price came with a lady and left with Tab Hunter; Georgia Brown and Anthony Newley arrived two hours late for dinner, threw a joint tantrum at finding we hadn't waited for them and left; Judy Garland sang the rudest song I've ever heard; Billie Whitelaw first met and fell in love with Robert Muller (they married); and Benny Hill fell for Jackie, then my secretary, and courted her with flowers. She thought he was sweet but not fanciable.

In October, at the BBC Television Centre in Wood Green, we made the first edition of 'The Big Noise'. Much against the cowardly nature of my disc jockey character, he's coerced into trying to talk a teenage rebel out of jumping off a fourteenth floor ledge. Told that the lad hero-worships him and wants to meet him, the quaking deejay is lowered from a helicopter to sit in terror beside the boy on the narrow shelf. David Hemmings, playing the delinquent, turns out to have no intention of jumping, only demanding the presence of the slimy broadcaster to tell him to his face how thoroughly naff he is. The dialogue by Muir and Norden had a knowing sparkle and everyone seemed to love the show, especially the new Head of Light Entertainment, Tom Sloan. He arranged a press viewing followed by a party on the fifth floor of the Centre. Since I was already involved in taping the series, I came up from the studio after the party had started. I walked in the door, Sloan saw me, clapped his hands for attention and called out, 'Here he is, here he is! Ladies and gentlemen, may I present *our golden boy!*' The journalists applauded with warmth but the tremor I felt had a distinct chill about it.

The six shows were the best thing I'd ever done on TV. I can say that with impunity because they no longer exist. In the 1970s, a producer named Michael Mills was commissioned by BBC TV to reduce the size of their archives and he destroyed about eighty per cent of the recordings in the library. 'The Big Noise' vanished without a sound.

The first viewer reaction to our premier show was uncertain. They said they couldn't understand why I was playing such a nasty man. The second show, in which I hid the exhausted 'Beatles' from their fans in my maiden aunt's bed-sit to her (Irene Handl's) girlish delight, did a little bit better.

In the third show, Warren Mitchell played a consistently unlucky agent who suddenly gets a break. A record by a rock singer he represents becomes a surprise number one hit. He can book the lad into every club and concert hall in Britain at top money. But there's a slight hitch – the singer can't travel half a mile before being incapacitated with travel sickness. My deejay character comes up with a crooked solution – miming look-alike impostors – with predictably disastrous results.

I thought the show was terrific. Viewers thought otherwise. The Appreciation Index for this show wasn't just small, it was infinitesimal. It was like US comedian Fred Allen said about all the sincerity in Hollywood: you could fit it inside a flea's navel and still have room for three caraway seeds and an agent's heart.

The BBC rescheduled the last three broadcasts to a later hour and they did even worse.

It seemed that this brilliant little show was my poisoned chalice. Tom Sloan stopped calling me his golden boy, and light entertainment producers stopped calling me altogether.

The phone went quiet. Television bookers didn't return my calls. It was so unthinkable I'd never thought of it. At the age of thirty-six, my career in TV comedy was in serious trouble. The magic gold of my alchemy was turning back into base metal.

23

DILIGENT IN THE DOLDRUMS

1965–1966

Some thoughts on failure, a period of dramatic docimasy, an adjustment of partnership with increased income at a price yet to be paid – then an impressionist outwits and a councillor is outwitted. A Mad Movie man maddens but a dream pacifies

Perhaps real individual failure lies in the squandering of potentiality, a volitional waste of one's ability. If you paint signs when you could paint sunsets, invent jingles when you might compose symphonies, foregoing eventual achievement in favour of instant reward, that may be regarded as personal failure.

If this general definition holds true, then I can put it together with my fairest assessment of my own capabilities, both as a man and as a professional, and take some satisfaction in the conclusion that I am no failure. At each stage of my life, I have taken stock of my talents and set my targets as high as I've dared. While a few of my contemporaries have generously thought me worthy of greater challenges than those I have essayed, the full exercise of what wits I possess has usually guided me to attempt only the attainable.

If, in living up to your best expectations of yourself, you make incidental miscalculations, over- or underestimating your gifts as you go along, you had better learn from such setbacks, and learn to like them too. The bumps are often the best lessons in the negotiation of the darker passages of your progress. In comedy, every laugh you don't get teaches you as much as the laugh you do.

Reflections like these followed what I've called my golden boy period, my luckily long honeymoon with show business when most people assumed I knew what I was doing. Since no great comedian has ever risen high and higher in a smooth, unbroken curve without dips, how much less could I, a safe distance from greatness, expect to continue my ascension. Instead, I sniffed the ill wind for good scents.

Almost immediately, as if cued by my first major flop in comedy, the drama producers were stirring.

Over the next two years I did more dramatic work than in all the twenty-eight years since. Several reasons may have combined for this burst of histrionic opportunities. First, the collective effect of some halfway decent stage work, my narrative job on the TV version of Loesser's musical, and some slight intellectualisation of a clever but unpopular series like 'The Big Noise'; all must have made me seem less of a comic and more of an undiscovered luvvie. Second, producers were fashionably attracted to offbeat casting at this time. The broad US comedian Jackie Gleason had triumphed as Minnesota Fats in *The Hustler*, nightclub gagster Red Buttons had scored in *The Longest Day*, and suddenly there was a rash of dramatic opportunities for funnymen to turn tragic on both sides of the Atlantic. On British TV we saw straight play roles for Bruce Forsyth, Alfred Marks, Dave King and others from the illegitimate theatre. Lastly, comedy paid better than drama. It followed that, since I was out of favour with the Light Entertainment Department, I'd be grateful for honest toil at union rates. I was, although there was a slight lack of imagination in the sort of parts I was offered and took. My greasy disc jockey was the key to what was thought suitable for me. Thus, I played the eponymous hero in a two-hour Bernard Kops play, *Enter Solly Gold*, directed by Stuart Burge, in which conman Solly steals a rabbi's clothes off a line and, impersonating him, occupies a wealthy Jewish household, helping himself to their wealth while helping them to a fragile happiness. In other plays, I portrayed a couple of philanderers, a swindler and a fake spiritualist. In Reuben Shipp's *The Taxman Cometh*, I was a bankrupt playwright who seduces his tax inspector's plain secretary so as to persuade her to destroy his files. With Ian Hendry as my disbarred lawyer, I contributed an oily Cypriot crook to *Beware Greeks Bearing Gifts*; another cockney conman to Robert Muller's *Take Three More Girls*, a seedy radio ham who hires an even seedier Bill Owen to spy on his wife in *The Bug*; I even won a drama award fron the *London Evening Star* for a one-man play called *The Flip Side* as a lone all-night TV linkman who tries to hold his falsely cheerful on-screen self together while, during breaks, his desperate phone calls to his wife cause his mental breakdown. I saw it lately. I was such a ham the make-up girl had to glaze me. My cufflinks were pineapple rings.

My favourite drop of acting was in a half-hour piece by Ray Galton and Alan Simpson called *Friends in High Places*, in which I appeared as fifty-eight-year-old George Gosling, fat, bald, worn out and miserably married to a shrewish Patricia Hayes. When he wishes that he were thirty years younger, some idle angels, Arthur English and Frank Williams, decide to grant his wish and, of course, his troubles double. Ray and Alan wrote me such wonderfully lugubrious soliloquisings over the miseries of ageing, plangent with the ring of truth and pity, that some viewers wrote to say they were moved to tears. Now that I'm seven years older than poor old George, I know how they felt.

Curiously, while I was checking and revising the previous two paragraphs, Prichard phoned with the offer of a dramatic role. I am adding these words during a break in filming in an unfinished office block at 60 London Wall, London, E.C.1, on the hottest of June days. I am playing Giles Lederman, a cold and calculating financier, in Guy Andrews's *All Or Nothing At All*, a 3-part drama, produced by Brian Eastman and directed by Andrew Grieve. It's due for transmission by LWT in November, 1993, starring Hugh Laurie and Pippa Guard. Age has its advantages. At sixty-five, I feel far more assured about my ability as a character actor than I ever was with my endeavours a quarter of a century ago.

While I was very grateful for all these exercises in dramaturgy, I was also agonising over losing my way in comedy. MMA, the creative consultancy I had formed with businessman Henry Howard and musician Malcolm Mitchell, was doing well enough to move from our cramped Greek Street office to something larger in Wardour Street, then onwards and upwards to a luxurious suite above The Pair of Shoes Casino in Hertford Street, next to the Park Lane Hilton. Hooray for income, but I was fast tiring of sterile meetings in advertising agency offices. I wanted to hear happy laughter and know that I was the cause of it and I told Henry so. We sat in his tastefully designed office with its soft felt-covered walls and subtle lighting, being very reasonable with each other: 'Henry, you've been my manager for over three years now, but you're not really an agent.'

'You're absolutely right. We need someone in our company with more show business knowhow to handle your affairs. Your name's been invaluable in opening doors for us so far but now we're up and running, well, what's to stop you getting up and running too?'

Henry smiled reassuringly and offered me a cigarette. He was an attractive man, a year or so my senior, with a warm gaze and a frank manner. We'd met socially in the 1950s and then, when his first marriage collapsed, he'd quit the mattress and bedding business and approached me with a proposition. If I'd provide the small initial finance to get started and contribute my ideas, while Malcolm Mitchell donated his musical talent, he would head a new sort of service company for the big advertising outfits, supplying jingles at first, but then establishing itself as a conduit between the agencies and the entertainment world. We'd own a third each.

Malcolm was an old friend, so like me in appearance that people took us for brothers. The three of us each worked hard at what we could do best and our little concern thrived, to the point where we were commissioning work from world-class names like Nelson Riddle and Henry Mancini.

Henry rose and went to the door to call Malcolm in from his desk. 'Bob's feeling a bit held back, frustrated at having to attend so many meetings and so forth. He feels he needs an experienced agent to advance his performing career.'

Malcolm said, 'I quite agree with you, Bob. Me, I'm happy working a few weeks a year round the nightspots with my trio. But you, you should be doing the big dates for bigger money. Isn't that right, Hank?'

'Yes, Bob, let's do this. You pay a higher percentage of your earnings into the company to compensate for the loss of your availability, and that will cover the cost of appointing an agent to improve your bookings.'

'I'm still a one-third partner, aren't I?'

Both my friends earnestly assured me that I was. Perhaps I

should have known that I had just fashioned the thin end of a wedge.

Henry called in two agents, Alf Preager and Monty Bond, who informed us that my weekly cabaret salary was a joke in the business. I'd been doubling the Bailey Nightclubs, that's playing two a night for seven nights, for seven hundred pounds. Stan Henry and John Smith, owners of Bailey's, had done good enough business with me to raise this to one thousand pounds with an annual guarantee of twelve weeks minimum. Now here were these two guys in our office telling us that my income-to-earnings ratio was a laughing stock. They renegotiated at once, raised my weekly stipend to seventeen hundred pounds and I never saw them again. The bookings just came in by phone, I signed the contracts, went to the venues, played the weeks, and my commission was deducted automatically. I was developing my nightclub material and technique with every week in joints like the Ace of Clubs, Worksop, or the Carlton Cabaret Club, Chesterfield, packing them in despite my absence from the TV screen as a comedian, or perhaps because of it. Similarly, what was left of my marriage was surviving despite my absence from home, or perhaps because of it.

Peter Webster, boss of Blackpool's Central Pier entertainment, offered me the 1965 summer season for six hundred a week with a guarantee of fifteen thousand, six hundred pounds if the show ran less than six months. Once more my little family joined me in St Anne's for the duration of the school holidays. The show had opened to only passable reviews for me, so I was glad of strong support from ventriloquist Neville King, and a youthful Mike Yarwood in his first stage show. Yarwood taught me a useful lesson. For a Sunday concert in St Anne's he playfully borrowed a few gags from my closing spot at the Central Pier. I found out about it and asked the advice of our amiable impresario, Peter Webster, who told me I ought to play my part as the star of the show, send for the offending support act and give him such a thorough dressing down that he would never do it again. Harry Butterworth was duly sent scuttling round to Yarwood's dressing room and, between houses, he sauntered in to see me. I took on an avuncular air.

'Now listen to me, my lad – learn, mark and inwardly digest!

You do NOT steal another entertainer's act. You do NOT steal from a friend. Taking my material is theft. You want to steal from me? I'd sooner you sneaked in here while I was on stage and picked my pockets! Now run along and NEVER do it again.'

Yarwood smiled brightly and left. I was trembling with the effort of simulating anger, my nerves quite frayed and my head aching. Three snorts of malt whisky later, I was walking along the backstage corridor to plant a couple of props in the footlights when I heard a burst of laughter from the Zio Dancers' room. A voice was raised and I recognised it. It was *mine*. More laughter. The door wasn't completely shut and I peeked in through the crack. All the members of our cast were sitting in a semicircle around Yarwood, who had assumed my stance and physical mannerisms. He was saying, 'You want to steal from me, my lad? Better that you skulk like the low thief you are, await your moment until the STAR is onstage, enthralling the simple people who have paid to see HIM, then creep into my dressing room and *pick my pockets of what gold I possess*! Now run along and NEVER do it again!'

How they laughed, how I blushed. Then I ran along and NEVER did it again.

Ever since that evening, every time I've been tempted to over-react to some minor transgression by a colleague, I've heard Yarwood's masterly burlesque of my pomposity in my mind and looked for a better way to deal with things. And, like everyone else who's ever worked with him, I've come to have great respect and affection for Mike Yarwood.

At a Variety Club Luncheon celebrating my fortieth year in show business, he spoke, not as himself but as me. When he sat down, his face was slick with sweat.

'How do you do it?' he muttered. 'I've only been you for eight minutes and I'm knackered. You've got to keep it up for a whole sodding lifetime!'

One morning early that summer in St Anne's, I was washing my car on the forecourt of the house I'd hired when a small man approached and addressed me with an officious air. 'Monkhouse, isn't it? I'm Councillor Whenham. You've heard of me.'

I had indeed. After our opening night at the Central Pier he had complained to the *Blackpool Gazette* that my material was blue and offensive, then led a clean-up campaign to have all the comedy in every local show censored by a committee which he would lead. His outcry had fizzled out as soon as its small political purpose had been served, but not before Webster had been persuaded to cut out half of a very well-received sketch of mine called 'Candid Capers'.

The idea was simple but effective. I'd roam through the audience, conducting a quiz about what they could see on the stage and passing out little prizes for good answers. Then we'd play back a tape recording of the whole thing but with different props on display. I kept the gags simple. For example, the first time we went through it, a chorus girl would hold out a large pair of earrings and I'd ask woman in the audience, 'Madam, do you ever wear things like that?'

Answers would vary from, 'No, I never wear them' or 'Sometimes, but I'm not wearing any now' to 'Yes, if I'm going to a party' and so on.

As we played the answers back, the earrings would be replaced by a frilly pair of panties. That harmlessly ribald gag had to be cut, along with five or six others, all because of Councillor Whenham's self-serving attacks.

'Yes, I do know you. Is there something you wanted?'

'It's just that I'm thinking of buying a new car,' he said, tapping mine with his walking stick. 'Nothing like this, of course. Something more sensible.'

Holding my temper, I told him that my monthly car magazine had recommended a newly imported Japanese car for ease of parking and maintenance and extraordinary petrol economy. He thanked me curtly and walked back to his house, which I now realised was only a few doors away from mine. A week or two later I saw his new red Japanese car parked outside his gate. I jumped into my own car, drove to a garage and bought a two-gallon can of petrol.

Every night, when I came home from the show, I sat up with a whisky or two and a good book. At about one a.m., I walked quietly from my house to Councillor Whenham's, unscrewed the petrol cap on his car and topped up the tank.

A week or two passed and I was in my driveway, waxing my car this time, when he pulled into the kerb, got out of his new motor and slapped its roof proudly.

'Well, as you know, I'm no fan of yours, Mr Monkhouse, but I'll give you your due, you know about economical cars. I've done my first four hundred miles in this little beauty and not yet used up one tank of petrol!'

As he stood there, his narrow chest stuck out, his Alf Garnett moustache bristling with pride, I wondered how many other people he'd told so far. I also wondered how long it would be before his sanity was doubted.

I filled up his tank every night for a further two weeks, by which time I was told that he was worrying his colleagues at work and in Council with his far-fetched boasting about having a car that did eight hundred miles to the gallon. Then I stopped adding fuel to his tank and started removing it every night, using a long rubber tube, my now empty can and a spot of lung power. Suddenly the man was barely getting ten miles to the gallon. His exhausted figure was seen all over East Lancashire, pushing his gas-guzzling vehicle. One morning he knocked at my front door. 'I wonder if you could assist me, Mr Monkhouse. It's that car you recommended. At first, it was absolutely wonderful, it was giving me a thousand miles to the gallon. Now I seem to run dry every few hundred yards.'

He blew his nose emotionally and I almost felt sorry for him.

'I wonder if you'd oblige me by coming with me to the car dealer who sold me the thing. Give me a bit of moral backup, as it were. I can't get them to understand over the phone. We'd best use your car, what with mine acting up and that.'

I told him I didn't mind at all. I didn't add that I wouldn't have missed it for worlds. We drove to a famous Blackpool motor trader and I went with him into the office of the manager. I stood just behind Whenham so that I could watch the expression on the face of the man sitting at the desk. Whenham wasted no time in preliminaries. 'Look, I bought that car off you for economy and, to begin with, economy was what I got. A most satisfactory economy. Up to around a thousand miles to the gallon.'

The set of the manager's face shifted from patient to numb.

'Now, for the past fortnight or so, I can hardly go the length of our road before the car's used up every drop. All right, I've given it quite a bit of thought and I reckon I'm on to the answer. The Japs put some sort of thingy in every car they export, some doodah in the engine that makes it get the highest mileage out of the juice, right? And, after the first thousand miles or thereabouts, the *doodah melts*!'

The manager's eyes met mine. I allowed my eyes to cross slightly and lolled my tongue out of the corner of my mouth. Then I re-focused and moved my eyes to indicate Whenham. The message was 'this man's two spanners short of a toolkit'.

'I'm right, am I not?' Whenham was continuing. 'No, it's quite all right . . . ' as the manager started to speak, 'I don't want to know any of your precious trade secrets, thank you. I've no time to spend on campaigning against Jap imports. All I require from you is that you put in a new thingy, doodah, whatever it is, so that I can get the proper miles per gallon I'm entitled to – and we'll say no more about it. Fair enough?'

I waited with Whenham while the manager whispered to his head mechanic and two assistants were despatched with Whenham's car keys and a can of fuel. They soon returned with the little red car and it was raised on the grease rack. The mechanic fiddled unconvincingly with the underside and the manager suggested coffee back inside his office. Whenham snorted and muttered, 'Doesn't want us to see what's being done!'

His car was waiting for him out in front, tank filled and ready to go. We said goodbye and I watched him drive off. The manager was standing behind me. 'That man's on the Council, you know.'

'So I understand.'

'Jesus! And I thought *we'd* still got a few parts on order.'

After that, I left Whenham's car alone. He was now getting a perfectly satisfactory forty-five to fifty miles to the gallon, but what comfort was that to him? He, who had once gloried in a miserly motorist's heaven of a thousand m.p.g.!

Just before I quit Blackpool after the illuminations at the dark end of October, I saw Whenham's little red car parked on the grassy area of the pavement outside his house. A very honest sign on its rear end said, 'FOR SALE, AS NEW. 2,400 MILES ON CLOCK. ONLY DOES 50 M.P.G.'

By the end of the summer, I'd made up my mind not to wait any longer for a TV opportunity that wasn't going to knock. If TV Light Entertainment wasn't about to give me a break, I'd make my own. Denis and I had once packaged a sitcom for the BBC. Now I planned to be my own employer and create a series I could back with my own money.

Once while in America I'd pursued a show for myself that never did come to Britain, a re-working of silent film dramas, imposing silly plots and a zany soundtrack, under the title 'Fractured Flickers'. Being a fan and a keen collector of silent films I didn't much like what was being done to them, but work is work. I didn't much like the man who provided copies of some of the films either, a freak of nature named Raymond Rohauer. Now I reckoned I needed him. Having made contact by phone, I flew to a meeting with him in New York. 'Ray, here's my proposition. I've got a very large collection of silent comedies, nearly all of them known to be in public domain, the few remaining almost certainly out of copyright too. I want to make a show called "Mad Movies" with me as the host. I'll use my own library of film with others I can hire from the film historian and curator, Phil Jenkinson. I don't know who'll buy the series from me, I don't even know whether or not I can sell it, but I do know there's only one man in the world who'll try to stop me – and that's you.'

Rohauer didn't smile, he just acknowledged the truth of my statement by slitting his eyes and licking his lips with what could have been a forked tongue. He was a stocky, flabby man in his forties, with tight wavy brown hair over a porcine face that made him look like a pig in a wig. His reputation had made him feared by all private film collectors. They had come to dread his dogged pursuit of them through the courts, his obdurate insistence upon his ownership of imprecise rights to the motion pictures they had preserved, the sheer implacability and unreasonable greed that had made him awesome even to some of the more venal lawyers he engaged. I knew of naive hobbyists who'd been so terrorised by him that they eventually surrendered their film collections into his hands for nothing more than his promise not to prosecute. Sometimes he obtained what he called 'quit claim deeds' from the widows of silent film pioneers for a token sum, using the documents to scare off other claimants to the films he appropriated. With the threat of tireless litigation, indictments, interdictions, injunctions, and other legal delays of every kind, Rohauer's nuisance value made him a better ally than foe.

Simply having his name on the credits of my series would protect me from lesser predators.

'I'll want an all-expenses paid trip to England, viewing facilities to see all the footage, plus ten per cent of sales worldwide,' said Rohauer, picking his porky nose.

Please don't get the idea that I hated the man, I didn't. He just seemed to me to be unnecessarily unkind, naturally vicious, cold, mean and repulsive, that's all. You can't waste all your time and energy hating everyone who's like that. Well, you can, but it does you no good and them no harm. Hatred poisons the hater, not the hated. I won't have anything to do with it.

Back to London and my partners, where we agreed to set up a company called Comix Ltd, sharing everything three ways. I'd supply the films from the thousands I'd amassed since starting to acquire out-dated film hire libraries when I was sixteen years old. Over the ensuing years, I'd spent a fortune on saving old films. Now I hoped they'd save me. It was also my lot to assemble the shows, edit the movies, script the half-hour shows, record the voice-over commentary and link the clips on camera. Malcolm would write, arrange and conduct all the music. Henry's job would be to set up the production company and direct its activities. While he sold Eyeline Films on the idea of deferred payment, I persuaded Richard Williams to make us animated titles for the pilot at cost. Since he was skint and *Roger Rabbit* twenty years away in his future, I got them.

We all moved so fast that Jeff Inman was directing me on the home set in the Goldhawk Road Studios, Shepherd's Bush, only seven weeks later. Rohauer grudgingly OK'd the pilot show and we were ready to let it loose upon the box-watching world. First, however, we had to stick to a deal I'd struck with Brian Tesler, once my youthful BBC producer for most of our 'Fast and Loose' shows, now the boss of ABC TV's programmes. In exchange for a little extra financial help from his company, he had secured first refusal on the whole thing. Supposing he didn't like it. I'd have to come up with my own dough to repay the loan and I'd already ventured as much risk capital as I dared.

I thank God for the clips of Buster Keaton in *Cops*, Mack Sennett's *Love in a Police Station* and Tesler's schoolboy sense of humour. He ordered thirteen shows with options for thirteen and thirteen. In the event, we made all thirty-nine. They aired on the ITV network as the early Saturday evening crowd-catcher, and we sold them to thirty-eight countries over a period of sixteen years. Everyone made a few bob, including some of the clowns.

By arrangement with the Motion Picture Benevolent Fund, I located nine of the actors who'd appeared in our 'Mad Movies' between 1910 and 1927 and sent them certified cheques. One original Keystone Kop was eighty, in a charity home bed, and not expected to live long enough to spend the money. I sent it anyway. A few months later I asked after his condition only to be told by the matron that the old boy had no sooner got his loot than he ran off to Mexico with a twenty-year-old nurse. Comedy keeps you young, you see.

'Mad Movies' was doing well with the public but there was no use kidding myself. It just wasn't doing the trick of reviving my popularity with TV producers. They saw it as a kids' show. I needed to come up with something better if I was to protect my future as a desirable booking into my middle years. My marriage was crumbling fast now, held together only by our mutual concern for protecting our children from emotional damage. Something had to be done to save my career from crumbling too.

I remember a bitter October night in 1966 when I sat alone in our garden, wrapped up against the cold and staring at the stars, willing my mind forward, uselessly straining as if to pierce the black curtain that hides tomorrow and see what the future held. I dozed off for a moment and, as I snapped back to consciousness, I knew I'd had an odd sort of dream.

I was part of a laughing crowd, moving through a well-lit park at night towards a sort of illuminated palace in the distance. I asked a man where we were going and he said, 'Hurry up! It's New Year's Eve! It's 1999!' When I looked up again, the palace was very near and a sign in lights over the entrance said 'Bob Tonight'. Such a foolish dream. I've never been superstitious so I dismissed it. I didn't believe in dreams. But then, I told myself, they do say that they can come true whether you believe in them or not. I went to my single bedroom, an adapted first floor sitting room next to the master bedroom where my wife slept, feeling absurdly comforted.

24

ANOTHER *ANNUS MIRABILIS*

1967

After some bad playing of second fiddle comes the close call of the African jungle, the distant roar of the London greasepaint, and the happy chatter of the presses. An agent becomes a lifelong friend, and a family is divided as mother and son reunite

My seven-year-old daughter and twelve-year-old son spent most of Christmas Day, 1966, leaping in and out of a big swimming pool under a cloudless blue sky. The temperature was in the high eighties but my wife and I were kept cool by northerly breezes and mint juleps. We were enjoying the hospitality of the Melrose family in the flower-filled grounds of their home in a very exclusive suburb of Johannesburg but, as we joined in the light conversation and frequent laughter, we concealed a fair amount of tension. When Ronnie Quibell had come to London to book the British artistes who would support the American Barrie Sisters on their six-week tour of South Africa, I'd grabbed his offer. At that time British Actors' Equity had no objection to their members working in the Republic and, as well as longing to see the country, I felt that the trip might offer one last chance to repair a damaged marriage.

As soon as we arrived at the Jo'burg hotel, optimistically called The Sunnyside, it was apparent that it would take more than sharing a bedroom again to make things right between us. Along with that chagrin, I began to wonder if I'd made a wise move in accepting second billing to a singing duo well established in the States but quite unknown to the British TV producers and bookers who would read about it in the theatrical papers back home. I might appear more washed up than I was. Having only surrendered top billing twice before in a dozen years to two trendy hit parade toppers, I was finding my professional pride hard to swallow. While I chafed about that and my untimely absence from the TV scene as we entered the new year schedules, my wife and I were both suffering from another kind of guilt and anxiety. Six weeks was the longest we'd ever gone without seeing or living with our oldest child, Gary. Although we had explained our journey to him and had his OK, we still felt awful about not being with him at Christmas time. Still, if you have to put on a brave front, you might as well do it under a sunny sky beside a sparkling pool with your fist wrapped round your sixth highball.

Once my fellow performers began their rehearsals, I got the measure of the show that would take us from Jo'burg to Cape Town, East London, Port Elizabeth, Durban, Pieter Maritzberg and back to the capital again. As I watched from the empty stalls, a kind of mischief came over me.

So what if our posters and programmes read 'THE BARRIE SISTERS SHOW! STARRING THE BARRIE SISTERS, with Four Supporting Acts! British TV Star Bob Monkhouse'? If I couldn't close the show, I could still top it.

My remaining days before our opening night were spent in assiduous absorption of everything pertinent to South African life: topical issues, national celebrities, popular characters on radio, mockable politicians, everything indigenous that I could joke about and our audiences would not expect a visitor to know. Nights, I sat at a desk in a small office provided for me by the hotel, ripping my basic act apart and reconstructing it to make every line suit the inessive case, with the seamless inclusion of gags about everything Suid Afrikaan from Van Der Moewe to Jan Smuts. I hunted the record shops for Peggy Lee's song 'I Love Being Here with You', had it orchestrated and copied for our musicians and wrote myself an opening lyric to fit that included every local reference which had defied my efforts to invent a spoken joke about it. By the time our first audience filed into the great Civil Hall, I was ready with three short compère spots and a first half closing act that had to do or die.

The show was very good. Barry Kent sang superbly; Ben and Adam, Israeli folk singers calling themselves The Dudaim, scored well with the largely Jewish crowd; Roy and Jackie

Toaduff knocked them dead with their clog dancing finish; and the Barrie Sisters closed the concert with an immaculate performance that pleased everyone. As for me, in Arthur Askey's favourite phrase, modesty forbids. Suffice to say (another of Arthur's pets), by the time our company had been moved on, I had been moved up. Hastily reprinted posters and programmes announced 'COMEDY STAR BOB MONKHOUSE with Full Supporting Programme. Special US Guest Stars, The Barrie Sisters'. Good as they were, I was stronger. In the immortal words of scriptwriter Spike Mullins, never turn your back on a full-grown comedian. It might bite.

As our tour drew to a close, my wife flew home to London ahead of me, mainly to catch up with the children's missed schooldays. Alone in my hotel room, I smoked the cannabis that our musicians had gathered from the hedgerows whenever their coach halted for the call of nature to be answered. It did nothing for me.

After three or four nights puffing pot, I found out what the musicians meant by 'a bad trip'. Since South Africa I've never taken any sort of hallucinogenic drug, chiefly because I don't want my consciousness expanded one iota more than it already is. At my age now, an acid trip is popping round to the corner shop for a packet of Rennies.

I don't do depression very well. Those final days in Jo'burg were about as close as I've ever got to it, I suppose. My problem is, I try to get serious about what's wrong and the very effort starts me laughing. I say to myself, 'You're depressed? OK, I've got the set-up. What's the punchline?'

> *I tried that Positive Thinking stuff*
> *but I knew it wouldn't work*
> *and, sure enough, it didn't.*

In the midst of this anomalous condition, Doug and Diane Cullinan came to my rescue. She had been one of BBC TV's brightest singing stars, Diane Todd, a petite Liz Taylor *doppelgänger* with an operatic range. He was the handsome scion of the man who'd discovered the Cullinan Diamond. As Doug told it, his forebear had been shuffling about in one of his diamond mines when his boot kicked a half-buried beer bottle.

Thinking he'd caught one of his workers on the sauce, he'd taken a closer look and slowly realised he was holding the biggest single diamond ever found. Its greater part became a centrepiece of the Crown Jewels.

Seeing my discombobulated state, they suggested a safari. We agreed that I'd pay for a week at Mala Mala Game Reserve for all three of us if Doug would drive the seven hundred miles there and the same back. He gave Gilbert the week off and we went. Gilbert was the Cullinans' princely looking chauffeur. They had lent me his services and a limousine during my stay. He'd turned out to be a self-educated, well-spoken companion and we got along very well. Due to the segregation laws it was impossible for us to eat or drink together at any good restaurant or bar, so I'd buy food and beer and we'd share it in the car. Once I asked him if there was anything I could send him from Britain.

'Can you get an American magazine for black people called *Ebony*?'

'I've seen it on sale. I'll buy you a subscription.'

'No, thank you, it would never get through to me here. Just buy a copy for me and send it wrapped inside some right wing paper.'

'Do you think all this talk of a blood bath, a black uprising against the white minority, do you think anything will come of it?'

'Oh, for sure. In confidence, right? Well, first there will be riots, just like in the French and Russian revolutions. Then, suddenly, the white population of this country will be swept into the sea.'

'Will you have to take part?'

'Oh, for sure.'

'What about Major and Mrs Cullinan?'

'What about them?'

'You'd never harm them, would you?'

Gilbert turned his finely sculpted face to me with the offended hauteur of a Bantu nobleman.

'How could you even think that? The boss and his wife have done everything for me and my family. I love them very much. I could never harm them in any way. Never.'

'Forgive me.'

'Of course.'

There was a silence in the car. Then Gilbert said, 'I have a private arrangement with the gardener who works for Colonel and Mrs Vandenberg. I'm going to kill them for him. And he's going to kill Major and Mrs Cullinan.'

I waited for the funny punchline. There wasn't one.

At Mala Mala we stayed in rondavels, the round guest houses traditional in South Africa. At night, the loudest noises were the roar of the air-conditioner and, from the roof, the creaky sounds of that curious rock badger called the hyrax. Each dawn we breakfasted together at an open-air trestle table before our Great White Hunter came to fetch us in his jeep. His name was Basil and he looked like the little bald man Benny Hill used to slap.

We were amazed at how invisible wild animals can be. Basil would drive through the veld for an hour or so, then stop in one of the more thickly forested parts and silently gesture around him as if to say 'get a load of this'. We couldn't see anything to get a load of. He had to whisper. 'To our left, between the nearest trees, three giraffes staring at us.'

We still couldn't see them. With a sigh, Basil would slide out of the driving seat and let his feet touch the ground. Immediately, the previously motionless creatures would take off and become as plain as day.

A few times Basil let one of us drive. My turn came as we headed through a sea of grass about three feet high. I wasn't going very fast when I thought I saw a light brown stump or anthill sticking out of the grass about four yards ahead and I braked. The thing turned and we saw two blazing cat's eyes looking at us. The young lion stood up and growled. I said, 'Any suggestions?' and immediately five more lions rose to their feet all around us.

Basil said, 'Full speed ahead', so I stepped on the gas and steered through the widest gap between the startled beasts. Two of them chased us for twelve yards or more, one getting close enough to take a swipe at the back of the jeep that I could feel in the front of it.

Over a picnic lunch in a clearing, Basil said, 'I know those boys. They look quite big and fierce but they're still only cubs. They were larking about, those two that chased us. We weren't in much real danger.'

Doug signalled to me to join him and I walked with him round the back end of the jeep. The spare tyre fixed to the rear was slashed through.

On the third day there, with three more to go, we were about an hour from the lodge and using our cameras to record zebras as fat as butter, their striped haunches reminding me of the seaside postcard mothers-in-law of Donald McGill, when the sounds of the game reserve took on a new type of growling. From behind us appeared one of the staff, a tall Kenyan girl with skin the shade of cognac, wearing a blazing red and orange caftan and turban, riding along our rutted trail on a battered little motor scooter. She stopped, dismounted and asked, 'Mist' Ma'house?'

I said, 'That's me.'

She held out a folded cablegram. Since I never fear the worst, I opened it with nothing but curiosity. It said, 'BOB MONKHOUSE, MALA MALA GAME RESERVE. MOST URGENT YOU RETURN LONDON SOONEST. HOST SUNDAY NIGHT AT THE LONDON PALLADIUM NEXT SUNDAY ONLY WITH OPTION. FEE AGREED WITH HOWARD. CONFIRM. REPLY PAID. ALEC FINE.'

Somewhere in the trees a bird gave a mad, whooping laugh. I concurred.

We were on our way within two hours, the Cullinans less bothered about our abandoned vacation than excited for me about my summons home.

In the plane leaving Jo'burg, I read the cable for the fortieth time. 'NEXT SUNDAY ONLY WITH OPTION'; did that mean what I hoped it meant? That if I did a good job in three days' time, they'd take up their option to use me again the following week? I settled down in my seat and started making notes, writing down every notion that entered my head. If this great chance was going to pay off, I needed all available ammunition. I was still far from sleep when we landed at Heathrow.

The taxi driver at the airport knew me. 'Glad to be 'ome, Bob?'

'I certainly am.'

'St John's Wood, isn't it?'

'No, thanks. Take me to the London Palladium, please.'

'What you doing there then?'

'Hosting the TV show this Sunday.'

'Won't be no telly people there yet, will there?'

'There won't, no. I just want to walk about on the stage for a bit and get the feel of the place.'

'Nervous, eh?'

'No, not nervous. Just bloody determined.'

I haven't inflicted many press clippings on you in this history but, at this point, a couple of quotes will explain what happened next with a contemporaneous observation that I may now lack. It just so happens that a benign publicist named Tony Barrow was looking after my promotion later in the year and kept a scrapbook. An uncredited article in *TV Weekly*, dated 8 June 1967, is headlined 'BOB'S BIG SUCCESS – *FROM A 'ONE WEEK' PALLADIUM BOOKING!*' It reads:

The man with a thousand and one gags, Bob Monkhouse, this week finishes one of the most astonishing television excursions of his career – compèring the last LONDON PALLADIUM SHOW in the present series on Sunday. He was booked as host for one week only, when the 11-year-old show was sinking low in the ratings. He transformed it. He also transformed himself. He's stayed altogether for 13 editions, having conquered the most gruelling task in television on Sunday night. His was one of the strangest contracts in the television history of that theatre. Every week, he got bigger, louder, longer laughs. So the officials booked and re-booked Bob and he kept re-shuffling his cabaret engagements in order to return to the Palladium. And now it's a foregone conclusion that the host who put the ailing warhorse back into the top 6 shows of the week will return soon with a fair contract.

The *Evening Post* of 12 June says:

BOB'S THE MAN FOR THE NEXT BIG SHOW

and continues:

The eleventh season of Palladium shows closed last night with a pretty average bill with little to relieve the set, stale pattern. The one thing that has made the present series at all interesting has been the long overdue recognition of Bob Monkhouse. He has been around in the business for many years, and in many ways was a pretty big star. After all, everybody knew the name. But for some reason the really plum jobs seemed to escape him. Then he stepped into the Palladium hot seat and came up trumps. He has approached the thankless task of compère in a fresh, friendly manner. His humour has been infectious and clean. Never has there been the slightest trace of smutty jokes, and for that I thank him more than anything else. It has been a Monday morning topic of conversation for three months now, with people in offices and factories swapping Monkhouse's witty lines from the night before. Each Sunday, when one feared his invention must fail, he'd appear as de Gaulle, Francis Chichester, Mick Jagger or Jayne Mansfield, to make the evening his own. Encore! If the Palladium has to come back, and its late success ensures it, it will take Bob Monkhouse to carry it.

Please forgive my vanity in including these favourable reviews. I just felt that I'd rather have them tell you about the way it was, than try to pussyfoot round the facts myself. In one of the many clippings I found in Barrow's scrapbook (nearly all of them kind; the *Daily Express* said I was 'sometimes too slick and glib for comfort' and the *Bolton Evening News* commented, 'Monkhouse jokes too quickly for older viewers'), there's one review syndicated around at least five papers, including the *Yorkshire Post*, the *Northern Despatch*, the *Oxford Mail* and the *Nottingham Post* and the *Shields Gazette*, dated 10 June. It says:

And so we say 'farewell' to the present series of London Palladium Shows, hosted and hoisted to new heights by Bob Monkhouse, who has been called a 're-find' by ATV chief Lew Grade. The master showman said, 'The Palladium Show will be back and Bob with it. He's our golden boy.'

And I thought I'd finally grown out of that. Still, this time I reckoned I'd earned the epithet. Luck and labour had got me out of the doldrums.

During this uplifting experience of re-discovery, I became allied with one of the two people who would most affect the rest of my life. Henry Howard asked me to meet an agent called Peter Prichard. 'I'd like your opinion of the man. Tuesday morning at eleven all right?'

He was in the office with Howard when I got there. I didn't know then that Peter would always be everywhere before anyone else. At this stage, I knew this Prichard chap only vaguely. We'd met a few times in Leslie Grade's office, where he'd worked his way up from general dog's-body to the European representative for the top US variety host, Ed Sullivan. I knew he'd managed Mario Lanza in Rome, and a number of visiting American stars in Britain, the likes of Lanza, Johnnie Ray, Gene Barry and Robert Horton of *Wagon Train*. Meeting him again, he struck me as a tall, well-formed and well-tailored man, with a distinctly London accent and an easygoing manner. His upper eyelids had a slight tendency to droop at the outer corners, giving his translucently blue-eyed regard an oddly sad look. He had full cheeks and light brown hair, slightly wavy. His handshake was firm and dry, and I said I was pleased to meet him again, even though I had no idea why.

'Bob, I'm delighted to tell you that Malcolm and I have convinced Peter that it's high time he left the umbrella of the Grade organisation and formed his own agency, Prichard Howard Management. He'll be taking an office with us here and acting as your future agent and manager.'

'Oh,' I said.

'He's got a nice raft of working performers that he's bringing with him with the blessing of Lew and Leslie but, of course, you'll be his major star. Peter here understands that, with the way things are going for MMA, well, I just haven't got the time to spend on your personal management. Obviously, we're hoping you'll volunteer to increase the percentage of your performing fees as currently deducted, in order to cover additional costs.' The briefest pause. 'Because all this wonderful success of yours means you can't contribute as much of your creative talent to our company, but yet you remain a one-third partner.'

'I see,' I said.

Howard then suggested a commission percentage that I found unacceptable. He *agreed* that it was *totally* unacceptable. Peter suggested we should take our time and think it over, these things could be worked out. I asked what would happen to the two agents who'd appeared one day and increased my cabaret fees by seventy per cent, never to be seen again. Peter said there was no need to worry about them, he'd take care of it. I asked Peter how long he thought our arrangement should last. He said these things had a life of their own, it was better to go from day to day, week to week, let matters decide themselves. I said I wondered what direction my career ought to take from now on. He thought that would depend on so many unknown factors but he was certain we could look forward to a very good future. During this platitudinous exchange, I came to the conclusion that I liked and trusted this fellow who wasn't handing me a line of bullshit or making the slightest attempt to sweetheart me into believing that he could achieve miracles like so many other agents had. I stood up and said, 'Good! Well, I've got my solicitor to see about the apartment my wife wants to live in. You don't handle any hit men, do you?'

The Palladium success brought me a huge rush of work and I accepted it greedily and thoughtlessly. Without stopping to consider how I'd used up every good idea I had in the concentrated material that had been packed into the Sunday night shows, I flung myself into an Anglia series called 'Carnival Time'. During the previous few months, a dental mechanic named Wally Malston had submitted some good topical gags and I had persuaded him to give up his day job and work with me for a retainer plus fees for material used. Together we travelled to Clacton on 6 June to meet my co-host Pete Murray, producer John Paddy Carstairs, and the first nine competitors who wanted to be crowned 'Miss Anglia'. I was over-confident and careless, my private personal situation providing no excuse for my burdening the clever but inexperienced Wally with the responsibility for the entire script so that I could spend hours on the phone, planning my domestic split. The first transmission was on 8 July. Barrow's scrapbook becomes harrowing reading at this point. Since I imposed flattering reviews upon you a few pages ago, perhaps I can make amends with this comment from the *Essex County Standard* of Colchester:

Comedian Bob Monkhouse and disc jockey Pete Murray lead the

*so-called fun each week in Anglia's Carnival Time. Where
Monkhouse attempts urbanity, he achieves smugness. Where he
believes himself side-splitting, he is merely painful. His eye-rolling
lechery during last week's demeaning miniskirt contest had to be
obscene to be believed. One can only feel sorry for the courtly
Murray who seems too debonair to realise that a man may be
judged by the mean company he keeps.*

We visited twelve towns with this trashy circus, me and Pete
gabbling our crosstalk before lunch on the dusty stages of sweaty
town halls and civic centres in Scunthorpe, Cleethorpes,
Bedford, Lincoln, Hull, Corby, Skegness, Hunstanton,
Northampton, Gorleston, Peterborough and Felixstowe. In the
afternoons we capered inanely through slapstick rubbish in fields
and car parks and swimming pools, while Life Boat Crews tried
to tow Swimming Clubs into jets of cold water, mini-mokes raced
against clowns on bikes, Bagpipe Bands wailed and local blades
frolicked through feathers and soot.

No one else took that much notice of 'Carnival Time' so it did
little damage. In many ways, 1967 turned out to be as much my
annus mirabilis as that which I'd enjoyed a decade earlier.
Thanks to the persuasion of my Aunt Ella in Port Elizabeth and
Jackie's gentle but persistent urging when I returned from South
Africa, I had written a long letter to my mother. In it, I expressed
all the increasing regret I had felt during our long estrangement,
explained the breakdown of my marriage, related the ups and
downs of my career, and told her that I loved her and longed to
see her. She replied with a cautious letter, inviting me to visit her
at her home, 'Madeira' in Ashurst Drive, Goring-by-Sea, Sussex.
I went and was received with guarded kindliness. We exchanged
further letters and, beside her signed 'mum', she drew a little
cartoon of her pet dachshund. That touched me quite a lot. By
summer's end I had been to see her three times and was feeling a
tremendous relief, although my only attempt to discuss the roots
of our years of animus was immediately quashed with a quick
frown and a dismissive flutter of her hand. She didn't tell me she
was having radiation treatment for cancer. Late the following
year she was to succumb and fall into a coma which would last
until the next summer of 1969.

When she died I felt no particular sense of loss for two or three weeks. Then Jackie made some quite inconsequential remark in no way connected with my mother and it triggered my pent-up grief. I collapsed with sorrow and loss, grieving not so much for her death than for her life, racked with regret for the lack of all that could and should have existed between us. For several weeks afterwards my conversation was subject to lapses. I'd simply lose the hang of what I was saying and start to become uncontrollably distressed. Having to go onstage every evening in Bournemouth was a blessing. This may seem strange to you if you haven't experienced some similar relief from the oppression of bereavement.

There's a term I'd often heard show people use: Doctor Theatre. You can hurt yourself quite badly while onstage and be quite unaware of it until you come off. I discovered that you can also leave your dressing room in an extremity of melancholy and forget all about it as soon as your foot hits the boards. For two hours or so you're free from sadness or remorse because there's a show to be done, in this case a high-speed, knockabout farce.

It's impossible to contemplate personal desolation while you're cantering around a set full of doors, yelling barmy dialogue and dropping your trousers. By the time the curtain's come down, you've had a little holiday from heartache. For all that Jackie has done to bring me in closer touch with my deepest feelings, I am still not one to wallow in woe if I can avoid it. Even now, writing these words, I can feel the tug of emotions reawakening the uncomfortable awareness of my failure to break down my mother's defences and make her widowhood that much happier, no matter what the cost to me. It shouldn't be up to the parent to come to the child and beg forgiveness for a mutual mistake with shared responsibility. In such circumstances the father and mother have given what they can and that includes the gift of life; now the child has the chance to repay through the subordination of ego in the interests of filial love. I can tell you that I will never forgive myself for failing in that duty, but then again – yes, I will, because I don't have to write like this every day or read my own words. I'll be writing and reading something else, using work as I've always used it, to keep myself contented and well distanced from sad thoughts.

My driving ambition over the years, backed by what I believe is very little actual original talent, has been in part a way of keeping useless, wasteful worry at bay while I've got on with the positive activity in hand. Mind you, I'm not quite as nifty with this evasive trick as I used to be. Ever since Jackie unblocked the channel between my outer mind and my inner heart, it's been harder to whistle in the dark. I've involved myself more and more with the kind of charity work that puts me in deeply moving situations. As well as the belief that I ought to do what I do, that it's my duty, there may be an element of self-punishment in it. When I see the under-fives with cerebral palsy being assessed at the London branch of the Peto Institute that my colleagues and I support through SOS, I can't deny the pain that is part of my compassionate hope for them. Once I could have averted my mind. Well, I detested my ability to do that. I knew what I was up to and I hated myself for it. I remember standing in a room at the Turk's Head Hotel in Newcastle, away from my young wife and children for a whole week, literally hugging myself with the glee of freedom. Then I caught sight of myself in the mirror and my shame was overwhelming. So I went for a very brisk walk and made up a parody that I did onstage that night.

I'm glad that's changed. If I hadn't grown up and away from that, I might be shaking with horror at the very thought of my inhuman coldness. While I shall never embrace guilty self-judgement as a daily penance, I take comfort from the fact that I'm not incapable of it.

★ ★ ★ ★ ★

Gary was excited about his mother's new home in Holland Park and fully accepted the idea that I had to remain behind at Loudoun Road to sell the property. His schooldays were ending and we were taking him to look at some of the adult residential centres run by the Spastics Society so that he could choose. At first he favoured Cambourne, near Redruth in Cornwall, but later on he was to settle upon Kyre Park, a beautiful old mansion by a lake, close to Tenbury Wells, Worcestershire. It would be his other home for over twenty years.

His thirteen-year-old brother spent his school holidays serving in a shop specialising in old military uniforms. Every day he took three buses and a train to Camden Passage in Islington, N1, having impressed the shop owner there with his knowledge of Nazi paraphernalia when he'd called as a customer. His school was now Holland Park Comprehensive, with fellow pupils like fifteen-year-old Jonathan Routh, son of my old 'Candid Camera' compatriot, eleven-year-old Nicholas Korner whose dad was jazz musician Alexis Corner, John Huston's sixteen-year-old daughter Anjelica, and the children of such luminaries as Tony Benn, Roy Jenkins, Lord Queensberry, Lord Kennet, and the novelists John and Penelope Mortimer. The school had a better cast than my entire Palladium season.

We entered my daughter at Fox School, an easy walk from her new home, and I flew out to Aden on 2 August to entertain our troops, minus the twenty-five showgirls from Raymond's Revuebar in London's West End who'd volunteered to accompany me. Army command had signalled Arthur Watson of Combined Services Entertainment that they couldn't guarantee the girls' safety as all their units in Aden were on standby in the danger stage that comes before red alert. Nice stuff for the act:

All the way over on the flight I could feel something hitting my left knee.
It was my right knee.

Already Peter Prichard was lining up work, one of my Polaroid ads had won a 'Clio' award at the American TV Commercials Festival, the new Yorkshire TV company wanted me to host their 'grand opening night' with Frankie Vaughan, a film I'd made for Exide called *Getting Your Share* was scoring a big sucess as a trade education exercise, radio hired me to chair a new series titled 'Mark My Words' with Katie Boyle and John Junkin, CBS records asked me to make my first single release singing 'I Remember Natalie', Willis Hall invited me to illustrate two of his books with my cartoons, and Denis Norden had written me a wickedly funny role as the trendy psychiatrist in the new Shirley Maclaine-Richard Attenborough movie, *The Bliss of Mrs Blossom*. Enough? Well, apparently not for the fellow I was at the time.

While I was still living from week to week as the Palladium host,

I'd picked up the merest whisper of ATV's new secret acquisition from Europe, some sort of game that could be played by viewers from their own homes. Hungry as ever, I had gone in search of this mysteriously titled show. I was to find not so much a show as a way of life.

25

'THE GOLDEN SHOT'

– ROUND ONE –

*In which boy wants show, boy loses show, boy storms
show, boy gets show, impresario gets robbed and Bernie
the Bolt gets his name*

I first heard of it in May, with two more of the season's Palladium
shows to go. I didn't know exactly what it was, I only knew I
liked the sound of it – 'The Golden Shot' – and that Lew Grade
had bought it from Germany for ATV. A new show, an exciting
title, to be made by the TV boss who had just told the press that I
was his 'golden boy'! I thought, 'I'd like to get that series.' When
I found out what it was, the best single idea for a game show in
over a decade, then I *knew* I'd like to get that series. Word was
out that my old friend Colin Clews was going to produce it, so I
arranged to bump into him accidentally in the bar at the
Borehamwood Studios, bought him a pint and me a whisky and
asked what he was up to next.

'Haven't you heard?' 'Clewsie' gave me a lazy, blue-eyed gaze
that said he knew very well that I'd heard. 'I'm in charge of a
Nazi firing squad.'

'Need any help with it?' He'd been glad of my suggestions on
other shows, ever since he had directed my 1957 series, 'Do You
Trust Your Wife?'

'As I understand it, I'll be getting your help, Bob. Bill Ward
has more or less decided to ask you to compère it.' Now he
seemed genuinely surprised. 'He hasn't spoken to you then?'

Feeling jubilant, I said, 'I expect he's talking to Peter Prichard
right now. Well, it'll be great to be doing a hit show together, eh?
I hear it's a beaut.'

'Clewsie' sank the second half of his beer and gave me his best
sardonic smile. 'Wait till you see it, it's more of a brute.'

236

As I drove to my new agent's new Hertford Street office in my Palladium car, a deep blue and silver Buick Riviera I'd bought to celebrate the upturn in my fortunes, all I could think of was the safety and security of hosting another series, perhaps even alternating six months of the Palladium with six months of the new show. It was easy to park my show boat vehicle beside the London Hilton. This was 1967 and half the recently installed parking meters were vacant. As for driving with a whisky or two inside me, Mrs Barbara Castle had yet to introduce her November blow to the club trade, the breathalyser.

I couldn't wait to break the news to Prichard. In a way I was to become accustomed to over the next quarter of a century, he let me finish. Then, as straightforward as he'd always be, he shook his head as if in sorrow at the childish fancies of all performers who wanted the moon.

'Sorry, love, it's gone.'

Gone?

'Lew saw that Canadian singer, Johnnie Ray . . .'

'Jackie Rae?'

'Yea, him. Apparently he was playing the part of a quiz show host on that Charlie Drake programme the other night and Lew liked his style.'

I couldn't take it in. A few minutes ago I'd got 'The Golden Shot' in my sights, now it was a misfire – I'd lost it to another host. I knew Jackie Rae, a charming singer and record producer, briefly married to Thora Hird's film star daughter, Janette Scott. He had hosted Granada's late-fifties 'Spot the Tune' ably enough. Up till this moment I liked him. Now I wished I could get him deported back to Canada.

I drove home feeling angry with myself. A valuable writing day of preparing topical gags for my last two Palladium shows of the season had been wasted on my pushy optimism. My wife had tickets for the National Theatre that evening. I sat and watched Tom Stoppard's ingenious *Rosencrantz and Guildenstern Are Dead* without following a word of it. We argued on the way home and I couldn't bring myself to tell her about my disappointment during the day. To have described the failure of my hopes would only have provided further justification for contempt. She told me she'd set a date in October for her and the children to move out of our St John's Wood home and into the Holland Park mansion flat.

Alone in my makeshift bedroom I looked through the newspapers and tried to write jokes inspired by the news of the day.

The news of the next day was that 'Sunday Night at the London Palladium' was to end.

'But it's a hit again, Peter!'

'Yes, love, Lew wants to take it off while it's back at the top. Have it remembered as a success. It was his baby, after all, his and Val Parnell's. So it'll finish this June, though they're not announcing that yet. But there's an offer of four nights' cabaret in Mansfield at the Doom-Doom Room . . .'

The cabaret casino was in Macclesfield and it was called the Boom-Boom Room but Peter's name for it was better.

For the final Palladium show I persuaded three previous hosts to join me on the stage – Bruce Forsyth, Jimmy Tarbuck and Norman Vaughan. We sang a parody of 'Dearie, Do You Remember When . . .', listing the most memorable events in the history of the show, launched by Tommy Trinder in 1955. Tommy couldn't appear, he wasn't well enough, but we used his recorded voice as though he were phoning and his then still familiar catchphrases,

'Trinder's the name! T.R.I.N.D.E.R., pronounced Chumley!
I'm gonna sing to you – ha ha – you lucky people!'

The show came off the air at nine p.m. with the cheers and applause of the audience combining to produce the famous 'Palladium roar', a sound that no other theatre has. In the aftermath of such happy excitement I didn't feel much like going home to sadness and tension so I invited Wally Malston, Tony Hawes and Jackie to dine with me at Isow's in Brewer Street. Jack Isow had copied the idea originated by a Broadway eaterie of putting the names of its most famous patrons on its chairs. When we arrived for dinner my morale was lifted when he showed me a new addition to the leather seating. There among chairs elegantly painted with such illustrious names as Leslie Howard, Charles Chaplin, Jack Benny, Rex Harrison, Ginger Rogers, Cary Grant, Vivien Leigh, Danny Kaye, Al Jolson and

Ronald Reagan was one bearing the words 'Bob Monkhouse, of All People!'

'The Golden Shot' made its debut that summer after much touting in a vigorous publicity campaign hailing it as 'the liveliest LIVE show ever!' One press review responded with 'It's the deadest DEAD duck ever!' I watched the first show from a hotel room in Gateshead with increasing discomfort. It seemed to me that to dislike what I saw would be giving way to a cheap sort of satisfaction. Yet there was so little to like. Jackie Rae was affable but obviously very nervous and uncertain of what was going on around him.

Its Teutonic origins revealed their worst qualities in the stolid style of the production, allowing no humour or excitement to interfere with the plodding procedure of the game. The central idea was still excellent but no attempt was made to sell it to the viewers. Quite simply it was this: a TV camera is mounted on a big crossbow, looking through the sights at the target, so that a contestant sitting at home anywhere from Orkney to Penzance could see it and, using the telephone, direct the blindfolded cameraman to aim at the bullseye and fire the bolt. But the German target designs were so dull, just geometric designs with roundels. The three hostesses were lovely but languorous, the two musical interludes intrusive, the guest star served no purpose other than to fire the bow at an apple and the world's least attractive armourer was instructed to arm the bow with the world's least attractive catchphrase: 'Heinz, the bolt!' You could almost see his swastika tattoos. 'Clewsie' had been right from the start; it was a brute of a show.

Having concluded that I was lucky not to be presenting this calamity and so suffering condemnation by press and public alike, I was puzzled when Peter phoned to say I was wanted as the guest star for the tenth week. The fee was insignificant and the inconvenience considerable as it meant travelling from Liverpool to Elstree and back again for my midnight jobs at Jack Murphy's Cabaret Club in Duke Street. And who was watching 'The Golden Shot' now anyway? Its Saturday ratings had plunged. 'I know, love, but it's a chance for you to show 'em a thing or two on that set.'

I got the message.

Having made sure the set was standing, I drove out to the studio and looked it over. The guest had to fire the bow using a joystick in a glass booth. The booth looked like the one featured in a frequently seen soap commercial of the day where a man went into a phone kiosk which turned into a bathroom shower. I sought out my pals in special effects and had the booth rigged to do the same. Next, I consulted the props men and they agreed to build what I'd drawn. Then came the script which I wrote and rewrote in an office adjoining the one occupied by Colin Clews. He eventually wandered in and asked what I was writing so busily. When told it was my guest appearance for next week's show, he laughed.

'Come off it, mate, Jackie Rae'll never learn that!'

'How is he with cue cards?'

He laughed again and sat, shaking his head, 'You're a crafty bastard.'

Looking through what I'd written, he added, 'It's funny, very funny. But you won't get these props and set changes made in time.'

'They're half done already.'

'A very, very crafty bastard. So you do a great guest spot, who's going to see it? Lew and Bill won't be watching, they've lost interest, and there'll be no recording for them to send for.'

'There could be, couldn't there?'

'You want me to tape it?'

'Or have it filmed on 16mm, just in case.'

There was a long pause while he considered the additional costs I wanted him to meet. He looked again at the script.

'OK, OK. I need you all day Friday to rehearse this. Who's going to play the midget and who's going to pay him?'

'Johnny Vyvyan, and I'll pay him if it's not against ATV policy.'

'I'll ask Alec to book him officially.'

'Clewsie' stood, walked to the door and gazed back at me with a kind of wonder. 'If I ever want to study for the crafty bastardhood,' he said, 'I'll come to you.'

On the Monday after my first appearance on 'The Golden Shot' there were phone calls buzzing from Sir Lew Grade's office to

Bill Ward and from Bill Ward to Colin Clews and from Colin Clews to me. If I had been hoping for congratulations and praise – and I had – I was sorely disappointed. It seemed I'd hit the target and shot myself in the foot at the same time. Both Lew and Bill were seething and it soon emerged why. My spot on the show had run three minutes longer than planned and, as a result, a song had had to be abandoned so that there would be time for the finale, the 'golden shot' itself when a winning contestant fired for the one hundred pound prize. As luck would have it, the song that had been cut was a plug for a new record release that Lew had personally promised to EMI, a company closely associated with ATV. Embarrassed and irate, he could identify only one obvious source of his irritation – me.

Peter was very relieved when he knew a recording had been made. He told his godfather Lew, 'Just look at the show. Just sit down with Bill for a moment to see what happened and why.'

So they did and what they saw was this:

Half an hour of the usual stuff, tedious as ever, with no audience reaction other than cued applause where required. Then I was announced and my first appearance brought a crack of laughter that registered on the Richter scale. I was dressed as a big target, the golden bullseye over my middle. The absurdity of anyone showing up at an archery contest in such an idiotic costume delighted the previously bored crowd. A fusillade of gags followed as I removed my outer costume to reveal a Tyrolean outfit in the style of William Tell, put an apple on my head and did some comic business with a curved crossbow that could shoot round corners. Then I announced that I had my own private armourer, 'Heinz the dolt!' A four-foot tin of Heinz Potted Shrimp was wheeled on and tiny Johnny Vyvyan climbed out, dressed as a stormtrooper with a spiked Prussian helmet and carrying a gigantic door bolt. We plunged into a fast and crazy routine in which I fired at various objects he was holding up, each of them rigged to explode when hit and shower the stone-faced little man with their contents. The laughter was just as explosive, roars of hysterical mirth and applause bursting from two hundred and fifty people who had been spending an evening starved of any semblance of fun.

When I started stuffing Johnny feet first into a large cannon, Jackie Rae must have been wondering what had hit him.

Unrehearsed, he was rooted to the spot by his need to read his lines off idiot boards.

I ran into the glass booth to fire the cannon and rattled off a few funny lines while Johnny was secretly replaced by a dummy. On a signal that Johnny was out and clear, I pressed the firing button. There was a hell of a bang with confetti and red smoke, the dummy soared fifteen feet in the air and its spiked helmet stuck firmly in the bullseye.

The crowd went wild and Jack Parnell, watching the show on the screen of a TV monitor in the bandroom, waited for the din to diminish before giving his orchestra the downbeat. Precious seconds were ticking by.

Then the music from the then famous soap advert filled the air and, just as in the familiar commercial, the lighting changed to make a silhouette of me as my firing booth became a shower stall. A cascade of water hit me from above and I washed myself, working up a lather with the detergent already in my clothing. If an audience ever howled with laughter any longer and louder, it could only have been in comedy heaven.

As they viewed the recording, it was obvious to two showmen as experienced as Lew and Bill that there had been no way in which any performer or producer could have prevented the audience reaction from spreading my spot three minutes longer than the allotted time. They also must have seen something they liked.

On the Thursday of that week Lew sent for Peter. ATV's light entertainment booker Alec Fine joined the meeting and Lew told them to do a deal for me to take over as host on 'The Golden Shot' as soon as possible. A fee of two hundred and fifty pounds was mentioned. Peter wished he could help them, especially as he had been Lew's protégé and appreciated all the help and advice he'd been given when starting up his own agency, but what could he do? He'd got me booked in cabarets for at least a dozen Saturdays to come, all for lucrative fees. Cancelling such bookings would be difficult enough but suffering the loss of income to his fledgling business would be crippling. Lew must have eyed him with a mixture of antagonism and admiration. He recognised a good negotiating point when he heard one and if he admonished Peter for using such a gambit, that would surely bring the very reasonable answer from any star pupil to his master, 'Guv'nor, you're the one who taught me.' It was due to Peter's talent far more than mine that Lew eventually authorised Alec to pay the unheard of fee of seven hundred and fifty pounds per show. I was to take over on the fifteenth edition. 'But if the show's not increased its present rating by fifty per cent by the time we get to show twenty-six,' said Lew, 'I'll dump it.'

Within a few hours Peter had cleared the decks and I was free to spent the next ten days reconstructing 'The Golden Shot' in an attempt to turn it around and make it a success. I grabbed a free ticket to a land-selling junket on Grand Bahama and got away from it all for a deep think. By the time I was flying home again, I thought I had all the answers.

I hadn't, of course. But I'd come up with enough ideas to revitalise the stilted format. Out would go two of the languid hostesses, only vivacious Carol Dilworth remaining, later to become wife to Chip Hawkes of the Tremeloes and mother to Chesney Hawkes of more recent pop fame. In would come quaint Norman Chappell as my comedy amanuensis, an ever helpful valet to provide comedy interruptions during the live scenery changes. The seven wearisome stages of the original game were simplified into only four: home contestants used their phones to aim the bow at the central detonator in each of four apples, thus blowing them to smithereens, the successful marksmen qualifying for a place in the studio next week. These four players then handled free-standing crossbows, aiming at a more difficult target to win a bronze prize. The two with the highest scores qualified for the silver stage, using the joystick to aim at an even tougher target. Finally, the week's best archer tackled the 'golden shot' itself, trying to sever a thread. If it broke, a glittering shower of gold coins gushed on to a chute and clattered into the winner's treasure chest below. (Previously, hitting the bullseye had caused a sagging bag of money to fall to the floor with a dull flop, and another dull flop was just what I was determined to avoid.)

Cutting repetitive rounds allowed more space for human interest, time to talk to the competitors and get some laughs. But more space also created the need for greater continuity, a natural flow that would make it easy to return to the story of the show. To provide this framework each week, I used a single theme: circus, British history, sport, space exploration, the arts, any subject that would inspire pictorially thrilling targets, engaging musical ideas, appropriate comedy interludes and attractive star guests.

My first show kicked off with a historic reunion of the RAF Skyrockets Dance Orchestra conducted by Paul Fenoulhet. Our detonating apples were located in barrage balloons over the skyline of London in the blitz. Anne Shelton sang a wartime medley and then the free-standing bows fired at models of Luftwaffe bombers diving through the sweeping beams of our searchlights, the flying bolts exploding the enemy aircraft seconds before they could drop their deadly cargo. Comedy guests from 'Much Binding in the Marsh' were Richard Murdoch, Kenneth Horne and Sam Costa. After a comedy routine, they fired on behalf of their charity, the RAF Association.

The target for the silver shootout was a marvellously accomplished model scene of the kind only the artisans at ATV could produce. Sitting in the booth operating the joystick, the contestants were given the point of view of a fighter pilot, homing in on a choice of three enemy planes of increasing difficulty and prize value. It was only just possible to shoot down all three in thirty seconds and our second player, a decorated and one-legged ex-RAF rear-gunner named Basil 'Ginger' Cody, did it. Then, in an atmosphere as tense as the thread he had to split, he fired a perfect bull and won the golden shot as well. As Anne Shelton presented him with the treasure chest and his other prizes, the official Band of the Royal Air Force played their stirring march anthem and cheered the winning hero. I promise you, there wasn't a dry eye in the house.

Though our switchboards were jammed for over two hours with congratulatory calls, the national press took no account of us until the second week. For this, Tony Hawes and I designed old time Music Hall targets, drawn in the style of Donald McGill's vulgar seaside postcards and based on such songs as 'My Old Man Said Follow the Van' and 'Any Old Iron'. The set resembled a typical variety stage of fifty years earlier and our two musical guest stars were eighty-nine-year-old Hetty King dressed in top hat and tails singing 'Piccadilly', her success of 1909, and seventy-eight-year-old Randolph Sutton recreating his beloved 'On Mother Kelly's Doorstep' from 1925. Our comedy guest was dear old Sandy Powell, who gave us his hilariously inept ventriloquist sketch and then fired a winning bolt on behalf of the Variety Artistes' Benevolent Fund. Once again the golden shot was won, this time by a sixty-eight-year-old ex-chorus girl. Luck was smiling on those early shows. This time the papers noticed us: 'A Bolt Out of the Blue!', 'Golden Shot Bobs Up' and 'On Target at Last' were three headlines that conveyed the new opinion of the series. A quarter of a century later, it's difficult to communicate the extraordinary warmth with which these shows were greeted.

Someone suggested that it was due to a combination of singular factors: the drama of an over-ballyhooed series failing and then surviving, a follow-up to my own return to public favour at the Palladium, and a lack of anything comparably energetic in that season's TV amusements. During the third week, my wife and children moved out.

The show achieved a fifty per cent increase in its ratings in only five weeks. Lew was about to extend our Saturday run past its twenty-sixth week when a chance remark made him reconsider. His young nephew Michael Grade had gone to see a James Bond on a Sunday afternoon but had been turned back by the length of the queue. He told his uncle, 'The cinemas are always full on Sunday afternoons because there's nothing worth watching on television.' Lew must have figured that he had the ideal family entertainment for Sunday teatimes and it wouldn't cost the folks the price of a Bond film. After consulting the other network chiefs, he switched the 'Shot' to its new slot and phoned Peter. 'Obviously you'll adjust Bob's fee.'

'Lew, I wasn't thinking of an increase this soon.'

'Yes, very funny, I'm talking about a downward readjustment to accommodate the fact that you won't be losing cabaret work.'

'You know comedians, Lew, Bob thinks he's made a turkey into a hit.'

'Which could be a long runner, over a year, two, three even, you make more by taking less, you follow me?'

'But can you be sure of a long run with a different host?'

'Peter, how can you do this?'

Since neither of the parties involved will ever tell me what was really said and I've had to imagine the above conversation, I can only suppose that Peter finally got his chance to reply, 'Guv'nor, you're the one who taught me.' I only know that I continued to be paid seven hundred and fifty pounds a week and that a year later, while I was walking out of the studio gates at ATV, Lew's chauffeured car stopped beside me, the rear window hummed down, Lew shouted 'Robbery!' and the window hummed up again.

At my suggestion, Humourless Heinz had been released from his duties as armourer and allowed to return to the Reichstag or Brazil or wherever. In his place a mild-mannered special effects expert named Derek Young was assigned the care of the crossbows, their adjustment, cocking and loading. Since the previously used command to load had lacked euphony, I suggested that we use an alliterative phrase such as 'Bartholomew, the bolt' or 'Basil, the bolt' or 'Benjamin' or 'Barnaby' or 'Bertie' or 'Beauregard'.

'What's wrong with Derek?' asked Derek, 'I think Derek's a nice name.'

'No question, but this isn't about your real identity, Derek. You're playing the role of the armourer and if we pick the right name, repeated eleven times in each show, it'll become a popular catchphrase.'

'Derek, the bolt?'

'Doesn't quite make it. How about Bart? No? Benson? Broderick?'

None of my names suited his taste and he expressed grave doubts about his being able to accept the job if he couldn't keep his own name. I begged him to reconsider. He was just right for the part, a diligent technician of pleasing appearance, and I didn't want to lose him. Two days later he appeared at my elbow in the studio canteen. Eyes downcast, visibly embarrassed, he muttered a word I didn't quite catch.

'Sorry, what did you say?'

'Bernie,' he repeated flatly.

'Bernie?'

'It's the wife's idea. I still don't like it but she does.'

'Bernie, the bolt? What made her think of that?'

'I think she had an old boyfriend by that name,' said Derek with a sigh.

A year later the phrase had entered the national vocabulary.

Without any encouragement, our studio audiences began to join in every time I drew breath to utter, 'BERNIE! THE BOLT! PLEASE! THANK YOU!'

Towards the end of 1968, ATV decided to move the production to the major city of the Midlands area the company was franchised to serve, Birmingham. This meant using the existing provincial staff and crews and, of course, a different armourer would replace the Borehamwood-based Derek.

Once again Derek appeared noiselessly by my side at the canteen bar. I ordered him a lager. We drank in silence for a while, then he asked, 'What are you going to call him then?'

'Who?'

'The next bloke, the one who'll be doing my job in Birmingham.'

'Well, we can't change the catchphrase, Derek. Whoever takes over, we'll have to call him Bernie the Bolt.'

'But . . . but *I'm* Bernie the Bolt!'

'Well, yes, until we start the new series, then someone else'll have to be Bernie the Bolt.'

'But you can't do that to me,' said Derek, 'I'm picking up good money opening fêtes!'

Two further blindfolded 'Bernies' were to guide the giant crossbow in the Birmingham years, Alan Bailey and, for the final three years, popular Johnny Baker. But to me and many, Derek will always be the first and most famous Bernie the Bolt. He's retired recently but I know he still treasures his year of fame.

So by 12 January 1969, the 'Shot' had moved again, this time physically. Proved to be a success as a Sunday teatime fixture, we were now ensconced in our new but old home, the technically out-dated rabbit warren known as the Aston Studios in Birmingham.

Everyone there was patiently or impatiently waiting for the completion of the new studios in the heart of the city, briefly styled 'The Paradise Centre'. This name instantly suggested a soubriquet for the comparatively dilapidated Aston Studios: 'Hell Motel'.

26

'THE GOLDEN SHOT'

– ROUND TWO –

In which a run-down studio runs us up the ratings, a brace of contestants is mislaid, and a comic genius takes steps to be laughed at

Murphy's Law – 'Everything that can go wrong will go wrong' – acquired an addendum at Aston: 'And everything that can't possibly go wrong will also go wrong.' Once, when essential equipment broke down five minutes before we were due on air and I asked if it could be mended, a senior technician said, 'I don't know, we're running a little bit short of string, chewing gum and hope. Thank God we can stick things together with shit.'

On the screen, our disasters began with the very first Aston transmission and never quit. Light bulbs overloaded and burst, my radio mike picked up local taxi controllers, phone lines to home contestants suddenly died, cameras went down, crossbows warped out of alignment, safety solenoids failed, tape decks jammed and tangled their tapes, an apple loaded with far too much gunpowder blew up in a ball of heat that set fire to the curtains – they were right, I thought, as I chattered at my number one camera in an attempt to keep some sort of show together for bemused viewers, this *was* Hell Motel. I could see the flames.

But as chaos maintained its reign in subsequent weeks, a small phenomenon slowly developed. Veteran viewers, now accustomed to technically flawless shows, felt a twinge of excitement at the return of accident-prone live TV. Younger viewers, unaccustomed to seeing stars tripping over unfixed carpet and electric guitarists struggling with blown fuses, found our disarray fascinating. Students began to grant our accursed populist efforts cult status. Critics who had long deplored my nonchalant slickness now relished my public discomfort and found my panic-stricken strivings to conduct a crumbling catastrophe curiously appealing. The weekly spectacle of a smoothie-chops with egg dripping off his chin was winning me friends I never had before.

The unflappable John Pullen was producing when we lost two contestants during transmission: a Mr Henry Doak and a Mrs Flo DeMange, phoning from Rawtenstall and Didcot respectively, had shattered their pippins the previous week and duly arrived at our ramshackle studios at noon on this fateful Sunday to join two other players in a short course of instruction, all four meeting for the first time. When, I now wonder, did love first bloom? Was it as the new armourer invited them to share a common trigger? Could it have been over a canteen lunch of ATV's boiled ham and coleslaw?

Or did passion ignite all unseen as they sat beside one another in the circle seats during rehearsal while the rest of us were engrossed in trying to make order of disorder? However it happened, I suspected nothing as I introduced the four players to the viewers and conducted each of the bantering interviews. Mr Doak from Rawtenstall and Mrs DeMange from Didcot defeated their opponents at the free-standing crossbows and so qualified to compete in the silver stage of the game.

Ironically enough in view of what happened, the theme of that week's show was 'Great Escapes'. Targets offered animated scenes from *The Wooden Horse*, *The Count of Monte Cristo*, *Albert R.N.* and *The Colditz Story*, with the star of the last film, John Mills, as our special guest. While I joked with John and introduced Del Shannon to sing 'Runaway', Mr Doak and Mrs DeMange ran away. Nobody missed them till Shannon was into the closing bars of his 1961 hit. Then the floor manager noticed that their chairs were unoccupied. He instituted an instant search while the song ended and I led the applause, then announced the duel for the silver prize.

Let's welcome back the two successful survivors from the bronze combat, Henry Doak and Flo DeMange!

The people clapped and two total strangers walked towards me. I addressed them as Henry and Flo and they didn't argue. One of these two imposters won a washing machine and the other cracked the golden-shot for three hundred pounds. If the studio audience detected any difference between the mysterious new-comers and the pair who'd won at the bronze stage, none of them showed any sign of it. And there was never a single phonecall from a single baffled viewer. What could people have thought? That Doak and DeMange had come back in disguise? That the first pair were fakes and the second genuine? Was no one paying any attention at all?

As you'll have guessed, the floor manager had used his initiative and grabbed the first couple he could lay hands on, pulling them out of their seats with an urgently whispered, 'Just go along with whatever Bob says.' Placidly, they had done so and done rather well out of it too.

Of Mr Doak and Mrs DeMange I can tell you nothing more. They vanished and we never even saw the going of them. We received no enquiries from distraught families and our staff were too busy to make any of their own.

I like to think they were two lonely people who experienced love at first sight and eloped. In Wally Malston's less romantic view, 'They lost their bottle and pissed off.'

Because the old Aston main auditorium was a converted cinema, the stage and stalls had been removed to form a studio floor around which cameras and scenery and actors could be moved. The audience sat in the circle, unable to watch much action directly and following most of the productions they came to see by staring at TV monitors suspended from above. They really might as well have stayed at home. I hated that set-up and had persuaded Dickie Leeman, newly assigned to this penance, to built the 'Shot' on two levels, connected by a handsome staircase. This enabled the comedy to be done on a platform right in front of the people, while the rest of the action could take place down below. Terrific idea. Perfect for accidents.

At one point it seemed that everyone in show business was a kind of lemming, eager to come on the show solely to fling themselves down our staircase. Alan 'Fluff' Freeman lost a shoe halfway up and did it again halfway down. When I told the endearing magician David Nixon that he was to be 'this week's

shooting star', he took a step back in mock modesty, missed his
footing, only just saved himself from toppling and said, 'Bit early
in the day to see a falling star!' Tony Blackburn cracked a joke,
got a laugh and was so surprised by it that he backed away from
the audience in alarm and somersaulted down eight steps. His *ad
lib* was, 'I think I just became a slipped-disc jockey!' Matt Munro
tried to slide down the banisters and nearly broke his coccyx.
You might suppose that this deathtrap would have discouraged
celebrities from coming anywhere near the show. But for one
great clown it was a magnet.

My home phone rang. 'Bob? It's Norman, Norman Wisdom.
Can I come on that show of yours, please?'

'My God, yes. When?'

'Soon as possible.'

'Are you free next Sunday?' Harry Secombe had been booked
but had begged off, saying he was sick. Maybe he'd seen that
staircase.

Norman jumped at the booking and turned up at the Aston
Studios on the following Friday. He took a look in the deserted
auditorium and came back to the receptionist's desk. 'Excuse
me, miss, but where's the staircase? For "The Golden Shot"?'

'The staircase for the . . . oh, they strike the set on Mondays
and build it Saturdays.'

'I can't wait till tomorrow, miss, I need to rehearse on it now.'

'But there's no one here to put it up.'

'Well, where is it? I'll put it up.'

'It's all in pieces in the scene dock. You couldn't put it up by
yourself.'

'Bet I could if you helped me!' Norman was so eager, she
laughed.

'Wait, let me make a couple of phonecalls. I'll see if we can get
it built first thing in the morning.'

The stairs were in place by eleven a.m. and Norman was
rehearsing on them by eleven-o-one. The next day he persuaded
John Pullen to start early and instead of our usual stagger-
through plus one camera rehearsal, we managed three full
rehearsals of the comedy segments. By the time we went on air at
four-thirty p.m., Norman must have been up and down the
twenty-three steps well over a hundred times. He was fifty-two
years old and no more exhausted than a dog track hare.

I opened the show by announcing that I now had an assistant. Norman pelted up the stairs. 'Not yet, Norman, I'll tell you when.'

Norman hurled himself down the stairs. 'And here he is!'

Norman sprinted up. 'I didn't say your name.' Norman bounced down.

'Norman . . . ' He whizzed up.

'Wait for your full name.' He fizzed down.

' . . . Wisdom!' Now he couldn't get up the stairs for trying. His legs entwined, he tripped and fell, his knees seized up, both legs stiffened, he tried to climb with rigid limbs, tumbled and caught his head between the struts of the balustrade, all of these wonderful acrobatics while anxiously repeating at the top of his voice, 'Coming!' At last he overcame all his physical problems and arrived beside me in triumph. And I said, 'All right, I'll send for you if I need you.' Norman fell all the way to the bottom of the staircase.

Soon it was time for the first of our phone contestants to shoot. Norman fought with Bernie for the right to load the bow. I summoned him upstairs and told him he could be Bernie's assistant, he could be the one who fetched the bolts. He ran downstairs to tell Bernie this, then he realised he had to run back upstairs to fetch each bolt from me and then run downstairs to give it to Bernie. The studio audience grew near-hysterical as Norman found different ways in which to negotiate the stairs. Their laughter was so unrestrained as to make the producer wonder who would surrender to fatigue first, them or Norman. But to me, witnessing this virtuso display of athletic comedy taking place all around me, it seemed that the more they laughed the more inventive he became, and the more inventive he became the louder they laughed. It was an unvicious circle.

When the time came for Norman to fire the crossbow himself, I told him he had to make an entrance. 'But I'm already 'ere,' he complained. ''Ow can I enter if I'm 'ere?'

'Use the stairs. Walk up them with dignity.'

Grumbling, he slouched down. Announced, he zigzagged up with what was meant to be dignity, nose in air, hands flapping dismissively.

'No, not like that. Do it in a more manly way. Be masculine.'

Now he charged up, chest out, shoulders up, shadow-boxing

and growling, threatening men in the front rows, clambering on to women's laps like a pet. As with my very first visit to the show two years before, some dispensable singer had his ballad quietly dropped from the show to make room for unstoppable mirth as Norman continued, inspired by appreciation, finding a seemingly inexhaustible source of delightful silliness in the ways in which the human body can behave on a staircase. After the usual climax of the golden shot itself, there was time for Norman to take one last skipping run up the twenty-three steps to acknowledge the audience's ovation. In all the years I have watched great performers take instinctive advantage of a situation and exploit it past the point of all foreseeable possibilities, I have never seen anything quite like that single, unrecorded performance on an otherwise forgotten Sunday afternoon twenty-five years ago. The little genius, who'd almost driven me to homicide during the mercifully brief run of *Sauce Piquante* in 1950, had me ready to forgive him anything.

27

'THE GOLDEN SHOT'

– ROUND THREE –

*Wherein a bolt from the heavens silences holy
opposition, a false sense of security causes too close a
shave and a nasty cut from a razor, safe harbours are
found at Thamesside and in Sydney and Hong Kong –
and an Aussie entrepreneur prophesies survival*

Freshly installed at the new ATV Centre in the centre of
Birmingham, we said goodbye to the snags and snares of Aston's
deterioration. Instead, we said hello to an agglomeration of
adjectives beginning with un:- untried computers, unfamiliar
lighting rigs, untested sound systems and a thousand more
unpleasant and unexpected technical traps for the unconvers-
ant. Me, I was undismayed at the prospect of an unpredictable
series which could remain unconstrained and occasionally
uncontrollable.

Guest stars continued to queue up to appear, keen to be part
of the mayhem as rogue bolts spun into the prize displays,
moving targets ran wild or jammed, contestants clammed up or
became hysterical, high-tech colour cameras turned everything
green, chimpanzees ate the target apples, music tapes went
haywire and Clement Freud simultaneously pan-fried an
omelette and set fire to my tie. Wally and I wrote comedy
routines for Ken Dodd, Shelley Berman, Peter Sellers, Stephanie
Powers, Terry-Thomas, Gracie Fields, Sacha Distel, Eric
Morecambe and Ernie Wise, Ella Fitzgerald, Mike and Bernie
Winters, Des O'Connor, Tom Jones, Liberace, Cilla Black – in
terms of top-of-the-bill names we were scraping the top of the
barrel, to uncoin a phrase.

The show was attacked in the press by a lay preacher from

Redditch who complained that we were demonstrating 'weapons of Satan' on a Sunday. We invited the self-styled 'priest of truth' to come to the studio during final rehearsal so that we could show him how safe our crossbows were. He turned out to be a supercilious bore who viewed all our explanations as contemptible. As we went on the air, he took his place in the middle of the studio audience and began to pray loudly in English, Latin and French. I was trying to deliver my opening gags with his voice droning in the background and, of course, I wasn't able to get a single laugh. *Ad lib* lines were wasted. Phonecalls from bewildered viewers began coming in, asking if we had cross-channel interference from a religious transmission. While I hurried through the four telephone contestants, our floor manager tried to silence the chanting priest to no avail. Next came the round when the previous week's apple bursters joined me at the free-standing bows. Still the priest continued his litany, although others in the audience were hushing him now and shaking him by the shoulder.

I must now explain that in 1969 the Independent Broadcasting Authority rules required us to accept all contestant applications in rotation. That had often meant rather unlikely marksmen sometimes appeared on the screen, one so overweight she had to fire from a chair, another so short he had to stand on a box. On the day we had invited the praying mantis, we were also playing host to a lady contestant with a double disadvantage. She was partially sighted and had a nervous twitch in her head and upper torso that could have KO'd Rocky Marciano.

Once the audience had seen her large magnifying spectacles almost dislodged by the violence of her first spasmodic shudder, there was no way to prevent the note of rising delirium in their suppressed laughter. Sympathetic as they might normally have been, this new element of lunacy in the proceedings was too much to bear.

The priest's recital moaned on and the lady took aim as best she could. Then the inevitable happened. She pulled the trigger and twitched at the same time.

The bolt flew high and struck the metal frame at the top of the target, bouncing up and back into the studio where it struck the barn door on an overhead light and plunged downwards into the studio audience. Guess who it hit. Just take a guess. That's right.

It cracked sideways onto the skull of the priest, knocking him cold. Silenced at last, he slid slowly out of his seat and onto the floor. A cheer went up in the studio such as I've seldom heard, cameramen and crew joining in with the studio audience. While two St John's Ambulance men removed the unconscious Holy Joe, we completed the show without further incident.

Afterwards, our press officer said, 'Just goes to show the preacher was right all along. Our crossbows may not be the weapons of Satan but they can be dangerous for some.' It also just goes to show that you shouldn't try to monopolise God on His busiest day of the week.

By 1970 Jackie and I were accustomed to a working routine: the weekly forty-five-minute show on late Sunday afternoon, then off in the car for seven nights in cabaret at Tito's, Cardiff, or the Golden Garter, Wythenshawe, or the Shakespeare, Liverpool, or the Wakefield Theatre Club or the South Shields Latino or Worksop or Batley or St Agnes or Cleethorpes or Middlesborough or Glasgow or Luton or Blackburn or Derby or St Helier or Sheffield or Swansea or Newcastle or – you get the idea. I worked in every kind of nightspot, from the glamour of La Ronde in Loughborough with its perfumed air conditioning to the squalor of the Candlelight in Oldham, where you walked through the door to be hit by a fog of armpits and chip fat. Cabaret work only stopped for summer seasons. Six months of 1969 were spent on a farce called *Uproar in the House* with Sue Nicholls in Bournemouth's Pier Theatre. The following summer we lived in Sawdon, a village near Scarborough, while I tackled the Floral Hall in *The Golden Show* with Ronnie Hilton and Les Dawson. 1971 had me back in farce at Weston-Super-Mare's Playhouse, vying for laughs with David Jason and Bill Treacher in *She's Done It Again*.

All this activity was carefully arranged around visits to and from my three children. As for hosting 'The Golden Shot' every Sunday of the year, doing it had become second nature. It existed in a world of its own, separate and apart from the rest of ATV's programming and, as with all things familiar, good and bad habits had formed. Cosily turning out a show every week for five years, I had grown much too sure of myself. I was involving myself in every aspect of the series, designing more complex targets, conducting a nationwide collection of trading stamps (it bought six dialysis machines and HRH Princess Alexandra accepted the cheque), even bringing friends of mine on as guests, like the socialist millionaire Len Matchan, who pledged £100 for every charity that could phone in before the show ended that evening (it cost him £3,300). If I saw an attractive new product in the shops, a music centre or a portable TV, I'd suggest it to the man in charge of buying our prizes. In a few cases, the companies that made the products would express their satisfaction at seeing their goods displayed on the screen by giving me something from their range. It may have crossed my mind that this was improper but the thought was shrugged off.

I certainly never even suspected that I was giving in to a worsening habit that would bring my downfall and dismissal.

The newly appointed head of light entertainment at ATV's Borehamwood centre was Francis Essex, the gifted pianist-composer I'd first met in 1948 at the Amersham repertory theatre who had then become a highly regarded producer in BBC TV's variety department. There he'd made my first series of the sitcom 'My Pal Bob' and a lavish musical special starring Cyril Fletcher, Terry-Thomas, Jill Day and me called 'Beat Up the Town', appointing me his associate television producer. I asked him, 'What exactly *is* an associate television producer?' and Francis said, 'An associate television producer is the only man in television who'll associate with a producer.'

He moved to ATV, and when I did the same we made more programmes together. I regarded him as a good friend with whom I'd lost touch when he went to Scottish commercial TV as their chief of entertainment. Now he was my new boss and I felt that it made my position even safer. I was wrong. The memos from Francis began at once. He'd seen the show with Len Matchan and was 'appalled at such a flagrant display of the Old Boys' Act' of which there was to be no repetition. Claims for expenses by my favourite freelance designer were disallowed and Francis had to dismiss him. He sent memos couched in the sternest terms on every aspect of the series that displeased him, making it clear that he had detected our smugness and would not allow 'the lunatics to run the asylum'. If I had been less assured of my own unassailable job security, I might have had the sense to proceed with caution.

An advertising executive named Bob Brooksby invited me to a Monday lunch at the Caprice. He told me that Wilkinson Sword were launching a new double-bladed razor and wondered whether it could be part of a prize on our show the following Sunday as the exposure would be a feather in his cap at his agency. I liked Bob and wanted to help. Perhaps we could assemble a sort of His and Hers Beauty Package, assorted cosmetics and aftershave lotions with a course of treatments at a local health centre. The new razor could be displayed as part of the men's toiletries. Bob loved the idea and said if I could wangle it he would owe me another lunch.

Before we left the table Bob handed me a brown envelope, saying, 'It's a little gift, don't look inside now, open it later.' It turned out to be an Olympia Press book from Brentano's in Paris called *The Shy Photographer*. Banned in Britain, it was very filthy by the standards of the day but it made me laugh and I have it still, although there was soon to come a moment when I would be tempted to chuck it on the fire.

The following Sunday the show went on the air as usual. A load of razors and blade dispensers had been delivered to the studio and freely distributed among the staff. One set was duly included as part of the bronze prize for men and the brand name could be seen briefly but clearly on the screen. Wally and I took home a set each and thought no more about it. After all, what did it amount to? A pound's worth of perk, that's all.

Jackie and I spent Monday in Worcestershire visiting Gary at Kyre Park Spastics Society Centre where he was then resident. He was angry with me for sending him the wrong sort of gloves and had refused to watch me on TV the previous day. With a pen clutched between the first and second toes of his right foot he had scratched out the listing of the show printed in the *TV Times* and written 'No more no'. Although his mood soon improved and he forgave me my mistake, his action was uncannily portentous.

On Tuesday morning there was a phonecall from Francis's secretary to say that he'd be passing by St John's Wood after lunch that day and needed to see me on an urgent matter. He arrived at my door in his usual chirpy, brisk way and asked Jackie to excuse us while we settled by the open fire in the living room. My worst expectation of his reason for calling was a warning that my gags with Anne Aston were becoming too suggestive for a

Sunday teatime. He took a deep breath and said it in one sentence.

'Bob, when I was told a week ago that you had been seen and overheard accepting a bribe to advertise a shaving product on an ATV production I could hardly believe it, but I decided to wait until Sunday to see if it was true and, sure enough, you did it and I'm afraid that's the end of the series for you, old chum, although we'll agree to announce it to the press as your resignation, reluctantly accepted by us – OK, fella?'

My throat dried up and I actually felt myself blushing like a school cheat.

'I wasn't bribed, Francis, I mean no money was involved.'

'If you say so, but a pretty fat brown envelope was seen to change hands.'

'That was just a book. It's upstairs, I'll show it to you.'

'No need for that, is there? You tell me that no money was involved and I'm relieved to hear you say it. Still, there it is, the company can't have the host of one of its top shows using it to advertise products for his friends. So I suggest we announce your departure from the series as from the week after next. Perhaps you'll have Peter Prichard tell Alec Fine, yes? That's the bargain then – you step out of the picture quietly and I accept your story that there was no money in that envelope. No fuss, no scandal. Sorry, fella.'

We walked to the front door.

'Francis, I put you in a rotten position. We've been friends for many years and it must have been very difficult to choose between your priorities, whether to warn me not to go ahead or let me fall into the trap. But you're an officer of a public company and your duty to that responsibility was inescapable. No hard feelings.'

That's what I should have said to him but I didn't.

I just muttered a crestfallen goodbye and watched his Jag disappear down Loudoun Road with wretched mortification. I'd really screwed it up this time and for what? A quid's worth of shaving kit and a dirty book in exchange for weekly national TV stardom and about £35,000 a year. Jackie and I had only just struggled out of the debts I'd incurred in my calamitous night club venture in Newcastle (of which more later). I sat down in our big L-shaped sitting room, stared into the fire and contemplated my outstanding talents: greed, sticky fingers and a petty dishonesty were the only ones that I could think of.

Neither Peter nor Jackie ever reproached me. In fact, after Jac had absorbed the seriousness of the situation, she gurgled and said, 'And you always shave with an electric razor anyway!'

Francis was as good as his word. No whisper of the real reason for me leaving my golden series after five years of success ever reached press or public. Well, not until now. He even arranged for shy Johnnie Baker, the latest 'Bernie the Bolt', to surprise me with the presentation of a gold wristwatch at the end of my last show. It was inscribed, 'To Bob – Love and Peace from All on the Shot'. I had to smile. Then I had to smile again when I read the statement given out by ATV to the newspapers. It took me back to that day in 1946 when I stood in front of David Hand's desk in Moor Hall, Cookham, while he gave me the heave-ho from G-B Animation. It said, 'Bob is being released to find opportunities for his abilities elsewhere.' All it lacked was the reference to a broken morals clause.

★ ★ ★ ★ ★

The saga of 'The Golden Shot' doesn't end here with my secretly ignominious retirement, ill-gotten wristwatch and all. It just gets even more absurd. If you'll adjust your sense of the ridiculous up a notch or two, I'll complete the tale after the next few pages. First, let me sketch in briefly the events of the next two years or so. While my place on the series was taken by my good friend Norman Vaughan, the ill wind that had overblown my ego also did me some professional good. Now that I was free of my exclusivity with ATV, Peter immediately negotiated a deal with Thames TV for a sixty-minute special called 'The Bob Monkhouse Comedy Hour', with an option for five more hour-long shows. Within a further week he had fixed me a six-week series of comedy shows in Australia, to begin on 12 April 1972, on Channel Nine from Sydney. I quickly completed a series of TV commercials selling a sort of fruit junket called Nestle's Sweetheart but it was no sweeter to me than the news that my second son had secured himself a place at Bedford College in London University. Although my older son Gary was used to my frequent visits in Worcestershire and regular weeks staying at

Loudoun Road, he took a great interest in my trip to Australia and gave it his blessing by drawing a plane flying there and back with the return date in red capitals on its side.

Abigail cried when she heard I'd be gone for eight weeks but cheered up at once when I promised to bring her back a koala and a kangaroo.

'If one's a boy and the other's a girl,' she said hopefully, 'they might have babies.'

We taped the first Thames hour on 30 March and Jackie and I took off for Sydney on 6 April. Making the Aussie series was a total joy and over so fast that we were able to laze around in the sun in Fiji for a couple of weeks. There we met a TV tycoon named Reg Grundy on holiday with his family. I confided him the facts about my dismissal from the 'Shot'.

'Swear to God, Bob, I've had worse set-backs than that and if I've learned one thing about show business, it's this – if what you do can make money for somebody else, you'll be doing it.' And then Reg added prophetically, 'I'll bet you this, mate – you'll still be a TV star in twenty years' time and it'll be me who's employing you!' With the screening of his company's new version of 'Celebrity Squares' on Central TV in 1993 with me as host, Reg was only one year out.

Jac and I came home via Hong Kong and Bangkok to rush from London Airport to Kyre Park where Gary had organised a welcome home party with party hats, balloons, sherry and iced cakes. The next day was my younger son's last half-term at his public school and we spent it together. I was thrilled when he told me that, after getting a degree in sociology at Bedford, he was considering a career in the entertainment industry.

'That's wonderful, perhaps I'll be able to help you.'

'Doubt it, dad,' he said. 'I want to be a cinema projectionist.'

After reconsideration he opted for the job of a TV cameraman but has finally settled for his current work as an educator.

While we'd been abroad, it appeared that my Thames show had been a success and the option had been taken up for five more. Meanwhile, Peter kept me alive on British screens with regular appearances on 'Jokers Wild', a comedy panel game that was about as genuinely spontaneous as Big Ben. Throughout 1972 and 1973 I kept active on radio with 'Mostly Monkhouse', twenty-six jokey halfhours with David Jason which I wrote myself. I was also busy writing something else, far more effective in career terms, which I'll tell you about before this chapter ends. I hadn't quite forsworn my membership of what Colin Clews had called 'the crafty bastardhood'.

Throughout the summer of 1972, and for the following ten summers, Jackie and I drove round the Butlins Holiday Camps, where I appeared on stage from one o'clock every morning until 2.30am. During one such week, in between these strenuous trips, I had strained my back lifting Gary out of my car and so had to do my cabaret act sitting in a high-backed chair. As I creaked offstage to my changing room, supported by a redcoat and a walking stick, I overheard an admiring holidaymaker remark to his wife, 'It must come as second nature to him, pissed or not.'

The second of my Thames specials, co-scripted with Tony Hawes, and titled 'The Bob Monkhouse Disturbance' aired on 22 November 1972, to the sort of fulsome praise against which I was defenceless. One provincial critic wrote, 'A banquet of spicy comic invention that makes my mouth water in anticipation for Bob's future feasts of fun.' I'm afraid she must have found the next sad mess inedible. Taped the following March, it was a vastly over-ambitious satire on censorship, far too complex to be shot in the two studio hours allotted. The resulting half-completed disaster had to be re-edited into a thirty-five minute oddity that was excreted at eleven p.m. on an April Wednesday when we all hoped no one was paying attention. Not surprisingly, Thames bosses sought to cancel their option for any further shows but were persuaded to take one more chance with me. Hawes and I wrote it with studio simplicity in mind and we recorded it in June without mishap. Philip Jones, the shrewd and kindly head of Light Entertainment at Thames, was so relieved he immediately agreed to modify my contract and buy a series for me to host called 'Quick on the Draw' in which my cartooning knack was lightly tested against a panel of celebrity sketchers. This worked well enough for a second series in 1974, the year in which Jackie and I spent the first of two gloriously happy months in cabaret at the elegant Mandarin Hotel in Hong Kong. More important to this chapter, it was also the year in which 'The Golden Shot' began to loom into my life once more and for the last time.

28

'THE GOLDEN SHOT'

– ROUND FOUR –

*How the crossbow backfired on two reputations and the
prodigal son returned for the last supper; two favourite
tales are told of an aimless archer and a clueless
anarchist and a final crafty stroke is confessed*

After my departure from 'The Golden Shot', its new host,
Norman Vaughan, had taken to it like a cat to water. 'These are
the jokes, folks,' he would say in desperation, waggling an
invisible cigar Groucho-style, once adding, 'I feel as wanted here
as a lobster in a jockstrap.'

Always a nervous performer, his biggest TV success had been
as the chatty host of 'Sunday Night at the London Palladium',
where his vitality and eager charm proved very popular. A
decade later, the physical complications of moving contestants
and guests around the cluttered studio seemed far more daunting
to him. As he confided to me when he inherited the job, 'Listen,
Bobby, it was one thing to nip on between acts at the old
Palladium, twinkle the baby blues, say "swinging" and "dodgy"
and put the next turn on. Nerve-racking enough, that was. But
here I am ten years older and I'm supposed to be funny for forty-
five minutes while I'm directing traffic!'

On the strength of his return to regular TV exposure and the
expectation of his renewed drawing power, the Bailey
Organisation booked Norman into all its cabaret clubs. Despite
his great talent and popularity, he was forever fearful of failure,
packing everything he could think of into his act, from Jennie
Lee Wright for glamour and George Truzzi for slapstick to a pair
of midgets scuttling around inside Mardi Gras heads. We had a
rare and happy reunion when he was playing the Bailey's

Cavendish in Sheffield in early June 1973. I was working at the Jesters, Mexborough, and Jackie and I joined him and his wife for dinner at the Hallam Tower. Bernice said frankly, 'He's not enjoying the TV series or these cabarets, are you, Norman?'

Norman has always been funniest in his modesty and honesty. 'They won't let me out of my contract. I mean, there I am, trapped every Sunday, making a cockup of it, the ratings are down and I want out. Everyone can see it but them. You know what everybody says to me? "You want to get off that show, Norman!" That's all I hear, wherever I go. "You want to get off that show, Norman!" Taxi-drivers, railway porters, hotel porters, they all keep saying the same thing: "You want to get off that show, Norman!"'

At that exact moment, the elegant head-waiter glided up to our table, deftly distributed four giant menus, bent towards Norman discreetly and murmured in a charming French accent, 'You want to get off zat show, Norman!'

The phrase became our shared private joke until a few months later when ATV finally released Norman and announced that the new host of 'The Golden Shot' would be Charlie Williams, the beloved black Yorkshire star of Granada TV's 'The Comedians'. My phone rang and I picked it up to hear Norman's familiar 'Ooh!'

'Where are you?'

'Bobby, Bernice and I are at London Airport, off abroad for three weeks in the sun, can't be bad. Just went through passport control, bought some duty free, waiting for the plane, sitting here, an airport baggage handler walks by, what does he say to me? Go on, what did he say?'

'You want to get off that show, Norman!'

'Right, right! And what did I say, Bobby, what did I say?'

'What did you say, Norman?'

'I *AM* OFF THE BLEEDING SHOW, MATE!'

We laughed together, I wished them both a happy holiday and, out of professional curiosity, made a point of watching Charlie make his debut on the series the following Sunday. Then I watched the second Sunday and the third. Some things you don't believe the first couple of times.

I answered the phone a day later and Norman went, 'Ooh!'

'Where are you, Norman?'

'London Airport, Bobby, just landed, waiting for baggage, *had* to phone you. No need to tell me how poor Charlie's doing. Three minutes ago I'm walking across the tarmac from the plane and a bloke driving a luggage truck spots me, he stops, he gets off, he crosses over to me – and what did he say, Bobby, what did he say?'

'What did he say, Norman?'

'He said, "*You want to get back on that show, Norman!*"'

Charlie's popularity was then at its peak and his agent, Stanley Joseph, could demand and get £4,000 a week for his services, a sum worth seven or eight times as much today. The mistake was to assume that a relatively inexperienced comic, only recently a pro footballer, nurtured into popularity through short clips from his repertoire of largely racial jokes, could step into an established game show and wing his way through its myriad traps and snares without coming a cropper.

Charlie had warmth, lovable looks, a hundred funny stories and a laugh that could ripen apples, but he couldn't *ad lib* a gargle. If a nervous contestant said, 'How do you do?', Charlie was stuck for an answer. Put this fact together with the distorting effect Charlie's new and tremendous popularity had worked upon his ego, and you have a formula for the show business equivalent of a serious trainwreck. Any pity engendered by his inadequacy was nullified by his blithe ignorance of it. Charlie just didn't know how bad he was on that show. He figured he could chuckle his way through three-quarters of an hour of lumbering disorder and keep his public devotion intact. Well, I thought, maybe he could. I was wrong, he couldn't.

When the public takes to a performer as it had taken to Charlie on the vulgarly popular Granada series, it will forgive early mistakes made during the first intoxication of his sudden fame. Then, if disappointment persists, it simply averts its gaze.

As the viewing figures began to dwindle again, the blame was put on bad casting. It hadn't been fair, it was argued, to throw a fledgling comedian in at the deep end, too much had been expected of him, he would have to be rescued by on-the-job training. Sure, like you could teach me to sing opera or divine water or run a four-minute mile. It's as true of the entertainment business as it is of racing: horses for courses. Some comedy performers understand farce, some conquer the concert halls, others shine in film roles, sit-coms or the circus. To succeed in any of these media one requires either genius, exceptional ability or great dedication. Hosting a game show calls only for the last of these, great dedication, combined with a high degree of enthusiasm and a fair amount of facility. That's all it takes but it takes all of it. If the executives responsible for setting up this often despised and widely misunderstood form of amusement fail to recognise the need for total commitment from the team on the shop floor, they become vulnerable to an error of judgement like the casting of Charlie Williams. It all but destroyed the career of an endearing entertainer whose continued rise to sustainable stardom required only sagacious guidance, and the lack of which left him adrift in what was already a shrinking, sinking pool of clubs. It was a crying shame.

Lew Grade must have been in the process of deciding what to do about 'The Shot' and its decline when something made his mind up. I suspect it began with an appearance I didn't make.

Bill Ward had approved my booking for a spot on 'Sunday Night at the London Palladium' on 6 January 1974, in support of the top of the bill, Engelbert Humperdinck. My rehearsal went so well that Jack Parnell's orchestra applauded me, a tribute they normally reserved solely for visiting musicals greats such as Erroll Garner and Stan Getz. It had the effect of making me heady with excitement at the prospect of doing the show that evening. Then came disappointment – the live transmission was cancelled just thirty minutes before we were due on air because of a bomb threat.

While I was feeling bitterly balked, a good report on my contribution must have been made and I was immediately re-booked to top the bill myself on 17 February. Naturally I used the same well-rehearsed material with even greater confidence, featuring a strong parody of ITV's then top-rated religio-pop show 'Stars on Sunday', and I hope you'll forgive me if I boastfully count the evening among my better moments. During the next four weeks I couldn't have guessed what arguments included my name in the upper echelons of the ITV network. Jackie and I were too busy enjoying capacity business at The Talk of the South, Frank Manzi's stunning new nightspot in Southend, where his zany son Lou heckled me every night, inspiring me to some spontaneous ripostes that have remained in my armoury of squelchers ever since:

> *What size of shoe does your mouth take?*
> *This is what comes of drinking on an empty head!*
> *Waiter, serve this man a Durex so he won't reproduce.*
> *I know where you were when brains were handed out ...*
> *getting an extra helping of mouth!*
> *May the wind at your back always be your own.*
> *I need you like Van Gogh needed stereo!*

(We grew to love Lou and his indomitably glamorous future wife, Marion. Today they are our next-door neighbours in Barbados.)

Jac and I were back at home with Gary and Abigail on a March Monday, watching a hired 16mm copy of *Dumbo*, when Peter phoned.

'Lunch, love, this Wednesday, 20 March, Alec Fine, Francis Essex, 12.30, Charles's Necropolis in Greek Street.' You had to know Peter pretty well to figure out that he meant a Greek restaurant called the Akropolis in Charlotte Street.

Francis came right to the point as soon as we'd ordered our meal. He offered me a return to 'The Shot' on the strict condition that I was to be engaged merely as the presenter or compère without any control over the programme content. I suggested we cancel the food and disperse. Peter and I left the restaurant but Alec pursued us and reasoned with us on the pavement: 'Accept, for God's sake. Francis knows you'll probably change the whole damn show but he can't actually say so. He's representing ATV's official position. Just take the job, eat your moussaka and no one will give a damn what you do to the show as long as it goes back up the ratings.'

We rejoined the table and Peter immediately surprised me, which really shouldn't have surprised me by this time: 'Fine, Francis, we'll come back on "The Shot" on your condition if you'll accept our condition. Al Berlin in my office showed Bob an American game called "Hollywood Squares" and he liked it very much. You take an option on that show and, when Bob's done a good job on "The Shot", you give it to him.'

A lot of fine tuning went on but it was all over bar the shooting. While I figured out a new look for that, a deal was struck. Jackie and I went to work in Hong Kong for the month of May where I spent my days planning a format facelift: all contestants would be celebrants, enjoying birthdays, wedding anniversaries, reunions or divorces. The targets would represent important events that had taken place during that week in history. A new signature song, 'This Is Your Golden Day', would be commissioned from Stephanie De Sykes and Barry Blue. Winners would choose their prizes from treasure chambers called the Bronze Room and Silver Room, where dozens of gifts would dazzle them. And my hostesses would be Anne Aston, the sweet-smiling lass who couldn't add up the scores correctly:

She has to take her sweater off to count to two, folks!

and the demure Wei Wei Wong, a Chinese dancer with a wonderfully offbeat way of delivering insults at me:

Wei Wei, she say, if Bobby wore sound-proof trousers,
no one would hear a word he talking about.

Neither of those lines was used on the air, of course; far too shocking for a Sunday. Dennis Berson, a masterly gagwriter from Leeds, joined the team to provide cleaner and funnier jokes and we met to rehearse on Saturday, 2 July. During everyone else's lunch break, alone in the studio, I went over every detail of the re-vamped show, touching the props, moving from place to place, utterly absorbed as I jotted down my notes of continuity phrases, one-line gags and thoughts *tant soi peu*. Becoming aware of being watched, I looked up into the amused gaze of Francis Essex. He said, 'I've been standing here watching you for ten minutes. I've never seen a man so happy.'

The series ran nonstop for the rest of 1974 and up to its final edition on 16 March 1975. Norman Vaughan and Charlie Williams accepted my invitation to return and we sang a farewell song together. Francis presented me with a 16mm film of the last show, the only existing record of the occasion. We had already begun rehearsals for 'Celebrity Squares' at Borehamwood and I knew it was the last time I'd ever see those famous crossbows. As Jackie and I left the end-of-series party and drove north for a week's cabaret at Fagins in Manchester's Oxford Road, we reminisced about many extraordinary moments in the eight-year story of 'The Shot':

. . . the contestant who disappeared from the contest because she'd gone to the lavatory just before she was due to appear and, when she heard her name being called over the public address system, jumped to her feet so violently that she knocked herself out on the loo door.

. . . the Asian restaurant proprietor from Stafford who simply could not stop talking in one continuous flood of heavily accented enthusiasm, keeping up his prodigious monologue in praise of everyone and everything related to the show right up until he fired the bolt, missed the target, fell silent for a few seconds and then called out in a clear sing-song, 'Oh, shitty me!'

. . . Alton Douglas, a fine warm-up comedian, who'd taken over the show when I'd lost my voice, conducted it with immaculate skill and afterwards announced, 'If that's what you have to do to be a star, I quit!'

. . . and my favourite, which is why I've saved it for next to last: the Man from Wergs. We were halfway through our first series from Aston when this contestant came on the phone to aim the bow and obliterate an apple:

'Hello, who's calling the Golden Shot?'

He gave his name and, as per our contestant researcher, I said, 'And you're from Wolverhampton.'

'Wergs.'

'What was that?'

'I'm not from Wolver'ampton, Bob. I live in Wergs. That's *near* Wolver'ampton I grant you, but it's not actually *in* Wolver'ampton. You want to 'ead north on the A41 . . .'

'And what do you do for a living?'

'Ah, now that rather depends on what you mean by the words "for a living", Bob. That implies I work for what's called "a living wage" whereas it is my contention that the salary I am paid for the job I do is less than any man can be expected to live on, Bob.'

'I know how you feel, sir. Last week the company cashier asked me how I wanted my week's wages – heads or tails.'

'It's all very well to make a joke out of it, Bob, but for us as finds it very 'ard to make ends meet, that sort of flippant remark can cut to the quick.'

I decided to cut my losses instead.

'Well, if you're all set to aim and fire, your apple is the one on Isaac Newton's head, OK? You have thirty seconds in which to hit it, starting – *now*!'

'Right a bit, right a bit, right a bit, right a bit . . .'

'You're going off the target altogether, sir.'

'Oh, sorry, Bob. Left a bit, left a bit, left a bit, left a bit . . .'

'Sir! Hold it! Stop the clock. You're way off to the other side of the target now. Can you see the target all right?'

There was no reply.

'Hello? Sir? Can you see the target?'

Another hesitation, then: 'You see, I *told* the man.'

'Er – what man is this, sir?'

'The man from Rumbelows.'

'From Rumbelows?'

'When he came to take the set back Wednesday.'

'Take the set back. Your television set has been taken away.'

'You've got it in one, Bob.'

A certain amount of asperity must have entered my voice: 'You mean you're sitting at home, trying to play this game *without a television set*?'

Another pause.

'Sir?'

'There's no call for sarcasm, Bob, no call at all. I am not *sittin'* at 'ome.'

'I'm sorry.'

'I'm in a phonebox.'

Ten million viewers are watching this. With an effort, I control myself.

'If you're in a phonebox, sir, then you can't see a TV screen, can you?'

'Calm down, Bob, don't lose your rag. I can see *five* TV screens as an actual matter of fact.'

'Where?'

'In the window of Curry's. The phonebox out of which I am speaking at this moment in time is situated in a Wolver'ampton 'igh street, Bob, facing Curry's. They leave all their tellies in the window switched on over the weekend. I can see five of you, Bob, clear as day.'

'OK, then we'll put the target back on the screen again. Can you see it now?'

'No, it's still you.'

'It can't be me. We're transmitting a picture of the target.'

'Wave, give us a wave.'

'All right, the camera's on me again and I'm waving, OK?'

'You're not waving, Bob.'

'I AM WAVING!'

A final pause.

'Oh, bugger. That's not you at all. They've left 'em tuned in to the bloody BBC. Well, here goes nothing – FIRE!'

Our blindfolded cameraman pulled the trigger and, unbelievably, the bolt hit an apple and blew it up. The audience cheered. I cheered. It was the weirdest public event I ever presided over.

And finally, the bomb threat. You may remember the IRA bombing atrocity in Birmingham on 21 November 1974.

That horror rallied entertainers associated with the Midlands for a fundraising concert on behalf of the bomb victims at the Birmingham Hippodrome on 5 January in which I introduced Frankie Vaughan, Noelle Gordon, Stan Stennett, Keith Harris and Orville, Dave Ismay, Diana Dors, Alan Randall, Lance Percival and others. Prime Minister Harold Wilson sat in a box and didn't even smile when I said, 'Watch out, that's where Lincoln got it.'

Even if the end of 'The Golden Shot' had not been already decided upon, we would have had to take seriously something we'd laughed at from the very start – our weekly bomb threat – and consider cancelling the series. Because we had to make a live transmission so that telephone contestants could see what they were aiming at, we ourselves became a natural target. Ours was one of the only two live light entertainment shows with an audience present (the other was the revived Palladium show). So week after week, month after month, some anonymous voice phoned in a bomb threat. At first we announced these to everyone in the studio so that those who wished to leave could do so before the show started. After a year or so, we didn't bother, although the police asked us to tape all incoming calls on a Sunday. So it was that our classic call came to be recorded for posterity. The call came at 4.10 p.m. A bored duty officer spoke first, identifying himself. Then he heard a densely Dublin-bred accent say:

'Sir, I have to inform you of the presence of a two-pound gelignite bomb hidden in the studio where "The Golden Shot" is due to begin shortly. Take note that the device has been well concealed and timed to explode during the early part of the programme, causing maximum damage to anyone foolish enough to remain in the vicinity. Failure to take immediate action to abandon the area must be the responsibility of those in charge of the studios. You will now confirm that you have understood all that I have said.'

Wearily, the duty officer asked, 'Is this a hoax?'

After a stunned pause, the Irish voice answered, 'How the fuck did you know that?'

At one time I think everyone in the Birmingham ATV Centre had a cassette copy of that tape. So end the annals of one of British television's silliest and best loved shows. Well, almost.

A few pages back I mentioned that, during my absence from the series. I busied myself writing something other than scripts and far more effective in career terms. You may also recall that an early wireless comedian once censured me as 'a very persistent and impudent little fellow'. Here's further proof of it: I persuaded a friend in the stationery business to supply me with one hundred and eighty different samples of envelopes and notepaper, all the pages headed with specimen addresses in a wide range of fonts and colours. Over the two years I wrote three or four letters every week, using different pens and writing styles. All of these were addressed to Sir Lew Grade in subtly varied ways. Every one of his phantom correspondents wanted Bob Monkhouse back as the host of 'The Golden Shot'. What's the old saying? 'If you want a job done well . . .'

29

THE JACK OF CLUBS

1: Musicians

Clubland maxim: never assume a musician understands anything other than music, like human speech

Musicians are not normal human beings. They are a species out of the Twilight Zone with something different in their brains. This alien something manifests itself as the ability to write, read and perform music but it also takes the place of certain thought processes that normal people have. That's how you can spot a musician right away, without him having to pick up a piccolo or sit down at the zither. They're all marching to the beat of a different drummer. And he's not their regular man.

You doubt me? I once did cabaret at a classy night spot called The Plantation near Chester. There were five numbers in my act at the time so I was punctual for band call at seven p.m. The bass player and drummer accepted my dots but the pianist peered closely at each page of music and growled, 'Is this pencil? This is pencil, isn't it?'

I said, 'Pencil? No, they're photocopies.'

'They look like pencil to me. I play ink. Proper ink copies, not bloody pencil. I thought you was supposed to be a star.'

'The originals were in ink. These are photocopied from the originals.'

Rubbing at the music with his thumb, the pianist was sneering now. 'This is never ink, this is pencil, don't kid me. Well, you can find someone else for this job. Some bugger as'll play bloody pencil.'

As he stormed off into the night, the bassist said, 'That's it then. You'll not find another piano player as can read round here, not on a Saturday night, not in time for your show.'

A harrassed manager appeared. 'Now, Mr Monkhouse, you've not let Arnold go, have you? He's the best sight reader in the Chester area during the present shortage.'

I said, 'Couldn't I work with your regular dance band?'

The two musicians sniggered.

'Regular dance ba – we have a rock group, Mr Monkhouse! Disco dancing! Your agent said you wanted proper musicians who could read and I moved heaven and earth to get you Arnold.'

'But he doesn't read pencil,' I explained.

'Well, you should have thought of that,' he answered inexplicably. Frantic phonecalls followed throughout the evening as the customers arrived.

Twenty minutes before show time the exhausted manager came to my cramped dressing room with the news that a deputy accompanist had been found. The bassist and drummer had already rehearsed the material with me and I could only hope that whatever pianist was rushing to my aid could follow my cues without preparation. At ten-thirty I was standing in the kitchens behind the door that led to the cabaret room, listening to the disc jockey chattering to the crowd as he waited for the manager's signal to introduce me. Peering through as waitresses traversed, I could see that no one was seated on the piano stool. Then, as the deejay began my intro, a big man in overalls pushed past me into the main room. His once-white boiler suit was smeared in a dozen hues of decorator's paint from collar to ankle and he carried a canvas bag of Dulux cans and brushes which he dumped on the stage beside the piano, unzipping and stepping out of his working chrysalis to reveal the dress-suited pupa from within. Some tables applauded. The big fellow nodded in acknowledgement, sat and drowned out the conclusion of the deejay's announcement with some arpeggiate sweeps of the keyboard. I thought I heard my name, came bouncing on to the dance floor and went into my opening number. Or rather, I tried to. The player painter did something that lesser musicians would never have attempted, let alone brought off. He proceeded to transpose all five of my songs into the key of C. It's not easy to sight-read unfamiliar tunes set in F flat and E flat and play them in C. It's pretty well impossible for a really good singer to follow suit, let alone a performer of limited range like me, once described by a critic in the *Independent* as 'vocally impaired'.

Nevertheless, with desperate misjudgement, I attempted to sing my opening song in the key imposed, failing and so switching to a lower octave, changing upwards again, then settling for a sort of declamatory recitative of my perky lyric which a moment's sober consideration would have told me would be comedy suicide. The audience must have thought I was drunk, drugged or mad. Of course I should have cut the other four numbers but in those days my act was tightly routined and my gags were going well enough to lull me into a false sense of security about taking each musical hurdle as it approached. Needless to say, I fell at each one. I came off to bewildered applause tinged with hostility.

I couldn't blame them. I felt just as bewildered and hostile as the customers who had paid good money to hear me either shrieking my parodies at them as a strangling soprano, growling them inaudibly low or yelling them like a ham actor. I resolved to cut my songs down to three in future – opening, false tabs, closing – and, in fact, I've done that ever since. The bass player returned my dots to me as I changed my clothes in the dressing cupboard and I asked him, 'What the hell was all that about? He played everything in the wrong key.'

'Yeah, he always does that, does Big Phil. You just have to follow him, that's all you can do with Big Phil.'

I saw the pianist on my way to my car. He was standing under a lamp, counting the cash he'd been paid.

'Excuse me a moment. Why did you play all my music in C?'

'I do that. I'm known for it.'

'But why?'

'Sounds better,' he said and walked away to his van. I imagined hiring Big Phil to paint my house white and finding him painting it black because it looked better.

Over the years of cabaret in clubs, pubs, holiday camps, banqueting suites and assorted fleshpots, I've worked with musicians who've stood behind me on the stage in plain view of the audience while I've been labouring to amuse and done a wide variety of things. They've fallen asleep, read comic books, written letters, ransacked their nostrils, swigged from bottles, argued amongst themselves, changed their clothes, shot craps, exercised with a bullworker, listened to personal stereos, sharpened pencils, sprayed their breath, even heckled me. On one memorable occasion I was onstage at the Pig and Whistle, Butlins, Barry Island. It was one o'clock in the morning but the audience was lively. Then slowly I lost their attention. Following their gaze, I turned and joined the crowd in watching the pianist. He had unscrewed a thermos flask and was totally absorbed in the process of extracting frankfurter sausages and lowering them into his mouth without breaking them. When he had finally eaten all of them, screwed the top back on to the flask and daintily wiped his fingers on my music, he was very startled by our cheers and applause.

By reducing my musical needs to only three items, i.e. an opening number . . .

> *How do you open a cabaret act*
> *When you'd rather open a vein?*

. . . followed by verbal comedy for the greater part of an hour, I had solved the problem of having the trio onstage behind me all through my act, diverting the audience's attention by mending a lawnmower or dissecting a cadaver or whatever they might have come up with next. All I had to do was invent a bit of business to get them off after the opener and a cue to get them back on for my false tabs, the song which apparently concludes the act but which is only a dummy ending, enabling the performer to milk the applause and accept the gracious implication that an encore is required. I'd just have to put up with the trio's presence for the brief duration of the closing jokes and then do the real finishing number. To this end I devised the simplest of gags to send them off. One musician would have a drink onstage near him. After the crowd had applauded my opening song, I'd do a few gags about the trio . . .

> *One on keyboard, one on bass, one on drums, two on cannabis*
> *and all three on probation . . .*

. . . then I'd kid the manager of the joint or a similar authority figure of the evening, adding that he'd promised me a drink which had failed to materialise. Suddenly seeing the glass of booze that one of the musicians had brought on with him, I'd retract my accusation and grab it, thanking my generous host.

That was the cue for the musician's one and only spoken line. It was written in huge black capital letters at the bottom of the music he'd just played. It read:

(AFTER BOB TAKES GLASS, SAY: 'THAT'S MINE!')

I'd then misunderstand his meaning and assume the glass contained a urine sample (I told you this was simple), hold it up to the light and say . . .

You can sell your organ, young man, your monkey's dying.

. . . and other vulgar lines. Then I'd ask him if I could keep it, he'd nod yes, and in gratitude I'd tell the trio they could take an 8000 bar rest. Exit the trio, I had the drink I needed to wet my throat for the rest of the act, the routine couldn't be simpler. But some musicians could.

The first night I restructured the act this way was on Sunday, 19 April 1964, playing two clubs a night in the Leeds area. The booker was Burton Brown, an agent with a nice line in sardonic humour. Once in the 1950s when I was trying to interest Wardour Street in using me as an actor in films, I asked Burton, 'Do you think I should send round lots of eight-by-ten glossy photographs of myself to all the casting directors?'

Burton said, 'Yes, of course. Then all the people who are not going to use you will know exactly who it is they're not going to use.'

He'd got me six hundred pounds for the week at the Ace of Clubs in Leeds, doubling the first three nights at Kettlethorpe and the last four at Doncaster, making a total of fourteen cabaret shows, plus a radio programme called 'Workers' Playtime' on the Thursday in Hull for an extra fifty-five pounds.

After my bandcall at six p.m. from Teddy Joyce at the Ace, having carefully familiarised the pianist with the drink gag, I drove to Kettlethorpe and rehearsed with their trio, again explaining the purpose of the drink business with equal clarity. I ate in some local botulism dispenser, studying the map and working local names into my material. Then, at nine-thirty I went onstage at the club in Kettlethorpe.

The opening song went as well as usual and so did my lines about the club, the trio and the manager.

He's a very sexy man. There, I said it. Toughest contract I've ever signed. Besides, he promised there'd be a drink for me onstage but I can't see – ah, there it is!

I picked up the glass. It was empty. I looked at the pianist. He shrugged. I showed the empty glass to the crowd.

See what happens in this dump when you ask for a dry wine?

Not one of the great *ad lib* lines of all time but it gave me the chance to recover, hand the glass to the pianist and tell him to go away. After the show, I asked him why there had been nothing in the glass. He said, 'I was thirsty.'

'You drank it?'

'Yeah, well, you said at rehearsal that it was mine.'

I told him I'd explain it to him again tomorrow and drove back to Leeds.

When I picked up the glass of whisky and soda in the Ace, it was full. So was the pianist. He belched, 'Hey, that's my drink!' That knocked out my witty urine sample lines. We struggled briefly over ownership of the drink while he built up his part with, 'C'mon, c'mon, letsh have it!' I let go of the glass and its contents spilt over him. He staggered a bit, winked at me and cried out, 'Teamwork!'

You must forgive our piano player, folks – he's Yorkshire's only living brain transplant donor!

The following evening I talked to the Kettlethorpe pianist in the corridor behind the stage which served as a communal dressing room and garage for the manager's motorbike.

'Look, all you have to do is say "That's mine" – two syllables, right?'

'When you pick up the drink?'

'Yes.'

'Who's is it then, yours or mine?'

'You pretend it's yours but it's really mine.'

'But it's not mine, it's yours?'

'That's right, it's really mine.'

'But if it's yours, what am I doing with it?'

'You're pretending it's yours. It's just a gag, for God's sake!'

'I don't get it. What's funny about it?'

I was beginning to wonder that myself.

'Look, just do what I'm asking you. It gets you and the other lads off the stage for fifty minutes, doesn't it? Saves you sitting there all through my act, OK?'

As I went into my opening that evening I didn't notice an extra microphone that had been hastily rigged up near the keyboard. I rattled off my first few gags, then picked up the glass of whisky and turned to the crowd, thanking the manager and waiting to be interrupted. When the interruption came, it was deafening. The pianist had his lips close to the newly installed mike with the volume at its highest. Reading very deliberately from a piece of paper in his hand, he boomed:

THAT . . . IS . . . MINE . . . !

The audience was astonished and a little unnerved by this announcement.

There seemed to be no connection between what I was doing and this sudden thundering statement. They had no idea what the pianist was talking about. I tried to explain, cutting to the end.

It's his glass! I've taken his glass!

Then to the pianist,

Can I keep it?

The pianist had forgotten this was his cue to nod and be dismissed. He just looked at me blankly, then lowered his head to the mike again and repeated,

THAT . . . IS . . . MINE . . . !

Someone giggled nervously. I decided the best thing to do was to milk it.

Pardon?

This was so unnecessary it appeared funny. The people laughed. My co-star remained stuck in the groove. With slightly less conviction he muttered,

That's mine.

Then in a fit of honesty, he told the audience,

It's not really, it's his.

All I could do was mug at the people and send the band off with an assortment of insults.

Those boys make me think of Glenn Miller. I wish they'd get on a plane and disappear.

By this time I had lost a little bit of confidence in the entire drink bit. But I was stubborn and felt sure it would eventually play. At the Ace I located the pianist and found him sober.

'Look, if you say "That's my drink", you kill my next three gags where I pretend it's your specimen. Please just say: "That's mine!" as if it is yours and don't add any words of your own.'

'Oh, now I get it!'

Confident now, I ran through my opener, scored my first few laughs and reached for the whisky. As I did so, the pianist rose to his feet in mock anger. He shook his fist at me and shouted as loudly as he could:

Oy! That's my piss!

I have to admit he got the biggest laugh of the evening.

30

THE JACK OF CLUBS

2: Change Is

We meet a cheat who charms, a pair of tramps, a choir of nuns, and learn how to work the 'mint blinder'. Ron turns Rasputin and money goes down the plughole in Bath Lane

With one important difference, Ron Markham's business technique was like that of a stage magician. You know the man's a trickster, it's understood that he'll deceive you – 'Here's your ten pound note, I set fire to it, it's vanished, abracadabra! Here it is, inside my pocket, I return it to you with thanks' – the difference being that Ron didn't return the money.

His disarming charm was that of the confessed conman, a cardsharp who declares his hand before the bilking, the dip who enquires in which pocket you keep your wad so as to minimise mutual inconvenience.

Combine this conciliatory honesty about his dishonesty with the almost handsome features of a renegade rabbi; domed forehead above which sat thick, black ropes of hair, combed from the sides over a balding crown; gleaming black eyes which took refuge in slits during his frequent smiles; expressive, long-fingered, white hands; a persuasive and carefully modulated baritone; a deliberately lopsided manner of walking, standing, tilting his head and elegantly balancing himself sideways on to you, elbows in and palms up, as if to express an attitude simultaneously apologetic, uninvolved and stylishly laconic. With this small arsenal of assets, he assaulted the punters who crowded into his Dutch auctions across the north-east, telling them he was about to rob them, robbing them, telling them that he'd robbed them, and sending them out feeling sure that they'd robbed him, thoroughly pleased with the phony bargains with which he'd fleeced them.

Ron said he'd once been an actor in the Morecambe Repertory Company and had appeared on the West End stage in *Pacific 1890*. Whatever truth there was in that, by the time he wrote to tell me of his 16mm film collection, offering a few titles for sale, he was the Lord High Auctioneer of junk in the north-east of England. He and his delightfully eccentric wife Louise had seen me in cabaret several times without introducing themselves. I replied to his letter suggesting that they did so when I next appeared within easy range of their home in Ponteland and I listed my forthcoming weeks at La Dolce Vita and the Cavendish in Newcastle, La Strada and Wetherells in Sunderland, the Latino and second La Strada in South Shields, La Marimba in Middlesbrough, Tito's and La Fiesta in Stockton, La Ronde in Billingham . . . in those days you couldn't throw a stone in any Tyne- and Teesside High Street without hitting a black-tied bouncer.

Jackie and I liked Ron and Louise on sight, so much so that we broke one of our strictest rules and accepted their invitation to stay with them during these cabaret engagements. Louise was kooky but a good cook, with comfortable proportions, unruly red curls, full lips, huge turquoise eyes, and a small son from a previous marriage who once introduced us to a useful domestic expression by banging on the outside of the lavatory door and demanding, 'Are you doing tinkle or plops?'

Ron had two larger sons, also from an earlier espousement, and the five of them lived in a ranch-style house in Darras Hall, Ponteland. It was cheaply lavish, with big picture windows, vivid nylon shag-pile sparking static under your feet, wine-hued flock wallpaper with bright brass bas-reliefs of galleons and primitive masks, curtains of large rainbows and sunbursts, patterned glass doors and black Formica surfaces everywhere you tried not to look. Ron's 16mm projector was set up in the spacious living room, where he showed modern film copies of dubious provenance on a free-standing tripod screen. Jackie and I would come back after the midnight cabaret in Gateshead or Jarrow, I'd bath and get into my pyjamas and we'd sit up till dawn watching *Taras Bulba* or *633 Squadron* or *The Pawnbroker* or any of Ron's covertly obtained prints. It was film buff heaven. I was with the woman I adored, doing enjoyable work, making nice money, relaxing with funny friends; it all seemed too good to last and, of course, it didn't. Ron would eventually bring me to the brink of financial ruin. In the meantime, we had a lot of laughs.

Once the Markhams lent us their Rolls-Royce Silver Shadow to drive to the clubs. We did the first floorshow at La Bamba, Darlington, and returned to Sunderland for the midnight stint. When I came off the stifling dance floor, the audience overflowing from the tables to sit in heaps around my feet so that I was restricted to two steps in any direction, Jackie was in alarmed conversation with one of the bouncers.

'Don't ask me how they got into your Rolls, pet! I just heard them singin' in the back seat, told 'em to gang away but they're too drunk to move!'

'What's the trouble, Jac?'

'Two tramps, they've broken into Ron's car and won't come out.'

We could hear their boozy warbling as we gingerly approached the car.

Sprawled across the back seat were two of the filthiest human beings I've ever seen, their torn overcoats bound with string, battered hats pulled over balaclavas, faces thick with grime. The bearded man was holding a quarter-full bottle of turpentine to the black-toothed mouth of the female vagrant and they had both vomited on to the pavement outside the open car door. We asked the bouncer to call the police. 'Ah, y'see, the club manager likes to keep the coppers out of any trouble like. And me, I'm not allowed to manhandle anybody who's not on club premises. You'll just have to coax 'em out like.'

Well, we tried ordering them out, we tried entreaties, friendly persuasion, threats, inducements, finally begging them to quit the car on the grounds that 'it's not our car, it belongs to the Chief Magistrate'. That was just too much for Ron and Louise. They abandoned all pretence of their hobo identities and howled with helpless laughter. After gasping with relief, Jackie and I joined in. Later I asked, 'What about the puke on the pavement?' Ron said, 'Serendipity. It was already there. We just moved the car alongside it. You've got to take advantage of every gift life offers.'

More extravagant practical jokes followed. On a later trip

Jackie and I were greeted in the arrival lounge of Newcastle's airport by a mother superior leading a group of nuns from a convent in Jesmond. After presenting me with a Bible with my name embossed on its leather binding and thanking me for all I'd done for local charities, the nuns escorted us to their monsignor's chauffered Bentley. As we were driven to the Markham's house, we saw little knots of well-wishers standing on corners along the route, each with one or two nuns among them. They threw confetti and waved banners that said 'GOD BLESS YOU, BOB!', 'SAINT BOB, WE LOVE YOU!' and 'BOB, FOR THE LOVE OF CHRIST!' When we reached Ron and Louise's door, we found the big sitting room filled with nuns, all of whom prostrated themselves as I entered. Ron, faking embarrassment, said, 'They want to sing you some hymns, Bob.' As they struck up 'Climb Every Mountain', one comely nun opened her habit to expose her nude body and came forward to embrace me. Louise tried to pass round the sherry while we all broke down in happy hysterics. One pro stripper, the local Amdram members and their *The Sound of Music* costumes had answered Ron and Lou's call to spoofery.

Occasionally I was drawn into Ron's stunts. Tyne-Tees Television News archives may still have footage of my heavily disguised auctioneer selling plots of land on the moon. This lark was taken quite seriously and I 'sold' several lots at bargain prices to buyers keen to leave the property to their descendants as an investment in future times when an overcrowded earth and cheap space travel would render moon acreage priceless. The joke's underlying purpose was publicity for Ron's Oxford Salerooms. He'd hired several cheap shops around the north-east and sometimes set up his auctions in the assembly halls and hotel reception rooms of smaller towns. Like a superior market trader, Ron flogged every conceivable form of trash to his gullible gatherings. He bought anyone's bankrupt stock, fire-damaged trumpery, factory rejects, discontinued lines, remnants and gimcrackery, cases of trinkets and gewgaws seized and sold off by HM Customs, chaff, fag ends and crap by the crate. I remember watching in wonder while he demonstrated a classic manoeuvre of the street market grifters. Using three tacky, almost unsaleable bits of bagatelle, displayed briefly in a flattering spotlight while his reassuring tones purred through the microphone, Ron's spiel went like this:

'First let me show you a genuine twenty-four-carat, eighteen-jewelled, self-winding, wafer-thin ladies' watch, designed by Christian Dior and selling like hot cakes in Bond Street at sixty guineas.' (Ron had bought these fakes from Hong Kong at forty-three pounds a gross, about six shillings or 30p each.) 'Now look at these, five pairs of perfect, fully fashioned, seamless, reinforced, Hollywood nylons, as commissioned by MGM Studios in Culver city, LA, for the film *My Fair Lady*, and sold to my agents as surplus when the studio realised all the girls would be wearing long skirts. Audrey Hepburn's loss is our gain!' (The stockings were slightly flawed rejects from a Nottingham factory costing about one shilling or 5p a pair.) 'Lastly, I have a precision tooled optical instrument you may recognise from TV, since these are the exact binoculars insisted upon by Peter Scott and David Attenborough, the ultimate in pin-sharp magnification of wildlife, whether it's out in the fens or through your neighbour's window.' All three items were handled with loving care, caressed by Ron's respectful touch and clever manipulation. Even the plastic, migraine-inducing binoculars took on a precious aura.

Now the cost of all this culch came to about a pound. Settling for no more than a four hundred per cent mark-up, Ron wanted a mere five pounds for the lot. Here's how he went on to get his price:

'Now, my friends, I'm going to ask a simple question and the first person here to give me a correct answer is going to get a prize, a reward, a once-in-a-lifetime opportunity. Here's the question: do you trust me? You were first to reply, sir, it's your lucky day. Will you trust me now? You will? You won't be sorry, I promise you that. Are you married, engaged, or just enjoying yourself? Good, I'd like to make the special lady in your life a little present. How would she like to have these? Five pairs of Hollywood nylons, valued at fifteen shillings a pair, that's a total of three pounds fifteen shillings – *would* you, I didn't say *will* you, I said *would* you – and you're on test here, my friend, I'm testing your trust in me – *would* you give me ten shillings for them? You would, very good, you should. Now put your ten shilling note on the table, go on, don't be afraid, no one will touch it. There we are, one ten bob note, and with your permission I'll just fold that money around the five pairs of stockings valued at seven and a half times that amount. There it is, safe and sound, within plain sight of all.

285

'NOW! A sixty-guinea watch, solid gold, encrusted with gems inside, and I won't take forty pounds, I won't take forty-five pounds, don't waste my time, I want fifty pounds for this beauty. Why not? That's a saving of ten quid under the price at Asprey's. Ah, but this gentleman said he trusted me and I promised him a reward, so *would* you, sir, consider this worth a fiver? Yes, I thought you would! Well, I'm not letting you have it for a fiver, I'm not ready for the funny farm yet, thank you very much! But listen, I just might give it away. I might, I'm in a silly mood today. Tell you what, you fold your fiver in two and we'll gently wrap it around this beautiful timepiece and lay it on the table. NOW! These high-tech, light-weight binoculars have precision ground lenses for use by MI5, James Bond stuff come true. I couldn't buy one pair like this for a hundred pounds but our Government gets them cheap! Bulk buying from the USSR has shrunk the cost of these babies to only twenty pounds each. Sir, are they worth one pound? Then trust me one last time, sir, put a one-pound note on the table and I'll place these unique, optically powered Soviet-made binoculars upon your quid.

'Now, my friends, you all heard this gentleman say that he trusted me. And you heard me promise him a reward for that trust. Sir, I'm about to do something now that'll make you think I'm crazy. But remember that my business is built upon good will and word of mouth. Here on the table you've got articles worth eighty-three pounds fifteen shillings. You've also got a cash total of six pounds ten shillings in notes of the Royal Mint! That's a grand total in goods and readies of NINETY-FIVE POUNDS FIVE SHILLINGS! And I'm going to let you take the lot, sir, six pounds ten in cash and all the superb goods, for how much do you suppose? Half price? A quarter of the price? One tenth of the price? How about less than one nineteenth of the price? Yes! It's all yours – for a *fiver*! How can you lose? Done! Good luck, you'll never be luckier.'

The excitement aroused by what Ron called his 'mint blinder' usually resulted in the sale of up to a dozen more nylons-watch-binocular packages at five pounds each, without the inclusion of the cash provided by the first lucky customer who'd had the privilege of buying back his own money. He left, well pleased with the envious glances of other punters and the good-humoured grunts of 'lucky bugger'.

The Markhams took a great interest in my eldest child and arranged for him to take a holiday in Matfen Hall, a charitable residential institution about half an hour from their home. Gary enjoyed his visits there but liked their house in Darras Hall better. The Newcastle airline staff became quite used to helping me carry my son on and off their planes as he began to stay with Ron and Louise for a week here and there. They discovered some wonderful ways of laughing him out of his bad moods, having quickly learned to tell the difference between his moments of real distress and his frequent artificial fits of bad temper. When he was just angry for no reason and, eyes tight shut, began to slam his right foot on to the wooden frame of his wheelchair over and over again, they called it a 'perf' and held a mirror close to his face. Inevitably, Gary would take a scowling peep to see what was happening and find himself staring at his furious reflection. It nearly always dissolved his tantrum into chuckles.

It was a happy friendship until the Sunday afternoon Ron hypnotised me. We were alone in his house, Jackie having gone with Louise to visit friends.

Ron said, 'What's your ambition?'

I was sipping camomile tea and smoking a Player's Number Six, a brand supplied free to my London partnership since our successful promotion of it. We'd produced some bright cabaret packages to tour the holiday and caravan camps, with dancing girls dressed in Player's colours, free samples of the new cigarettes and Engelbert Humperdinck, in his previous incarnation as Gerry Dorsey, singing songs to cough along with. After a short think, I said, 'Like I told you last night, lately I've had a foolish fancy to open my own nightclub.'

'That's right, you told me. Yes, of course. But you also said you wanted to give up something.'

'Mmm? Oh, smoking, yes. Well, the desire is there so I suppose one day it'll grow so strong I'll just stop.'

'I've helped a few people to stop, you know. Yes, I was fooling around at a party once and I said I could hypnotise people. You know, I just said it, for the fun of it. Anyway, this girl asked me to stop her smoking. Sort of challenged me. Everyone started egging me on so I did what I'd seen Peter Casson do on the stage. "Lie back, your eyelids are getting heavy, as I count to ten you'll grow sleepier" – all that malarkey. Well, it worked, she went under, out like a light. So I told her that from now on every cigarette she lit would taste like shit. Then I told her she would forget everything except the instruction about the cigarette and that she'd wake up on the count of three. I tell you, I was damn glad when she did. Then, of course, everyone wanted to give her a fag and, sure enough, she lit it and spat it out.'

'She was just playing along with you, joining in the gag.'

'No, it was Mireille Gray, the singer, you know her. She's never smoked since. I've done it quite a few times since then too. It doesn't always work. The subject has got to want to do what I suggest. I can't make anyone do something that's against their will.'

There was a long pause while I watched my cigarette smoke wheeling up a sunbeam. What the hell.

'OK, Ron, let's give it a go.'

He moved me from my chair at the table to a long seat that was upholstered in cerise candlewick with buttercup-yellow lightning flashes all over it, told me to lie back and relax with my eyes shut. I remember thinking I could never have relaxed on that fabric with them open. For about ten minutes, Ron murmured his persuasive phrases along the lines he'd described. I was beginning to feel rather foolish and a little embarrassed for my friend. Nothing was happening to me. I decided to tell him so. Then I wondered why I wasn't telling him. The sensation reminded me of smoking pot in that South African hotel room. I was immobilised, aware of my thoughts but unable to act upon them. His words were obtundent to my nerves so that I lay in a dead calm, without alarm or the need to break free of my inertia. I seemed to lose track of his words, conscious only of their sound and not their meaning. The sensation deepened to a dream state in which I felt myself floating in a waveless sea, almost as insensate as a baby in the womb, reposeful and placid. How long I remained suspended in this ataraxy I'm not sure. By the time I drifted back to normal consciousness, Ron was on the other side of the room, pulling a curtain against the brilliance of the late afternoon sun. Its new position in the sky suggested that about half an hour had passed. He said, 'Here are the girls. They sound very chatty. Do you fancy a breath of air?'

I sat up as Jackie and Louise came in and said, 'Let's go for a drive.'

Louise said, 'We were just going to make us all something to eat.'

'I fancy a breath of air. We won't be long. See you both later.'

I kissed a surprised Jackie and went straight to Ron's car. As we drove into Newcastle I felt a suppressed itch to do something. This restive urge made me edgy but the idea of smoking didn't occur to me. In the centre of the city, Ron turned up a sloping road and stopped, saying, 'This is Bath Lane. See that door? That used to be the old Piccadilly Club, belonged to Dennis Stafford, the murderer. You remember the case.'

Stafford, who'd been in prison most of his life on various charges, started working for Newcastle's night-club bosses at the Dolce Vita in 1965. I met him there and found him menacingly intense when he asked me to shorten my eighty-minute act. 'If I lose gambling time because of you, it upsets me.' He moved to the Bird Cage, taking over the Piccadilly Club in 1966. The following March, 'The Playboy Villain' was jailed for life for the murder of Angus Sibbet, who'd been found shot in his E-type Jag. I was glad I'd cut my act.

There was a notice fixed to the neglected door of the club and, encouraged by Ron, I got out of the car and went with him to read it. 'Someone's put in an application for a drinks licence,' he said. 'This gives notice of their intention to reopen unless objections are lodged. Of course, they might drop the whole idea if someone bought them out.'

We copied down the name and address of the applicant and drove back to Darras Hall in silence. While Jackie and I got ready for work, Ron found a phone number to go with the name on the notice and called the man. As we were leaving for the first of evening jobs in Spennymoor, he told me, 'Two thousand pounds'd see him off. He'd leave the field clear for that much. Says the licence would be in the bag for anyone with a clean reputation.'

'What's he talking about, Bob?' asked Jackie as we drove away.

'How'd you like the idea of us having a nice little business ticking over up here? Nothing too ambitious. Just a small cabaret club, selling snack food and booze, with a bit of live music, some disco, good singers. What do you think?'

'What do I think? I think you're off your head even to consider it, darling. You haven't got time to worry about running a nightclub in Newcastle. What do we know about being licensed victuallers? Or catering or employing bartenders and cleaners and waitresses and men to fix the lights and the sound, men to repair the toilets and chuck out drunks? And why in Newcastle, in direct opposition to the Bailey circuit, Stan Henry and John Smith, who give you so much work? And things up here are getting tougher. We live in London, Bob. If you wanted to try owning a club, why not invest in a going concern somewhere nearer? That's what I think.'

I heard her good sense while knowing I was going to ignore every word of it. In my mind, there was no turning back from my newborn dream. We'd go ahead with our application for a licence to open a club in Bath Lane to sell alcohol, tobacco and food, with a door charge for dancing and cabaret. Ron would do it all -supervise the construction and decoration, plumbing and electrics, organise our suppliers, install beer pumps, kitchen and bar equipment, hire staff, book musicians and entertainers, arrange publicity and advertising, printing of menus and tickets, all the thousand-and-one tasks for which he had no previous experience whatsoever.

All I had to do was pay for it. Jackie remembers my frequent use of the words, 'I'm doing it because I want to. No one can be made to do anything they don't really want to.' She thought I was irrationally fixated. Now we both believe I was responding to suggestions that Ron had made while I was in a mesmerised stupor, even including the repetitious use of those phrases. Certainly, my behaviour was totally at odds with my nature. Within the next few months I had underwritten a twenty-five thousand pound loan from Newcastle Breweries Ltd, guaranteed another seventeen thousand to our electrical contractors, paid bills to our builders that totalled fifty-three thousand and poured thirty thousand pounds into an account from which Ron drew daily to buy the countless requirements of this dauntless, senseless venture. Journalist John Stevenson wrote:

WHY CHANGE MEANS SO MUCH TO BOB
As a comedian I don't think I've improved at all in the past four

years. From now on I won't get funnier – just older.' That's Bob Monkhouse, one of the shrewdest entertainers in show business, explaining his reasons for taking the biggest gamble of his career. At a time when Northern clubland, after years of boom and easy pickings, is going downhill fast in hard times, Bob is plunging over £130,000 into launching a new club in Newcastle upon Tyne. As a club it will be different – until someone duplicates the exercise. Called 'Change Is', Bob's club is so designed that it will not be the same place from one week to the other. The floor levels can be permutated fifteen different ways. The sound equipment is the best available. The decor is mainly a question of projection on to curved walls. One week Change Is China – with menu to match. The next week Change Is – you name it and Bob and his club staff can supply it. Monkhouse admits that Newcastle is 'over-clubbed already'. But he adds: 'This is a swinging city where they appreciate value. And if we succeed here, there will be a chain of clubs like this – maybe a dozen across the country. WHY TAKE THE RISK? Says Bob, 'I'm not knocking my life as a comedian. Let's face it. I love being an entertainer, but as a comedian I've reached my peak.' The cost of 'Change Is' keeps changing too – ever upward. Bob hopes that it too has reached its peak.

We opened our doors, with the previously unheard-of admission charge of one pound, on 9 February 1969. My engagement diary for the period shows a punishing, nonstop schedule of work. The dough had to come from somewhere. I was grabbing every job in sight to finance my money pit.

Mind you, Change Is was a beautiful club. Denis Norden's son Nicky had suggested the name. Brian Eatwell, the award-winning designer of the film *The Bliss of Mrs Blossom*, designed three circular levels: the reception area, a first-floor eaterie-disco and top-floor cabaret arena. For an extra eighteen thousand quid, the massive concrete floors had been made soundproof. Our giant, state-of-the-art speakers were blowing out eardrums years before laws had to be made to lower decibel levels in discotheques.

Hidden movie projectors created amazing effects all around the curving walls, transforming the rooms into jungles, deserts, ice caps, ocean liners, observation balloons above the Rocky Mountains, submarines, funfairs and zoos. Not that I saw much of it. Costs were still soaring and profits, despite our apparent popularity, very disappointing. I didn't know that Ron and Louise were becoming more interested in playing their glamorous roles as hosts than paying enough attention to staff fiddling, petty thievery and embezzlement at the door. Louise had begun to sing with the band, displaying the lovely voice that would eventually bring her a good living as a cabaret and recording artiste in countries all round the world. Jackie and I keep cassettes of Lou's songs in our cars and play them often. The cover pictures show a slimmed-down sophisticate, far removed from the scatty Mrs Markham we once knew.

Ron was in heaven, introducing the entertainment. We booked wonderful performers like King Crimson, Lambert-Hendricks-and-Ross, Max Wall, Bruce Lacey and The Alberts, Blossom Dearie, Mark Murphy, poet Ivor Cutler, Alan Price, Ronnie Dukes and Ricky Lee, nude parodists Dickie and Dottie, funny Bobby Pattinson, and the outrageous comedian John Paul Joans, who might have become Britain's Lenny Bruce but for a tragic hit-and-run accident that left him with cerebral damage. Good friends of mine who were in the vicinity would pop in and perform – Alan 'Fluff' Freeman took over the disco and Clement Freud's skill as a stand-up comedian was never more appreciated. And if the crowd still called for more, Ron Markham himself would entertain. Can you imagine how? You're right, as a hypnotist. Unwary celebrities, among them singer Selina Jones and Margaret Lockwood's actress daughter Julia, were called upon for Ron's one a.m. experiments as a stage Svengali.

Whatever spell he had cast on me began to wear off after the first year.

By autumn I was exhausted from the amount of work I was having to do in order to keep Change Is open. I wanted to close it down but that would have meant my having to settle up personally guaranteed loans from the brewery and the bank, besides completing some large deferred payments to contractors. I had, as they say, a tiger by the tail. Then one day I phoned the bank in Newcastle to check on the safe arrival of funds I'd transferred to our Change Is account as working capital for the last quarter of the year. It had been cleaned out.

'Yes, Mr Markham withdrew all the cash last Monday, Mr

Monkhouse. I'm glad you called. Your assistant manager at the club has been round to see us. It seems that neither Mr or Mrs Markham has been seen at the club all this week and the young man was quite worried about wages for the staff.'

Ronnie Markham was gone. Change Is wasn't.

A hurried consultation with my accountants showed that it would cost me nearly thirty-two thousand pounds to shut the club down and meet the company's debts. I was sitting at a desk in MMA's splendid new offices in Egyptian House, Piccadilly, when Henry Howard asked me to step into his office. He actually said that. 'Would you step into my office for a moment, Bob?' After I'd stepped in it, he said, 'How's Change Is doing?'

I told him.

'You know, Malcolm and I were both very hurt that you didn't share that enterprise with us.'

'But it's been an idiotic disaster, Henry. You'd both have lost a bundle.'

'That's not the point really. A man has partners, there's an obligation. Never mind. I was happy to help you with it in any way I could. You chose to trust that Markham fellow. Now I understand he's flown the coop. It's all been rather unfortunate. Anyway, both Malcolm and I feel that we now need a change in company structure and we'd like to relieve you of the burden of your responsibility and give you the independence you seem to need to follow your own career while retaining some participation in the fruits of your own success.'

In short, they wanted me to give up my third share in the company. In exchange, I would have an investment in my own future with Peter Prichard. No one had to hypnotise me into agreeing. And I was too tired to argue.

31

THE JACK OF CLUBS

3: Change Isn't

After a competitor is benevolent and Kenya provides a break, Romark does the trick, does the decent thing, curses a bit and does time

Peter Prichard set up shop with Joan Anderson as his partner in a mews off West Eaton Place, representing Clive Dunn, Anita Harris, Clodagh Rogers, Jack Douglas, Tony Hawes, Ray Alan (and Lord Charles), plus me and a few others. As well as having 'The Golden Shot' to occupy my Sundays, I was beavering away in the trenches, plying my trade in some of the worst toilets in clubland's often tawdry history. While it was a pleasure to play well-run fun palaces like The Double Diamond in Caerphilly or The Wooky Hollow in Liverpool, it was a grubby grind in filthy fleshpots that paid less and required so much more in terms of physical effort and loss of self-esteem. No matter, I needed the money so I took them all on. One smelly strip joint in Wolverhampton called 'The Lady Eve' was closed down by the police two days before I was due to appear. By the time I turned up, it had reopened under a new name, 'El Club Caliente'. I had to follow a stripper who sat on a Coke bottle and made it vanish. The audience wasn't quite as high class.

Another manager or two later, Change Is was still losing money. Then, one October Monday, I was in Birmingham, ready to host 'The Miss Night Club Contest' at Bailey's La Dolce Vita. Stan Henry showed up at rehearsals and asked me to have a coffee with him during one of the breaks. Ever since he'd started his hugely successful Bailey Organisation with John Smith, Stan had been a good friend of Jackie's and mine. He and John had even attended the opening night of Change Is and wished us well.

Now he sat, bolt upright and fashionably attired as usual, turning his normally humorous gaze upon me with a pitying expression.

'We're both forty-something, aren't we, Bob?'

'I'm forty-one, Stan.'

'That's what I mean. Not too old to make our money over again.'

His hair was gingerish-fair, his cleanshaven face plump and pleasant, his accent gently Geordie, a very clever, very fairminded man.

'I'm not completely broke, Stan. I'm just a bit damaged, that's all.'

'I had a man sitting in a car outside your place last Saturday. Every time someone went into the club, he clicked his clicker. All told, three hundred and eight bodies passed through your portals, Bob, three hundred and eight.'

I said that I thought that sounded better than usual.

'This morning I had someone else sneak a look at your Saturday night takings, never mind how. According to your books, you only had sixty-two customers in the joint all night. They're robbing you blind, bonny lad.'

I felt sick. I'd been up to Newcastle immediately following Ron's desertion, then again after a second and third change of manager, giving my loyal staff a pep-talk, assuring them that their jobs and wages were safe, declaring my faith both in them and the eventual recovery of the club with their help.

Now this.

'Do you want rid of it, Bob?'

'Oh, my God, yes, Stan. I'd pay someone to take it off my hands.'

'Leave it to me. Let my canny lads take a look at your figures and do a few sums. How busy are you?'

'Frantically. But I've cleared the decks in late November so that I can spend two weeks in Newcastle trying to put things right.'

'Scrub that. Take Jackie for two weeks holiday abroad instead.'

After a nineteenth birthday party for Gary at Kyre Park, Jackie and I took Stan's advice with a fortnight in Mombasa, Kenya. Only one thing about Gary had me slightly puzzled. He had written R.O.N. with his right big toe. When I explained that Ron had gone away, Gary had opened his diary at the atlas pages and tapped Africa. Since I'd already used that same map to tell him where I was going with Jackie, I couldn't unravel his message. I thought he was just a bit mixed up.

I'd wanted to see Kenya ever since 1956, when film director Terence Young commissioned Denis Goodwin and me to write some additional dialogue for a fierce jungle drama called *Safari*, with Janet Leigh and Roland Culver supporting Victor Mature v the Mau Mau. We met the heroic star in a Wardour Street office and found him to be a good-natured Goliath with two things on his mind. He wanted some wit in the script and he didn't want to go to Kenya to film it. 'There's nothing in that goddam jungle that we haven't got on the studio backlot *minus mosquitoes*! I hate mosquitos more than I hate crocodiles. And do you know how much I hate crocodiles? *More than I hate mosquitoes,* that's *how much I hate crocodiles!*'

Denis and I said we could see how to insert some laconic humour for Culver but felt that the adventure and love scenes might resist our best endeavours in the short period before the film unit embarked for East Africa. Mature snorted. 'We'll be back in a week and you'll be handing the rewrites in at the studio day by day.'

'But the shooting schedule in Kenya's two months, Vic,' said Young.

Mature just snorted again. A year later we attended a press showing of the completed film and a wry Irish actor named Liam Redmond told about the day the cast arrived at the first African location. 'Terry Young took Vic Mature down to the riverbank. Says he, "You'll paddle your canoe towards camera and then, as you pass by . . . " 'Says Vic, "Forget it." Says Terry, "What does that mean?" Says Vic, "It means forget it, colonel! I'm not paddling any goddam canoe. That's not a river, that's croc city!"'

Liam told us that Young enlisted the support of his technical adviser, a big game hunter in khaki shorts, who said, 'There's no problem, Mr Mature. Crocs can't abide noise. We'll just raise a bit of hell with the drums and they'll make themselves scarce for half a mile.'

'Forget it, will you? There's no way I'm putting a thin canoe between my arse and the jaws of a goddam crocodile.'

'Look, sir, I'll camp here all night and fire off my elephant gun every hour. By morning there won't be a single croc between here and Nairobi.'

'Well now, I'll tell you what's wrong with that idea,' said Mature, turning away. 'One of those fuckers might be deaf!'

A week later the unit was back in England. A lesson in star power.

When we returned to England on 10 December 1970, my first phonecall was to Newcastle. Stan had assumed control of the club and put his own team in to run things. He told me not to worry.

Gary came home for Christmas, bringing gifts of old magazines he'd collected and books he'd appropriated from the staff and other residents. As he sorted these out from a cardboard box and presented them to his brother and sister, mother and me, I saw at the bottom of the box a postcard addressed to Gary that solved my little puzzle about Ron Markham. He had sent the card to Gary a month earlier. The stamp was South African, postmarked Durban.

By the summer of 1971 we'd forgotten about my club owning madness. My bank balance had recovered its equilibrium so Peter was turning down the sleazier dates once more. I had attended my last AGM for Mitchell Monkhouse Associates in a very friendly atmosphere. Jackie and I had enjoyed ten days on Grand Bahama, me doing nightly cabaret at the Lucayan Beach, Freeport, and a holiday in Cyprus. By the time I opened my summer season at Weston-super-Mare, I was out of debt and clear of Change Is. Stan was now calling it Bloomers and it was doing fine. As for Ron Markham, he wasn't Ron Markham any more. He was Romark.

Promoting himself, he had hired a Durban theatre and his two-hour presentation of hypnotism had become the longest running one-man stage entertainment in the history of South African show business. He came back to England and starred in his own TV show on BBC 2, 'Romark – The Man and His Mind'. 'How did he do it?' wondered the *News of the World* in December 1973. Rather confusingly, the Sunday national newspaper claimed to have found the answer in Hollywood, where the forty-seven-year-old ex-salesman had mesmerised film celebrities at the

Playboy Clubs and talked his way on to America's biggest chat shows. Ron was quoted as saying, 'Instant stardom – that's what's happened to me over here.'

He told the paper that after learning to develop his powers from an Austrian expert in hypnology, he'd spent seven years as a clinical hypnotist with a long list of patients. After a domestic break-up, he'd found his true *métier* on the Durban stage, calling himself The World's Most Remarkable Brain. A Hollywood impresario came under his spell and made him an offer.

'Up near Sunset Strip, famous names like Zsa Zsa Gabor swirled around the theatre where Romark was appearing,' claimed the press report in one bizarre phrase, going on to describe how Romark had cured the travel sickness of Shirley Jones, 'TV favourite and the stepmother in real life of pop idol David Cassidy', and fooled TV star David Janssen into naming himself as his own favourite actor. In his BBC TV series, Romark said, he'd be discovering a needle in a haystack, finding just one word that a total stranger has secretly chosen out of 130,000 in a dictionary, and completely outclassing 'anything Uri Geller can do'. In the event, the twenty-minute shows didn't quite live up to these promises and, before long, Romark was seeking headlines by putting a curse on soccer manager Malcolm Allison and his Crystal Palace team. When that made the tabloids, he decided there was more capital to be squeezed out of this cursing lark.

'CONMAN ROMARK CURSES THE *SUN*' headed a full page in that paper, with the sub-headline, '"Your sales will slump if you expose me," he says.' Below, the *Sun* reported that the 'self-styled hypno-therapist and psychologist' had said, 'I prophesy that the *Sun* and the *News of the World* are trying to expose me as a fake. The curse is that both newspaper circulations will plummet when that article appears.' Murdoch journalist James Lewthwaite gave 'the former bankrupt' more column inches than he might have wanted. When he wrote that 'the unsuccessful actor' had a nameplate outside his 'luxury flat near Harley Street' which said 'Dr R. Markham' although he had no medical qualifications, Ron answered him, 'I did not call myself a doctor. The porter typed the name and put it up when I moved in.'

Lewthwaite took TV critic Hilary Bonner for a ten-pound

consultation and had to admit that Romark's suggestion that her hand was made of steel made it impossible for either him or Hilary to bend her hand for an impressive length of time.

Sadly, 'the world's most remarkable brain' let Ron down. I'd had no contact with him since he'd absconded with my money ten years earlier, then suddenly he got in touch with my solicitor and volunteered to appear in my defence at the committal proceedings against me for conspiring to defraud authorised film libraries out of their lawful rentals by owning a private movie collection. When he shuffled into court, it was plain that he'd had a stroke.

The left side of his face sagged slackly. His left arm hung limp and he dragged his leg. Still the eyes glinted with Ron's old familiar intensity. After affirming, he spoke briefly with some slurring. 'I gather it's the modern films from Mr Monkhouse's collection which are in question. Well, I sold him most of them. They were mine. They're ex-library prints sent for destruction because they were of no further value to the film hire libraries. I knew the rubbish disposal company that was supposed to destroy the copies. I paid them a few quid to pass the copies on to me and tell their clients that they'd burned them. If a crime was committed by obtaining the films in that way, I'm the one who committed it, me and the disposal company, not Monkhouse.'

It was a noble effort but the magistrate dismissed him and committed me to trial at the Old Bailey, a tale that's told in another part of my annals.

The Times of 29 May 1982 reported, 'TV HYPNOTIST JAILED FOR ROBBING MOTHER'. It said that Ron had plundered his ailing mother's fortune to set up a new home in Hollywood. 'Markham, aged 55, had denied 14 charges of theft and fraud and his wife pleaded not guilty to being a party to them.' It seemed that while seventy-nine-year-old Emma Goldman was gravely ill, her son and his new wife, Ursula, had taken £68,000's worth of her silver, antiques and jewellery. Ron had forged letters and his mother's signature to withdraw over £47,000 from her savings accounts. The judge sentenced him to eighteen months imprisonment and his wife to nine.

A few years later, I was taping a show with Paul Daniels when

I heard that Ron had died. I asked Paul if he'd ever heard of Romark.

'Oh yes. He was a total fake.'

Not total, Paul. I haven't smoked a cigarette for twenty-five years.

32

SILENCE IN COURT

Scotland Yard v Me

The DPP spends a million pounds prosecuting, fifty-two thousand pounds are spent defending. The cost in anxiety and fear is not calculable

A letter came from a stranger. It said, in part, 'If the worst thing you ever have to go through is a two-year court case, consider yourself lucky.'

In retrospect perhaps, I can accept that. During those two years, however, I couldn't. Although, with Jackie's help, I strove to be philosophical, I found the experience of criminal prosecution immensely dispiriting. There's something about preparing to fight a faceless foe, whose weapons are of unknown power and whose motives for attacking you are largely incomprehensible, that saps the will too much to do more than go through the motions of self-defence like a dazed loser. I was told I could be facing a custodial sentence. That possibility seemed to me an outrage and an affront, but how long can a man remain outraged and affronted? I'm not very good at summoning up either feeling, let alone sustaining the mood for two years. I had to settle for my usual pathetic devices, alternating hours of blank detachment lightened by childish flippancy with sinking myself in the laborious homework required by my QC, writing reams of meticulous details about the acquisition of every one of the eighteen hundred films in my collection, many of which had been siezed by the police and housed in quite unsuitable conditions for their safety. It's an understatement to say I just wasn't ready for this. Just as I hadn't been ready for David Jason.

The six years prior to my arrest on a warm summer evening in 1977 had lulled us into the consistently fulfilled expectation of daily contentment. We'd spent our 1971 summer season at Weston having riotous fun with Jason and, before his fame in 'Eastenders' as Arthur Fowler, Bill Treacher. The farce was *She's Done It Again!*, rewritten by Michael Pertwee from a Guy Bolton 1930s original in which my role was played by Robertson Hare. Bunny, and later Brian Rix, had played a naive rural vicar whose wife presents him with sextuplets. Jason was a nutty professor, hurtling round the stage in a curly white wig and beard in a beautifully timed frenzy of comic falls and treble takes. He was as well cast for his part as I was miscast for mine.

At the end of our first night the cast did the finale walkdown to take their bows. Jason received nothing less than a roof-raising ovation. As I followed him on to the stage, the sound level dropped to a more restrained volume. I made a sixty-second curtain speech of farewell, the whole company bowed and the curtain fell. Oh dear, no, I thought, this won't do.

The second night was slightly different. I came on first for my final bow and then introduced the cast by name, one by one. Jason entered last and again received his well-deserved acclamation, which I now led. I made a three-minute curtain speech, ending with a strong laugh, and the curtain fell. Hmm, I thought, a bit better, but I'm supposed to be the star of this thing and a brilliant, as yet unknown youngster is stealing the show from under my disjointed nose. Each evening my curtain speech got longer and funnier. I changed it quite a bit each night so that the cast would laugh naturally. Then a couple of holidaymakers stopped me in the street to say, 'Thanks for a good laugh the other evening. He's a caution, isn't he? The little old man!' Aha, I thought, they think he's a little old man. Before curtain up that evening, I gathered the cast onstage.

'First I want to apologise for the length of my curtain speech, it's grown far too long' . . . (Loyal murmurs of protest) . . . 'The thing is, the management wants to keep it all in' . . . (More murmurs of agreement) . . . 'Well, I've said it's not fair on you to keep you all in your makeup and costumes while I'm standing out here doing gags. It gets too late for some of you to even get a meal. So here's the plan. I'll come out and do the curtain speech in one, on the part of the stage in front of the closed curtains. You all use the time to get cleaned up and into your own clothes. Then, after ten minutes, I'll say, "Now please say goodnight to the wonderful actors and actresses who entertained you tonight – but this time, as themselves!" We'll take the curtain up, you can take your bows as usual and have an early night.'

They were all very grateful and it worked well for the rest of the summer. Jason still stole the show, winning actual gusts of laughter that could be felt from the stage. My curtain speeches scored every night. And when Jason took his final bow without his wig and beard, nobody knew who the hell he was.

Was I sneaky, looking after my status like that? Maybe, but then I think that's part of my job. If you're the ticket-selling name on the marquee outside the theatre, it's up to you to protect the value of that name. If something threatens to undermine your reputation or standing, you must do your best to correct it. I deplore stars who throw their weight about, cutting other performers' lines and laughs. There's no need for such intimidation.

A bit of ingenuity can save everyone's face. It says something about the sweetness of Jason's nature that my guileful scheme never became apparent to him throughout the run of the play. I had to explain it to him twice, a year or so later. 'You diseased cow!' he said, inaccurate in the particular but capturing the spirit of truth.

Although I had to quit 'The Golden Shot' for a while, club work was plentiful and pleasant. Other good things happened besides those I've already recounted: Prichard fixed up my first season of one a.m. holiday shows for Butlins, a terrific multiple booking that had us touring round the camps for the next eleven years; my divorce became final; a charity campaign I'd initiated resulted in my presenting many wheelchairs, designed by Lord Snowdon, to the disabled in Lancashire and Cheshire; and Change Is gave a last kindly gasp when Stan Henry called at our home and left behind a briefcase containing a generous amount of money. He told Jackie, 'This is not for that pratt you sleep with, pet, it's for you. You deserve to get back something for all the aggro he put you through.'

I decided that she hadn't been put through nearly enough aggro yet so, as I have related, Jackie and I were married at St Marylebone Register Office on 4 October 1973.

Two years later, my return to 'The Golden Shot' was replaced by the first run of 'Celebrity Squares', a success which led to 'I'm Bob, He's Dickie', six hour-long specials with Dickie Henderson. The week after the first of these, the cops came calling at our Bedfordshire home.

I came home from the Borehamwood studio after a hard day of scripting the new series with Dick Vosburgh and Gary Chambers. After I'd stubbornly insisted on struggling for over an hour with a sketch idea that just wouldn't come together, my patient colleagues left me to it. As they went through the door on their way to the canteen, I heard one say to the other, 'It's like watching Cyclops trying to thread a needle.' The other responded, 'More like a kamikaze pilot working out his pension plan.' I got up and went with them.

When I got home, Jackie had prepared a glorious dinner to dispel my frustrations and I decanted a suitably grand wine to match.

Mellowed, I was setting up a film to watch in the cinema when the doorbell rang. Jackie came in to tell me there were three police officers asking for me. I cursed and said something about it being a hell of a time to call round to ask me to do some concert for police widows and orphans and went to fetch them through the house.

Claridges is very old, its middle part built in the sixteenth century, with oak-beamed ceilings and an inglenook fireplace in the central room. We bought it in 1975, selling Loudoun Road to a US businessman who didn't mind the inconvenience of living opposite a new, noisy school for the children of Americans in England. After Jackie had checked out a dozen houses for sale about one hour up the M1, placing us within easier reach of clubland and all the major TV studios north of London, we found our home on a dark, wet night during a power cut. The owners' daily cleaner flashed a torch around the place and we fell for it, fourteen rooms including four bathrooms and two kitchens, three acres of landscaped garden with an outdoor swimming pool and cabin, integral double garage and the most beautiful weeping ash you ever saw. Important to me was a very large room that could be converted into a private cinema with a projection booth and racks of films stored along the walls behind giant sliding panels. Ironically, it was to this room I conducted the Chief Inspector, Detective Sergeant and Detective Constable, who promptly informed me that I was under arrest.

At first I thought they were joking. Then it became clear that they weren't.

'You're serious,' I said stupidly.

'Of course,' said one. 'We're from the Serious Crime Squad.'

Now that did sound like a joke. Not a good joke, a rotten joke. 'On what charge?'

'Conspiracy, sir. Have you any 16mm films on the premises?'

'Just a few.' I swept back the first of the six big panels to reveal about a hundred cans of film standing edgewise on the racks, the titles displayed on the forward rims.

'We shall have to seize all those, sir. Put them in our car and take them to Marylebone police station.'

'I hope you've got a big boot,' I said, opening the other five panels.

In the end we had to pile all the film cans we could into the police vehicle and stack the overflow into Jackie's white Granada Ghia. With both cars groaning under the weight of everything from *Citizen Kane* (1941) to *King Kong* (1933), we left our Bedfordshire village for London at about nine-thirty p.m. They didn't finish interrogating me till four a.m., complete with mug shots and finger-printing. How I managed to furnish them with so many coherent answers during the five hours of questioning, I'm unsure. Every film title on the cans had to be recorded in longhand while I was required to explain exactly how I'd come by it. As you know by now, I have a retentive mind for things that interest me and subsequent examination of my answers showed them to be a hundred per cent accurate. Hooray for me.

The next morning we pulled back the curtains of our bedroom in Claridges to see twenty-seven cars parked around our front gates and a throng of reporters waiting patiently for our house to show some sign of life. There was only one sensible way to behave and that was to cooperate with the press as openly as I had with the police. I dressed and went down our gravel drive to allow photographs to be taken and answer all the questions. Colin Pratt of the *Daily Express* was the first person to explain to me what the charges really were. 'You're accused of conspiring to import copies of feature films belonging to Columbia Warner and other film distributors without having the rights to do so,' he informed me. 'They say you've plotted to defraud for eleven years.'

'Thank you, Colin. But what exactly does that mean?'

'Buggered if I know.'

Buggered if anyone knew. The arrest on 11 July was followed by three more conspiracy charges at Marlborough Street on 16 November. Now we learned who I was supposed to have conspired with. It was a film buff from Acton who had sold me a few titles, copies which he had legitimately imported from the USA, where they had been publicly advertised for sale. My legal advisers were baffled. How, they asked, could a buyer conspire with a vendor?

As the case dragged on through countless expensive delays, I had a few unpleasant glimpses of what the general public had made of the story. My daughter was with me when I stopped to put petrol in my car.

'Who's a naughty boy then, eh, Bob?' said the pump attendant. 'They give you back all your mucky porno films yet?'

Others thought I'd been pirating films, making clandestine copies of blockbuster movies for sale, or that I'd received stolen goods. I won't bore us both by detailing the misery of the two years before I was brought to trial at the Old Bailey on 6 June 1979. Jackie was staunchly supportive, both of me and to her increasingly sick mother, and Prichard, though four years younger than I, was my strong older brother. He'd been there beside me through every stage, from that first inquiry room grilling in the small hours to the grindingly dull meetings with my solicitor and counsel. As a special constable, attached to West End Central, he understood police procedure. He was said to wear the only constable's uniform that had been picked apart, re-cut and tailored by Robbie Stanford, Tailor To The Stars. With two commendations for courage from the Chief Commissioner of Police, my agent and manager was often on patrol in dangerous circumstances. Francis Essex remembers the night he took his wife Jeanne to The Talk of the Town, a glamorously appointed theatre-restaurant on the Hippodrome corner of Charing Cross Road. They'd gone to see Cleo Laine and Johnny Dankworth but, after dancers and singers in exotic costumes had provided the first half of the entertainment, the compère announced a bomb scare. As the crowd shuffled out into the night, Francis led Jeanne to where he'd parked his Jaguar. He saw a constable bending, peering in at the back seat of his car. With a light laugh he asked, 'Does The Talk of the Town get many bomb threats like this, officer?' To his astonishment, Constable Prichard straightened up and said, 'Yes, sir, and they'll keep getting 'em until they book some of my bloody acts!' Then, classy as always, Prichard moved off into the night without looking back. In 1992 he went to the Palace to receive the OBE for his voluntary work, especially with the St John's Ambulance and the Entertainment Artistes' Benevolent Fund. Not bad for a cockney kid who left school at fourteen.

My counsel, Anthony Hidden, QC, advised me to be punctual, respectful and conservative in my dress. All he needed was an impudent comic in a vicuna coat to alienate the judge and jury. I must have looked a real victim in that dock; whey-faced in a Polish paper suit, a martyr to ignorance.

My daughter came to court to provide moral support but, although I'd appealed through Henry Howard for Raymond Rohauer to appear in my defence, corroborating my account of how I'd acquired the silent features which had been confiscated, neither felt free to respond in any way. Nat Cohen, for whose company *Carry On, Sergeant* had been made, told the court that he'd given me several 16mm films, 'as a gift to a sincere collector'. He added that he couldn't see that 'merely being in possession of a film deprives the domestic film libraries of their rental fees for the same film', as the prosecution charged. 'How many times a day can they rent it out? How many times can a person watch it? And if the person hadn't got his own copy, how do we know he'd hire it?'

By chance, the arresting officers had found a thankyou letter among the films which revealed that I'd lent one of my movies to a young friend. It was argued that the lad would have had to pay a ten pound hire charge to show the film if he hadn't borrowed it from me. As a result, Terry Wogan, appearing uncomfortably for the prosecution, was forced to admit that a letter thanking me for the loan of a film for a birthday party was written by his ten-year-old son Andrew, but added, 'Bob once lent me a book as well – was he diddling the Maidenhead lending library?' The judge ticked him off but the jury loved it.

After eleven days of disagreeable absurdity, with Liberal leader Jeremy Thorpe fighting a rather more scandalous accusation in the next court, my judge dismissed my jury, declaring that there was no case to answer. I was awarded costs, both for the committal proceedings and my defence, given a gold star and acquitted. I had been warned to expect a three-month trial. Humiliated and sitting wretchedly in the dock, I had listened to vile insinuations about my dishonesty and perjury from the prosecutor while having to maintain my silence in court. Well, enough of that! So sure was I that the idiotic case against me could not prevail much longer, I had smuggled some props into a cupboard in a back room of the court where the accused waited to be called: a dozen empty film cans, a champagne glass and a bottle of Moêt et Chandon. As soon as my name was cleared of all the charges, I gave the press photographers half an hour to assemble, then sat outside the Old Bailey on a pile of cans, toasting my exoneration.

Two ironies. Because I wanted the readers to infer that I'd be given back my impounded movies, I'd quickly scrawled short film titles in black capitals into strips of white sticky tape and stuck them on to the edges of the cans. Randomly selecting one-word titles for maximum clarity in the press photographs, I'd written such names as *Whoopee, Sunnyside* and *Cops*. One 'lost' Buster Keaton feature that I'd never seen crossed my mind and I included it – *The Sap-Head*. At last I heard from Henry Howard, via Prichard: 'As you know, I represent Raymond Rohauer's interests in the UK. He wants to know where Bob got his copy of *The Sap-Head* which Rohauer owns, and he wants it surrendered into my care immediately.' Since the film didn't exist, I didn't feel that I was such a big sap-head myself.

The second rueful smile came from Japan. It was also labelled with one-word names: Sony, Akai, Hitachi, Panasonic, Mitsubishi, Aiwa, JVC, and all the other makers of video cassette recorders. Within three months of my trial, Beta and VHS machines were baffling British adults as they knelt before each Nipponese box of tricks and strived to tape their own copies of some of the same films of which I had been dispossessed. Ten years were to pass before I gave up all hope of regaining the greater part of my film collection. My successful defence had failed to establish my right of ownership without each film title requiring its individual claim in civil court. I had been awarded costs in the total sum of £23,000. It had cost me over £52,000 to defend myself. I suppose you could say I went private but I got NHS. The lesson? Innocent you may be but, from the moment a copper says you're nicked, you're losing money.

Prichard, who'd had to refuse a fortune in work for the next three months, now did some masterly hustling.

'How'd you and Jackie fancy a cruise on the *Queen Mary*?'

'You mean the *QE2*.'

'Yeah, love, only two cabarets to do, maybe a late show for the crew, and you sail up to Cape Town and back.'

'You mean the North Cape.'

'Whichever. Radio Two wants you for thirteen "Punchline" shows and a Music of the Movies Gala Night, Dr Barnardo's want you to film an appeal, a week's cabaret at Night Out, two nights at the Skylight, Sheffield . . .'

'The Starlight, Enfield.'

'It wouldn't surprise me. Weeks at Caesar's Palace, Luton, the Lakeside in Frimley Green, Wakefield Theatre Club, oh yeah, and Francis Essex called. He's going to give "Celebrity Squares" a rest.'

'Oh, that's a shame, Peter.'

'He wants to talk to you about doing something called "Family Fortunes" instead.'

I wondered what that was.

33

FAMILY FORTUNES

We asked one hundred people, 'Name a TV host who isn't going to hang around where he's not wanted if he can hang around where he is.'

Around the world, family fortunes varied as the 80s began. The Afghans were called on unexpectedly by their neighbours, the Soviets. The Iranians fell out with their neighbours too and warred with the Iraqis. The Thatchers began their second year at Number Ten and the Reagans began their first in the White House. Our little family at ATV was in trouble for screening 'Death of a Princess', a rather confusing depiction of barbarism under Islamic rule, resulting in the expulsion of our ambassador from Jeddah and the loss of £200 million in British exports to Saudi Arabia. I was in trouble too, for saying that Foreign Secretary Lord Carrington had offered the Arabs the hand of friendship, one that had previously belonged to the producer of the programme. That was on 'Summer Royale', the Sunday night variety show along Palladium lines but staged at Nottingham's principal theatre in a bit of barndoor closing by ATV, suddenly aware that it seldom acknowledged the local assets of the region it was franchised to serve. Despite my diplomatic indiscretion however, my family fortunes were on the upturn. Francis Essex had seen and snapped up Mark Goodson's latest game show hit in the US, 'Family Feud', needing only to alter the title and dump the touches of battlin' Rocky Mountain hillbillies from the American original. While he was offering me the show, Michael Grade had bought another Californian game, 'Card Sharks', intended as a LWT vehicle for Bruce Forsyth. After studying his acquisition more closely, Grade called Essex: 'Have you still got Monkhouse under contract? My people have just picked up a show in the States that'd be perfect for Bob, Francis. Bruce Forsyth wants to do it but, to be very frank, it's not his style at all. It's a wisecracker's showcase, tailor-made for a slick talker like Bob, so if you want it ... look, I'll tell you what. Do you want to unload that "Family Feud" thing on me in exchange? I believe it's very physical, much more Bruce's kind of thing. We'll do a straight swap, what do you say?'

'Michael, I say you're wonderful, just like your dad, but not even the great Leslie Grade would have got away with this. No deal.'

So while we went into the studio with a working formula, Grade & Co agonised over how to re-vamp 'Card Sharks', a game of pure chance, into the game of skill required by the IBA. With added quiz questions determining the outcome, they came up trumps with 'Play Your Cards Right'.

The relative strengths of the two formats are demonstrated by the fact that 'Fortunes' is still a popular success while the Forsyth show left ITV's schedules with the host's departure for the BBC, returning only when he became available again, the show needing its star more than the reverse. The secret of the game I hosted for four seasons lay in the simplicity of the survey concept, 'We asked one hundred people ... ' Two families muster five players each. Pairs of players, one from each family, try to guess the most popular answer gathered from the public in response to a simple question with several possible answers: 'What do newlyweds need most?' (A home, car, money, a baby, a bed), 'What's the first thing you do when you wake up in the morning?' (Get out of bed, wash, clean teeth, yawn, go home), 'Name Britain's most common Surname' (Smith, Jones, Brown, Robinson, Patel). The winner is the player who names the more popular public response. Then, advised by the family, he or she opts to play or pass on the task of coming up with the remaining answers to the survey question. If you've seen the show this will seem pretty easy to understand, but British viewers couldn't cotton on at all at first. We'd been on for ten weeks or more and people were still asking what the game was about. We were learning too, having to ditch questions that inspired answers the censor didn't appreciate:

> *'Apart from the Grand Prix, name a dangerous race.'*
> *'Arabs.'*
> *'What do little children miss most on holiday?'*
> *'The toilet bowl.'*

By the start of the second series the ratings zoomed to fifteen million and above. Spike Mullins, a comedy writer of antic genius, came up with some wonderful lines, named our computer Mr Babbage in tribute to the British inventor of the very first one in 1837, and suggested we try celebrity teams. The Montagues of Beaulieu challenged the Baths of Longleat with wondrous results. Asked to name a high street shop, Lord Bath said, 'Harrods'. The honourable aristocrats were foxed when asked to name a food you have to peel. After running out of time, one said, 'Peeling's the sort of thing that the staff does actually,' while another snapped out of her deep thought with the triumphant cry, 'Haggis!' Lord Montague didn't hesitate for a second when asked to name a bird you'd see in an English garden. 'Peacocks!' he blurted.

My favourite contestant came as the maternal head of an Irish clan, introduced by our announcer as, 'The Thicke family!' The studio audience chuckled so I stopped the taping, the third of three shows that evening. 'Sorry, ladies and gentlemen, we're going to start the show again and, please, this time try not to laugh when this charming family is introduced. I know it's amusing to some but let's be fair. It doesn't give them much of a chance if they start off being laughed at because of what would be seen as a rather racist attitude. Sorry, but we'd get a thousand angry letters.'

Sure enough, the audience was as good as gold the second time around. Their self-control was about to be more severely tested. Our researchers had come up with six popular answers to the question, 'Name something blue' – sky (33), sea (30), baby's eyes (13), male baby clothes (8), Oxford/Cambridge (6), Smurfs (5). The eldest Thicke son gained control of the board by guessing the top answer, sky. His mother, next in line to play, prompted him vehemently, 'Play! Play! We'll play, Liam!' I now approached this middle-aged matriarch of the Thickes from Newtonards and repeated, 'We asked one hundred people to name something blue.'

'Sure, and he's answered that. Sky. We've done that question.'

'Well, we have to try to find the other five answers which we got from the public when we asked them to name something blue. OK?'

She peered about her without signalling comprehension.

'We asked a hundred ordinary people, all kinds of people, old and young, rich and poor, all over the United Kingdom . . . ' I rambled as much as I dared to give her time to think . . . 'and as you can see, thirty-four out of a hundred said sky. What else do you think the other people said when we asked them to name something blue?'

Bewilderment faded from her expression as enlightenment dawned. With endearing hopefulness, she said, 'Was it my cardigan?'

I began to dread the second round. In answer to the survey request to 'name something that's deserted in winter', a hundred people had replied variously with nudist camps (29), swimming pools (27), seaside (24), parks (12), Oval/Lords (5). Once more I faced this plain lady with her dyed frizz of ginger hair, her catalogue frock and her anxious stare.

'We asked one hundred people to name something deserted in winter.'

There was no hesitation this time. She was ready. 'My cousin Elsie,' she said. The audience hooted and she turned on them angrily.

'It's not funny! With five kids in the house and Christmas comin' up!'

Graham C. Williams, our likeably fearless producer-director, arranged a studio party to celebrate our hundredth edition. Francis Essex had been succeeded as Light Entertainment chief by Jon Scoffield, a saturnine but elegantly handsome designer who'd achieved a brilliant track record as the producer of extravagant musical showcases for such stars as Tom Jones, Julie Andrews and Liberace, plus some award-winning specials. No one was more impressed by this than Scoff himself. Capable of great kindness and the kind of charm that could kill a diabetic, he was also the victim of total self-enthralment. Today, it must be said, Scoff is a highly regarded and hardworking freelance professional with a realistic perspective. But in 1983, if he didn't like you, he was no day at the seaside. Here's the exchange I had with him at the party, as well as I can remember it, which is very well indeed: 'Well, Jon, a hundred shows, eh? Here's to the next hundred!'

'Oh, I doubt that.'

'Doubt what?'

'I haven't decided whether I really want even one more series. I'm inclined to think that four seasons are enough of this sort of thing.'

'You mean I can't even count on one more?'

'Oh dear, please, don't push. It's undignified for a man in your position.'

That was all that was said. Perhaps it was meant humorously, perhaps it was the blether of rosy wine, but it was enough to set off the clangour of alarm bells in my cerebellum, that darkroom where we develop our negatives. Within thirty minutes, I was giving Prichard a verbatim report. He reacted with soothing and deceptive mildness.

A few weeks later I met Spike Mullins at my daughter's flat in Barons Court to write my spot for 'Live from Her Majesty's', another variety mixture compèred by Jimmy Tarbuck, a fine comedian with a manner as gentle as a Mike Tyson seduction. Spike wondered why I seemed so jumpy. 'What's up? I can 'ear yer ulcers burstin' like popcorn in a microwave.'

'I don't know. I feel as if I were enchanted by a cantrip.'

Spike rubbed his white beard. 'A cantrip? Isn't that what a Yank makes when 'e goes to the bog?'

'No . . .'

'While an Englishman goes "tooderloo"? Sunday, I'll 'ave to go to church and confess these jokes.'

'. . . it's a kind of spell, Spike. Ever since this morning, all the way here in the car, I've had this weird sensation that something is happening that will change my whole direction. Not that I believe in extra-sensory perception.'

'You gotta believe in something, mate. Me, f'rinstance, I believe I'm gonna get pissed tonight.'

The bewitched feeling persisted throughout the day until Prichard phoned just after we'd completed the script and as I was about to leave for home.

'Are you sitting comfortably, guv'nor? Right then. I've just finished a long meeting with Jim Moir who, as you know, is Head of Light Entertainment at the BBC. I've negotiated a three-year deal for the time being. You host a score of peak-time game shows each year and a dozen fifty-minute chat shows on Monday nights, BBC2's top spot. Congratulations! How does it feel to be fifty-five years old this year and starting a new career?'

Over a period of four days in the following May, Jackie and I went from a Monday lunch at Blackbeard's in Freeport, Grand Bahama, to a Monday dinner in France, Tuesday lunch in Canada and dinner in a Polynesian village, Wednesday lunch in China and dinner in Italy, Thursday lunch in Mexico and dinner at the Top of The World, Orlando, Florida. The last named rather gives the game away. At the invitation of 'Union Jack' Hayward and Edward St George's wife, Lady Henrietta, we'd flown to Grand Bahama from New York. While in the Big Apple. I'd spotted several unknown comedians for my new chat show, among them Rita Rudner, Emo Phillips and Steven Wright. I gave a charity concert performance in Freeport's handsome theatre to raise money for the island's orphanage, then flew over to Orlando in the Port Authority's private plane. At Disney World and Epcot, I met up with my first BBC crew for nearly twenty years – and they were all Americans. Together we spent three days shooting links for 'Disney Time' and eating our way round the world. Mexico gave me heartburn.

In June I was back home and making my first pilot show at the BBC Television Centre in Wood Green, from whence I had crept so ignominiously after 'The Big Noise' had ended with a whimper in 1964. Under the benevolent eyes of chubby Moir and the inventive Marcus Plantin, we spent long hours in the Acton rehearsal rooms trying to develop the skeletal format that I was now contracted to present. It was a quiz game based on bingo and titled 'Top of the Shop', the brainchild of two cockney lads whose only previous experience of TV had been doing warm-ups for Wogan's 'Blankety Blank'. Creating a successful game show requires careful building, hammering and testing. We tried every possible variation – using six contestants, then three, settling on four; trying bingo cards with sixty numbers, then thirty, finally only fifteen; making it from a single, continuous game into one that built in tempo through six rounds, then five, at last a mere three with a sudden death challenge for the two front-runners, a notion I disliked. I prefer the end game of a quiz to have the host onscreen with a single contestant in a suspenseful climax, with its timing under my control. Nevertheless, the pilot show was liked by everyone except Bill Cotton, the reigning monarch of popular programming, who told us all to try again.

Plantin suggested a 'golden bingo card' finish. The seed of this idea flowered at once: I'd stand by the winning player as we looked up at a display of numbers. For each correct answer to my simplest questions, the player could pick a number which would then light up as its own cash equivalent or change to a letter. Revealing seven letters amongst the fifteen numbers on display would spell out a 'dream holiday destination' like Madeira, Florida or Bermuda. While a scheme to transmit the shows live and run a national bingo game in conjunction with the *Radio Times* fell through, we renamed the series 'Bob's Full House' and made a second pilot. This time I loaded the show with gags: opening monologue, funny interviews with the four players, apt one-line jokes after every other answer. Then I dropped the comedy for the third, knockout round, using three-word questions to build up speed. A bright, brisk, balding Bishop named John produced the glossy result that had our bosses so fully satisfied that they lengthened the run of the series to twenty-two editions. It ran for six years, attracting the highest ratings, and I adored it. I adored 'The Bob Monkhouse Show' even more.

34

DREAM TEAM

Spreading the Blame

Happy to be judged by the company that is kept, unhappy about a taxing situation, but deeply appreciative of those made of the write stuff

I was very fortunate in my producer and director for the thirty hours or so of comedy that went under the eponymous title I'd rejected when the BBC proposed it thirty years earlier. John Fisher, a man so soft-spoken you have to hug him to hear him, looked like an ascetic monk in mufti, tall and willowy and softly creeping up on forty, with a kindly face tilted in dreamy abstraction. His deep passions were, still are, magic and comedy. I only ever saw him lose his temper once and I hope never to see it again. It was like watching Mother Teresa strangling a puppy.

Geoff Miles directed the three series of ten shows each, plus the Christmas compilations and a special edition with Joan Rivers, one of the exotic comics whom we first introduced to British TV. He had a moustache that came and went, brown unruly hair that he feared was doing the same, and the bluff, eager manner of a school captain. His barking laugh could shatter a glass eye at twenty paces. My other principal colleagues were the writers – Spike Mullins, a cynical sinker of infinite pints, already so old that he no longer left fingerprints, had written classic lines for Ronnie Corbett, many about his home town:

> *A weird area. Last week they held a Keep Britain Tidy paperchase.*

– Neil Shand, having forsaken sweet wine for dry wit, had steered the 'Des O'Connor Tonight' series through its funniest passages.

With his bashful charm gracing a delicious touch of malice, he'd also put some fine phrases on to David Frost's nimble tongue:

> *Bernard Manning can't be with us tonight. He's busy, closing down a Sunshine Home.*

– Dennis Berson, moodily dedicated or disgusted, unmarried and choosy, blinking behind Gestapo spectacles, standing his half-smoked fags on end like airfield smudgepots, slim, sandy, strictly hygienic but often unwell, he composed jokes like haiku:

> *Our local spiritualist bought an answerphone.*
> *Got a recorded message from Queen Victoria.*

Together with these talented men, I took on an army of comedians, burgling their best routines for gems and weaving them into a conversational exchange, persuading reluctant stars to repeat their funniest party pieces, bringing out the spontaneity in newcomers like Michael Barrymore, feeding stimulating straight lines to languid ladies like Sandra Bernhard, firing up eighty-year-old Bob Hope till he hit his youthful form:

> *Sammy Davis Jnr loves golf, hits a nice ball about ninety yards.*
> *His jewellery goes a hundred and ten.*

The guest list on those shows reads like a Who's Who of comedy: Ronnie Barker, Warren Mitchell, Tommy Cooper, Sid Caesar, Victoria Wood, Danny La Rue, Alice Faye, Denis Norden, Janet Brown, Steven Wright, Rich Little, Duncan Norvelle, Spike Milligan, Norman Wisdom, Kenny Everett, Marvin Hamlisch, Paul Squire, Julia McKenzie, Bernard Manning, Roy Jay, Rosemary Clooney, Larry Miller, Bernie Winters, Ronn Lucas, Libby Morris, Roy Walker, Anna Dawson, Mike Harding, Max Boyce, Max Bygraves, Paul Daniels, Yakov Smirnoff from Russia, Gerard Sety and Mac Ronay from France, Bertice Reading, Pam Ayres, Little and Large, Mike Reid, juggler Michael Davis, 'improvisationists' Monteith and Rand, the legendary US radio stars Bob and Ray, Hale and Pace, Les Dawson and the Rolypolys, Jim Carrey, Jimmy Cricket, Charlie Drake, Rita Rudner, Professor Irwin Corey, Russ Abbott,

Byron Allen, Kelly Monteith, Gary Wilmot, Sammy Cahn, Cosmotheka, Peter Cook, Siobhan McCarthy, Fascinating Aida, Robert Guillaume of 'Soap' and 'Benson' fame, Trevillion and Nine, The Flying Pickets, Tom O'Connor, Steve Landesberg, Liz Robertson, Martin Mull, Su Pollard, Kit and the Widow, Pete Barbutti, Lorraine Chase, Phyllis Diller, Derek Griffiths, 'The Unknown Comic' Murray Langston, Ruth Madoc, Ted Rogers, Emo Phillips, Michael Bentine, Karen Kay, Frankie Howerd and many more, all with the superb orchestral backing of Harry Stoneham.

If it was a lifelong dream come true, to organise and interview and present this comedy caravan, it was also a further education in comic technique. I sat two feet away from some of the world's finest exponents of the perfect pause, the subtlest shading of a word, the sidelong glance, the sudden switch of expression, mock shock, simulated sanctimony, shared secrecy, faked frankness, genuine on-the-spot invention, observing all the accoutrements and sheer savvy that came from long experience in the use of each one's unique flair. Later, it seemed as though I'd been topping up my understanding of what makes entertainment work in preparation for what would be a very different but equally rewarding job for the next three years. Meanwhile, my cabaret work continued unabated. Twice I was thrilled to accept the award as 'Comedian of the Year' from the club, pub and hotel trade. In 1985 I became a Brother Officer in The Order of St John, wrote a best-selling paperback called *The Book of Days* to raise funds for the S.O.S., the Muscular Dystrophy Fund and the Heart Foundation, and started a far more rigorous programme of charity work. I wasn't expecting to be in such sudden need of charity myself.

Our accountant, a much valued ally blessed with gentilesse but burdened with sepulchral tones, phoned to say, 'The Tax Inspector wants to dig up the drains.' This good fellow sounds like the voice of doom when he wishes you happy birthday but for this drains announcement he was perfect casting. Even so, I took the news lightly. After all, I'd been with the same distinguished firm of accountants since 1952, enduring their meticulous discipline just as I complied with Prichard's methodical system, ensuring that every pound I earned was recorded and the appropriate tax paid. What could be so wrong? The question was answered – or rather, not answered – by the Grand Inquisitor of the Inland Revenue, a holy crusader with a self-appointed mission to root out and expose the heresy of anyone ever getting paid in cash for anything ever, let alone forgetting a long-forgotten sixteen pounds they had mouldering in the Post Office at three-per-cent interest for seventeen years.

Of course, he didn't tell us that this was what he'd discovered. Torquemada didn't work that way. This fanatic demanded physical evidence of every penny earned and spent over a five-year span. He wanted all the books unearthed, our personal diaries for all five years, copies of all contracts, ledgers, cheque stubs, bank statements, share transactions, bills, receipts, air and train tickets, theatre and cinema tickets, insurance plans and payments, pension schemes, bond holdings, annuities, tips, loans, every emolument and pittance that concerned me or my family. Now that's enough paper to choke an oceanful of whales, apart from the thousands of man-hours needed to produce it. And who's going to pay for it all? And why am I asking when we both know the answer?

So Jackie and I and our accountants worked very hard indeed for the next three and a half years, searching for some mistake that we didn't know we'd made without a clue to what it could be. In the meantime the Tax Inspector had mislaid half the papers we'd submitted and ordered us to deliver duplicates. More expense. We eventually identified the lost Post Office deposit but the unreported sum that had accrued was so piddling that we couldn't believe that it was the cause of our investigation. You must be waiting for the punchline by now. There isn't one. After four years of dredging through our files with the threat of punitive measures and unspecified fines hanging over us, we were told that the Hanging Judge had resigned and the ordeal was over. Well, as Robert Maxwell said to Lester Piggott, you've got to laugh, haven't you?

As John Junkin once said to me, 'If I had my life to live over, I'd live over a decent Chinese restaurant.' Junkin's literate wit and fluent phrasemaking had delighted me since I first met him, one of Joan Littlewood's young, hungry and trailblazing actors at the Theatre Royal, Stratford East. Our paths often crossed during the following quarter century, sometimes on charity jaunts, often in Gerald Campion's much-missed Gerry's Club. In that Shaftesbury Avenue cellar John spent countless evenings with fellow thespians, weaving convoluted parodies and puns. His boozier ripostes were often the most memorable. When actor Edward Judd spoke of 'theatrical euphoria' and Gerry asked what that meant, Junkin explained, 'It's as in the directorial phrase, "You five stand over there and euphoria." ' He could be gently bitchy . . .

Has Freddie Starr learned wisdom? Or is he stealing someone else's act?

. . . or less gently, as when he wanted to place an ad:

For sale: photo blow-up of Clive James and a set of darts.

More often though, his humour had an endearing daftness about it:

A sailor I once knew crossed the equator with a steamer and got an imaginary kettle that runs round the centre of the earth.

Tall, bald, a bit deaf, a microphone-shaped cigarette lighter dangling from a cord round his neck, a port and brandy in mind and a *Guardian* crossword completed in no time, Junkin joined the 'Bob's Full House' team as Shand left in 1987. We've worked together ever since in close friendship.

One taping day, he drew me aside after a short session of greeting and instruction for our eight contestants for that evening's two recordings. 'The little blonde in the grey pullover, Bob, she's very unhappy about something.'

Sure enough, the twenty-year-old waitress from Warwick seemed sulky and defiant as we rehearsed the game in the studio. During the break, I got two cups of tea and approached her. 'Fancy a cup?'

'No.'

'How are you enjoying yourself so far?'

'Not much.'

'I'm sorry. Is there anything I can do to cheer you up before the show this evening? I'm paid by the laugh, you know.'

'Ha ha.'

'What's worrying you?'

'Look, I'm here, aren't I? I'm going to go through with it, all right?'

'You don't have to.'

'What?'

'You don't have to do the show if you don't want to.'

She stared at me in disbelief, then her green eyes widened with hope. 'But . . . but what'll happen to me?'

'We'll just send you home safely. A standby contestant can play instead.'

'Oh, yes, yes, thank you!' she cried, flinging her arms around my neck, then bursting into tears of happy relief. 'Thank you, oh my God, thank you!'

I laughed, 'But what made you apply to be on the show in the first place?'

'I never,' she choked, wiping her face with tissues from her handbag. 'It weren't me as wrote in. It was me twin sister. Then she met a bloke and went to Canada. So mum said as 'ow I 'ad to take 'er place or we might be in really serious trouble. Can I 'ave your autograph? It's not for me, it's for my mum. She likes you.'

Don MacLean, the only comedian containing fluoride, once told me about a young writer of topical gags. 'I know you write your own cabaret material, Bob,' he smiled, displaying more enamel than the Ming dynasty, 'but this lad's good for a few gags straight off the headlines.'

The lad was good for far more than that. Colin Edmonds officially joined the 'Family Fortunes' team in 1982 and was now spending his creative energies on my TV bingo quiz, working prolifically with Paul Alexander and Gavin Osbon. Jackie and I virtually adopted Col; a small, slim, balding DIY enthusiast, sharp-featured with darkly darting eyes, given to expressive movement and playful self-effacement, single then but married today to an entrancing BBC vision-mixer named Kathryn, mother to lovely Lucy who was conceived at our Barbados home. Col's ear for wordplay and coincidence is unerring. On the day Robert Mugabe became President of Zimbabwe, Col identified him as a backward Yorkshireman: 'Mugabe spelled backwards is "ee-bah-gum!' Within moments of HRH Prince Andrew announcing his engagement, Col was observing how much TV affected the royal family: 'Anne's already got a Phillips and Andrew's getting a Ferguson.' When a naval contestant said that he was always glad to weigh anchor, Col said he understood the feeling because 'I once worked on the butter counter in Sainsbury's.' As you may have gathered, I love the writers of sound, workable comedy. Survival of the fittest should give way to survival of the funniest, then at least we can die laughing. All of us play with words like toys. The English language is an adventure playground with a treasure hunt, full of puzzles to solve and silly meanings to be found. But there's also broken glass in the sandbox.

35

NEW DISCOVERIES

Spreading the Fame

*Prospecting for talent, the BBC strikes fools and gold. A
sixty-four thousand dollar question is asked and a sixty-
fifth birthday approached, with work in progress but life
lightly threatened*

Some of us, myself included, can write our pain, encapsulating
and sealing it away in a one-liner like a devil trapped in a bottle,
defenceless against our mockery. There are good reasons why so
many powerful comedy writers and comedians come from
underprivileged backgrounds. As Sigmund Freud wrote,
'Humour is used as a weapon by the have-nots against the haves.'
I'm also aware that much of my comedy has its origins in
emotional deprivation. There's a certain amount of hurt pricking
the conception of lines like:

> *I was not wanted. Two weeks after I was born*
> *my mother tried to have an abortion.*
> *To give you some idea of my sex life with my first wife –*
> *she got divorced in white.*
> *The main problem with growing old is*
> *the future's not what it used to be.*

As for what drives a person to want to stand up in front of the
largest possible number of people and deliver his jokes out loud,
this is an ambition which at this point begins to occupy the minds
of my little team as 'Bob Says Opportunity Knocks'.

Jim Moir invited me to host the famous talent contest
originated by Hughie Green, coincidentally on the fortieth
anniversary of my appearance on the wireless version when I

introduced Denis Goodwin for his debut as a comic. The producer was Stewart Morris, a giant veteran for whom I'd compèred a BBC TV Royal Variety Performance in Edinburgh a year earlier. Some men are built like Greek gods. Stewart's built like a Greek restaurant. He's affectionately known to his colleagues as Attila the Ton. During our first year, he was to audition over a thousand aspirants and produce a first series of thirteen fifty-minute shows. I wanted to accompany him around the UK as much as I was able, being anxious to involve myself with the project from the bottom up. There were other worries too, like how much comedy I should include in my links between the acts. I didn't want to be seen as though competing with our amateurs. Both Moir and Morris were complaisant. 'Just be the benevolent old maestro, Bob, battle-scarred and wordly-wise in the ways of the biz,' Moir advised and Morris added, 'But put in plenty of funnies.'

The audition process had firm rules. Each successful applicant was allotted an approximate time of day to appear at the venue, usually a local dance hall. Our team sat behind a trestle table facing the performing area. We provided a rehearsal pianist, a microphone, speakers, a TV camera and monitor.

Morris had decreed that every auditionee should be given not less than three minutes and not more than six, that all would be treated with respect and, no matter how gob-smackingly frightful they were, none of us should laugh except at those who meant to be funny. It wasn't easy to stop sympathy for the truly irredeemable turning to hysteria. One application form had a colour Polaroid attached showing a middle-aged lady with hair the colour of smoked salmon posed energetically on the stage of a smoky pub, glittering blue gown slashed low to show the customers where her lung power came from. Now we saw her in the flesh, seemingly the victim of some horrifying accident. She came forward on crutches, her left arm and leg encased in plaster, wearing a neck brace and with thick crepe bandages bound all round her torso. The same sparkly blue gown had been slashed even more extensively, cut all the way up the right side so that it could be wrapped around her over her bandages and held in place with several big nappy pins. One of her eyes was swollen shut but the other one gleamed with the determination that had brought her out of some hospital bed, hell-bent on getting her chance to be on the telly. We all gazed respectfully at this indomitable matron as she made her painful way to the mike and our pianist struck up her music. She sang 'Let's Get Physical'.

Our powers of self-control were to be even more severely strained. Eight enormous railway workers dressed as Russian cossacks turned up at our Manchester auditions, held in a dancehall where the polished floor was elaborately sprung to give bounce to the dancers' steps. When they went into the traditional Russian dance where the dancer assumes a position as though sitting on air and kicks his legs forward in turn, this band of Goliaths did it in unison. Their combined weight, crashing down again and again on to the resilient wood, made it begin to undulate alarmingly. As their taped music thundered out, drowning our cries of rising concern, the oblivious dancers bounded on and the elastic dancefloor stretched and recoiled in oceanic waves of reaction. Our TV monitor vibrated across the table and crashed to the floor. Coffee cups and pencils went shuddering away. Our secretary stood in an attempt to reach a mobile phone that was rattling towards the table's edge, couldn't keep her balance and fell. Morris was gripping his heaving chair and bellowing at the heavy giants to stop the dance. I actually felt seasick. God knows how it might have ended – with a splintering collapse of the sprung beams, pitching us all below into the subterranean waters of the Medlock, perhaps – but for the dancers' own cassette recorder, source of the deafening music, succumbing to the same forces as everything else, smashing on to the floor and falling silent.

We arrived at nine a.m. for the Cardiff auditions and Colin Fay, our senior floor manager, pointed out a figure sitting at a cluttered table in the window of a nearby tea-bar. 'I wonder what he's going to do for us?'

We laughed. The man had travelled from home in full make-up and costume: the traditional minstrel black-face with whitened eyes and lips, a curly black wig, shiny black suit, white gloves and floppy black bow tie. When we eventually got to him, around midday, he gave his music to our pianist and we settled back for the inevitable. He sang us a medley of songs made famous by Vera Lynn.

On a freezing cold February morning in an unheated dance hall on the outskirts of Glasgow we sat bundled up in our topcoats, scarves and gloves to watch the Scottish hopefuls shiver with more than nerves. While listening to a very thin young woman playing 'Ramona' on the musical saw, I glanced sideways to where the next performers sat waiting their turn and noticed that Fay was remonstrating with a small man who had stripped to the waist. The angry little man disappeared into the gents' toilets, then came back again wearing an old raincoat. When his number was called, he cast off the coat and walked on to the performing area dressed in only a baggy old pair of underpants and thick brown socks. He was about sixty years old, stringy but not hairy, with tattoos on his forearms and the knotted muscles of a manual labourer. With great passion and no ability whatsoever, he sang 'I, Who Have Nothing'.

We struggled to keep straight faces. When he'd finished, Morris thanked him courteously with the usual 'We'll let you know' and the wee fellow stalked off in a vexed manner. It was just too intriguing for me to resist. Excusing myself, I followed him into the large toilets where he was getting dressed, pulling a worn shirt over his bristly grey head, muttering to himself in exasperation. I said, 'That was very unusual. What exactly was the idea behind that?'

He looked at me disgustedly and shouldered on his braces. I tried again. 'Was it your own idea to sing in underpants and socks?'

'Christ!' he exploded bitterly. 'It's yer mon! It's yer bloody mon!'

'Pardon me?'

'Yon eedjit wi' the glasses. Says I couldna gae on TV wi' nae clothes on. I told him, that's the whole point. It's a political statement! To stand there wi' nothing on and sing yon song. "I . . . I, Who Have *Nothing*!" Ye've got to have *nothing*! Ye've to be bollock nekked! Och, but him, he says, "Oh no, sir, nobody wants to see yer genitals on their TV screens, ye must wear pants."'

'I see.'

'Do you? I doubt it. Destroyed the whole purpose of wha' I was attemptin' tae achieve. What's the point o' singin' that song wi' yer underpants on? It makes a mockery of what's meant to be a harsh satirical protest!'

'I'm sorry. Did he ask you to keep your socks on too?'

His innocent blue eyes looked at me blankly.

'Och, no, that was my idea. Yon floor's fucking cold.'

The first series of 'B.S.O.K.', or Bobnox as it came to be called within the BBC, was nothing short of sensational. The ratings went sky-high and our grand finale, transmitted live from the London Palladium, was seen by twenty-four million viewers. Two delightful lads from Neath named Rosser and Davies attracted a massive vote with their original comic songs at the piano. Today they are also well established as comedy scriptwriters. During the three years that I presented the show our discoveries included Brenda Cochrane, who has gone on to international recording success, ballad singer Jane Harrison, the ebullient Welsh entertainer Mike Doyle, Johnny Casson who has found success with Granada TV's 'The Comedians', comedy illusionist Brodie Fry, and impressionist Darren Day, recently back at the Palladium playing the eponymous hero in *Joseph and the Amazing Technicolor Dreamcoat*. My fellow writers and I had learned a lot, endeavouring to help aspiring comedians with their material and shape their routines for the show. Some soaked up new ideas like a sponge, others like a stone.

Before the third series had ended, Prichard grew even more enigmatic than usual. 'Opportunity is still knocking, guv'nor, but not here and not yet.'

Within a few weeks he let me in on the secret in his new Regent Street office.

'I've been having a few meetings with Woolf Phillips.'

'You mean the old bandleader? I thought he was in Los Angeles.'

'No, not Woolf Phillips. The head of entertainment at ATV.'

'It's Central now, Peter. Do you mean Tony Wolfe?'

'He wants you to look at a couple of shows. "The $64,000 Question" and "You Asked For It".'

I knew both shows from the 1950s. The first was a quiz that had dominated US ratings from its first edition in 1955 until its collapse in a famous scandal about backstage corruption just over three years later. It had a foolproof construction that had provided the matrix for numerous rip-offs. Glamorously refurbished, I thought it might have the appeal of a 'Mastermind' with money.

The other show depended too much on rare film footage. What had been rare thirty-five years before was now commonplace. At our first meeting, I suggested bringing back 'Celebrity Squares' but Tony, his rounded face composed in cordiality beneath a cap of grey hair, demurred. 'With the greatest respect, Bob, we want you to come home to Central with something dazzlingly new.'

The new and dazzling 'Bob's Your Uncle' resulted, lavishly staged by the inexhaustible Nigel Lythgoe. Newlyweds in wedding finery competed in 'love boats in the sea of matrimony', took a 'run for fun' around our arena and manhandled giant props for the chance to fire 'cupid's bow' and win a car. Opinion was divided on its qualities so, after twenty-six extravagant outings and with the unflappable Richard Holloway inheriting Wolfe's chair at Central, it was superseded by the return of the popular 'Squares' game. Silver-maned Peter Harris, once my senior floor manager on 'Golden Shot' and director of 'The Muppet Show', sits at the helm of both '64' and 'Squares', a dear man with all the calm self-control of a Yorkshire terrier on speed. And that, professionally speaking, brings me up to date.

I regard the future with hope, the past with gratitude. Last year, when I talked with Dr Anthony Clare on his Radio Four programme, 'In the Psychiatrist's Chair', he asked me how I felt about my death. I answered without hesitation and with no intention of surprising him with my answer. I said simply that I had made all the necessary arrangements to make things as easy as possible – my will was written, my life well insured, such matters as the disposal of my various collections (of original cartoons, paintings, films, videos, stamps, books, clocks, etc.) had been planned – and there was nothing much more I could do about it really. He found my reply extraordinary although I'm still not sure why. Perhaps I owe him a more thoughtful response.

I'm rather relaxed about death. From quite an early age I've regarded it as part of the deal, the unwritten guarantee that comes with your birth certificate. If I were told that I had only six months to live, I'd just try to sleep faster. Should the cause be incurable and painful, I'd opt for a voluntary exit. Like most of us though, I'd prefer death to sneak up on me as subtly and slowly as a windscreen sneaks up on a gnat. As for funerals, I rather like them. Such nice things are always said about the deceased, I feel sad that they had to miss hearing it all by just a few days. I've noticed that as, growing old, I attend more and more of them, the size of the attendance at one's funeral depends less upon popular respect and more upon the weather.

Perhaps my reaction is common to people born with a tendency to accept life's conditions with equanimity and humour. As Mel Brooks said, 'If Shaw and Einstein couldn't beat death, what chance have I got? Practically none.' Seriously though, ladies and gentlemen . . .

Although I've always loved the noise of laughter, I really can't fear the coming of quiet.

On Sunday, 24 January last, having broken off from writing this book to drive to Scarborough and back for a cabaret at Butlin's Grand Hotel, I had a little reminder of my mortality. Coming out of our wine 'cellar' to replenish the fridge with some dry whites, I reached out to turn off the light switch. Since the light didn't go out, I pressed harder with no result. I looked at my right hand and found that I was pressing my fingers into the wall beside the switch. I knew I was very tired from the journey but I was surprised at my confusion. Carefully turning the light out, I walked into the kitchen carrying the wine bottles and said to Jackie, 'I coong swidda lide uff.'

She laughed patiently, thinking I was being silly as usual. I was bewildered at myself. Thinking I must sound like the characters who spoke backwards in David Lynch's TV serial, I tried to say, 'I sound like someone out of "Twin Peaks"' but it came out as, 'I soun'ike sunun ouda "Tim Pee".' I tried again with the title and turned it into 'Tinned Peaches'. Giving up, I put the wine away and went to look at TV in the drawing room. A few minutes later Jackie brought me a cup of Earl Grey. She put the cup down, smiled at me, then did a double take. 'Your face!' she said. 'What's wrong with it?'

I hurried to the big sitting room mirror in the alcove that leads to the garden and saw my right cheek was sagging curiously. 'Thash funny,' I said, my speech normal now except for the sluggishness of my lips at the right corner of my mouth, 'I think it might be Bell'sh Palshy.'

Half of Neil Shand's face had suddenly slid south during our work together on the bingo quiz and the condition was diagnosed as Bell's Palsy, passing off in about a week. Jackie and I pored over *The Family Medical Guide*. No, I didn't have the required droopy eye. Our good Dr Dry was summoned and she lost no time in arranging for me to be examined at the Saxon Clinic in nearby Milton Keynes. Jackie drove me there rather fast and another doctor diagnosed a stroke, my brief disorientation and facial sag being due to a cerebral aneurism.

A cat-scan detected no haemorrhage and yet another doctor revised the nature of the problem as an infarction or death of brain cells caused by some interference in the blood supply. My carotid arteries were observed as functioning well and within a few days my face was back to normal. My speech cleared up rather more slowly and I bit my lower lip every time I chewed my food, but only for a week or two. They all asked me to cut down on my wine and whisky and I am trying, since a fourth doctor warned me that over-indulgence at my age can cause impotence. Anything as nasty as that has to be rolled up in a joke to reduce it in size:

> *Recent studies show that alcohol diminishes your sexual capacity.*
> *It's called cirrhosis of the lover.*

I suppose the most revealing aspect of my blip was my own reaction: fascination. I've noticed this happening before. Driving south alone on the A1 in a snowstorm, I braked too hard and my car waltzed round and round rather gracefully until it hit the roundabout I'd braked to avoid. During this slow spin I wasn't at all fearful, just very, very interested.

In Los Angeles, when Jackie and I were staying on the fourteenth floor of the Beverley Wilshire, we were woken just after six a.m. by a tremendous noise.

Jackie thought a room service trolley had crashed through our bedroom door. The din consisted only partly of shattering glass and the scream of tortured metal. A bright yellow light was slowly blinking on and off outside our window, as if a police helicopter were swinging to and fro in the sky. 'My God!' I shouted over the racket, 'that's the sun!'

'It can't be, Bob, it's going on and off!'

'No, it's not. The hotel's swaying! We're having an earthquake.'

Jackie, sensibly terrified, dived under the blankets and pulled at me to join her but I wasn't going to miss this show. I was over at the big window, looking at the Californian landscape doing the mambo. Not only were palm trees swaying, just like they do in popular songs, so were entire buildings. It was the most amazing sight I'd ever seen and I was transfixed by its terrible allure.

As the massive shock began to subside, Jackie was still calling for me to come away from the window so I did, but only to snap on the TV and watch a couple of newsreaders recovering from the surprise of finding themselves literally shaken by events. It seemed the epicentre had been nearly five miles away in an old part of town, where highways had split into huge gaping rifts, flyovers had crumbled to rubble and many local buildings, constructed before the laws requiring earthquake precautions, had fallen flat. After-shocks followed during the day and we were told that the cataclysm had registered a seven-point-four. Jackie, who had recovered her composure quickly once the danger had passed, scolded me for my stupidity.

She knew as well as I did that my indifference to the risk of broken glass from the window had nothing to do with courage. My audacity isn't that of the brave man, only of one infatuated by the inevitablity of the inexorable. Similarly gripped by the irresistible force of certain music, Maurice Ravel's *La Valse* for example, I surrender all volition to the unstoppable drive towards its resolution. It's more than a resignation to overpowering forces, it's a consuming curiosity about their nature that deadens panic. Just as I have little concern for unavoidable physical pain, excessive heat or cold, other than to take note of it, so I react to anything life-threatening over which I can have no control as a totally absorbed observer. It's no intellecutal decision, there's no time for that. It's more like the immediate reflex of the deer, caught in headlights of an approaching car, that simply stands and stares.

Tomorrow my manuscript goes to be published. Once again, wheels will begin to turn which I am powerless to halt. A deer in the headlights. This is my last chance to abandon the whole project, protect myself from your criticism and disapproval, withdraw from the risk of distressing friends and family by some of what I've written. It's not too late. This page and the pile of pages which precede it, now sitting neutrally on my desk, can be consigned to the shredder or the furnace and never seen by anyone except for the four people who have read eighty per cent of it – my publishing editor, Mark Booth; my daughter Abigail; Jackie, and our funny friend, Wirral comedian and disc jockey Peter Price. They have each prevailed upon me to make tiny modifications, deletions and additions, writing more to clarify or less to avoid giving unnecessary offence. They've also pointed out to me that some readers, perhaps those who already hate me, will hate me more. If I appear to have led no more than a shallow and philandering life of selfishness, artfulness and vanity, then that will have as much to do with the reader's judgement as it has to do with the truth. At the start of my story, I promised to tell you about my life as honestly as I could. I also explained that there was a lot I couldn't tell you because it was more about other living people than it was about me. Their privacy has been reasonably respected and that was the deal I offered you, a subjective view excluding nothing but those things I have no right to tell.

It's been said that an autobiography is the last refuse of scoundrels, but the prospect of biography lends to death a new horror. Oscar Wilde wrote, 'Every great man has his disciples, and it's always Judas who writes the biography.' Though by no means great, I may have been my own Judas here and there. Shall I play safe and junk the whole thing? No, to hell with it. It's the only life story I've got to offer and, please God, you found it as funny to read as it was to live. Finally abandoning humour in favour of movie buff solemnity, I'll settle for the epitaph given by Marlene Dietrich's Gypsy to Orson Welles's Cop in *Touch of Evil*:

> *He was some kind of a man.*
> *What does it matter what you say about people?*

The End

INDEX

334

4